75th Anniversary

D-DAY

A MILLENNIALS GUIDE

Edited by Jay Wertz

Monroe Publications

For orders and information, please visit:
www.monroepublications.com

Monroe Publications
1152 Mae Street #242
Hummelstown, PA 17036

ISBN: 9781732631502

Printed & bound by Caskey Group, York, PA

Book design by Barb Justice

Cover Photo: *Omaha Beach, called St-Laurent-sur-Mer Port once it was secured, became the main point of arrival for reinforcements and supplies for weeks after D-Day.*
(Photo courtesy of National Archives and Records Administration)

Dedicated to

Robert Immanuel "Bob" Maher

1944-2018

History Education Innovator

Bob Maher illustration
by Zack Fry

CONTENTS

The Past

The Present

The Future

Captain Richard "Dick" Winters stands in the Schoonderlogt Estate gateway in Holland in October 1944. He was commander of Company E, 506th Parachute Infantry Regiment, 101st Airborne Division and later a battalion commander. After World War II Winters willingly shared his wartime stories and leadership advice with historians and the public because he believed in passing on the lessons of history.
(Albert Krochka, U.S. Army Signal Corps)

Introduction

So-called "milestone anniversaries" have always peaked interest in events. On a personal level they merit something extra—Silver (25 years) and Golden (50 years) wedding anniversaries, "Over the Hill" birthdays (30, 40, 50 or 60 years old), etc. Milestone years for historic events foster wide interest and carefully planned commemorations—the American Bicentennial and the World War I Centennial, for example. While 100-year anniversaries are certainly the most widely recognized and celebrated, for World War II the 75th Anniversary is generating major commemorations.

Why are these commemorations so significant? Two reasons, I believe. First, World War II affected people around the globe into the late 20th century politically, economically and personally. The world that entered WWII was not the world that existed after it. The second reason is that the longevity of humans has continued to increase, so many surviving veterans of D-Day and the war, now in their 90s, are still with us, and some will attend D-Day commemoration ceremonies. This probably will be, however, the last milestone anniversary with World War II veterans present. In the future it will be up to others to understand, remember and commemorate their lives and deeds.

That is what prompted me to create this guide, to continue passing the legacy of D-Day from one generation to the next. The term *A Millennials Guide* used in the title is a popular culture reference to people born between 1986–2000, who in 2019 are young adults. Generational labels might sound insulting to some, but they are used statistically and to identify traits common to individuals in that age group, including traits based on the progress of technology and society in the formative years of their lives. In my opinion, millennials, as a group, do not think as much about history as prior generations did. Their lives are consumed with technology, with what defines their lives today, and what defines their hopes and wishes for the future that will be their world. But without knowledge of history, there can be no defining, no real understanding, of who we are as individuals and as societies. Without reading, writing and understanding history, individuals and societies have no direction to guide them in the future, and they risk subjecting themselves to exploitation by those who would falsify the past for their personal agendas.

My generation, the "baby boomers," will soon follow the "greatest generation" into eternity. It will, therefore, be up to millennials to carry on the stories and meanings of World War II, the people involved, the lives lost and the lives saved, and the dramatic changes the war wrought. I made this guide to help you, the millennials, continue to learn, remember and pass on these stories. The decision to use the moniker "millennials" was mine alone—a device to involve new readers in this vast, fascinating and important history. If you don't like to label, blame me. But I do hope you will gain some satisfaction and insight from the contents of this book.

I also believe, however, there is something for everyone in this guide—from those who may have only recently heard the term *D-Day* to those who have read, studied and immersed themselves in World War II history all their lives. I assembled a group of 18 writers who have contributed the wonderful chapters of history, thought, interview and information in this guide. They range from distinguished historians who have published many recognized works, to contributors who are just beginning to add their names to the collections of World War II history. They have brought a variety of styles, perspectives and areas of research to the book. I hope that you will get to know them by reading the biographical entries following this introduction. I must pay special recognition to Gerald Swick who, besides contributing chapters to this book, acted as executive editor. We were in constant collaboration. In baseball terms, he was field manager to my role as general manager; in moviemaking terms, I was the director and he was the editor. He helped pull the diverse styles and content of these written works together. Without his help I would never have been able to complete this book.

Finally, it would have been impossible to create a work of this quality without a first-rate staff of people contributing their special skills and knowledge. I have authored a number of works of history with the same people acting as book designer, publisher, mapmaker, photo editor, researcher and proofreader. They have made this book a work to be read and enjoyed. You can find their names and titles listed in the back of the book. It is my sincere hope that readers everywhere will use this guide and have fun doing it. If something in it propels one person to read further, to visit a place of history, attend an event or perhaps speak with a World War veteran, and then remember and pass on the experience, this guide has done its job. Thank you for the opportunity to share this history with you.

-Jay Wertz

Phillips Ranch, California

About the Contributors

CHRISTOPHER J. ANDERSON is a historian who is well versed in many aspects of American history, with special expertise in the Normandy Invasion, the *Band of Brothers* television series and 101st Airborne Division, as well as the American Revolution. As the former editor of *WWII Magazine* he edited and wrote about all areas of the U.S. involvement in that war. Chris is also one of the original creators of the Stephen Ambrose Band of Brothers Tour and continues to lead tours for the organization. He was a personal confidant of Major Dick Winters, commander of Easy Company, as well as many other veterans of WWII.

EDWIN COLE BEARSS is among America's foremost authorities on American history and historic preservation. He was a member of the U.S. Marine Corps in WWII, wounded four times in the Pacific Theater. His long and storied career with the National Park Service includes serving as its chief historian from 1981 until his retirement in 1995. He received the Department of the Interior's Distinguished Service Award, its highest honor and one rarely given during an employee's term of service. Two awards are named for him: The Civil War Preservation Trust Edwin C. Bearss Award for leadership in the preservation of Civil War sites (he was its first recipient) and the National Park Service Edwin C. Bearss Fellowship Award. He has authored 14 books and co-authored *Smithsonian's Great Battles and Battlefields of the Civil War* with Jay Wertz. Ed has been a frequent speaker at Civil War Round Tables and other historic symposiums, pacing their rostrums without using a single note, without accepting payment and without delivering a single dull moment. In his 90s, he continues to be a much sought-after guide for historic tours worldwide.

COL. ROBERT J. DALESSANDRO (USA ret.) is currently the Acting Secretary of the American Battle Monuments Commission (ABMC) and former Executive Director/Chief of Military History, U.S. Army Center of Military History. Considered one of the U.S. Army's foremost experts on battlefield interpretation, he is widely published on the lifeways and material culture of the American soldier. He is editor of the *Army Officer's Guide* and coauthor of *Organization and Insignia of the American Expeditionary Force, 1917–1923*; *Willing Patriots: Men of Color in the First World War*; and *American Lions: The 332nd Infantry Regiment in Italy in World War One*. He is a member of a number of professional organizations, including the Society for Military History, American Association of Museums, and the Company of Military Historians.

ROBERT IRVING DESOURDIS received Master of Science degrees from Massachusetts Institute of Technology and Worchester Polytechnic Institute. As a Solutions Architect, Master, he has worked on development of simulators for the Department of Defense, public safety communications, and many other projects. The author and contributor for eight technical books on emergency and safety communications, he is currently assisting in the writing of Edwin C. Bearss's memoir. The two met in 2011 on a tour of European battlefields.

MATTHEW DEWINDE was born in Rochester, New York, and attended the State University of New York at Fredonia, where he earned a bachelor's degree in Social Studies Adolescent Education and History. He is currently a 7th and 8th grade social studies teacher at Eisenhower Middle School in Liberal, Kansas.

DENNIS EDWARD FLAKE is a seasonal Interpretive Park Ranger for the National Park Service at the Eisenhower National Historic Site in Gettysburg, Pennsylvania. He has interpreted history at six other national parks since retiring from the pharmaceutical industry in 2010. He holds two graduate degrees, including an MA in history, and he is the author of four history books and numerous articles and book reviews. He is a U.S. Navy and U.S. Public Health Service veteran.

WILLIAM FLOYD JR. has written for *Military Heritage, History Magazine* and *America in WWII* and authored a short biography, "Robert E. Lee's Indispensable Man, A History of Walter H. Taylor." He is presently working on *The Engineering Life of Robert E. Lee,* a book about Lee's experiences in the Army Corps of Engineers from the time he graduated West Point until he resigned from the Union Army at the beginning of the Civil War.

MARTIN ROBERT GALLE was born 1964 in Munich but raised in Landau/Rhineland-Palatinate near the French border, where he was surrounded by traces of more than 2.000 years of military history. At the age of 17, Martin volunteered at the historic French Maginot Line Fort of Schoenenbourg and later became a guide there. After serving in the German Army he made his career in the hotel industry and later became a battlefield guide, focusing on the American involvement in WWI and WWII. His grandfather, Col. Ernst Goth, commanded German forces above Omaha Beach on D-Day. This led Martin to research the Normandy Campaign from the German perspective. He is currently the honorary curator of the Westwallmuseum Bad-Bergzabern (WWII Siegfried Line Museum). www.Otterbachabschnitt.de

MIKI GARCIA began her career as a newspaper reporter and covered a wide range of stories from across the world. She is the author of five books including *Filipino Cooking by Mike Garcia* and *Rebuilding London: Irish Migrants in Post-War Britain.* Her latest, *The Caribbean Irish: How the Slave Myth was Made,* will be published in November 2019. She has a master's degree in journalism from City, University of London.

LOWELL DEAN GYTRI is professional actor with a BA degree in theatre from Minnesota State University Moorhead. He is known for roles in feature films, episodic TV and national TV commercials. In addition to acting, Lowell serves as a film industry technical advisor on rural living, firearms and archery. He held the office of district captain (DCAPT) and currently serves as a coxswain in the United States Coast Guard Auxiliary. He has also conducted interviews of World War II veterans for the *War Stories: World War II Firsthand*™ book series. He divides his time between his home in Big Bear Lake, California, and his farming/ranching operations in West Central Minnesota.

SHARON GYTRI is on the staff *War Stories: World War II Firsthand*™ book series as interview coordinator, researcher and indexer. As a retried secondary school teacher of English, speech and theater she gained experience in puzzle making. She also taught speech communications at California State University, Los Angeles. Sharon now acts as a movie and TV casting director for background and local principal actors in Big Bear Lake, California. Two of the TV series she worked on were nominated for 2018 Golden Globe awards. She also has been an auxiliary flotilla commander and assistant district staff officer of publications for a Southwestern region of the U. S. Coast Guard Auxiliary.

LEE W. JONES earned his doctorate studying under Arthur M. Schlesinger Jr. at the Graduate Center (City University of New York). His dissertation subject was "The William Remington Story," a McCarthy-era spy case, written with the sponsorship and collaboration of Joseph L. Rauh Jr., the prominent civil rights attorney who defended Remington. A veteran history teacher in New York City, Lee has written for various magazines including *The Nation, America in WWI* and *World War II.*

DANA LOMBARDY was a contributor to the *Encyclopedia of World War II: A Political, Social, and Military History* and numerous other military history books and publications. Dana was publisher of *World War One Illustrated* magazine from 2013 to 2019. His *Streets of Stalingrad* wargame received multiple awards. His work appears at LombardyStudios.com.

ERIN MAHAN, PhD, is Chief Historian of the Office of the Secretary of Defense and Director of the Pentagon Library. She previously served as associate research fellow at Center for the Study of Weapons of Mass Destruction at the National Defense University in Washington, D.C. As Chief of the Division of Arms Control, Asia, and Africa in the Office of the Historian at the Department of State (2004–2008) she edited several volumes in the *Foreign Relations of the United States* series. She is also the author of *Kennedy, De Gaulle and Western Europe* (Palgrave, 2002) and many shorter works, and is co-author of *The Great War: A World War I Collector's Vault* (2013), in addition to being general editor of the *Secretaries of Defense Historical Series.* She is currently finishing a co-authored book on the Nixon administration's arms control policies. She served on the National Historical Publications & Records Commission (2010 to 2019) and on the Historical Advisory Board of the World War I Centennial Commission from 2014 to 2019.

SANDRO MONETTI is a multi-award-winning journalist, author and broadcaster. Frequently seen on CNN and the BBC as an entertainment expert, this Beverly Hills–based Brit is the editor in chief of *Hollywood International Filmmaker Magazine,* the author of bestselling biographies of movie stars Mickey Rourke and Colin Firth, and is a British Academy of Film and Television Arts Los Angeles board of directors member. He has also written acclaimed plays and screenplays and counts *Saving Private Ryan* among his favorite films.

GERALD D. SWICK has worked as a magazine and book editor and was web editor for the various sites of Weider History magazine publishing group. He has written for the *Encyclopedia of World War II: A Political, Social, and Military History* and *The West Virginia Encyclopedia,* as well as *American History, America's Civil War, Armchair General, The Games Annual, Game News,* and other magazines, and is author of the *West Virginia Histories* book series. His work has been honored with a literary fellowship in nonfiction writing and an Associated Press Lifestyles Writing excellence in journalism award. His *Once, in America* history blog appears on his website, GeraldDSwick.com.

GERHARD L. WEINBERG, PhD, is an internationally recognized authority on Nazi Germany and the origins and course of World War II. As a youth he emigrated with his family from Nazi Germany to the United States. He served in the U.S. Army during the occupation of Japan, then earned his PhD at the University of Chicago. In captured archives he discovered *Hitler's Second Book: The Unpublished Sequel to MEIN KAMPF,* which he also edited and annotated. He served on the faculties of the University of Michigan and University of Kentucky. He is the William Rand Kenan, Jr. Professor Emeritus of History at the University of North Carolina at Chapel Hill. Professor Weinberg is the author or editor of numerous books and articles on 20th century European and world history including the pivotal *A World at Arms: A Global History of World War II.* He received the 2009 Pritzker Military Museum & Library Literature Award for Lifetime Achievement in Military Writing, and he currently sits on the Museum's Presidential Counselors advisory board. He is the recipient of a 2019 American Spirit Medallion from the National WWII Museum.

MARK WEISENMILLER is an author-historian-reporter living and working in Florida. He has worked for most of the world's major international news wire services, including United Press International; Deutsche Presse Agentur; Agence France Presse; Inter Press Service; the Associated Press, and the Xinhua News Agency, and he has written for *America in WWII* magazine. For more information, please visit the website of www.alkapressinternational.com.

JAY WERTZ is the author of seven books, including four volumes in the award-winning *War Stories: World War II Firsthand™* series. Other book-length publications include *The Native American Experience; The Civil War Experience 1861–1865* and *Smithsonian's Great Battles and Battlefields of the Civil War* which he co-authored with Edwin C. Bearss. He has completed five graphic histories of World War II campaigns for Monroe Publications' World War II Comix imprint. Jay has been a columnist for *Civil War Times Illustrated, America's Civil War, Historynet.com* and *GreatHistory.com;* a feature writer for *Aviation History* and *Armchair General* and a columnist, feature writer and contributing editor for *America in WWII.* His 44-year film and TV career in Hollywood includes working on TV series, commercials, feature films and acting as producer-director-writer of the award-winning 13-part documentary series *Smithsonian's Great Battles of the Civil War* for *The Learning Channel* and *Time-Life Video.*

A tabloid vendor in the Whitehall District of London displays the long-feared news headline of September 3, 1939.
(Image courtesy of the Library of Congress)

The Past

WHY THE 20TH CENTURY WAS SO VIOLENT

Gerhard L. Weinberg

IF ONE ASKS WHY THE 20TH CENTURY WAS SO FILLED WITH CONFLICTS, one needs to first look at the extent to which the national states into which the world was increasingly divided attempted to expand and acquire colonies. They then came to engage each other in a terrible world war with one of the belligerents, namely Germany. Germany, insisting that one world war was not sufficient for the century, started a second. Furthermore, as the colonial empires Europeans and Americans had created disintegrated, there were conflicts within and between the new states that emerged as a result of this process. As we will see, two of the major powers involved in the century's developments, Germany and the United States, did learn important lessons that reduced the level of conflict in the second half of the century to wars of a local rather than worldwide scope, but there was still a substantial quantity of that local type.

Early 20th Century Conflicts

When the 20th century started, there were three conflicts growing out of national colonial expansion already under way. In the southern part of Africa, the British were fighting a war against the Dutch settlers there, the Boers. This fighting had begun in 1899, continued until 1902, and came to include the British establishment of what were called "concentration camps" into which large numbers of Boer civilian families were herded with little attention to their subsistence needs. While the British in effect came to dominate the area, resentments lingered for decades.

Another conflict already under way was one growing out of the prior war between the United States and Spain. One American colonial acquisition resulting from its victory in that war was the Philippine Islands. A revolt against the newly imposed American rule by Filipinos, who wanted independence rather than just substituting one colonial master for another, began in 1899 and came to be called the Philippine Insurrection. The insurgents were effectively subdued by 1902, with the U.S. forces commanded by General Arthur MacArthur, father of World War II general Douglas MacArthur. Many within the United States, however, had reservations about the U.S. assuming the role of a colonial power, when the country had gained independence in a revolution against colonial master Great Britain. This sentiment led to the passage by the U.S. Congress of the Philippine Autonomy Act of 1916. The concept of moving the Philippines toward independence would later influence a further highly dramatic development.

The Tydings-McDuffie Act passed by the Congress in 1934 provided that the Philippines would become independent in 1944 with the United States giving up its military bases in the islands in 1946. When, in the years 1940–41, Britain would not cave in to Germany after the latter had crushed France, Belgium, and Holland, German leaders wanted Japan to attack Britain under circumstances that they projected would lead to Japanese seizure of Malaya, Singapore, the Dutch East Indies, as well as other French and British colonial possessions in Southeast Asia. The Japanese responded that they planned to seize all those areas but not until 1946. The Germans realized that this date was picked as one when American forces would no longer be in the Philippines, on the left flank of any such Japanese advance. Since the plans of Adolf Hitler called for a war with the United States after the conquest of most of Europe, with Britain crushed then rather than much later, he promised to go to war against the United States as soon as the Japanese did so as part of their conquering push into Southeast Asia. It was on the basis of this assurance, which the Japanese checked on a few days before striking, that they moved up their timetable from 1946 to 1941, attacked the USA on December 7, 1941, and were promptly joined by Germany and Italy (Hungary, Romania, and Bulgaria also declared war on the USA in December 1941). It was thus ironic that the American conquest of the Philippines would draw the United States formally and actively into World War II.

The third conflict that began in 1900 and lasted into 1901 was an anti-foreigners uprising in China that is generally referred to as the Boxer Rebellion. The efforts of the "Society of Righteous and Harmonious Fists" were a reaction against the incursion of European, American, and

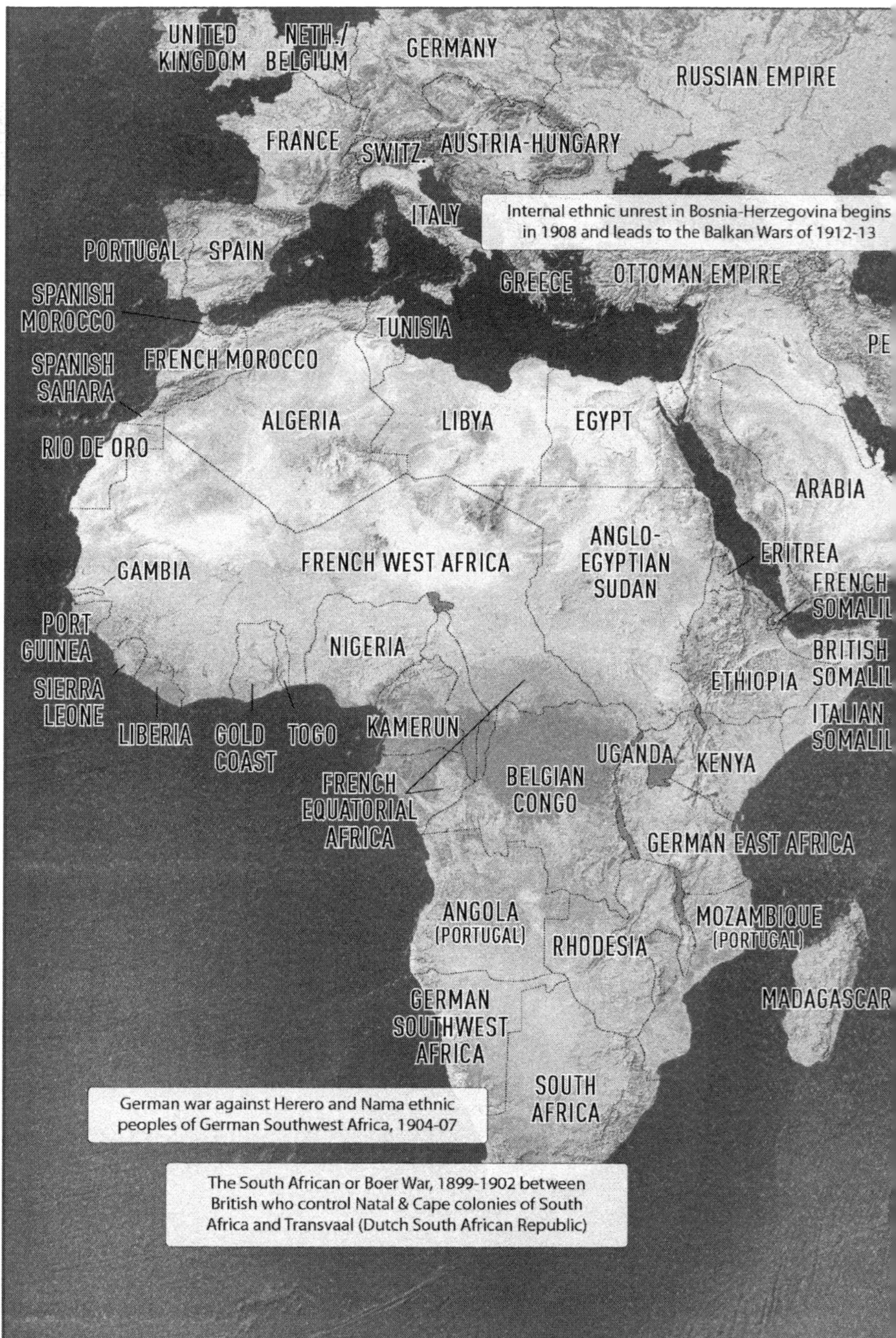
UNITED KINGDOM
NETH./ BELGIUM
GERMANY
RUSSIAN EMPIRE
FRANCE
SWITZ.
AUSTRIA-HUNGARY
ITALY
Internal ethnic unrest in Bosnia-Herzegovina begins in 1908 and leads to the Balkan Wars of 1912-13
PORTUGAL
SPAIN
GREECE
OTTOMAN EMPIRE
SPANISH MOROCCO
TUNISIA
SPANISH SAHARA
FRENCH MOROCCO
RIO DE ORO
ALGERIA
LIBYA
EGYPT
ARABIA
GAMBIA
FRENCH WEST AFRICA
ANGLO-EGYPTIAN SUDAN
ERITREA
PORT GUINEA
NIGERIA
SIERRA LEONE
LIBERIA
GOLD COAST
TOGO
KAMERUN
ETHIOPIA
UGANDA
KENYA
FRENCH EQUATORIAL AFRICA
BELGIAN CONGO
GERMAN EAST AFRICA
ANGOLA (PORTUGAL)
RHODESIA
MOZAMBIQUE (PORTUGAL)
MADAGASCAR
GERMAN SOUTHWEST AFRICA
SOUTH AFRICA
German war against Herero and Nama ethnic peoples of German Southwest Africa, 1904-07
The South African or Boer War, 1899-1902 between British who control Natal & Cape colonies of South Africa and Transvaal (Dutch South African Republic)

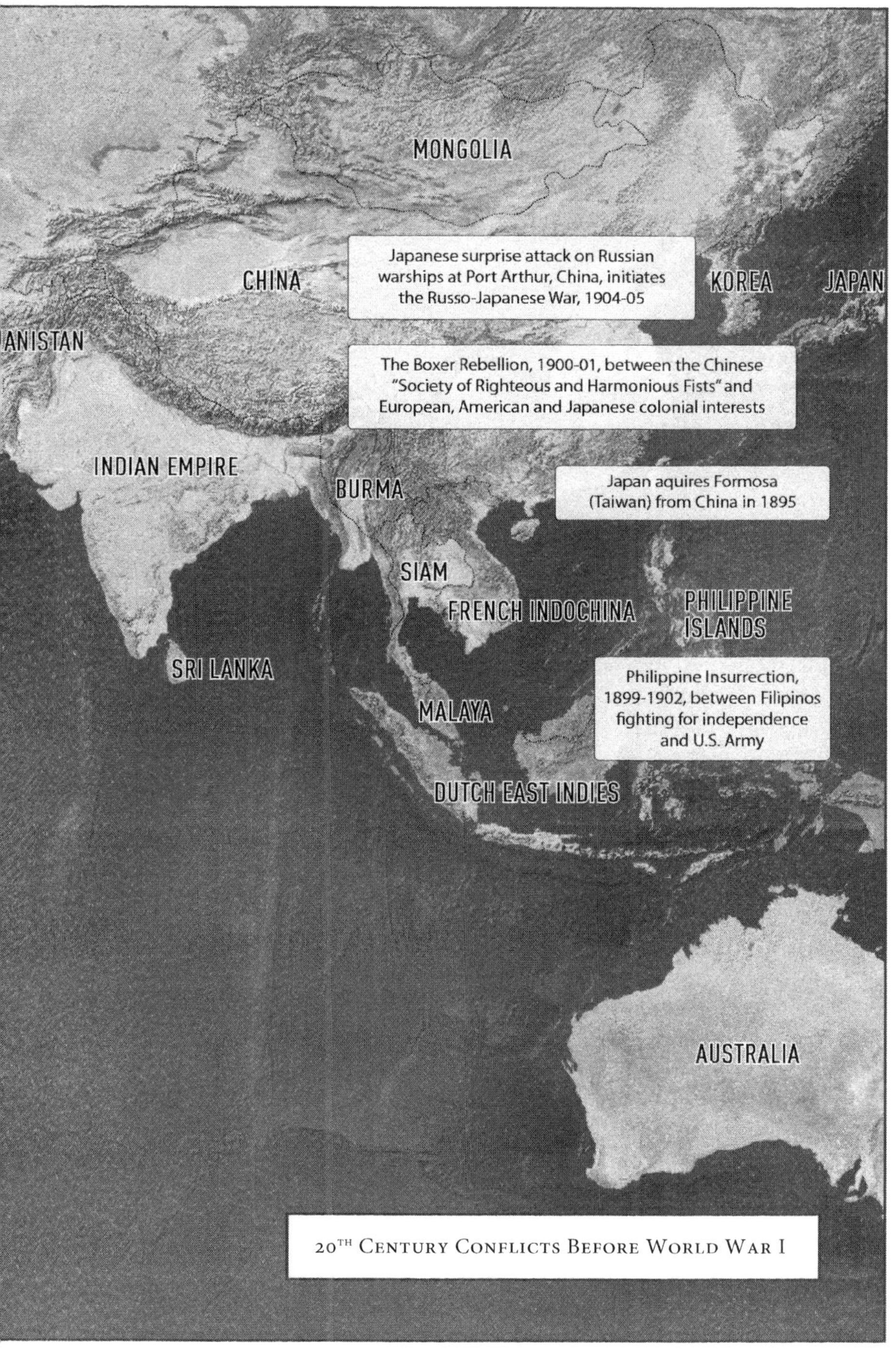

20TH CENTURY CONFLICTS BEFORE WORLD WAR I

Japanese colonial interests and measures into China as well as the activities of Christian missionaries in the country. Some foreign diplomats and missionaries were killed, and the foreign legations in the capital were besieged. Expeditionary forces from Britain, France, Russia, Germany, Japan, Austria-Hungary, Italy, and the United States relieved the situation but were also involved in considerable fighting, looting, and slaughter. Here was a further development in the process of colonialism that would on the one hand inspire the Japanese to attempt a greater role in controlling China and, on the other hand, lead to an American policy in an opposite direction—that is, a defense of Chinese independence with an "Open Door" for foreign commerce.

Japan, which had already fought a war with China, and had in that war seized the island of Formosa (Taiwan), saw its ambitions soon after the suppression of the Boxer Uprising rise in the northeast Chinese area of Manchuria and in Korea. This was in conflict with ambitions of Russia, which had in prior years expanded to the shores of the Pacific Ocean. The Russian port of Vladivostok on the Pacific was closed by ice much of the year, and the Russian government had leased Port Arthur on the Liaodong Peninsula from China as a port that was open practically year-round. The government in Tokyo decided on war with Russia and initiated hostilities in 1904 by a surprise attack on the Russian warships at Port Arthur. This war lasted into 1905 and was ended by the Treaty of Portsmouth, which was mediated by American president Theodore Roosevelt. As a reward for his effort, the Russian government gave the American president a Siberian crane, which lived in the Washington D.C. Zoo into the 1950s. This war had had the special aspect of an Asiatic country defeating a European one. The effect of this victory on the thinking of some in Japanese ruling circles makes it easier to understand Japan's subsequent willingness, even eagerness, to expand at the expense of European powers and the United Sates.

By the time the Russo-Japanese war ended, something very much resembling a war had broken out in the German colonial territory of Southwest Africa as the local Herero people, and later the local Nama people, rose in revolt against colonial masters and settlers who impinged on their resources in an extremely limited economy. The German war against the Herero uprising lasted from 1904 into 1907. German forces led by General Lothar von Trotha not only killed fighters. They systematically slaughtered civilians, drove many others into the desert or moved them into concentration camps as the British had done with Boers, in effect reducing the population by 75%. It has been thoughtfully argued that this first modern genocide came to have a major impact on the subsequent development of

German military policy and practice. (See Hull, *Absolute Destruction: Military Culture and the Practice of War in Imperial Germany*, in bibliography.)

Soon after the end of bloody fighting in the southern portion of Africa, the drive of European imperialistic powers produced a war on the continent's northern shore. As the Islamic- led Ottoman Empire declined during the 19th century, European powers adopted different and at times shifting policies toward it. Sometimes one or more tried to support and maintain the Ottoman state, but at times they tried to take portions of it for themselves. The main developments in this process that need to be noted for an understanding of what happened in the 20th century were that Britain came to have a predominant position in the Egyptian portion of the Ottoman Empire, while France acquired a form of control over the Tunisian portion and also began establishing control of Algeria. It should not be surprising that under these circumstances, Italy, which had acquired some colonial territory in the northeast corner of Africa but had been checked there in 1896 by a local defeat at Adowa (or Adwa) in what is now Ethiopia, might look toward the area now known as Libya, situated between the British and French areas of influence and across the Mediterranean from its own coast.

In 1911 Italy began what can be called a war of conquest against the Ottoman Empire. The fighting raged both in Libya and on the Mediterranean Sea, and during the fighting the Italians also seized the island of Rhodes and what came to be called the Dodecanese Islands in the Aegean Sea. The peace signed in 1912 in effect turned Libya over to Italy, and while the Dodecanese were not to remain under Italian control, in effect the islands remained under Italy until after World War II. The obvious weakening of the Ottoman Empire by its struggle with Italy has to be seen as tempting the Balkan states to take advantage of the situation by getting together to take from that declining and busy empire whatever they might be able to acquire.

World War I

The Balkan League of Serbia, Montenegro, Bulgaria, and Greece in fact initiated its attack in what has come to be known as the First Balkan War in 1912 even before the treaty to end the Italo-Ottoman War was signed. The armies of the Balkan League won a series of battles, and in the peace signed in 1913 almost all Ottoman lands in Europe were lost to Serbia, Greece, and Bulgaria, while Albania became an independent state. The Bulgarian government was not satisfied with the country's share of the spoils, attacked Serbia, and lost the Second Balkan War to Serbia, Greece, and Romania later in 1913.

It was an incident related to the process of the decline and dissolution of the Ottoman Empire that, in combination with the reaction of other European states to the emergence of a unified and highly ambitious Germany, came to lead to what is at times called "The Great War" and is now more commonly referred to as the First World War. The Ottoman province of Bosnia-Herzegovina had come under the control of Austria-Hungary in 1875–78. It was annexed by Austria-Hungary in 1908, but there were all sorts of internal troubles among Muslims, Eastern Orthodox Christians, Roman Catholic Christians and national minorities. There were also external issues growing out of Serbian ambitions for further expansion after the Balkan Wars. It was out of these frictions that there came the assassination of the heir to the Austro-Hungarian throne while on a visit to Sarajevo, the territory's capital, in July 1914.

What made the Sarajevo incident so critical was the encouragement that the German government gave to the Austrian government to go to war with Serbia, which was held responsible for the assassination. Once the Austrians initiated hostilities, the possibility that Russia might support Serbia led Germany to declare war on Russia and, since Russia was allied with France, to declare war on France as well. German military planning was concentrated on quickly defeating France so that massive German forces could be sent to the eastern front against a more slowly mobilizing Russia. In view of German concern about delay in the west because of French fortifications on the German-French border, German troops were instead to move through neutral Belgium into France. It was this breach of prior treaties about Belgium that brought Great Britain and its dominions and colonies into the war on the side of France and Russia. Britain had previously warred against both these countries, but had worked out reconciliations with them in view of German ambition. Germany was building a huge navy in the early years of the century as a challenge to Britain's control of oceans.

Because the participants in the First World War had colonial possessions around the world, the fighting took place in the Middle East and parts of Africa and Asia, as well as much of Europe. It is essential to note how additional countries came into the conflict. Because of developments in the Second Balkan war, Romania entered the conflict on what came to be called the "Allied" side, while Bulgaria joined what would be designated the "Central Powers," led by Germany. The Ottoman Empire also joined the Central Powers because it feared further encroachment from Russia, Britain, and France. Both in view of a prior alliance with Britain, and in the hope of acquiring German colonial possessions in China and the Pacific, Japan joined the Allies. Italy had been aligned with the Central Powers, but found it more likely to be profitable in territorial gains to side with the Allies and fight against those with whom it had been associated previously. The failure of the German effort to secure a quick victory in the west led it to use submarines to crush its British enemy. This brought major trouble with the United States. After a temporary reduction of submarine attacks, the deliberate resumption of the submarine campaign in the Atlantic brought the United States into the war on the Allied side.

When the German naval records were captured by the Allies after World War II, they illuminated among other topics a major and lengthy controversy within the German authorities during World War I. Should the invasion of the United States begin on the beaches of Cape Cod in Massachusetts or the beaches of Long Island in New York? No such invasion ever occurred, but the debate illuminates the extent to which the war growing out of an incident in the Balkans had become global.

After Germany's forces had defeated Serbia, Romania, and Russia, it hoped to crush the Western Powers by a series of offensives on the Western Front. After some initial victories, these were halted. Reinforced by rapidly increasing American troops, the Allies began to drive the Germans out of French territory the Germans had earlier occupied, and they hoped to end the war victoriously in 1919 by major new offensives of their own. As the highest German military leaders saw their hopes of victory shattered and Allied advances threatening to crush, and not merely drive back, Germany's shrinking land army, they insisted their government ask for an armistice to end the fighting. The surprised German government followed this advice, and the equally surprised German home front dissolved into mutinies and revolutions. Some on the Allied side urged a continuation of the fighting until Germany surrendered unconditionally. Enormous losses already endured, however, and the likely continuation of very bloody fighting persuaded the Allies to agree to an armistice as long as the terms precluded a German resumption of hostilities—which it did. In subsequent years, many military and political figures in Germany, Adolf Hitler becoming the loudest and most prominent among them, would assert and actually come to believe these events occurred in reverse order. They would argue that the upheavals inside Germany came first and caused the need for an armistice, turning an imminent German victory into a defeat.

Europe Between the Wars

The German military victories on the Eastern Front had in 1917 led to a revolution that overthrew the Tsarist regime in Russia; subsequently, a Bolshevik movement, assisted by Germany, overthrew the successor

British-German naval battles
DENMARK
UNITED KINGDOM
NETHERLANDS
BELGIUM
France, Britain and later the U.S. battle Germany in trench warfare along the German borders with France and Belgium, 1914-18
On August 1, 1914, Germany invades France through neutral Belgium
FRANCE
SWITZERLAND
Italy enters war on Allied side in 1915 - Austria-Hungary gives Italy a stunning defeat at Caporetto, October 1917
World War I begins after the assassination of an Austro-Hungarian royal in Serbian-controlled Bosnia on June 28, 1914, escalates
SPAIN
PORTUGAL
World War I
TUNIS

Germany invades Russia in 1915 after beating back Russian army at Tannenberg in August 1914. In 1917 Germany reaches armistice agreement with new Bolshevik government after October 1917 revolution in Russia.

GERMANY

RUSSIAN EMPIRE

AUSTRIA-HUNGARY

Central Powers ally Bulgaria joins Austria-Hungary battling Allied nations of Serbia and Romania in Balkans

ROMANIA

SERBIA

BULGARIA

Just to the east of the map edge is Armenia - Turkish genocide in Armenia in April 1915

TALY

ALBANIA

GREECE

OTTOMAN EMPIRE

ICILY

Ottoman Empire joins Germany and Austria-Hungary in Central Powers - battles Allies in Turkey and other areas of the Middle East

CYPRUS

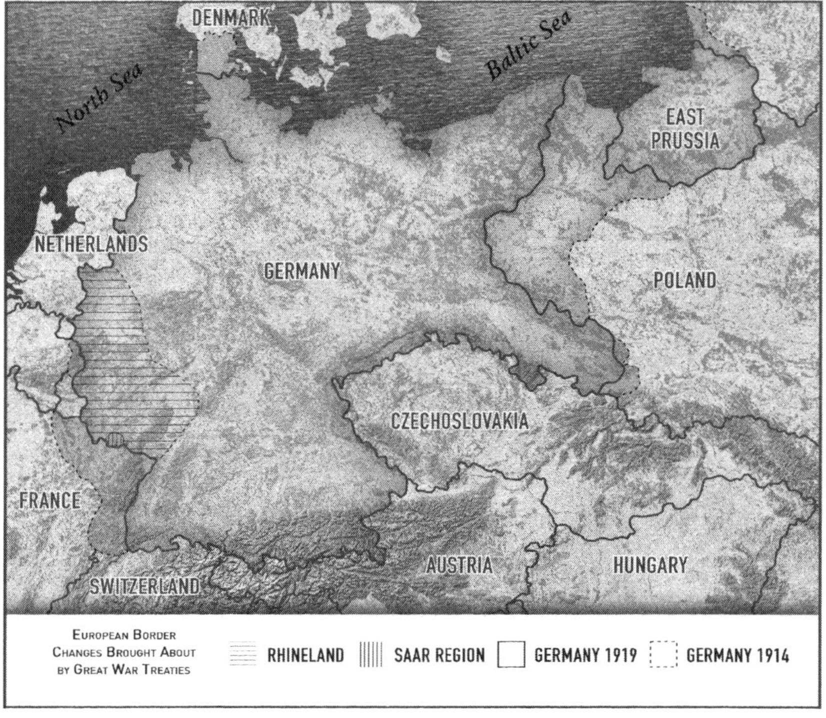

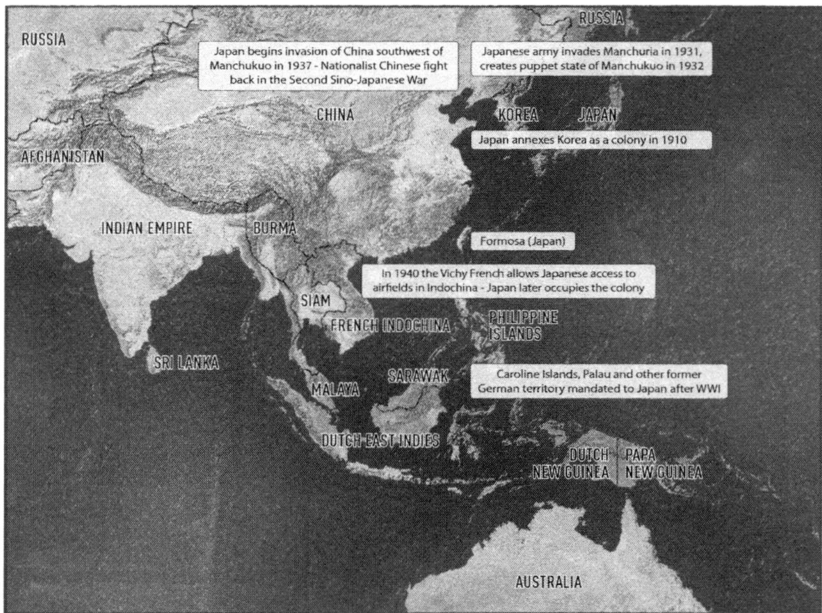

Japanese expansion in East Asia and the Pacific from 1919 to 1940.

government that had continued the war. In view of the Bolsheviks making peace with Germany, the Western Allies intervened in the Russian Civil War from 1918 to 1921, and in the latter part of that conflict the winning Bolsheviks also tried unsuccessfully to crush the revived independent Poland. The peace conference that was held in Versailles by the Western Allies to end their war with the Central Powers therefore took place while fighting continued in Eastern Europe and Russian lands all the way to the Pacific.

The peacemakers at Versailles tried hard to remedy what they believed had led to the terrible war now ended. They tried to adjust the boundaries in Central and Southeast Europe to the populations' nationality and provided for plebiscites (elections) where this was not clear, to allow a subsequent drawing of boundaries along national lines as expressed by the inhabitants. The colonies of Germany were turned over to the victors but under a so-called "Mandate" system as they moved to independence. Instead of following the prior practice of victors in war of imposing an indemnity on the defeated, the victors this time insisted that those who had initiated the conflict, Germany and Austria-Hungary, pay for the cost of repairing the damages caused by a war in which 99% of those damages had occurred inside the lands of the victors. In the hope of preventing a future calamity of the sort that had just occurred, the peace conference also created a new international organization, the League of Nations, whose charter became the first article of each peace treaty with the defeated.

The settlement put together at Versailles has been criticized as too harsh or too soft, but has rarely received a fair evaluation. One important aspect of it has even more rarely received the attention it deserves, and this issue will be stressed subsequently. At the peace conference in Vienna in 1814–15 to settle things after the wars of the French Revolution and Napoleon, the various separate territories in the Rhineland were turned over to Prussia in the hope of thereby deterring future French military adventures in Central and Eastern Europe. It worked that way for decades, but then the Prussians and Germans had twice used that area as a base for attacking to the West. At the 1919 Peace Conference the French argued that this barrier now needed to be utilized to prevent future German attacks to the West and urged that it be made into a separate state. The Americans and British saw this as a violation of the nationality principle that was to provide the basis for peace in Europe and obtained agreement to the area's retention by Germany through treaties of guarantee with France in the hope of thereby deterring any future German attack westwards.

The decision of the American people and government in and after the presidential election of 1920 to stop the earth and get off is generally discussed in terms of the refusal to ratify the peace treaties and to join the League of Nations. Surely as important was the refusal to ratify the treaty of guarantee with France and to maintain the armed forces that might be needed to implement it if the Germans were not deterred and utilized the Rhineland for a third attack westwards. Early in World War II Germany did invade and occupy France. That meant that in World War II American soldiers could not unload in French ports as they had done in the prior war but instead had to storm beaches. The cemetery in Normandy near Omaha Beach holds some of the thousands of American soldiers who paid with their lives for this portion of America's post-1918 policy.

The fighting inside Russia and between it and Poland has already been mentioned. Other violence also occurred due to the shifts in power during and immediately after the First World War. These include the massacre of about one and a half million Armenians in the Ottoman Empire in 1915–16 as well as the substantial violence that occurred as Turks left former parts of the Ottoman Empire, forcing Greeks to leave cities in the western part of a new Turkey that emerged out of the ruins of the empire. There were also local incidents of violence as some of the former pieces of Poland annexed by Prussia were returned to the revived Polish state.

The Armistice of November 11, 1918, did not end violence but the loss of about 30 million lives in the war and the vast destruction caused by the fighting provided an incentive to avoid open conflict. This hope for avoiding war was reinforced by the experience of two German innovations in the war. The bombing of cities far from the front by zeppelins and aircraft, as well as the employment of poison gas at the front, suggested that further development of these techniques of combat was likely to make future hostilities even more costly in lives and property. There appeared to be every incentive to reduce military forces and settle whatever problems in international relations might arise peacefully instead of by force of arms.

Japan and Italy Destroy a Fragile Peace

Under these circumstances there was a whole series of conferences designed to encourage a reduction of military forces both on the sea and on land, as well as a treaty, the Kellogg-Briand Pact of 1928 signed by 59 states, to do away with war altogether. There was, however, no agreed procedure to implement and enforce this concept. Two of the signatories, Italy and Japan, preferred to adopt policies ignoring the pact, and a third, Germany would absolutely insist on making a whole series of wars into which those two states decided to join.

In the cases of Japan and Italy their turn to violence was a continuation of prior policies. Japan seized Manchuria in 1931, took over adjacent portions of China proper, and moved into a real war with China in 1937. This conflict, which would last until 1945, was designed to assure Japan control of the whole country either directly or through a puppet regime. The horrors that Japanese forces inflicted drew worldwide attention, but the main long-term impact of the whole process was to enable the Chinese Communists to defeat a weakened Chinese Nationalist government in the Chinese Civil War of 1946–49.

The fascist government of Italy under Benito Mussolini moved to remedy the previous halt to its colonial ambitions in Northeast Africa by invading Abyssinia (Ethiopia) in 1935. In a conflict that saw the Italians use poison gas (as did the Japanese in their war with China) and also repeatedly carry out very large-scale massacres, the whole country was conquered. It would remain under Italian control until British forces crushed the Italian garrison during World War II and restored the country's independence.

Mussolini had hardly completed the conquest of Abyssinia in 1936 before he decided to intervene with substantial forces on the side of Francisco Franco's Nationalists in the civil war in Spain. From 1936 to 1939 the Nationalists fought to replace the government of the Spanish Republic. This conflict saw intervention not only from Italy but also from the Soviet Union on the Republican side; volunteers from several countries on both sides; and a special participation on Franco's side by a German air force unit sent by Hitler. Among other operations, this "Condor Legion" engaged in a bombing of the Spanish town of Guernica that was internationally condemned. It should be noted that in the Spanish Civil War Germany and Italy, which had fought on opposite sides in World War I, were sending forces to fight on the same side. *(See map on Pages 32-33)*

The Rise of Nazi Germany

The impetus for the century's and probably history's biggest conflict, World War II, came from Germany. In his speeches and writings, Adolf Hitler always distinguished himself from all other political leaders in Germany by derisively referring to them as "Grenzpolitiker" (border politicians) while referring to himself as a "Raumpolitiker" (politician of space). They would get Germany into wars causing numerous casualties to reclaim the bits of territory Germany had lost in the 1919 peace treaty and which, even if victorious, would leave Germany unable to feed its population from its own soil as before 1914. He, on the other hand, would lead the country into wars for space on which German farmers would raise large families both to replace the casualties incurred in war and create the need for further space until the whole earth was inhabited by members of the superior Germanic-Aryan population. All this could be accomplished, according to Hitler, only by a single-party government and required the extermination inside and outside the original Germany of all racially inferior but very dangerous Jews. By the beginning of the 1930s the National Socialist Party led by Hitler was drawing the largest number of voters in the country, and on January 30, 1933, he was appointed Chancellor of the country by its elected president, Paul von Hindenburg.

While consolidating power inside Germany, Hitler immediately initiated major armaments programs for the wars he intended Germany to initiate. The first against Czechoslovakia could be waged by more of the weapons Germany already had, while the next, against France and Britain, called for new dive-bombers and tanks. Victory in that war would make it safe for Germany to conquer the Soviet Union, a campaign that required no new weapons because, by what he considered a stroke of good fortune, the partly Germanic ruling elite in Russia that had before 1917 reigned over its "racially inferior" Slavic population had been replaced by total incompetents. That conquest would in turn facilitate war against the United States by providing the raw materials, especially oil, needed to conquer that "racially weak and confused" but far-away society. Since the weapons needed for that distant conquest, intercontinental bombers and super-battleships, would take time to develop and produce, he ordered initiation of their development and construction in 1937 as soon as the production of weapons for the war against France and Britain was well under way.

At the last minute Hitler called off the invasion of Czechoslovakia in October 1938 and, at a conference in Munich, settled temporarily for the acquisition of its border area inhabited by people of German background in what he thereafter always considered the worst mistake of his career. He made absolutely certain that no one would cheat him of war in 1939 as he believed British prime minister Neville Chamberlain had done in 1938. There would be a massive anti-Jewish pogrom throughout Germany in November 1938, the German media were instructed to prepare the German public for hostilities, and the German ambassadors to Poland, Britain, and France would be kept in Germany in the last days before Germany initiated hostilities.

In the winter of 1938–39 Hungary and Lithuania had been willing to subordinate themselves to Germany so it could make its eastern border quiet while crushing France and Britain. Poland had been prepared to make substantial concessions to Germany in serious negotiations but was not prepared to give up its recently re-acquired independence. Hitler therefore decided to attack it before striking in the West, or to fight the Western Powers right away if they honored a promise to Poland as they had warned Germany they would. If Stalin was stupid enough to join in attacking Poland and thereby provide a direct border with Germany across which the latter could by-pass the British blockade until Germany had won in the West and could turn on the Soviet Union, the German foreign minister could go to Moscow and give Stalin whatever he wanted since it would all be taken back later.

Like Hitler, Stalin believed and acted on the ideas he voiced. He thought it fine if what he considered the "capitalist" countries fought each other, and he would take measures to help the Germans conquer northern, western, and southeastern Europe and for the Soviet Union to attack Finland while the others were fighting. He would be surprised when the German agrarian expansionists, rather than capitalists, attacked the Soviet Union and he would be outraged at being for quite some time alone on the continent to fight them, unwilling to acknowledge his own responsibility for this situation.

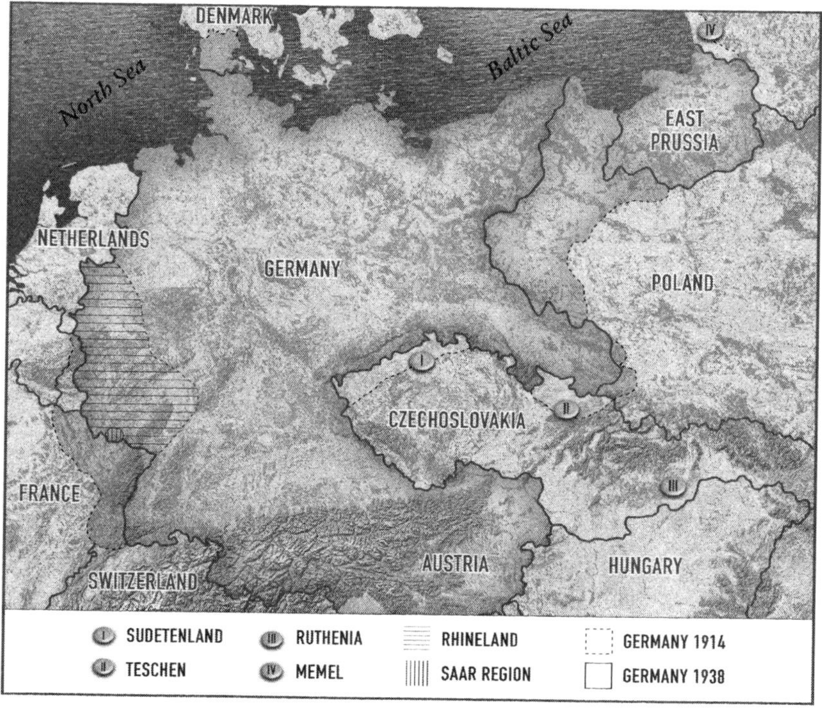

Under Hitler, by 1938 Germany expanded from the 1919 treaty borders through negotiations peppered with brutality. Saar and Rhineland were regained; Austria was annexed and areas marked I, II, III and IV were acquired.

A SHORT HISTORY OF THE EUROPEAN WAR

1939 to June 1944

Jay Wertz

THE CONCEPT OF TOTAL WAR, WHEN A COMBATANT SEEKS TO NOT only destroy the enemy's armies and navies but also to destroy the enemy's ability to make war and alter the fabric of its society, was hinted at in the wars of the 19th century. In the American Civil War the siege of Vicksburg, the burning of the Shenandoah Valley and Sherman's March to the Sea were examples of the total war concept. By the First World War, large numbers of civilian casualties were common. The siege of Verdun is but one prominent example.

In that war, the introduction of air combat was a clear indicator of where total war was headed next. In the 1930s Spanish Civil War (the dress rehearsal for the coming war) Dr. Weinberg describes the German Condor Legion's bombing of the Spanish town of Guernica. He notes that the indiscriminate bombing of the civilian population became the subject of a very famous painting.

"There is a story that may or may not be true that after the Germans occupied Paris in 1940 some German soldiers went into the studio of the painting's artist, Pablo Picasso, looked at some preliminary sketches of the painting and said to him: 'So you did that!' Picasso responded: 'No, you did.'"

The combination of leaders—committed to their goals often to the point of fanaticism—huge armies, vast navies, and most importantly, great advances in air power and other military technologies was going to make World War II a very bloody war. Total war would be taken to the extreme. And it all started in Europe with the Nazi invasion of Poland on September 1, 1939.

Poland—The War Begins

After the three bloodless coups, or "Flower Wars" as they are sometimes called, against Austria, the Sudetenland and Czechoslovakia, Adolf Hitler finally got his war. After setting in motion a "false flag" incident with a staged Polish attack on a German radio station near the border, German mechanized units supported by planes moved through the Polish Corridor—a strip of Polish territory between Germany and East Prussia that had been created by the Treaty of Versailles—and elsewhere along a more than 1,700-mile front. At the same time, an aging German warship supported attacks and internal violence in the former Prussian city of Danzig, which had been made an international protectorate by the same treaty.

Though the Polish military had mobilized after diplomatic efforts to stave off a German invasion failed, Polish leaders were unprepared for the onslaught of the German Wehrmacht. The million-man Polish army was organized in clusters, primarily along Poland's western border. They had minimal fixed defenses in these positions. Communication was all fed through the capital of Warsaw, slowing local response to the attacks and delaying commitment of Poland's sparse reserves.

The mechanized blitzkrieg (lightning war) of massed armor, born as a theory in the period when the Versailles Treaty greatly reduced Germany's military, was being put into practice. Airfields conveniently located in Germany and the new Nazi satellite countries on Poland's borders allowed the German Air Force (Luftwaffe) to track the ground invasion. The infamous Stuka dive-bomber provided a kind of aerial artillery with its screaming terror bombs. Unusually dry weather enabled German tanks and trucks to make good progress on Poland's roads.

On the first day German tanks were able to slice as deep as 15 miles into the Polish interior. They didn't advance unopposed. Polish tanks and light armored vehicles, primarily attached to infantry units, stood in the path of the German advance. Particularly in the north, where fog hampered German air cover, Polish troops with better defensive positions battled the attackers. Polish planes had been relocated away from the airfields that were among the first German bombing targets. Though no match for modern German aircraft, they did shoot down 70 enemy planes over the course of the conflict. However, such opposition was exceptional in the first days of the war.

It is a myth that Poland's famed cavalry riding horses and carrying lances attacked German tanks head-on. But their primary usefulness, to ride quickly to the enemy rear and cut off frontline troops from their support, was dampened by German air superiority and the rapid pace of the advance. As Polish units became surrounded and cut off, the Warsaw leadership attempted to man a second line of defense behind the Vistula River, but it was too late in forming.

As large chunks of the country and stands of troops were being scooped up by the German advance, the Warsaw leadership looked west for salvation. Between the wars France had given strong assurance in a pact to protect Poland from just this kind of German aggression. Great Britain backed France in the treaty. But the only response on September 1 from the Western Powers was diplomatic censure. Two days later, Britain and France declared war on Germany but took no direct action. The German high command left Germany's western borders lightly defended, in order to mass forces for the quick strike on Poland. It was a risk that paid off.

Not everything went according to plan for the German invasion. The armor was led, not by the imposing German tanks of later battles but by Panzer I and II models, which featured only a machine gun or light cannon. Only five armored divisions were fully equipped. Only four infantry divisions were mechanized, meaning they had vehicular transportation. The other 25 divisions operated as they did in World War I— they marched to the front along with horse-drawn artillery. Mechanical breakdowns were common. Congested roads and slow-moving units caused many logistics issues. Several times the panzers outran their gasoline supply. A better prepared and equipped army might have slowed or halted the German advance. But at that time there was no such army in the world.

Within a week German forces were closing in on the capital of Warsaw. There the advance was checked. Better defensive positions and Polish determination forced the Germans to besiege the city. It would be a temporary respite. Panzers continued to advance east to the Bug River while other Wehrmacht units reduced the surrounded pockets of Polish soldiers.

To add to Polish woes, 35 divisions of the Red Army entered Poland from the east. Josef Stalin, feeling safe with the nonaggression pact signed in August between Germany and the Soviet Union, and because his military had prevailed in a recently concluded conflict with Japan along the Soviet-Manchurian border, invaded Poland. All sorts of unconvincing reasons were offered to the world—the Soviets were there to protect Polish citizens from the Nazis; the communist country was just recovering lands lost in the

1920s war—but in reality, Stalin was trying to expand his holdings, while exposing his own eastern frontier to Germany as Hitler had predicted.

By arrangement with the Nazi government, the Red Army halted at the Bug River, which German units had already reached. Polish soldiers retreating to the southeast, if cornered, surrendered to the Germans rather than allow themselves to be captured by Soviet forces. By September 27, the Polish commander of the Warsaw garrison sought surrender terms. Poland's military chief and the country's political leaders had already fled to safety. No terms were given; the Poles accepted unconditional surrender.

The "Phony" and Winter Wars

Immediately after the surrender of Poland, Germany paused before moving on its next objective—the countries on its western border. Great Britain and France made efforts to mobilize for war, but if Germany had invaded the west immediately, the swallowing up of western territory would probably have been swift. Britain was still under the leadership of Prime Minister Neville Chamberlain, whose previous negotiations with Adolf Hitler led to the loss of the entire country of Czechoslovakia to the Germans. Disagreements in Chamberlain's own parliament colored the response to the Nazis, despite Winston Churchill's push for action.

In France, President Édouard Daladier was having even more difficultly drafting a response to Germany with his fractious government. The respite was much appreciated by Wehrmacht leaders who realized things that didn't work against Poland would have to be fixed before an invasion of the West. This period that lasted from October 1939 to April 1940 earned the moniker, the "Phony War."

Josef Stalin used this time period to accomplish some goals separate from those of his non-aggression pact partner, Germany. Exporting his signature campaign of terror, he first executed most of the Polish officers captured by his army in the September incursion. He then turned his attention to his neighbor to the northwest, the Scandinavian country of Finland, which had only escaped Russian rule as a result of the regional instability and treaties following the First World War. In a series of October 1939 conferences in which resolution was unlikely, Soviet foreign minister Vyacheslav Molotov made unreasonable demands for Finland to cede large chunks of land to the USSR. When this didn't work, the Soviets invaded Finland.

The action began on November 30 with 600,000 invading troops of the Red Army moving across common borders into Finland and the bombing of the capital Helsinki and other key targets. This was not blitzkrieg;

though outnumbering the Finnish army and air force, poor preparation for the frigid conditions and uneven leadership (Stalin had executed many in his own officer corps in 1937) bogged down Soviet advances. The Finns, adapt at conducting warfare in the snow and cold, scored a number of victories especially in the desolate tundra areas in the central and northern regions of Finland in what was dubbed the "Winter War."

In the end, the greater amount of men and resources of the Soviets forced the democratic government of Finland to come to the negotiating table, where they surrendered even more territory than was previously proposed. The country was forced to submit to the rule of a puppet Soviet government. It was a humbling the Finnish people would not forget. There was no cause for celebration among the victors however. The massive casualties and poor military showing by the Red Army made the USSR appear very vulnerable to the planned German invasion to which the Soviet leader was completely oblivious.

The Early Sea War—Invasion of Denmark and Norway

In April 1940 Hitler was on the move again. Objective: Norway, with the simultaneous consumption of his small neighbor to the north, Denmark. German naval leader Grossadmiral Erich Raeder had been anxious to snare Norway's fabulous ports for the Reich since the fall of Poland. German Kriegsmarine (navy) surface ships and U-boats had already been skirmishing with Royal Navy warships and engaging in commerce raiding for months. On April 9, Hitler escalated the war greatly by invading and capturing Denmark, almost more quickly than the tiny kingdom's royals could escape.

Norway was much more of a challenge. The Germans mounted their first (and only) large seaborne invasion of the war near the capital, Oslo, and at other key cities on the coast. For the first time in the war airborne troops were used to seize early objectives. But the British were waiting for them. Ship to ship and air to ship actions occurred along the coast and in the North Sea. The Germans were dealt a stiff defeat at Narvik, in the Arctic Circle region. British, French and Polish troops landed in Norway, but couldn't mount an offensive significant enough to slow down German gains.

By the end of May the forces of the Allied nations had greater problems and left Norway. Hitler was able to force Nazi rule on Norway, initially with a puppet government under Vidkun Quisling. The Germans also gained strategic port locations for their U-boat pens and a sea route from Narvik to transport valuable loads of iron ore from neutral Sweden to German steel mills.

Blitzkrieg in the West

Those greater problems for the British and French began on May 10 when blitzkrieg came to the West. Two German army groups, 75 divisions, crossed the borders of the Netherlands, Belgium and Luxembourg, supported by the Luftwaffe and paratroopers in *Fall Gelb* (Plan Yellow). Another army group of 19 divisions stood ready across the French defensive works of the Maginot Line on the German frontier. Most of the 99 divisions in the French forces were immediately mobilized under General Maurice Gamelin, the overall Allied commander. Together with the ground forces of the roughly 400,000-strong British Expeditionary Force (BEF) on alert in France they moved into neutral Belgium.

The German front was long and deep, though rear units quickly became delayed on the network of narrow roads. But the armored columns moved fast. First to go was the Netherlands. Its army and air force were no match for the Wehrmacht, and the ground forces quickly fell back from one defensive line to another. French motorized units did not arrive in time to help. While the Dutch were reeling, German forces pounced on the Belgian defenses along the Meuse River and established a foothold in the country on the first day.

The greatest tactical thrust, however, was along the same approach used successfully by Kaiser Wilhelm's legions in the Great War—through the Ardennes Forest in Belgium and Luxembourg. Within days, German tanks and infantry were threatening to cross the Meuse into France and cut off two French armies in the process. In the first six days of the campaign, May 10–15, the Allies encountered a series of setbacks. On May 11, the Belgian army gave up half the country by falling back to the Dyle River, a pre-determined defensive line where British and French troops joined them the following day. On May 13, a major tank battle was fought at Hannut, but the Allies failed to slow down the panzers advancing across the Belgian plain. To the south, panzers bridged the Meuse River in the area of Sedan, France, and began to roll over the French Second and Ninth armies.

On May 14, the Netherlands surrendered. The Dyle River line was probed on the 15th. Gamelin began to call his armies backing the Maginot Line to move north but their entry into the battle zone would be too late. Aggressive panzer commander General Heinz Guderian was already angling his forces to the northwest, to keep up with other German tanks racing across Belgium under emerging division commander General Erwin Rommel and others. The principal factors that began to slow down these tank columns were orders from army commanders, fearful the panzers would outrun their infantry support and fuel.

Not only were the Germans causing headaches for the Allied battlefield commanders, they were creating disruptions behind the lines. French politicians lost confidence in Gamelin and each other. Winston Churchill, named British prime minister on the first day of the invasion, had little success stiffening French resolve during personal visits to Paris. The crisis continued. An attitude of defeat fell over the French capital. Even as German units began to force the French, British and Belgians into a pocket on the coast in the last two weeks of May, the noise in the capital was reaching the intensity of the noise at the front. Marshal Henri Pétain, a hero of World War I was voicing the opinions of the armistice supporters while French president Paul Reynaud was upholding the side favoring continuing military resistance.

By this time BEF commander Lord Gort and other British military leaders were voicing another concern—saving their army. Now cut off from their base at Cherbourg on the Normandy coast by the German forces surrounding them, a daring plan to evacuate the BEF troops in the pocket centered on the French port of Dunkirk was launched. Using a combination of military ships and private vessels pressed into service, most of the British soldiers and some French, more than 330,000, were evacuated across the English Channel with this makeshift armada. Most Belgian soldiers and a French rear guard holding off a ground attack by the German infantry (the panzers were withdrawn to continue to conquer France) were captured. The Dunkirk evacuation was aided by a fine showing by the Royal Air Force, which minimized Luftwaffe attacks during the 10-day operation.

After the Dunkirk evacuation the fall of France came quickly. The shattered and divided French army continued to give ground to the pressure of hard-driving panzers with their dominant air support. The Somme River was crossed. The Germans entered Paris on June 14 and Reynaud's government caravanned south on an almost daily basis, competing for travel routes with a crush of civilian and military refugees. The vaulted Maginot Line fell to the Wehrmacht's Army Group C, except for a few French martyrs who refused to surrender. The Reynaud government fled the country. By June 20 a signal was given for negotiations and on June 22, with Adolf Hitler in attendance, French military representatives were dragged to Compiègne Forest to reenact the armistice of November 1918, but with different results. The French unconditional surrender was much graver than the German capitulation ending World War I that had given Hitler so much ammunition in his rise to power.

France was then divided into north and south regions on a border that roughly matched the German advance when hostilities ended. Paris and the northern part were placed under occupation control. The southern part was declared free and allied with Germany under an agreement worked out at the nearby resort town of Vichy. Marshal Pétain was named head of the new Vichy French government.

The Battle of Britain

London was becoming crowded with the deposed leaders of Western Europe. One of those was a minor general who made an ineffective stab with his French tanks at the German columns moving toward the coast on May 17 and 19. Charles de Gaulle had a lot of political savvy and was known to the Reynaud camp. He quickly established himself as a leader in exile, calling for Frenchmen around the world to join his force and oppose the German occupation.

While de Gaulle was building a reputation in front of radio microphones, Churchill and British war leaders were anticipating Hitler's next move. An immediate problem was to deny the Kriegsmarine the use of French ships, scattered primarily in Mediterranean ports controlled by the Vichy French. Although the Vichy admiral commanding the Marine Nationale, the French fleet, promised not to turn his ships over to the Germans, the British didn't trust his word. Beginning on June 3, the Royal Navy commenced *Operation Catapult* and for a month seized French ships in British ports and attempted to commandeer those in other harbors, mostly in North Africa. The two former allies exchanged shots but after a month, the threat of French warships joining the German navy was nullified.

The Führer spent a few weeks negotiating with his allies, including the Soviet Union, General Francisco Franco's fascist government of Spain and Benito Mussolini. The Italian dictator had quickly fallen into the shadow of the German leader; his early forays into North Africa *(see previous chapter)* and Albania in 1939 seemed to pale in comparison to German accomplishments in mid-1940. After remaining neutral for nine months, Italy declared war on Britain and France on June 11 and Mussolini sent Italian forces into France at the tail end of the campaign, but only so his regime could share in the spoils of war. His next attempt to rival Hitler would come in September of 1940 when four Italian motorized divisions crossed the Libyan border into Egypt, then stooped short of the main British force. Mishandled, the campaign would become a burden for the Berlin government. Hitler, however, had other things on his mind in midsummer 1940.

After the fall of France the Führer wanted to strike a foe he saw as wobbly from the rapid collapse of Western Europe. On July 16, after Admiral Raeder assured the German high command that a lack of warships made blockading the British Isles a distant hope, Führer Directive 16 outlined a plan to invade England. Preparations went forward for *Operation Seelöwe* (*Sealion*), a plan that Raeder considered a last resort. As Hitler made speeches attempting to sway the more conciliatory among the Brits into an armistice, the German army and navy worked together to plan this cross-Channel invasion. German planners in 1940 did not realize at first what they were in for—assembling forces on the coast, preparing air cover, deceptions and, of course, finding enough landing craft to make a strong initial assault against what was likely to be vigorous British response. They soon found out and the invasion was postponed.

The head of the Luftwaffe, Reichsmarschall Herman Göring, did not wait to learn the outcome of *Seelöwe*. On June 5 he launched some ineffective strikes against Royal Air Force (RAF) airfields. It was an inauspicious start, but as more German planes were moved to airfields on the coasts of occupied France and Holland, the campaign began to take off. Germany's plan for long-range bombers never came to fruition so the shorter distance across the English Channel from these airstrips increased the number and efficiency of missions by Luftwaffe tactical bombers.

Throughout July and August the air battle raged. The Battle of Britain, as this air war was called, began with strikes on airfields and military targets. A number of land facilities in southern England as well as sea convoys were damaged or destroyed. German bombing targets were expanded to other parts of England, Wales and Scotland. As they had in the skies over Dunkirk, RAF fighter pilots in Spitfires and Hurricanes went toe-to-toe with Germany's flying aces in ME-109Es and FW-190s, who were keeping watch over the bomber squadrons. German plane losses began to mount.

On the night of August 24 an off-target bomber dropped a payload in residential London. Churchill responded by ordering retaliatory strikes on Berlin by RAF strategic bombers the next four nights. While the August 24 London bombing was unintended, terror bombing was added to the German aerial campaign after the accident. Hitler liked the idea of turning up the heat on the subjugation of Britain with this move toward total war. The air strikes going both directions were accompanied by a war of words. Hitler threatened to level London. Churchill replied, citing the bravery of RAF pilots as a rallying point for British resolve. When the campaign to put RAF fighters out of action was changed to the bombing of civilian targets,

Britons called it "the Blitz." Hitler continued to postpone *Operation Seelöwe* hoping that achieving air dominance would bring Great Britain to its knees.

But it did not work out that way. By October 20, with mounting plane losses, Göring halted daylight bombing of the British Isles. *Seelöwe* was finally cancelled, an obvious casualty of the Luftwaffe not being able to control the skies over the invasion area and beyond. Luftwaffe night raids continued to cause devastation in areas of Great Britain through May 1941. Once begun, RAF strategic bombing of Germany continued unabated. The Battle of Britain reversed the direction of the wobbling opponent the Nazis thought they had in Great Britain. In the end, Britain's continuous development of air warfare from the days of the Great War, their system of command and control, and their use of early warning radar and other defensive concepts gave the British air force a distinct advantage over the roughly equal elements of plane inventories, performance and pilot skill. Once on its feet, Britain began to think about conducting the war in the direction of the German Fatherland.

The War in the Balkans

Standing idly by while the Hitler's troops conquered Poland and most of Western Europe, and during the Luftwaffe attempt to bomb Great Britain into submission, was too much for Mussolini, the father of fascism. He wanted his moment in the sun. Though Hitler had implored "Il Duce" ("The Leader") to not begin a new front in the Balkan states while the Nazis were waging war in Western Europe, by August 1940 Mussolini could wait no longer. After giving an ultimatum to the independent government of Greece in August 1940, his 162,000 Italian troops entered the country from bases in Albania at the end of October. The Greeks immediately mobilized and beat back the incursion through their northern border. They were so successful within a month they had the Italians on the run and the Greeks entered Albania from two directions. The British bombed an Albanian port in support.

In January 1941 Hitler wanted to intervene, but Mussolini convinced his big brother that he could handle the situation. By March, Hitler was fearful the Italian fiasco would allow the British to pour more resources into the Balkans (they had already begun to commit troops to Greece) and he began damage control in the region. All this new attention in the region was coming at an inopportune time because Hitler was planning to invade the Soviet Union and needed his southern flank secure. The German high command planned an invasion of Greece and Yugoslavia through adjoining countries.

With Bulgaria as well as Romania already in the Axis sphere, Germany was able to approach Yugoslavia from three sides. The country, formed from smaller Balkan States as a result of the treaties ending World War I, was briefly compelled to join the Axis at the same time as Bulgaria reluctantly agreed to the pact. But a regime change, encouraged by the British presence in Greece, kept Yugoslavia independent on the eve of the German invasion.

On April 6 mobile German forces entered Yugoslavia and quickly closed the borders. The Luftwaffe bombed Belgrade, the capital and cultural center for the Serbian majority, and other major cities. The tiny Yugoslav air force could not resist German air dominance, while ground forces along the frontier were challenged by the fast-moving panzer columns. To make matters worse, the second largest ethnic group, the Croatians, who controlled most of the country's coastal area, used the invasion as a justification to go after their Serbian rivals. By April 12 Belgrade was in German hands and Yugoslavia surrendered to Germany unconditionally on April 17.

Simultaneous to the invasion of Yugoslavia was the German invasion of Greece. On April 6 most of the Greek army was still in Albania threatening the Italians. They were cut off, and surrendered on April 23. British and Commonwealth (countries in the British Empire, in this case Australia and New Zealand) forces, and a smaller portion of the Greek Army held a series of lines in the mountainous northern areas of Trace and Macedonia. With the rapid fall of Yugoslavia, the German columns in that area continued south into Greece, joining the XII Army already in Greece. Overall Allied commander General Henry "Jumbo" Wilson made a slow withdrawal south to Athens and Kalamata, where the Royal Navy successfully evacuated the soldiers while under fire from Luftwaffe planes. Athens fell on April 27 and Kalamata a day later. Mainland Greece was in German hands.

The majority of Allies were evacuated to the large Greek island of Crete, south of the mainland. Under New Zealand commander General Bernard Freyburg, the Allies prepared to defend Crete against a German invasion from the air—Luftwaffe troops parachuting onto the island under airborne operations mastermind General Kurt Student. When, on May 20, the parachutists began to jump to various points on the island's north coast, they were met by furious fire. Freyburg was able to get about 40% of his force off the island by boat after fighting to the southern shore, but the Germans took 18,000 prisoners and the island. Casualties among the German paratroopers were so great, however, Hitler never authorized another major airborne operation after Crete.

The British and Commonwealth soldiers who made it out of Greece and Crete were transported to Egypt, across the eastern Mediterranean where the Royal Navy held the advantage over the Italian Navy, Mussolini's strongest military asset. Already, the British were having success in North Africa against the Italians. Six months earlier Mussolini made the mistake of ordering forces into Egypt and, in a situation similar to his adventure in Greece, the British commander beat back the attack and moved his forces into the Italian colony. The British were making a stand in the Near East.

The Battle of the Atlantic

Also in May 1941 a big news item brought attention to the ongoing Battle of the Atlantic, where German commerce raiders and U-boat attacks on convoys were frequently engaged by ships of the Royal Navy. As on March 11, when President Franklin D. Roosevelt's Lend-Lease program was enacted into law, U.S. Navy warships joined Royal Navy vessels in guarding the western routes of trans-Atlantic convoys, brings ships, war materials and other supplies from the "Arsenal of Democracy" to Great Britain, and later to other allies.

Kriegsmarine warships had barely ventured beyond the North Sea. That changed on May 18 when the new German battleship *Bismarck*, accompanied by heavy cruiser *Prinz Eugen* left the port of Gdynia in East Prussia and entered the Baltic Sea. Grossadmiral Raeder wanted the two ships to join two older battlecruisers then at Brest and add some surface punch to breaking up the Allied convoys. The two ships from Brest were delayed, but Raeder ordered the two surface ships to head for the Atlantic anyway. Spotters found *Bismarck* and its escort off Bergen, Norway. Royal Navy ships of the Home Fleet gave chase. On May 23, two British cruisers discovered *Bismarck* and *Prinz Eugen* north of Iceland in the Denmark Strait. The following day, a gun battle between the German and Royal Navy ships began. It ended with the *Bismarck* putting a deadly shell into HMS *Hood*, which sank the British battlecruiser.

The cat and mouse game continued for another few days. No sooner had the *Bismarck* entered the Atlantic than the battleship was ordered to make a run for the port at Brest by Raeder, who was having second thoughts. *Bismarck* and *Prinz Eugen* separated but *Bismarck*'s crew never saw France. The battleship was attacked by Swordfish biplanes launched by British aircraft carriers on May 27. The attack left it dead in the water and a British cruiser fired torpedoes into the *Bismarck*, sending it to the bottom the same day. In less than 10 days the maiden voyage of the Kriegsmarine's most powerful ship ended, and the German navy was again forced to rely on U-boats as its principal weapon.

Invasion of the Soviet Union –*Operation Barbarossa*

Italian setbacks in North Africa and the loss of the *Bismarck* were of limited concern to Adolf Hitler as he kept his eye on the prize. He never intended Josef Stalin to be a long-term ally. Stalin truly believed Hitler would honor their agreement (though the Soviet dictator would have likely double-crossed the Germans whenever he had the chance) right up to the point when German tanks began crossing the borders of the Ukraine, Belorussia and Lithuania. On June 22, 1941, *Operation Barbarossa* began.

The invasion of the Soviet Union was a mammoth struggle between two leaders—committed to their goals to the point of fanaticism—with huge armies, vast navies and great advances in military technology. Each leader maintained control over his military forces and population—people who were either dedicated to these leaders, to the prestige or survival of their national identity, or were coerced into obedience and sacrifice. Hitler and Stalin each were able to commit their economies and societies to total war. For Hitler, his motivation was the opportunity to expand *Lebensraum* (living space) for Germanic peoples while defeating the Bolsheviks he despised. For Stalin, it was to preserve the USSR with an eye to expanding communist rule and his own power beyond the borders of the Soviet Union of 1941.

The Eastern Front campaigns are so broad and complex that no short history can do justice to the subject. But the overall progress of the fight will be covered chronologically. The Germans advanced on a broad 2,000-mile (3,200km) front, from the Black Sea in the south to the Barents Sea in the north, utilizing 117 divisions of the Wehrmacht plus troops from Axis members Hungary and Romania as well as a few Italians. In the north Finnish troops became temporary allies, under Field Marshal Baron Carl Gustaf Mannerheim, who had led the Finns against the Red Army in the Winter War. The three million in the German forces were opposed by an equal number of Red Army soldiers, with the USSR having another million in ready reserve and millions more not yet mobilized. Manpower was the chief asset of the communists when *Operation Barbarossa* commenced.

The initial battles of *Barbarossa* involved three German army groups, with the destruction of the Red Army and Air Force their primary goal. Army Group North headed toward Leningrad; Army Group Center targeted the Ukraine with a goal of eventually capturing the USSR's capital,

Moscow; and Army Group South headed for the Black Sea area, Crimea and the oil fields of the Caucasus Mountains. In a few areas the Red Army fought the initial invasion, but they had weak defensive positions for resisting the Germans. A series of pincer movements on all fronts surrounded and captured large numbers of Red Army soldiers. Much of the Ukraine was overrun, and Kiev was cut off.

But as summer became autumn, the blitzkrieg columns were slowing as they approached the Soviet Union's major cities of Leningrad and Moscow. Heavy rains through November turned the roads into mud. Panzer armies that had raced ahead were curtailed by the supply logjam and slower columns of infantry units on the march. Despite the loss of millions of soldiers, the retreating Red Army positioned itself in lines blocking the roads to Leningrad, Moscow and southwest/Crimean Peninsula, the gateway to the oil fields. They were buying time.

One of Stalin's most brilliant decisions was to move key elements of Soviet society away from the assault, to positions beyond the Ural Mountains and the Caspian Sea. In the Soviet Union, there was plenty of *Lebensraum* to do this. Not just refugees such as women and children; schools, hospitals, whole factories were dismantled, moved and reset in the Asian sub-continent that was part of the USSR. From these humble beginnings, the Soviets began to build their response.

The frigid weather of December actually helped the German advance initially by drying or freezing the roads and landscape. The advance of Army Group North reached Leningrad and Russia's second largest city was put under siege. The Finns had gone on the defensive after regaining land lost in the Winter War and a small leak developed in the force surrounding Leningrad. Supplies trickled in, but not enough to avoid thousands of starvation deaths among the city's residents.

Army Group Center advanced to within 80 miles (130km) of Moscow (some German patrols got much closer) before grinding to a halt. Both these advances were slowed by the weather and local Soviet counterattacks. The Germans were beginning to discover they were not prepared for the Russian winter. In the slightly less frigid south, the Germans captured Odessa and were poised to enter the Crimea.

War Comes to the Sahara

As mentioned, after losing Greece and Crete the evacuated British troops returned to bases in Egypt. The British forces based in Egypt and elsewhere in the region under Middle East commander General Sir Archibald Wavell had been busy opposing the Italians and having success

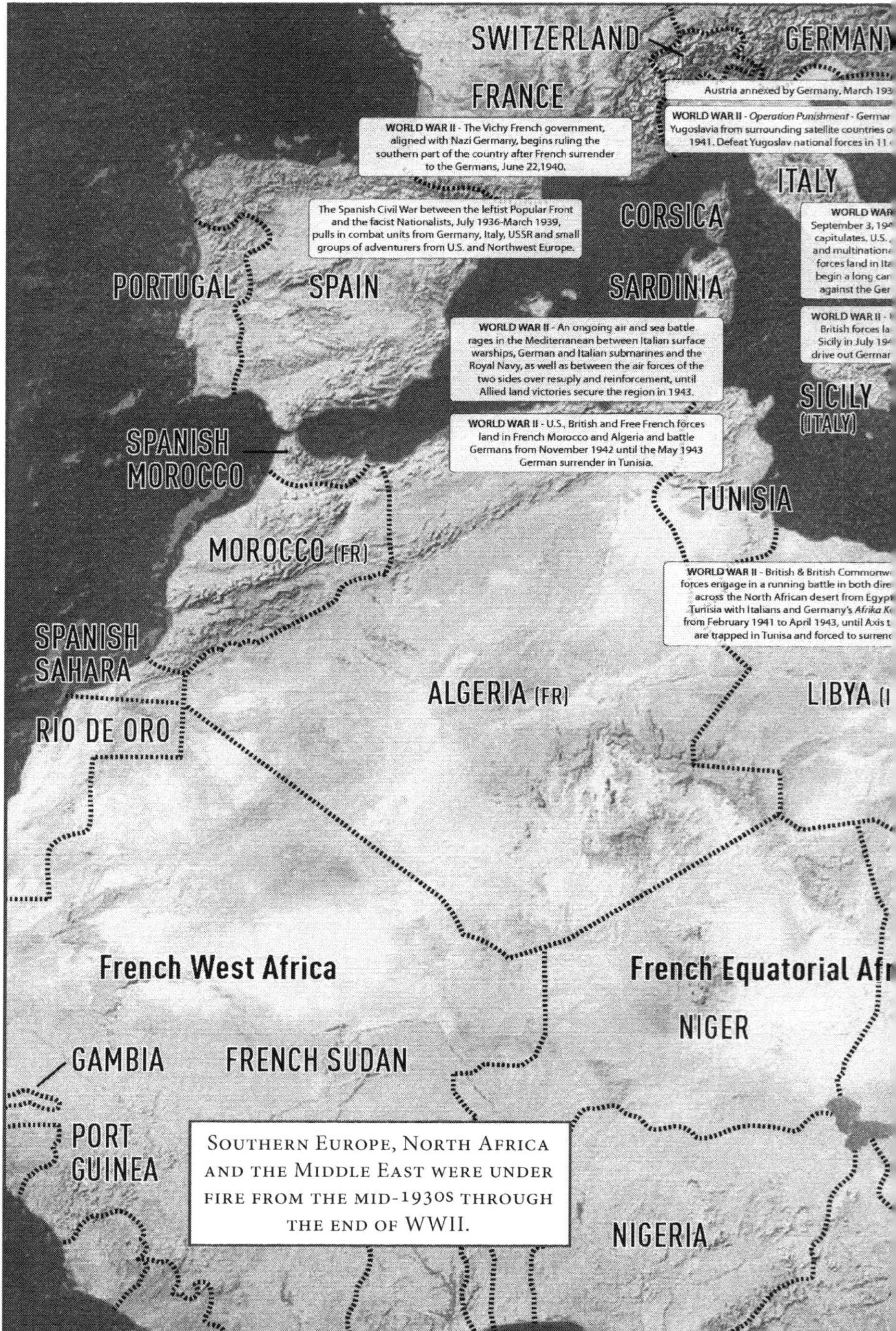

Southern Europe, North Africa and the Middle East were under fire from the mid-1930s through the end of WWII.

GARY
ROMANIA
SLAVIA
BULGARIA
NIA
es and occupies April 7, 1939
EECE
D WAR II - attack Greece, 1940. Greeks em back into and occupy it.
Black Sea
USSR
WORLD WAR II - The furthest limits of the Nazi invasion of the USSR were in the south and southwest, from the Crimea on the north edge of the Black Sea, to the peninsula between the Black and Caspian seas north of the Persian border. By November 1942 the German withdrawl against increasing Soviet pressure began.
TURKEY
WORLD WAR II - Germany invades Greece on April 6, 1941 - clears all British and Greek forces from Albania and Greece by April 28.
WORLD WAR II - Soviet forces from the north and British forces from the south invade Persia, August-September 1941 to secure oil fields. Persian forces offer weak, unsuccessful resistance.
WORLD WAR II - Germany defeats British & Commonwealth forces in Crete in May 1941
WORLD WAR II - German supplied Iraqui troops attack British in May 1941, but British forces defeat them and sign an armistice on May 31.
CRETE (GR)
CYPRUS
SYRIA (FR)
diterranean Sea
WORLD WAR II - British attack and defeat Vichy French forces in Syria to protect Middle East oil supply. June 1941.
IRAQ
PERSIA
PALESTINE
WORLD WAR II - Italians invade Egypt, September 1940 and are driven back by British forces which then enter Libya.
EGYPT
usiyya Muslim rhood guerilla war aly ends in 1931 - civilian deaths in entration camps.
SAUDI ARABIA
D
ANGLO-EGYPTIAN SUDAN
ERITREA
FRENCH SOMALILAND
Italians invade Ethiopia from Eritrea and Italian Somaliland and defeat independent rule of Halie Selassie I - October 1935-May 1936.
BRITISH SOMALILAND
ETHIOPIA
WORLD WAR II - British-led multinational force begins campaign against Italians in January 1941. By the end of November all Italian forces are defeated in Ethiopia, Eritrea and Somaliland. Ethiopia is restored to independent rule.
WORLD WAR II - Italians invade British Somaliland August 3, 1940

doing it. Not only did the British response to the limited Italian invasion of Egypt result in Allied troops moving far into Libya, but an Italian attack from Ethiopia (in Italian hands since 1935) to British Somaliland resulted in a British-led force of African colonials liberating that African independent state. In the spring of 1941 Wavell's forces also launched a campaign in Iraq and Syria against the Vichy French (an effort the Soviets later joined) to secure access to Middle East oil fields.

Turning away the potential invasion of the home islands and blunting Germany's attempt to control the skies of Western Europe had given British leaders and the people of the UK a resolve to reverse the losses they had incurred. Having handled the Italians, both on land and in naval control of the Mediterranean, Prime Minister Winston Churchill wanted to go on the offensive against the Germans; to attack, as he characterized it, "the soft underbelly of Nazi Germany." The British held both ends of the Mediterranean—Gibraltar in the west and Egypt and the Suez Canal in the east. In the middle of the vast sea, near Italy, was the British island of Malta. Control of the Mediterranean would be the perfect place to start such a campaign. But Hitler beat Churchill to the punch.

When the Italians began to fold in North Africa, Hitler sent to the region a Luftwaffe unit that specialized in bombing surface ships. He immediately followed this order in February 1941 with a commitment of ground units under a commander he liked, Lieutenant General Erwin Rommel. The force became known as the *Afrika Korps*, and the Germans were joined by the Italian units that remained in the desert, among the best in Mussolini's army. Almost immediately Rommel went on the offensive, forcing Wavell's force (weakened at the time by transfers to Greece) from El Agheila on the Libyan coast in Cyrenaica, west of Benghazi, to Tobruk. Australian troops landed in the port city to reinforce the British columns and Rommel's first attempt to take Tobruk failed. The *Afrika Korps* drive continued east and Rommel, whose tactical reputation gained him the moniker "Desert Fox," continued the advance, reaching across the border into Egypt before the end of April 1941. With the need to shift more resources to *Barbarossa*, Hitler forbade Rommel to advance further. The Desert Fox established a defensive position at Halfaya Pass.

Churchill replaced Wavell and the reinforced British force, named the Eighth Army, could not make much headway at first. Nor could Rommel's siege of Tobruk open that port to him. In November, Rommel's extended advance was hampered by British air and naval action sinking a large number of supply ships crossing to Libya from Italy.

This, coupled with new limited Allied attacks on his front (aided by British intercepts of German communication through the ULTRA decoding system) forced Rommel to withdraw to his base at El Agheila on December 4 to avoid being cut off by British tanks flanking him across the desert plateau to the south.

1942—The Tide Begins to Turn

December 1941 also brought the United States officially into the European War. Immediately after the Japanese attack on Pearl Harbor, the U.S. declared war on Japan, which in turn led to Germany and Italy declaring war on the U.S. President Roosevelt vowed the United States would support the Allies in a defeat Germany first policy despite the grave Japanese threat in the Pacific. American military personnel landed in the British Isles in 1942 and replaced British troops in a proactive occupation of Iceland to keep it out of German hands. The American impact on the war in Europe was not immediately felt—but America immediately felt the impact of war as the German U-boats, in their most productive year at sea, began attacking shipping on America's East Coast.

On the Eastern Front the local Soviet attacks against the Germans at Moscow were gaining strength. Stalin found a commander whose advice he would occasionally take: Marshal Georgi Zhukov, who commanded the central armies protecting Moscow. The German salients, the forward positions, were attacked on December 6, just as Army Group Center was settling into winter defensive positions. Success here encouraged Stalin to expand the attack along the entire front, against the advice of Zhukov and others. From January to April the Soviets, benefitting from increased manpower and supplies from the rear, engaged in this broad counteroffensive that gained ground, retaking hundreds of miles in some areas. The Soviets also benefited from supplies contributed by Great Britain and other Western allies, which arrived at Soviet Arctic ports. It would not be until mid-1942 that the Kriegsmarine would begin a concerted effort to disrupt these Arctic convoys.

By April German resistance stiffened and spring rains produced mud that slowed down the general Soviet offensive. Leningrad was still under siege and Army Group Center still held positions west of Moscow, but new developments were occurring in the south. Army Group South fought off a Soviet attempt to retake Kharkov in May, then advanced to the Kerch Peninsula under an emerging leader, General Erich von Manstein, and surrounded Sevastopol. Benefiting from favorable weather, the understrength German Army Group A retook Rostov, which had changed hands twice the previous November. Their next objective was the rich oil fields beyond the Donets River in the Caucasus Mountains. German Army Group B continued east toward Stalingrad.

The beginning of 1942 also brought new offensives in North Africa. In January Rommel advanced east to face a series of British defensive positions stretching from Gazala on the coast west of Tobruk to El Hacheim on the desert plateau. There he waited to build up supply reserves. The Luftwaffe pounded Malta and opened the sea lanes again to Italian merchantmen, bound for Libyan ports with supplies for Afrika Korps. In May, Rommel launched a successful offensive against the British line and forced the Allies to retreat to Mersa Matrûh. He then turned his attention to Tobruk. His concentrated attack began on June 20, and the garrison surrendered the next day. Rommel then defeated the main Allied force at their new defensive position at Mersa Matrûh. The British and their Commonwealth allies retreated into Egypt and by the end of June formed a defensive line at El Alamein, 60 miles (95km) west of the principal Egyptian port of Alexandria.

This new development caused Churchill to shuffle commanders again and Lieutenant General Bernard Montgomery was put in charge of the Eighth Army. "Monty" was in no hurry to drive the Afrika Korps out of Egypt. Supplies for Rommel, however, were again an issue as RAF attacks on his long resupply lines along the coast of Cyrenaica and the increasing shortage of Italian merchant ships offset German success in neutralizing Malta. As the logistics balance moved rapidly in favor of the Allies, Rommel was forced to attempt to break through the El Alamein line on August 31. ULTRA intercepts revealed Rommel's attack plan to Montgomery, but it was the inability to maneuver his gas-starved tanks against stout Allied defensive positions that caused Rommel to withdraw to his starting point within a week. Montgomery did not counterattack immediately and instead spent months preparing his army.

About this time, in July, a thousand miles or so to the northeast, German Army Group B was advancing rapidly on Stalingrad. Hitler could have thrown more forces at the very promising advance southeast of Rostov that was closing in on the Caucasus Mountains but the industrial city on the Volga River had a kind of hypnotic draw. Was it that the city was the namesake of his opponent? There is no hard evidence of this but he did want to take it. Unfortunately his commanders in the field had not carefully reconnoitered Stalingrad and failed to make plans to cut off the city from across the Volga. Also, the weaker units of Axis partners Romania, Hungary and Italy were assigned to protect the flanks of the

German line, while Sixth Army commander general Friedrich Paulus was ordered to advance his force headlong into Stalingrad's defenses.

British Commando Raids

In mid-1942 the Royal Navy was occupied in the Arctic, Mediterranean and Atlantic, and the U.S. Navy's Atlantic Fleet was taking a larger role in locating U-boats and guarding convoys. In the air, American long-range bombers, based at English airfields, began bombing German targets during daylight hours. The only fighting being done by the ground troops of the Western Allies was in North Africa.

The British did, however, stage commando raids in Western Europe. The largest of these was a partially successful raid of the German naval base at St. Nazaire, on the coast of Brittany, France. On March 28, British commandos propelled a stripped-down destroyer loaded with explosives into a secure waterway alongside the only Atlantic coast dock capable of berthing the German battleship *Tirpitz,* sister ship to the *Bismarck.* The exploding hulk severely damaged the docking facility and the *Tirpitz* was never sent there. (RAF bombers sunk it at Tromsø, Norway, November 12, 1944.) The commandos failed to damage any of St. Nazaire's U-boat pens, and the Allies suffered heavy casualties in dead and prisoners.

In order to test the Nazi defenses across the English Channel a raid-in-force was conducted with Canadian regulars, British commandos and armor to Dieppe, France on August 19, 1942. Faulty intelligence led the forces, which crossed the Channel during the night and landed at dawn, to face a much larger German force manning strong artillery positions. Most of the attackers, particularly the tanks, never got off the beaches. Hours later, the combined Allied force withdrew, leaving behind all of their equipment, many captured comrades and little damage done.

Operation Torch

In a series of conferences and meetings president Roosevelt and his advisors tried to lead Winston Churchill away from a strategy of defeating Germany via Mediterranean campaigns, "the soft underbelly," and toward the invasion of northwest Europe. The Dieppe disaster and many other factors led to the decision not to pursue an invasion of France in 1942-43. But Churchill did agree to the establishment of an office to plan the invasion across the English Channel (see *Planning the Invasion*, the next chapter). But Roosevelt wanted U.S. ground troops in action in Europe before the end of 1942. A previous plan for an invasion of Northwest Africa was resurrected and given the name *Operation Torch.* Because landing were to occur in French territories and that nation was then spilt in its loyalties, the invasion was American led, even though British units made up part of the force. Another part of the force were Free French fighters. It was hoped they would convince some of their countrymen to join, or at least not fight the Allies landing on their beaches.

Lieutenant General Dwight David Eisenhower was elevated to the rank of General and assigned to lead the campaign. He had just begun to organize U. S. forces in the UK after serving in the War Plans Division in Washington. The Combined Chiefs of Staff named Eisenhower as Supreme Commander, and "Ike" insisted on having a unified command, meaning he would control all service branches—army, navy and air forces—during the operation. This successful leadership model was used in all later campaigns of the Western Allies, and except for *Torch*, in which American major general Mark W. Clark was named Deputy Commander to avoid potential friction between the British and the French, second level commanders were appointed from the ranks of the two major allies.

On November 8, British and French forces landed in Morocco and Algeria. The Free French generally accepted the invaders as liberators while the Vichy French elements, aligned with Germany, fought the invaders until their North African leader, Admiral Jean F. Darlan, was convinced by the Allies to cooperate. In the meantime, Hitler ordered 140,000 troops with tanks and equipment to Tunisia, the objective of both sides.

At about the same time, in Egypt, Montgomery felt sufficiently prepared to launch an offensive to drive Rommel from El Alamein. On October 23, a day when Monty learned through ULTRA that Rommel was in Germany, he launched his attack and was able to penetrate the Axis minefield. Rommel returned immediately and the battle continued for two weeks as the British thrusts moved from one position to another. The *Afrika Korps* tanks lacked the fuel to keep up. Reluctantly, Hitler allowed Rommel to withdraw on November 4, after first insisting that he stand and fight at El Alamein. The withdraw spanned 1,400 miles from Egypt, entirely across Cyrenaica to eastern Libya. Montgomery was slow to pursue.

Once it was determined troops from Spanish Morocco, controlled by Franco's fascist government of Spain, would not ambush the Allied rear, British units took the first steps to advance toward Tunisia. There in November they clashed with the new German force under General Hans-Jürgen von Arnim. The only notable action was Arnim's mid-November seizure of key mountain passes from the part of the Allied line defended by the Free French. Then, torrential rains brought muddy conditions that effectively halted both sides in their tracks for weeks.

By late January Rommel's force, trimmed by breakdowns, attrition and skirmishes with the Eighth Army, arrived at Mareth, just across Libya's west border in Tunisia. Montgomery, still pursuing from a distance, was having supply issues of his own. Rommel hoped the two German forces could combine and defeat the Americans before Montgomery could join the Allied forces wet of him. Arnim, however, would not cooperate fully, even when Mediterranean commander Marshal Albert Kesselring came from Italy to intervene.

On February 14, in a series of actions in the area held by the American II Corps in the area of Kasserine Pass, German units struck repeatedly and gained ground on the Americans, whose officers and men were very inexperienced. But after one week the German offensive began to falter as resistance stiffened. Rommel was livid at Arnim's lack of cooperation but mental fatigue and sickness were also demoralizing the Desert Fox. He requested and was granted sick leave and departed North Africa on March 9. Spearheaded by Major General George S. Patton, who assumed command of II Corps, the Allies moved the Axis forces toward the sea, encircling them in a broad front. It was then just a matter of time before the remaining Axis troops would be crushed into a trap reminiscent of Dunkirk—but this time the Royal Navy ships standing off the Tunisian coast were not there to rescue the trapped forces.

Decision at Stalingrad

Army Group A was facing relatively light resistance during its Caucasian expedition but its supply lines were lengthening. And upon reaching the first group of oil fields the Germans found them ablaze. They continued on, but Army Group A's leader complained so much of the lack of supplies, Hitler sacked him and named himself replacement commander of the army group. Army Group B was also facing supply shortages and units short of manpower, but General Paulus, beginning in September, threw regiment after regiment of his 18 divisions into the smoking cauldron of Stalingrad where German bombing of the city and the Volga dominated the day, and street fighting continued into the night.

Though the Germans had units in every sector of the city, the building by building advances were achieving little. Stalingrad was degenerating into a stalemated killing ground like the worst trench warfare of World War I. Politically, Hitler could boast to the people about the great conquest of Stalingrad but militarily, little was being accomplished, except by the Soviets. They were quietly preparing a massive counteroffensive code named *Uranus*.

The Red Army bridged the Don River north of Stalingrad with pontoons. On November 19 it attacked the thinly stretched Romanian Third Army holding the German north flank. The Romanians were ill-equipped for repulsing the attack. Powerful Soviet T-34 tanks rapidly swept through their positions. A panzer unit sent to help barely escaped capture. The following day the Soviets crossed south of Stalingrad and forced back the Romanian Fourth Army. Within days the German Sixth Army was surrounded and cut off in the city. Hitler ordered Paulus not to abandon Stalingrad. Berlin airlifted supplies into the city, but only a trickle ever arrived.

In mid-December Manstein, whom Hitler appointed to command of a new Army Group Don (named after the nearby river) sent a panzer column to Stalingrad to open an escape. The force pushed its way toward the city, but Hitler would not allow Paulus to attempt a breakout to meet the German tanks only 30 miles away. Marshal Zhukov and Red Army planners had other offensives planned but held off until the German Sixth Army was defeated. That occurred in January 1943 when, broken down and starving, the Germans were rounded up by Red Army units combing the city. Paulus was captured the same day Hitler elevated him to field marshal in an empty gesture. He surrendered his army of about 90,000 survivors. Stalingrad was the turning point of the Eastern Front. The year 1942 started out with much uncertainty for the European Allies, but it began the trend toward victories that continued in 1943 against a still defiant Hitler and still potent Wehrmacht.

Invasion of Sicily and Italy

After Erwin Rommel departed from Tunisia, von Arnim could do nothing to break out from the Allied encirclement. The American II Corps was actually displaced from the line as the territory held by the German army shrank. Patton turned over command of II Corps to Major General Omar Bradley in order to prepare for the next Mediterranean operation, *Husky*. Surrounded, the 240,000 German and Italians remaining in North Africa surrendered en masse on May 13.

Operation Husky was the invasion of Sicily. Politically, the Italians were already wavering. Militarily, after the fall of Tunisia, they were about finished. Mussolini could only accept Hitler's decisions about what to do with his country. Erwin Rommel, named by Hitler to command forces in the mountainous northern part of the country, led a school of thought that threw most of Italy to the Allied wolves and created a strong buffer in the north along the Pisa-Rimini Line. Kesselring wanted to hold all of the country, and Hitler agreed, not wanting to lose Italy and expose the

Balkans to the Allies. Within months, Hitler reassigned Rommel to the Atlantic Wall and Kesselring then controlled all of Italy. The Germans decided to hinge their defense plans on what the Allies would do.

The invasion of Sicily, with an eventual invasion of Italy, was the Combined Chiefs' answer to what to do with the million members of the Allied military in the region. American military bosses never considered an invasion of Germany through Italy or any route other than via the northwest coast of Europe. But that plan could not be put into effect in 1943 (again, see *Planning the Invasion*). So they agreed with their British counterparts to *Husky*, to rid the Mediterranean of Axis dangers to shipping and to create additional airfields closer to Germany. Planning the invasion began months before the Germans surrendered in North Africa.

On July 10, 1943 American paratroopers and British glider troops landed on Sicily. Most were scattered in their objectives. Within 15 minutes the night amphibious landing of four assault divisions in the Seventh Army under Patton and the Eighth Army under Montgomery, took place on opposite shores of Sicily. High winds and surf complicated the landing but a beachhead was established. General A. Guzzoni commanded the Italian Sixth Army, though the German divisions were controlled by a Wehrmacht officer. Guzzoni counterattacked on the 11th, but the Allies ashore, supported by massive warship gunfire, turned away the attack. Guzzoni received permission for a fighting withdrawal, agreed to by Kesselring and this time Hitler didn't order a fight to the death. War resources were becoming too scarce.

While Montgomery was slowed by terrain and enemy troops taking the most direct route to Messina, the port city closest to mainland Italy, Patton's men advanced rapidly up the west coast and took Palermo on July 22. Patton received permission from his superior to continue a rapid advance toward Messina. While the Germans and Italians fighting with them conducted a series of delays, the evacuation of war materials began at Messina. Eisenhower ordered night bombing of the Messina Straits but the supplies, then the troops, crossed to the mainland during the day, when Luftwaffe fighters were in the air. All Axis men, equipment and supplies were off the island by August 17.

Political and military changes were already underway before the Allies took Sicily. The Italian king forced Mussolini's resignation and placed the former Supreme Leader under arrest. Hitler had him flown to Berlin instead. Hoping to avoid the terms of unconditional surrender, the new government under Marshal Pietro Badoglio pledged cooperation with the Allies. The Italian collapse propelled Eisenhower to order the most aggressive of several plans to invade Italy, *Operation Avalanche*.

The same day the Italians signed the surrender agreement, Montgomery's Eighth Army crossed the Messina Straits and landed without incident on the toe of the Italian "boot." Monty's advance up the toe was perceived correctly as a feint by General Kesselring, who placed an armored division across from the most likely landing beach, Salerno, a short distance south of Naples. Eisenhower announced the Italian surrender to the world on the evening of September 8. The Germans in Italy scrambled to recover tanks and other war supplies from Italians who were laying down their arms. That night Lieutenant General Mark Clark's Fifth Army, composed of U.S. and British divisions and commandos, landed in Salerno Bay. The landing went smoothly but was soon met by fire from Kesselring's massed armor on the ridge above the beach.

Allied naval gunfire, as in Sicily, helped the troops establish a beachhead. As he had planned, Kesselring mounted a counterattack with six divisions on September 13, but the II Corps withstood that and made some progress. Kesselring then began a withdrawal to prepared defensive positions. The Allies followed. In a short time they cleaned up the sabotaged port of Naples, and Montgomery, moving cautiously, secured the important airfield at Foggia, which would soon base Allied planes. Encouraged by the resistance of Kesselring and his determined troops, Hitler decided to make a stand in southern Italy, keeping Allied planes and ground forces away from Germany.

The Italian campaign was one in which weather and geography, as well as the Germans in well-prepared defensive positions, would have great influence. As winter rains began in October, southern Italy's rivers swelled, making large troop movements in the already hazardous mountain passes nearly impossible. The advance slowed to a crawl, and the Allies accomplished little after the initial September gains. This gave Kesselring the opportunity to carefully build his strongest defensive position south of Rome, the Gustav Line. The taking of Rome, which the Army Group Commander Sir Harold Alexander had predicted would occur September 21, was a long way off.

The Italian Campaign was also beginning to impact the coming cross-Channel invasion by delaying resources, mainly landing craft, from being transferred from the Mediterranean to England. As 1943 faded into 1944, the Western Allies had stabilized much of the Mediterranean. They were rapidly achieving air superiority in Europe over the Luftwaffe, as well as destroying Germany's war-making capabilities. They were even having greater success in containing shipping losses and sinking U-boats. But what to do about Italy was still very much uncertain.

Soviet Offensives Along the Front—January 1943 to April 1944

When the outcome at Stalingrad seemed certain, the Red Army launched an attack on four fronts to inflict maximum damage on Army Group Don and Army Group A. Retaking Rostov cut Group A off in the trans-Caucasian region between the Black and Caspian seas. Thanks to Manstein's efforts, one panzer army was able to escape but much of the rest of Army Group A met destruction over time. The Soviets retook Kursk and Kharkov. Manstein organized the remaining Army Group Don forces and counterattacked on February 20, driving the Soviet advance back east of the Donets River from Orel to just west of Rostov, except for a bulge surrounding Kursk.

Spring rains stopped Manstein's offensive. To that point there had been little movement in the line north of Orel. On June 5 Manstein began *Operation Citadel* to recover Kursk. The largest tank battle of World War II was fought over the next five days. Soviet superiority on the ground and in the air blunted the German advance and Kursk held. The Soviets began the second offensive of 1943 on July 12 and retook all that was lost in February. This precipitated a Soviet push all along the line held by the Germans in Army Group Center as well as the ongoing battle in the south. For the next three months the steady pressure drove the Germans back into the Ukraine and Belorussia.

Against Manstein's advice Hitler would not permit a withdrawal in the Crimea. Those forces were cut off and destroyed. Kiev was retaken by the Soviets in November. In January, 1944, Red Army forces in the north finally broke through German lines in relief of Leningrad, which had been under siege for more than 900 days. The Soviets then reorganized their fronts and continued to move west. Under unrelenting pressure the Germans found themselves with their backs against the Bug River and Carpathian Mountains, nearing the prewar borders of Poland and Hungary. Furious over the territorial losses, Hitler demoted Manstein, who had taken over command of Army Group South, and Army Group A commander Ewald von Kleist. He turned command over to the German leaders commanding in the center and north, who were faring little better in their retreat. This was the situation on the eve of the great Allied offensive in the West as the Soviets paused during the spring rains to prepare for their own big summer offensive.

The Road to Rome

In January, the weather was still a factor in the Allies moving forward and challenging the Gustav Line. Fighting was slow and difficult and once the line was reached, the defensive positions there were even stronger. The main road to Rome, Route 6, passed through the town of Cassino, which was strongly fortified. An abbey on Monte Cassino in the high ground above the town was the most difficult of the positions on the Gustav Line to overcome. Months passed with little progress as various attempts were made to take the position that could not be bypassed.

A controversial decision paved the way for an additional landing closer to Rome to put troops behind the Gustav Line. Controversial primarily because to execute the landing at Anzio, there would be a further delay of the timetable for the invasion of France (again, see *Planning the Invasion*). The affects were major. Nevertheless, the landing of 40,000 men was made at Anzio on January 22, but the plan went off course almost immediately. The forces established a beachhead but could not penetrate further. Instead of approaching the Gustav Line from the rear, the units that landed at Anzio were boxed in and had to cling to the small beachhead they had gained. Their only protection was fire from Allied ships off shore, dueling with the German artillery, and Allied air strikes when the Italian winter weather conditions cooperated.

Finally, after months of trying, Cassino was taken in May. Polish troops had the honor of taking the Monte Cassino abbey, which the German defenders had evacuated moments before. The Germans had to begin another fighting withdrawal to the Caesar Line but they could no longer hold positions below Rome. The VI Corps joined with the other American, British and multinational forces on the Road to Rome after the Germans that had bottled them up were chased away. There was still plenty of fighting to do in Italy. However, on June 4 Americans marched into Rome—the first Axis capital had fallen. Clark was questioned by some for hurrying to Rome rather than turning and attempting to trap the withdrawing German X Army. But there was also political value in taking Rome, though that development would be overshadowed by what would happen two days later, when the Germans were introduced to the beginning of another crushing blow, this time in France.

Conclusion

The German conquests of 1943-44, which placed most of continental Europe under Nazi rule, had additional consequences for the citizens of Germany and occupied countries. Total war came to these countries early and spread to other occupied nations as they fell. With aerial bombing by both sides, few areas of Europe, North Africa and the Middle East escaped damage, destruction and death. Dr. Weinberg explains:

"Certain features and related developments need to be mentioned for an understanding of the extreme violence of a conflict that would see well over sixty million persons killed, more than twice the number killed in World War I. As already mentioned, from the beginning, the Germans bombed cities to kill as many civilians and destroy as much property as possible. By 1942 the British came around to this policy, and in reviews of it in 1944 there was repeated reference to the idea that the Allies not only had to change the German government but also the general attitude toward war by the German public.

"A second feature was the initiation by the Germans of mass killing of civilians in the 1939 campaign against Poland with much repetition during subsequent fighting in Northern, Western, Southeastern, and Eastern Europe. In fighting against resistance and partisan forces both the Germans and Japanese engaged in wholesale slaughter of civilians. The German decision to extend the domestic program of killing the elderly and the handicapped into territory occupied in the fighting should also be noted.

"There was, furthermore, an essentially new attitude toward prisoners of war. In their campaign against the Soviet Union, the Germans killed or let die about three and a half million prisoners of war. The utilization of POWs for slave labor was certainly on a much greater scale than in any prior conflict. While the Germans were not as horrendous in their treatment of British and American POWs, of whom about 5% died in German custody, the Japanese murdered or let die over 28% of such prisoners. Chinese soldiers captured by the Japanese army were generally killed. It deserves to be mentioned that the Allied victory saved the lives of tens of thousands of seriously wounded German soldiers, since by the fall of 1944 the regime had completed the killing of its crippled World War I veterans and had initiated the killing of its WWII very seriously wounded veterans. The Allied occupation authorities halted this procedure in any hospitals where as a part of the routine it was still being practiced after the surrender of May 8, 1945.

"With the invasion of the Soviet Union on June 22, 1941, the Germans also began the systematic killing of Jews in what has come to be called the Holocaust. As Hitler personally explained in detail in November 1941 to the Mufti of Jerusalem, who was collaborating with Germany, this program was to be extended to the whole globe. In practice about six million Jews were killed in parts of Europe and Asia while the successful defense and eventual victory of the Allies saved the lives of the other twelve million Jews then alive."

If the Allies needed any further impetus for victory in the coming cross-Channel invasion, it was validated when millions of non-combatant Europeans, POWs and crippled soldiers were liberated from slavery, torture and death at the hands of the most violent and destructive dictatorship in the world to that time.

PLANS FOR THE INVASION

Gerald D. Swick

To a rifleman hugging the sand on Omaha Beach, D-Day was pure chaos: exploding shells, whistling bullets, the screams of the wounded and dying, small groups of terrified survivors not knowing what to do because their officers were all dead. As that rifleman prayed to live another five minutes he must have wondered, *Who the hell planned this?*

An old truism holds that no battle plan survives contact with the enemy. D-Day saw the pandemonium of Omaha Beach, the unintentional scattering of airborne forces, bombers far overshooting their targets, and the failure by virtually all Allied units to complete their objectives that day. Beyond the beaches came difficult and dangerous fighting in the hedgerows or deadly tank shootouts. Many an Allied soldier must have wondered if anyone back in London or Washington had any idea of what they were sending men into.

The Normandy Campaign actually involved some of the most extensive and imaginative planning in the history of warfare in order to overcome unprecedented challenges. Given the conflicting personalities of those involved (*See Allied Leaders*) and the differing opinions they held, it is remarkable they were ever able to agree on a plan. That the plan worked as well as it did is even more remarkable.

Planning to Plan

In *Cross-Channel Attack* Gordon A. Harrison wrote, "The principles that eventually shaped *Overlord* were developed early but their application was discontinuous, interrupted by diffuse experimentation and improvisation. Neither ideas nor planning can be traced along a single line from a clear beginning to the ultimate action."

In summer 1940, a year and a half before America officially entered the war, the U.S. Navy established a permanent observer in London (Rear Admiral Robert L. Ghormley) to discuss cooperation between the American and British navies. The U.S. Army sent observers on special missions and in spring 1941 established a permanent body to prepare for coordination of ground and air forces between the two nations, should the U.S. enter the war.

In January 1942, the month after America was pulled into the war by the Japanese bombing of Pearl Harbor, the Combined Chiefs of Staff was formed, consisting of Britain's chiefs of staff and their representatives and their "opposite numbers" in the American military, which had no chiefs of staff organization. (This led to establishing the U.S. Chiefs of Staff in 1942.)

First, the U.S. had to commit resources to protecting its Pacific bases from Japanese attack. Britain likewise was still in defensive mode. But both agreed the top priority was defeating Germany, the strongest of the Axis nations, while so much of its military was tied down fighting in the Soviet Union.

Roundup and *Sledgehammer*

British planners had already conceived *Operation Roundup*—arguably more wishful thinking than a plan, given Britain's weakness at the time. Once Nazi troops somehow became sufficiently depleted and demoralized and were withdrawing from France to defend the homeland, Britain would land slightly more than six divisions of infantry and six of armor around Le Havre and from Dequville to Dieppe to secure an area between Calais and the Seine, then free Antwerp and invade Germany.

A contingency plan, *Sledgehammer*, was to be implemented in late 1942 using whatever resources were available, but only if the Soviet Union was in danger of collapse or German forces in the east suffered significant defeats.

The initial version of *Roundup* was never taken very seriously, but it would go through multiple revisions by Anglo-American planners. One revision had three separate, nearly simultaneous, invasions going ashore at Pas-de-Calais and both sides of the Seine River, with follow-on assaults to capture Cherbourg and the Channel Islands. In November 1942, however, planning began to shift toward finding an area suitable for landing the entire Allied invasion force as a cohesive unit.

Go Slow or Go Now?

The British urged taking things a step at a time, building up resources and using air and naval power to wear down the Germans through bombing and blockades; this reflected Britain's capabilities at the time. American planners thought it gave too little attention to land warfare; this indirect approach was not, in their opinion, a war-winning strategy. They wanted a quick invasion of Europe, in no small part to take pressure off the Soviet Union lest it be forced to negotiate a surrender or become so diminished that its military collapsed. The Germans would then be free to shift combat units to France.

Soviet premier Josef Stalin also pressed his Western allies for an invasion soon, and President Franklin D. Roosevelt promised one would be made in 1942. American planners, therefore, generally supported the ideas of the revised *Roundup* plan, but logistics problems still led them to postpone the date to April 1943. Even that turned out to be overly optimistic.

Dieppe Disaster

Hopes for a quick cross-Channel invasion died on the French coast at Dieppe on August 19, 1942, when a British-Canadian hit-and-run raid supported by 60 U.S. Army Rangers (*Operation Jubilee*) turned into a disaster that cost more than 3,000 casualties. (*See the previous chapter for more information*) Whatever enthusiasm British prime minister Winston Churchill and his chiefs of staff had for a cross-Channel invasion was crushed, and American planners realized no such invasion could occur in the immediate future. Following Dieppe, Adolf Hitler ordered a massive program of fortification building along the French coast.

Casablanca

The first Allied invasion came ashore, not in France, but on the sands of Northwest Africa in November 1942. *Operation Torch* allowed Roosevelt to keep his word to Stalin, introduced green American troops to desperately needed combat experience, and provided a launching pad for cross-Mediterranean invasions favored by Churchill, who advocated attacking "the soft underbelly" of Southern Europe. (Torch *is explored more fully in the preceding chapter*)

Churchill, Roosevelt, and the combined Chiefs of Staff met at Casablanca, Morocco, January 14–24, 1943, to discuss strategic options once North Africa was cleared of German troops. Stalin declined his invitation to the conference, citing military pressures. In November two massive Soviet counteroffensives had encircled the German Sixth Army at Stalingrad; soon, 91,000 Germans would surrender there. The tide in the East appeared to be turning.

The leaders at Casablanca agreed to focus on winning the Battle of the Atlantic and gaining control of the sea-lanes across which American forces and millions of tons of supplies and equipment would travel to the United Kingdom. German U-boat successes against North Atlantic convoys reached their peak that March, but breakthroughs in decryption, along with high-frequency direction finding and new weapons, broke the back of the U-boat offensive, which collapsed in May.

With the Battle of the Atlantic won, tons of equipment began arriving daily at UK ports; even 1,000 locomotives and 20,000 rail cars made the crossing. American soldiers, sailors and airmen (along with women in military reserve units who performed tasks ranging from nursing to driving to postal services) were soon intermingling with British military and civilians; 1.5 million arrived before June 1944. Their presence was both welcomed and deplored. (*See the chapters Men and Women in Uniform – the Americans and Allied Flyers Epic Pub Crawl*)

The Americans still favored a cross-Channel invasion as the next step, but the British came to Casablanca well prepared to argue for invasions of the island of Sicily and then Italy. They carried the day, leading American major general Albert Wedemeyer to remark, "We came, we listened, and we were conquered." Both sides agreed, however, preparations for the grand assault on Fortress Europe must go forward.

'It won't work, but you must bloody well make it.'

One critical decision not made at Casablanca was who the Supreme Commander, Allied Expeditionary Force (SHAEF), was going to be. To keep things moving forward, British lieutenant general Frederick Morgan was named Chief of Staff to the Supreme Commander (COSSAC), responsible for coordinating British and American planning for the invasion. American brigadier general R.W. Barker would serve as his deputy.

Before long American general Dwight David Eisenhower, who had led the *Torch* landings and those at Sicily, and who had demonstrated an ability to work harmoniously with American, British and French leaders, would be named the Supreme Commander. Gradually most of the staff of COSSAC was absorbed into SHAEF (Supreme Headquarters Allied Expeditionary Forces) with Morgan serving as Eisenhower's deputy chief of staff. (*See Leaders of the Allies*)

Merging into SHAEF was still months away when, on April 17, 1943, Morgan held his first staff meeting. He said, "I want to make it clear that, although the primary object of COSSAC is to make plans, I am certain that it is wrong to refer to it in any way as a 'planning staff' (which) implies the production of nothing but paper. What we must contrive to do somehow is to produce not only paper, but ACTION."

COSSAC's assignment, Morgan continued, was to coordinate the efforts currently "being exerted in a 101 directions." He ended by quoting the Chief of the General Staff, who had said, "Well, there it is; it won't work, but you must bloody well make it."

Apart from considering German defenses, COSSAC had to study tides, weather, beach conditions, and port access to select the best landing sites, which had to be within the range of UK-based fighter planes. The Dieppe raid had proven a direct assault on a port city was folly. Normandy's Calvados Coast, across the Channel from Portsmouth, looked promising. Its wide beaches gave way to farms and small towns, and it was close to the port of Cherbourg, which, theoretically, would be captured within 48 hours and used for resupplying the troops.

COSSAC reported three conditions were necessary to launch *Overlord* in 1944: (1) Overwhelming air supremacy; (2) artificial harbors; (3) German mobile reserves in France could not exceed 12 divisions or 15 available from the Mediterranean and/or Eastern fronts.

Achieving Air Supremacy

In January 1944, Brigadier General J.H. "Jimmy" Doolittle took control of the U.S. Army's Eighth Air Force in England. As part of the plan to gain air dominance for D-Day he immediately changed the fighter pilots' top priority from defensive (protecting the bombers) to offensive (pursuing and shooting down enemy fighters). This shift plus the strategic bombing of factories left the Luftwaffe barely able to put in an appearance on June 6 and unable to prevent the carpet-bombings that were crucial elements of breaking out of Normandy in August. German general Heinz Guderian, often called "the father of the blitzkrieg," later said, "Lack of German air superiority in Normandy led to complete breakdown of the German net of communications."

In December 1941–January 1942 "ever increasing air bombardment" was identified as one means of wearing down Germany's resistance. The Royal Air Force at first used precision bombing during daylight hours but could not sustain the losses that produced, so the strategy switched to "area bombing" at night, which would hit civilian as well as military targets in hopes of demoralizing the German population. The Americans resumed daytime bombing when they arrived. Day and night, the Allies pounded infrastructure, aircraft factories, oil refineries, and other military and civilian targets.

As D-Day grew nearer, Allied aircraft bombed transportation infrastructure in France. In most cases, the Germans quickly repaired the damage, but several bridges over the Seine were rendered unusable to reinforcements sent to stem the invasion.

Additionally, in 1943 the RAF had begun airdropping weapons and ammunition, along with explosives and other needed supplies, to the underground French Resistance. For most of its existence the Resistance movement was small in number, and most involved were amateurs at war, radio communications, or intelligence gathering. Its numbers began to swell in the months before D-Day, after the Germans began requiring virtually all able-bodied Frenchmen to do slave labor in Germany. Thousands of young men who fled into the countryside were recruited for the Resistance.

In the months leading up to the invasion Resistance fighters carried out coordinated sabotage campaigns on transportation, communication, and power sources, along with attacks on command centers. Even more useful were the maps, photographs and other information they provided to Allied planners, adding badly needed on-the-ground intel to supplement air reconnaissance photos and radio intercepts.

Mulberries

To compensate for the lack of ports in the invasion area, an imaginative short-term solution was found for resupply: build two large, floating, artificial harbors (the second requirement identified by COSSAC) in England and tow them to France. Multiple supply ships could dock at these floating harbors, and their cargos would be carried to shore over flexible steel roadways. Code-named "Mulberry" (the next available name on a list of code names), one would supply Americans and the other Britons and their allied nations. The American Mulberry was destroyed in a violent storm 12 days after D-Day, but the other was repaired and remained in service until November 19.

The capture of Cherbourg ended up taking three weeks instead of two days, by which time the Germans had blocked its harbor with sunken ships. Had invasion plans not included the creation of the Mulberries, the ability to adequately resupply the men ashore would have slowed, if not stymied, the drive inland.

Limiting the German Response

The third COSSAC condition for invasion involved limiting the number of German forces in Northwest France and the enemy's ability to bring in reinforcements. A crucial element for meeting that condition involved subterfuge. It would be impossible to keep the Germans from learning of the buildup in England, so campaigns of misdirection and misinformation were undertaken to keep them from identifying where the invasion would come ashore.

Among the most famous parts of this deception campaign was the creation of "ghost armies" under *Operation Fortitude*. Phony tanks, trucks and other equipment were amassed and German observation planes allowed to fly over the "assembly areas." In Scotland, *Fortitude North* was designed to look like preparations for invading Nazi-occupied Norway. *Fortitude South* was assembled across from Calais, and German intelligence was led to believe that "army" would be led by hard-charging American lieutenant general George S. Patton Jr.

Additionally—and amazingly—Britain's counterintelligence services had identified the German spy network in England and had turned the spies into double agents feeding false information to Berlin. These and other deceptions convinced most of the German High Command the invasion would hit Calais, the closest point in France to England.

The German Preparations

Still, the deception wasn't complete. In mid-March Hitler, looking over intelligence about troop formations in England, said the invasion would take place in Normandy. Another who held that conviction even more strongly was the man Hitler had named commander of Army Group B in France: Field Marshal Erwin Rommel.

Famed as "the Desert Fox," Rommel had fought Americans in North Africa. He knew the Allies had to be stopped on the invasion beaches to keep them from building up overwhelming strength.

His superior, Field Marshal Gerd von Rundstedt, commander-in-chief, West, did not agree. Nor did Hitler. Rommel pressed them to position armor divisions close to the coast, not inland, because Allied air power could decimate the tanks on their way to the front. Hitler, despite his prediction about Normandy, still kept a large portion of the tanks in position to defend Calais and refused to let any armor move without his personal order.

Rommel did what was within his power to protect the beaches. He had obstacles placed below the water line to rip open ship hulls. By June he had 5 million mines sewed on the beaches and in the water (a fraction of the 60 million he wanted). Inland, more mines were put atop spiked poles in areas where enemy gliders might land; his men called them "Rommel's asparagus." He also had areas behind the beaches flooded.

When the landings came, he was in Germany, celebrating his wife's birthday and preparing to pay Hitler another visit to plead for more armor.

(For more information on German defensive measures and mistakes, see the Leaders of the Axis and Momentum Swings chapters)

One Invasion or Two?

Among the last major sticking points for committing to the Normandy invasion was the question of getting enough landing craft and naval support vessels. Landing craft and ship builders on both sides of the Atlantic had instituted 24-hour work schedules but still couldn't meet demand. Allied planners vacillated between continuing with a plan for two simultaneous invasions of France or cancelling the southern invasion and committing all available naval resources to *Overlord*.

Conditions in Italy settled the matter; the Allied advance up "the boot" had stalled. Accordingly, *Operation Anvil*, the invasion of Southern France, was postponed until August. Instead, "the highest possible tempo of offensive action" was to be used in Italy to keep the Germans from transferring troops to Normandy. Eisenhower also postponed D-Day from May 1 to June 1 to gain another month of landing craft construction. All of this gave *Overlord* the ability to transport five divisions for the initial wave, with follow-ons to come.

In addition to the amphibious assault force, 6th British Airborne Division and the American 82nd and 101st Airborne divisions would land behind German lines on the night of June 5–6 to disrupt communications and transportation, eliminate inland artillery positions and seize key bridges needed by the Allies.

Exercise Tiger

Initially, U.S. ground forces were expected to arrive in the UK already trained for amphibious assault, but some technical issues could not be solved long distance. An Assault Training Center opened at Woolacombe, North Devon, in Southwest England where the beach and inland areas resembled Normandy.

On April 24, 1943, a realistic amphibious training exercise, *Exercise Tiger*, began in the area of Slapton Sands after evacuating 3,000 residents of South Devon. Three nights later, nine German fast-attack E-boats slipped in, sinking two landing ships and damaging a third. More than 700 Americans died. *Exercise Tiger* continued, and more lives were lost in a live-fire exercise, bringing the total casualties to nearly 950. However, lessons learned from the tragedy may have saved lives on D-Day. Because of concern about morale, the events of *Exercise Tiger* were a closely guarded secret—and remained one until well after the war.

Offshore Support

No American warships were included for fire support in the original plans, but in February 1944 three U.S. battleships, three cruisers, and 31 destroyers were committed, along with minesweepers, PT boats, and other ships of war. Even the Coast Guard provided 60 cutters for search and rescue. The U.S. Navy set up special organizations, including Task Force 122 under Rear Admiral Alan G. Kirk, which had responsibility for operations and training for the cross-Channel assault.

Between March 20 and May 31 all required vessels—the largest naval armada ever put to sea—had been moved to England and were in a state of readiness. Once June 5 had been set for the invasion date (postponed to June 6 due to bad weather) American soldiers were moved into isolated camps—"cocoons"—and British military police kept them from visiting nearby towns.

When Eisenhower gave the go-ahead for June 6, the extensive planning for D-Day was done. Now it was up to the officers and men of the invasion force to carry those plans to fruition, and they did. To the officers and men hugging beach sand or hunkered down in hedgerows, this plan must have seemed at times like a haphazard mess, but the planning process paid off when they turned it into a successful invasion.

American generals wait on USS *Augusta* to land on Omaha Beach on June 8, 1944. From left to right are Maj. Gen. Hugh Keen, Lt. Gen. Omar Bradley and Gen. Dwight Eisenhower. *(Photo courtesy of National Archives and Records Administration Collections)*

LEADERS OF THE AXIS

Dana Lombardy

By early 1944 it was obvious to both the Allied and Axis countries that Nazi Germany was losing the war. This was the result of battlefield casualties in three years of fighting against the Soviet Union, the loss of North Africa and destruction of Axis power in the Mediterranean, as well as the reduction of the number of U-boats terrorizing the seas and the rapid Allied command of the skies over Europe.

Axis hopes in 1944 focused on three interrelated concepts:

1) Divide the Western Allies (Great Britain and the United States) from the Soviet Union and negotiate a separate peace;
2) Mount skillful and prolonged defensive actions to inflict huge casualties on the Allies that might result in negotiations for peace without a complete Germany defeat; and
3) Further encourage a cession of hostilities by wreaking widespread terror on Great Britain using the so-called "vengeance" weapons soon to be deployed: V-1 "Buzz Bomb" (the world's first cruise missile) and V-2 long-range rockets.

In hindsight these possibilities were wishful thinking. However, no matter how unlikely these outcomes were, the Germans fought tenaciously in 1944.

Fortunately for the Allies on D-Day, the Axis command structure was disorganized and dysfunctional, and the deployment and employment of the mobile, powerful German panzer (tank) divisions was piecemeal and fatally delayed.

These problems started at the very top of the leadership chain of command.

Adolf Hitler

Through his political savvy and ability to move the masses with stirring oratory, Austrian-born Adolf Hitler was the driving force behind the most dangerous political party ever created, the National Socialist (Nazi) Party of Germany. With violence, propaganda and measured benevolence he led the party and himself to complete control of a vulnerable Germany, scarred by the consequences of its defeat in the First World War. After he turned Germany into a thriving war economy and military power, Hitler then began to fulfill his prophesy of a thousand-year German Reich ruling Europe by warring against his neighbors. For a complete biography of Hitler from birth through the early German successes of World War II read *The World Turns to War*. Publication information in the accompanying bibliography.

In 1944, 55-year-old Adolf Hitler remained Führer and dictator of the Nazi state of Germany. He continued to be senior leader in execution of the pact between the three Axis countries: Germany, Italy and Japan. The Axis partners never cooperated militarily as closely as the Allied countries did during the war—a weakness that eventually undermined their strategic effectiveness. Instinctive decisions had often worked in favor of military success for Hitler in the early blitzkrieg campaigns, but that success could not be sustained.

There was a fatal flaw in Hitler's method of military success: he ran the campaigns in detail from his Führer headquarters, far from the battlefields. The Army's supreme headquarters was often ignored. Walter Warlimont, one of Hitler's staff officers, wrote: "The best the Army leaders could expect was occasionally to be summoned to a briefing." Arguments or debates were fruitless. Hitler's top aides ensured "that the 'Führer's genius' should win the day against the 'indiscipline of the generals.'"

By 1944, Hitler's method of micromanagement, plus hard and effective fighting by the Allies, led to major battlefield defeats in the Soviet Union and in the Mediterranean. Although the German Army was stubbornly preventing an Allied breakthrough in Italy, the Allied invasion of France was expected soon.

One example of the disorganized way the German Army prepared for the upcoming campaign in France was Hitler's management of the critical mobile reserve of fast-striking panzer divisions. At least ten of these divisions were under Panzer Group West commanded by Leo Geyr von Schweppenburg, a successful tank commander who led a panzer division in Poland and later a panzer corps in France and in the invasion of the Soviet Union.

Schweppenburg's initially powerful and mobile force was located near Paris, to be used against an Allied landing in Normandy or in the Pas de Calais area right across the Channel from England. Erwin Rommel, commander of the Normandy defenses, argued that the panzer divisions needed to be closer to the beaches in order to immediately counterattack the Allied landings since Allied air power would prevent rapid movement to the invasion area from positions further to the rear.

At first, Hitler agreed with Rommel, but then reversed himself, then finally settled on a compromise, giving Rommel three of Schweppenburg's panzer divisions. The rest of Panzer Group West was only to move forward with the express approval of the Führer. As a result, the arrival of the bulk of the critical panzer divisions to the invasion area was delayed—arriving too late, piecemeal, and badly shot up by Allied air power.

Hitler was a dedicated vegetarian and dog lover, a non-smoker who forbade smoking in his headquarters, and a hypochondriac who suffered from a variety of real and imagined ailments. As the Red Army closed in on his underground bunker in Berlin, he married his mistress Eva Braun and committed suicide with her on April 30, 1945, at the age of 56. His legacy remains as a mass murdering psychopath and one of the most vicious anti-Semites in history.

Reichsmarschall Hermann Wilhelm Göring

Reichsmarschall (Marshal of the Empire) Hermann Göring was commander of the Luftwaffe (German Air Force) from its creation in the 1930s. He also was an ardent Nazi who established the mechanism creating the feared Gestapo (secret police). A highly decorated fighter pilot in World War I, Göring's loyalty to Hitler earned him the designation as Hitler's successor until he fell out of favor with the Führer near the end of the war.

Initially, the Luftwaffe played a major role in the battlefield successes. Göring's attempt to manage the air attacks on Great Britain in 1940 failed to take control of the skies over the potential invasion areas. Hitler's disappointment with him grew when the Luftwaffe failed to supply a German army trapped at Stalingrad, and to defend Germany against the growing Allied air campaign that bombed at night and by day; by 1943 his influence had waned. By early 1944 the Luftwaffe was no longer able to inflict significant losses on the massive Allied bombing raids disrupting Germany's transportation and industrial infrastructure. Following D-Day the most effective German air missions was dropping oyster mines at night; five Allied warships and four other vessels were lost during June.

"Voice or no voice, the people can always be brought to the bidding of the leaders." -Hermann Göring, at the Nuremberg war crimes trials

Göring surrendered to the Americans on May 9, 1945, and was tried and convicted as a war criminal. He took poison on October 15, 1946, just a few hours before his planned execution. He was 52 years old.

Admiral Karl Dönitz

Fifty-two-year-old Karl Dönitz was commander of the Kriegsmarine (German Navy) in 1944. A U-boat commander in World War One, he was captured when his boat experienced mechanical problems in 1918. Hitler initially assigned him to rebuild the U-boat fleet in 1935.

Dönitz was a passionate advocate for submarine warfare and believed U-boats would be decisive in the next war. He also developed the highly effective "wolf pack" tactic of coordinated attacks by multiple subs to overcome the defenses of the convoy system. Frustrated with the poor performance of his surface ships, in 1943 Hitler promoted Dönitz to head of the entire navy.

By 1944 Germany had few remaining surface ships and the U-boat force had been substantially defeated in 1943 through a combination of improved convoy defenses, aircraft, radar, sonar and the Allies' ability to read Germany's encoded radio messages. Between June and August of '44 Dönitz's beloved U-boats sank seven escorts, 13 transports and three LSTs in the Channel, but at a cost of 18 subs.

On D-Day, Dönitz's Naval Group West fleet of surface E-boats (similar to U.S. PT torpedo boats) scored a few successes against the enormous Allied armada, but these results failed to slow the Allied invasion force. In early July the Free Polish cruiser *Dragon* and three Allied minesweepers were lost to naval commandos using human torpedoes. All Allied naval losses during D-Day and the Normandy Campaign constituted only a tiny fraction of their naval force in the Channel area.

"The reason that the American Navy does so well in wartime is that war is chaos, and the Americans practice chaos on a daily basis." -Karl Dönitz, *Memoirs*

An ardent Nazi, Dönitz hurried to see Hitler following the July 20 assassination attempt and proclaim his personal loyalty and that of the Kriegsmarine. The Führer named Dönitz his successor after Göring fell out of favor. Dönitz surrendered Germany unconditionally on May 7, 1945, but he had delayed the announcement long enough to allow tens of thousands of German troops and civilians to flee into territory controlled by the Western Allies in advance of Soviet forces. Tried and convicted of war crimes, he was sentenced to ten years in prison. He later wrote several books about his career and submarine warfare and died at the age of 89 in 1980.

Field Marshal Karl Rudolf Gerd von Rundstedt

Sixty-eight-year-old Gerd Rundstedt commanded *Oberkommando* (Supreme Command) West in 1944. He controlled Army Groups B (that included Normandy) and G (southern France). After the assassination attempt on Hitler in July, Günther von Kluge replaced Rundstedt. When Kluge committed suicide in August, Hitler put Rundstedt back in command for the German December Ardennes offensive.

Rundstedt served in World War One and in the postwar army. He retired in 1938, unhappy with Hitler and the Nazis' growing power. He obeyed when ordered to return to duty and commanded Army Group South in the 1939 invasion of Poland and the 45 divisions of Army Group A in the 1940 invasion of France.

Although Rundstedt's next army group, consisting of 57 divisions, had success in the invasion of the Soviet Union in 1941, Hitler replaced him for withdrawing in November without permission following a Soviet counterattack at Rostov. Rundstedt was quickly recalled again to duty in March 1942 as commander of *Oberbefehlshaber* (*OB*) West, the overall headquarters for the Western Front, with the job of building the fortifications known as the Atlantic Wall along 1,700 miles of coastline.

Rundstedt saw his new job as having limited strategic usefulness: "The value of these fortresses was insignificant because of their inability to defend themselves against a land attack." As the Germans retreated after D-Day, more than 120,000 soldiers were left behind in Atlantic Wall concrete outposts, which were eventually captured without tying down the valuable Allied mobile divisions. "I reported all this to the Führer in 1943, but it was not favorably received."

Once the campaign in Normandy was in full swing, Rundstedt had nothing to do. Hitler exercised strict control over the battlefront. Soon after D-Day, Rundstedt appealed to the Führer to allow him to create a reserve in order to form a powerful counterattack force. This required the release of infantry divisions from other areas of the Atlantic Wall in order to replace the mobile panzer divisions that were then getting ground down in the front lines. Rundstedt realized such a massive relocation of his divisions was politically impossible—Hitler had already ordered no withdrawal from any point in the Atlantic Wall. Rundstedt's request was denied.

A few days before being fired in July by Hitler, the field marshal wrote: "Our own losses are so high that the fighting strength of the divisions is sinking fast. The force is fighting heroically everywhere, but the unequal combat is nearing its end."

After the war, Rundstedt told Allied interrogators "If I had been given a free hand to conduct operations, I think I could have made the Allies pay a fearful price for their victory. But I did not have my way. As commander-in-chief in the west my only authority was to change the guard in front of my gate."

He was captured by the Allies but not tried for war crimes and was released after four years. He died in 1953 at the age of 77.

Field Marshal Erwin Johannes Eugen Rommel

When he died in 1944 just short of his 53rd birthday, Rommel was arguably the most popular field commander in Germany. Unusual for World War Two, he was also well known and respected by the Allied leaders and the public in the West as the "Desert Fox" for his operational prowess in North Africa where he led a German panzer corps (later army) and Italian forces.

As a young officer, Rommel was wounded in France in 1914 during the First World War. He recovered and then fought on the Italian and Romanian fronts, earning one of Germany's highest awards, the *Pour le Mérite* ("for merit"). In the postwar army, Rommel wrote *Infantry Attacks*, a textbook on infantry tactics. After teaching briefly at the War Academy in 1938, he became head of Hitler's army security detachment.

Rommel took advantage of his close proximity to Hitler to request one of the new panzer divisions that he then led in spectacular fashion in the 1940 campaign in France. His aggressive and daring style of leading at the front gained him command of the new *Afrika Korps* in February 1941.

For the next two years he scored surprising victories against the more numerous and better-supplied British and Empire forces in the sparsely inhabited North African desert but was decisively defeated in October–November 1942 at the Battle of El Alamein. Rommel conducted a skillful retreat after an Allied invasion force landed hundreds of miles behind him in Morocco and Algeria.

Promoted to field marshal, Rommel was evacuated from Tunisia before the Axis surrendered there in May 1943. In January 1944 he was appointed head of Army Group B, consisting of two armies covering the area from the Netherlands to the Loire River in France. Rommel concentrated on improving the defenses of the Atlantic Wall in Normandy before the D-Day invasion.

"[German commanders from the East] cannot imagine what they're in for here." -Erwin Rommel, in discussion with fellow field general, May 1944

Rommel argued with Panzer Group West commander Geyr von Schweppenburg about the best way to deploy and employ the German panzer divisions. At least one historian believed that a strong clash of personalities between them made it difficult for Schweppenburg to accept Rommel's reasons to move the panzer divisions closer to the possible invasion areas. The result was that the panzer divisions arrived too late to throw back or divide the Allied invasion forces.

"[The Allied] superiority in the air and in ammunition is overwhelming, the same as it was in Africa. I hope things will go better here in the West." -Letter from Erwin Rommel to his son Manfred, dated 17 days before the D-Day invasion on June 6."

Rommel shrewdly used the Normandy terrain to restrict and channel Allied tanks and attacks, but there was nothing he could do to offset the steady buildup of Allied divisions and supplies or to replace the relentless and crippling losses in the German divisions.

Badly wounded by Royal Air Force fighters that caught his staff car on the road on July 17, Rommel was absent when the German Seventh Army was destroyed in the Falaise pocket during the Allied breakout from Normandy in August. Implicated in the July assassination attempt on Hitler (although not directly involved), Rommel was forced to commit suicide October 14.

General Friedrich Dollman

Of the senior German commanders in France on D-Day, 62-year-old Friedrich Dollman had the least combat experience before June 1944. His Seventh Army was responsible for the defense of Normandy.

Dollman served as a young staff officer in World War One and rose steadily in rank in the postwar army. In late August 1939 he took command of the Seventh Army. Dollman's army did not participate in the conquest of Poland in 1939 and played only a minor role in the invasion of France in 1940. He then settled into comfortable occupation duty from 1941 to 1944.

Like Panzer Group West commander von Schweppenburg, Dollman did not get along with his boss Erwin Rommel, who could be intolerant of subordinates with contrary views. The Seventh Army leader was running a map exercise with his divisional and regimental commanders at Rennes on June 6 when 100 miles away the Allies landed at Normandy. He ordered Panzer Lehr and 12th SS Panzer Division to move to the front without waiting for nightfall, exposing them to attacks by Allied aircraft.

Rommel took direct control of the German defensive operations, circumventing Dollman. When a major Allied breakout attempt on June 26 penetrated Seventh Army's defenses around St. Lô, Rundstedt and Rommel were both en route to meet with Hitler. Dollman, apparently losing his nerve, ordered an immediate counterattack. He either suffered a heart attack or took poison on June 29. Second SS Panzer Corps leader Paul Hausser succeeded Dollman as commander of Seventh Army.

General Fritz Bayerlein

Forty-five-year-old Fritz Bayerlein commanded the German Army's elite Panzer *Lehr* ("Training") Division in the Normandy campaign. Initially held in reserve by Panzer Group West, the full-strength division moved into Normandy on June 7. Bayerlein's objections to moving in daylight were overruled by Seventh Army commander Dollman, resulting in serious casualties from Allied air power before the division got into combat.

Bayerlein joined the German Army at the age of 16 and fought in Word War One. He earned a commission as an officer in the postwar army and was a staff officer in a panzer division in the conquest of Poland in 1939. Promotions and further staff posts followed as he served in the invasions of France in 1940 and the Soviet Union in 1941.

Transferred to North Africa in October 1941, he was chief of staff for Erwin Rommel's Afrika Korps. He led the decimated unit in its long retreat from El Alamein. During some of the last fighting in North Africa he was wounded and evacuated before the Axis surrender in Tunisia on May 13, 1943.

Bayerlein began a second tour on the Eastern Front in October 1943 in command of the 3rd Panzer Division. The division distinguished itself in its breakout from encirclement in January 1944, rescuing four other German divisions in the process.

He then took command of the newly formed Panzer Lehr in May 1944, and the division played a major role in slowing the British advance on Caen in Normandy. On July 25 the division was bombed and nearly annihilated by 1,500 heavy bombers as part of the Allies' *Operation Cobra.*

"It was hell . . . at least seventy percent of my personnel were out of action—dead, wounded, crazed or numbed." -Postwar interrogation of Fritz Bayerlein

Bayerlein somehow scraped together 15 tanks and along with an SS panzer battalion, put up stiff resistance. The Americans opposite the shattered German line also suffered from bombs that fell short, but by July 27 German opposition began to crumble and the Allied breakout from Normandy intensified. Panzer Lehr was rebuilt and fought in the December German Ardennes offensive.

Bayerlein was held as a prisoner of war until 1947. He wrote about his wartime experiences and contributed to more than 20 studies in the post-war German Military History Program. He died at the age of 71 in 1970.

Colonel Ernst Goth

Most of the German infantry in France in 1944 was in weak fortress or static divisions. At Normandy on June 6, the strongest and most mobile field infantry division (made mobile mostly by horses with a few motorized vehicles) was the 352rd. Its defensive area included the landing zone designated as "Omaha" for the American 1st and 29th infantry divisions.

Despite Rommel's advice to move the entire division up to the bluffs above the beaches, the bulk of it was positioned well back of the coast on June 6. Just one battalion of the 916th Grenadier Regiment and a battalion of the 716th Infantry (Static) Division were initially available to resist the American amphibious assault. One historian described the fighting as one of the worst days in U.S. Army history.

The commander of Grenadier Regiment 916 was 46-year-old Ernst Goth, who had enlisted in the German Army in World War I, was promoted to officer rank and served in postwar and World War II staff positions. He was posted to the 916th seven months before D-Day. Goth remembered Rommel saying that Normandy was probably where the Allies would attack.

On June 6 Goth personally led the German defense, which included a counterattack by German reserve units, against an American attack on strongpoint WN69. Also that day he blocked enemy attempts to enclose Colleville and continued close-quarter fighting over the next seven days. He was awarded the German close-combat medal for his actions on D-Day and the following days.

Goth surrendered in 1945 and was a prisoner of war until early 1946. He was never accused of war crimes. He wrote his memoirs in 1983 and parts were translated by his grandson, Martin Galle, a contributor to *D-Day 75th Anniversary—A Millennials Guide*. Goth died in 1986 at the age of 88.

Conclusions

The disorganized and dysfunctional German command structure prevented an effective defense in France in 1944. Outnumbered German soldiers fought capably, led by veteran lower-level officers. In the end, it wasn't enough to stop the Allied breakout from Normandy and liberation of France.

Hitler may have thought he was "under the special protection of God," as he once said, but if the fates protected him against assassination attempts, they also smiled upon the Allies on June 6. Several key German commanders in the West were not present when the invasion started. Rommel, Dollman, and the German Seventh Army's division commanders were absent when the Allied invasion force landed on D-Day.

Historian Matthew Cooper summed up the reasons for the Axis defeat in Normandy in his highly regarded book *The German Army 1933–1945*: "The failure was due to the material superiority of the Allies, to the dispositions of the German [divisions], and to Hitler's intransigence."

Field Marshal Erwin Rommel inspects preparations among the static forces manning Germany's Atlantic Wall defense line. He expected the anticipated Allied invasion of France to land here, on the Normandy coast. *(Image courtesy of the National Archives and Records Administration Collections)*

LEADERS OF THE ALLIES

William Floyd Jr.

THE ALLIED LEADERS OF THE D-DAY INVASION ON JUNE 6, 1944, WERE men of diverse personalities and backgrounds who came together to push the invading German forces out of Western Europe and in so doing opened the long-awaited second front. This would eventually lead to ending the most devastating event of the 20th century. These were men who, at times, did not get along and seemed to be in competition with each other. However, they all had the same goal of defeating Nazi Germany. Supreme Allied Commander General Dwight Eisenhower sat at the top of this unprecedented war machine, using what he felt were the best strengths of his commanders while at times ignoring their squabbles and weaknesses. The German fighting force was still very strong at this point in the war, and an Allied victory was far from guaranteed. It was only through the determination and cooperation of these diverse forces that Germany would ultimately be defeated.

Dwight David Eisenhower

Shortly after the Cairo Conference between Churchill, Roosevelt and Stalin ended on December 1, 1943, Roosevelt made his long-awaited decision over when the Allies would open a second front in Europe with an invasion and who would be the supreme commander of the Allied forces in that operation. Stalin had pressed for this decision during the conference. On December 6 Roosevelt telegraphed the Soviet leader, "The decision has been made to appoint General Eisenhower immediately to command of cross-Channel operations."

One reasons Roosevelt gave for choosing Eisenhower over Army Chief of Staff George Marshall was his desire to keep Marshall in Washington. The commander had to be an American because the United States was contributing the most men of any nation to the invasion. British Prime Minister Winston Churchill warmly accepted Eisenhower as commander of all ground, sea, and air forces.

So here was 53-year-old Dwight Eisenhower who had not seen any combat in World War I, now being assigned to lead one of the biggest combat operations in history. Looking at Eisenhower's background no one would ever expect he would end up in this position. Marshall would tell Eisenhower that winning the war was now his problem.

Dwight David Eisenhower was born in Denison, Texas on October 14, 1890. In June of 1915 he graduated from West Point. He moved up the ranks and by 1940 was chief of staff of the 3rd Division in San Antonio. On February 16, 1942, Eisenhower was promoted to head of the War Plans Division. Later that year he was named commander of the European Theater of Operations and promoted to lieutenant general and named Supreme Allied Commander. He would lead a combined team of American and British officers in planning and carrying out the invasion.

Eisenhower proved to be a patient leader and seemed to get along with both American and British commanders, the only exception being the British general (later field marshal) Sir Bernard Law Montgomery. He found Montgomery to be arrogant, self-centered and not nearly as aggressive on the battlefield as he should be. During *Operation Goodwood*, a strong movement stretching from Caen to Falaise, Montgomery came up short of his pre-battle predictions. It was around this time that staff members at SHAEF (Supreme Headquarters Allied Expeditionary Force) began guessing who would be Montgomery's successor. Eisenhower even went as far as urging British prime minister Winston Churchill, "to persuade Monty to get on his bicycle and start moving."

Of course, Eisenhower's biggest decision was selecting the date for the invasion. The weather, phases of the moon, and tide patterns were crucial to deciding on the exact date. These factors restricted the possible dates to June 5–7 or 18–20. Bad weather on June 5 delayed the jump-off date, but on the morning of the 5th at 4:15 a.m. the decision was made to go on the 6th.

As the Allied invasion forces were boarding transports and landing craft bound for Normandy, they were handed Eisenhower's "Order of the Day". It stated in part:

> You are about to embark upon the Great Crusade, toward which we have striven these many months. The eyes of the world are upon you. The hopes and prayers of liberty-loving people everywhere march

with you . . . Good luck! And let us all beseech the blessing of Almighty God upon this great and noble undertaking.

Eisenhower's final service to his country was as 34th President of the United States (1953–1961). Dwight David Eisenhower died on March 28, 1969, at age 78 of congestive heart failure.

Sir Bernard Law Montgomery

General Sir Bernard Law Montgomery (promoted to field marshal September 1, 1944) was known as the hero of El Alamein for his stunning victory over German field marshal Erwin Rommel (the Desert Fox) in North Africa in 1942. Eisenhower had to deal with enormous egos and with Montgomery he got one of the largest. "Monty," as he came to be known, was called "insufferable" by Prime Minister Winston Churchill. One of the first meetings between Eisenhower and Montgomery in 1942 did not go well, as Montgomery reprimanded the American general for smoking. They would continue to butt heads throughout the duration of the war.

Montgomery was born on November 17, 1887, in London. He attended the Royal Military Academy at Sandhurst and commissioned into the Royal Warwickshire Regiment in 1908. In World War I he was wounded and spent the rest of the war as a staff officer. Montgomery began to make a name for himself during the 1940 Dunkirk evacuation with his handling of his 3rd Division. After El Alamein Montgomery commanded the Eighth Army in Sicily and on the Italian mainland. During the Normandy landings and for several months afterward he commanded all Allied ground forces. In September 1944 this command went to Eisenhower, which Montgomery bitterly resented. He went on to command the 21st Army Group. His arrogance and unwillingness to cooperate made him increasingly unpopular, especially with Americans.

In September the Allies launched *Operation Market Garden,* a plan conceived by Montgomery to use paratroopers and glider troops (the Market phase) to capture nine bridges in Holland, in the Eindhoven-Nijmegen-Arnhem area. Armor of the British XXX Corps, part of Monty's 21st Army Group, would simultaneously advance overland (Garden phase) and use the captured bridges to cross the Rhine into northern Germany and shorten the war. For a variety of reasons the force was not able to take the last bridge, at Arnhem, and *Market Garden* ended as a costly failure—over 10,000 casualties among the Airborne and 1,400 in XXX Corps.

The relationship between Montgomery and American general George S. Patton was strained. The Sicily campaign put them practically in competition.

The capture of Messina by Patton's 7th Army while Montgomery was bogged down outside the city was a blow to his ego. In perhaps Montgomery's biggest success he would lead *Operation Plunder*, the crossing of the Rhine River into Germany near the end of the war. This was the last natural major obstacle to the Allies crossing into Germany.

Bernard Law Montgomery passed away on March 24, 1976, after a long illness. He was 88 years old.

Omar Nelson Bradley

In July 1911 Omar Nelson Bradley from rural Missouri reported to Jefferson Barracks at St. Louis to take the grueling examination as an alternate candidate for the United States Military Academy. Afterward he thought he had failed the test miserably. Then three weeks later he learned he had passed and the primary candidate had failed and been disqualified. He was ordered to report immediately as a cadet of the class of 1915.

Bradley was born on February 12, 1893, near Clark in Randolph County, Missouri. During World War I he was assigned to guard valuable copper mines in Montana. In the inter-war years he created a training school for new officers that was adopted for use throughout the army.

After America's entry into World War II he served in North Africa under General Patton and commanded troops in the successful invasion of Sicily. Bradley played a part in planning for D-Day and led 1st Army during the invasion. On June 6 Bradley became so concerned with the situation on Omaha Beach that he seriously considered abandoning the beachhead and moving the follow-up units to the British sector or Utah Beach. He did not abandon Omaha Beach but called it a nightmare. He would later say, "Every man who set foot on Omaha Beach that day was a hero." America casualties at Omaha were over 2,000 in killed, wounded, or missing. By August 1, 1944, Bradley would be in charge of 12th Army Group.

On December 16, 1944, General Bradley was at Eisenhower's headquarters in Paris when word arrived that German forces had penetrated the American lines in the Ardennes region. This turned into what would become known as the Battle of the Bulge. In a lapse of judgment Bradley first thought these were simply spoiling attacks. This idea was soon set aside as Eisenhower and Bradley realized this was a full-scale attack involving over 200,000 German troops. Bradley's plan for a counterattack to cut off the Germans meant attacking from the north and south to squeeze off the bulge. The plan was a success in cutting off Germany's last gasp.

After the war General Bradley led the Veteran's Administration and later became the first Chairman of the Joint Chiefs of Staff. In 1950 he was appointed General of the Army with five stars. Omar N. Bradley died on April 8, 1981, and is buried at Arlington National Cemetery.

Sir Arthur William Tedder

British Air Chief Marshal Sir Arthur Tedder was named Deputy Supreme Commander under General Eisenhower on December 27, 1943, for the D-Day invasion that would occur approximately six months in the future. Tedder was born on July 11, 1890, in Glenguin, Stirling, Scotland.

During World War I he served in France (1915–1917), then in Egypt until 1919. After the war he served in the newly formed Royal Air Force, was promoted to group captain in 1931 and rose to commander of RAF Eastern Forces. When Britain entered World War II he was named head of RAF Middle East Command where he controlled Allied operations in North Africa and Italy. His forces played a huge role in disrupting enemy supply lines in the Mediterranean Theater.

His reputation as an effective air commander continued to grow. He became known for the "Tedder Carpet," a tactic that used multiple bombers to create a rolling barrage with high explosives and napalm ahead of advancing friendly forces.

He would become heavily involved in the planning for D-Day. After assuming his role as Deputy Supreme Commander, Tedder pressured Eisenhower to replace Montgomery as the Allied ground commander not long after the invasion began. He had disagreements with other commanders, both British and American. Field Marshal Alan Brooke, chief of the Imperial Grand Staff and chairman of the Chiefs of Staff Committee, said, "Tedder talks nothing but nonsense in support of Ike." In 1945 Tedder came close to being replaced, but that idea was quickly dropped. He would often disagree with Air Chief Marshal Sir Trafford Leigh-Mallory concerning air tactics at Normandy.

In the final year of the war Tedder travelled to the Soviet Union seeking better coordination between Russia and the Western Allies, especially during the Ardennes offensive. In May 1945 he signed the surrender document for Eisenhower.

After the war he served as the Chief of Air Staff and as a representative to the North Atlantic Treaty Organization (NATO). As a civilian he was chancellor of Cambridge University and served on the board of the British Broadcasting Corporation. He died on June 3, 1967, at age 76.

Sir Bertram Home Ramsay

At 2:23 p.m. on June 4, 1940, the British Admiralty gave the signal ending *Operation Dynamo*, the evacuation of Allied troops from Dunkirk on the west coast of France. Some 338,220 British and French soldiers were evacuated back to England in advance of the German offensive. The person primarily responsible for the successful transfer of this large force was Admiral Bertram Home Ramsay, for which he was knighted.

Ramsay was born into an army family on January 20, 1883, in London, but he chose to serve in the navy and was aboard his first ship in September 1899. He was known as a modernizer, determined to get rid of outdated ways of doing things. At the start of World War I Ramsay, then a lieutenant-commander, was serving on HMS *Dreadnought*, part of the Grand Fleet. He was later appointed to command the monitor *M.25* on the Dover patrol and by the end of the war was in command of the destroyer *Broke*.

During the inter-war years, Ramsay reached the rank of rear admiral. Named chief of staff to Sir Roger Backhouse, commander-in-chief of the Home Fleet, in August 1935, he asked to be relieved four months later after disagreements with his commander. In 1938, having reached the top of the rear-admiral list, he was placed on the retired list but returned to service in October 1939 when offered command of the Dover region. In May 1942 he was appointed as Flag Officer, Expeditionary Force, with responsibility for planning the Navy's mission for D-Day and became a deputy to General Eisenhower.

Ramsay's order of the day to his naval forces, May 31, 1944, read:

"Our task in conjunction with the Merchant Navies of the United Nations, and supported by the Allied Air Forces, is to carry the Allied Expeditionary Force to the continent, to establish it there in a secure bridgehead and to build it up and maintain it at a rate which will outmatch that of the enemy. Let no one underestimate the magnitude of this task."

Ramsay could not have been a more perfect fit for *Operation Neptune*. During his naval career he did not follow the normal path of advancement. Instead, he specialized in logistics, which turned out to be a ideal background for organizing the naval forces at D-Day. This operation would be his finest hour, responsible for moving enormous numbers of troops, equipment, and supplies to the Normandy beaches.

Unfortunately, Admiral Ramsay would not survive the war. He died in a plane crash over France on January 2, 1945.

Sir Trafford Leigh-Mallory

Trafford Leigh-Mallory's responsibility during the Battle of Britain (June 1940–April 1941) as Number 12 Group Commander was to protect England's Midlands from air attack. During this time he became embroiled in controversy with the commander of No. 11 Group, Keith Park, who was responsible for the area south of the Thames River. Park favored the use of individual fighter squadrons to intercept German planes while Leigh-Mallory favored a defensive tactic that used massive five-squadron formations. Such disagreements would be part of Leigh-Mallory's future as an air force commander.

Born July 11, 1892, in Mobberley, Cheshire, England, he attended Haileybury College and Cambridge University. His brother, George, was the renowned adventurer who famously said he wanted to climb Mt. Everest "because it is there." In World War I Trafford was wounded at Ypres. He later joined the Royal Flying Corps, flying reconnaissance and photographic missions. During the interwar years he served in a number of positions in the Royal Air Force.

In 1942 he was commander of air forces at the Dieppe Raid and was appointed Air Marshal of Fighter Command; in January 1943 he was knighted. He would become known for a deceptive technique of having high-flying fighters draw enemy fire while bombers flew at a lower altitude. Despite heavy political opposition, Leigh-Mallory was appointed Commander of the Air Forces of the Allied Expeditionary Forces under General Eisenhower, responsible for the coordination of air support for the invasion. Again he became involved in controversies, this time with the Americans and RAF Bomber Command. However, he was still able to substantially contribute to the Allied success of the invasion.

Leigh-Mallory was involved in planning and carrying out a number of important operations on D-Day and after the initial invasion including the Transportation Plan for the bombing of railroad facilities in France, which were being used by the Germans to move troops and equipment. He was also involved in *Operation Crossbow*, the plan to knock out launching sites used to fire missiles toward England. In late July he was heavily involved in *Operation Cobra*, the Allied plan for breaking out from the Normandy beachhead.

Leigh-Mallory was killed in a plane crash in the Alps on November 14, 1944, along with his wife and eight air crewmen, on his way to a new command as head of Allied air forces in Southeast Asia.

George Smith Patton Jr.

On December 18, 1944, Dwight Eisenhower summoned his senior commanders to a conference at Twelfth Army Group Headquarters at the French city of Verdun to plan a response to the recent German offensive in the Ardennes, soon to be known as the Battle of the Bulge. General Bradley at first thought the German offensive was simply a spoiling movement and not the massive operation it actually was. Lieutenant General Patton arrived at the conference with three proposed plans of action. Eisenhower told him, "I want you to command this movement under Brad's (General Omar Bradley) supervision." Patton told Ike he could attack in three days. Eisenhower added a day to make sure everything was ready; after all, Patton had to move his forces about a hundred miles before attacking. Patton's Third Army would slam into the German flank of two panzer armies with a full seventeen divisions, and elements of it went on to relieve the 101st Airborne Division at the Belgian city of Bastogne on December 26, 1944.

George S. Patton Jr. was born on November 11, 1885, in San Gabriel, California. He was descended from an old Virginia family that included a grandfather who was a Confederate colonel in the Civil War. As a child he was afflicted with dyslexia, struggling to read and write, but which he eventually overcame. After a year at the Virginia Military Institute, he attended West Point where he graduated as a cavalry lieutenant in 1909. In 1912 he participated in the Olympic Games in Stockholm, Sweden, finishing a very respectable fifth in the modern pentathlon.

In 1916 he served as an aide to Brigadier General John J. Pershing during the Mexican Punitive Expedition against Pancho Villa, and after the U.S. became involved in World War I he went with Pershing to France. Patton led the Light Tank Brigade in the battle at St. Mihiel and in the Meuse-Argonne offensive, where he was wounded.

In April 1941 Patton was promoted to temporary major general and made commander of the 2nd Armored Division. In November 1942 he helped lead *Operation Torch*, the invasion of French North Africa and in summer 1943 led the Seventh Army into Sicily, capturing Palermo and Messina.

The Germans knew that the Allied invasion of Western Europe was going to happen in 1944 and were convinced Patton would be leading it. The Allies took full advantage of the situation, creating an imaginary army with dummy inflatable tanks and other pieces of equipment. A captured German map showed German forces massing around the Pas de Calais, proof the plan was working.

After the American breakthrough at St. Lô, Patton's Third Army was unleashed on August 1, 1944. His forces drove rapidly east and then north seeking to encircle most of the German troops in Normandy. Stopped from closing the Falaise Pocket, Third Army swept across the Seine River and northeastern France. Reacting to the Battle of the Bulge, Patton reversed course and helped relieve besieged American forces in Bastogne. The Third Army experienced 281 days of almost incessant combat and advanced farther in less time than any other army in history.

After the war Patton was a harsh critic of the Soviets and of U.S. policies toward a conquered Germany. Injured in a traffic accident on December 9, 1945, he died on December 21.

Matthew Bunker Ridgway

Matthew Ridgway was handsome, graceful, and charismatic. General James Gavin described him as "hard as flint and full of intensity, almost grinding his teeth from intensity." General George Marshall once counseled Ridgway to "cultivate the art of playing and loafing." Ridgway moved up from major to brigadier general in 18 months. As a two-star he commanded the 82nd Airborne Division. Soldiers under his command would say, "There's a right way, a wrong way, and a Ridgway." Ridgway felt that God would preserve him until at least the final defeat of the Third Reich. He drove himself relentlessly and saw no reason not to drive others the same way.

Ridgway was born into an army family on March 3, 1895, at Fort Monroe in Hampton, Virginia, and graduated from West Point in 1917, returning the following year as an instructor of Spanish. He saw service in China, Nicaragua, and the Philippines. When World War II began he was working in the war plans division at the War Department. Within a few years he rose to the rank of Assistant Chief of Staff of the Fourth Army. In 1942 he took command of the 82nd Infantry Division and oversaw its conversion to the 82nd Airborne Division, which he would command in the Sicily invasion. The airborne assault on Sicily in July 1943 was planned by Ridgway and was the first major airborne assault in U.S. military history.

On D-Day he jumped over France with the 82nd Airborne, although he had not undergone paratrooper jump training—but he landed almost exactly where he was supposed to, managed to collect his 11-man team and set up a division command post. Promoted to command the newly formed XVIII Airborne Corps, he expected to lead the airborne portion of *Operation Market Garden*, an airborne and overland campaign in September to cross the Rhine at Arnhem, Holland. Instead, command was given to

Lieutenant General Frederick Browning, leader of the 1st British Airborne Corps. *Market Garden* failed to achieve its objective, and students of the operation have often speculated on whether it would have succeeded if the hard-driving Ridgway had been in charge.

On December 16, 1944, two German panzer units and the German Seventh Army began their offensive in the Ardennes. The XVIII Airborne Corps became one of the first units called upon to stop the offensive and expel the Germans from the northern part of the salient. Throughout, Ridgway remained calm and methodical. Historian Clay Blair, in *Ridgway's Paratroopers: The American Airborne in World War II*, wrote, "In the Bulge, he would become a rock to which many senior commanders would cling."

After the war Ridgway held the post of Deputy Chief of Staff of the Army and for a time commanded all United Nations forces in Korea. He was Supreme Allied Commander of Europe and Chief of Staff of the Army. He passed away July 26, 1993, at age 98.

James Maurice Gavin

In a French army barracks at Soissons, some 30 miles northwest of Reims, Major General James ("Slim Jim") Gavin—commander of the 82nd Airborne and at 37 years old the youngest commander of an American division—had just come back from a performance for his troops by the Ballet Russe de Monte Carlo. As he was beginning his dinner, he received a call from an old friend, chief of staff of the XVIII Airborne Corps, Colonel Ralph D. Eaton. He relayed to Gavin that Eisenhower's headquarters, "considered the situation on the Ardennes Front critical," and that the 82nd and 101st were to leave immediately for that area.

James Maurice Gavin was born March 22, 1907, in Brooklyn, New York. Orphaned in childhood, he was raised by adoptive parents in Pennsylvania. He quit school after the eighth grade and worked at odd jobs until he was 17 years old, when he joined the army. He completed a high school education by taking after-hours courses and was accepted at the United States Military Academy, graduating in 1929 as a second lieutenant.

By the start of World War II he had advanced to captain, but he would rise quickly through the ranks during the war. Promoted to colonel, he commanded a parachute combat team that helped spearhead the invasion of Sicily in 1943 and personally led it in stopping elements of the Hermann Göring Panzer Division. By D-Day he was a brigadier general and jumped with his paratroopers on the night of June 5–6. Elements of his section captured the town of Ste-Mère-Église and guarded river crossings on the flanks of the landing areas of Utah Beach. As a major general, Gavin took command of the 82nd Airborne Division when Matthew Ridgway was promoted to lead the XVIII Airborne Corps (*see above*).

In *Operation Market Garden* three months after D-Day Gavin's 82nd Airborne dropped at their designated areas near road and railway bridges near Nijmegen, Holland. After repeated attempts to capture the road bridge at Nijmegen, Gavin ordered an attack using boats to cross the Waal Canal. Despite heavy casualties that assault, accompanied by one supported with tanks, captured the objective.

At the Battle of the Bulge Gavin's 82nd Airborne fought heroically against the German incursion, sometimes armed only with rifles, grenades, and knives against German armor and often fighting in waist-deep snow, against some of the best German divisions. When the German attack ultimately failed, the 82nd went on the offensive. helping to force the enemy back through the Siegfried Line into Germany. On February 17, 1945, his exhausted troopers were relieved. After rest and refitting, the 82nd went back into action in April. It crossed the River Elbe, and on May 2, Gavin—dressed in his faded jumpsuit and carrying an M-1, received the surrender of the 21st Army Group.

During the war Gavin made more combat jumps than any other general in history. After the war he became chief of staff of Fifth Army, chief of staff to Allied forces in Southern Europe and commanding general of the U.S. VII Corps in West Germany. He would go on to serve as ambassador to France, 1961–1963. He died in Baltimore, February 23, 1990.

Courtney Hicks Hodges

Courtney Hodges, born January 5, 1887, in Perry, Georgia, is among the least known yet most important American generals in World War II. He would attend West Point for only one year because of failing grades but then enlisted in the Army as a private in 1906. By 1909 he had been commissioned a second lieutenant. He served in Mexico with General John J. Pershing, earned the Distinguished Service Cross during World War I and finished the war as a temporary lieutenant colonel. He later taught at West Point and became commandant of the Infantry School at Fort Benning. In May 1941 Hodges was promoted to major general. By February 1943 he was a lieutenant general in charge of the Southern Defense Command and Third Army. The following year he went to England where he served as General Omar Bradley's deputy commander in the First Army, a position he still held during *Operation Overlord*. In August 1944 he succeeded Bradley in command of 12th Army Group.

In mid-September his forces became involved in some of the most brutal fighting of the war, in the Hürtgen Forest. In a series of misguided engagements, Hodges sent one division after another into the bloody struggle. Before the fighting was over the following February eight American divisions had been decimated with 33,000 killed, wounded, or captured. Overall, the campaign along the Roer River cost the Americans 57,000 combat casualties, with 70,000 more lost to frostbite and other damage from the elements. In the end, as historian Carlo D'Este wrote, "the Germans remained in control of the vital Roer dams and the Allies were left with a hollow victory." Despite the disastrous outcome, Bradley and Hodges were praised by Eisenhower.

On December 19, during the Battle of the Bulge, Eisenhower ordered Hodges on the north with First Army and Patton on the south with Third Army to cut off the German advance at its base. After the German offensive had been stopped with the help of Allied air power, U.S. First and Third armies began their pincer movement on January 3 but were hindered by deep snow and many Germans escaped before the pincers closed on January 16. Hodges's forces continued to move toward Germany. Once across the Rhine River, Hodges's First Army and Lieutenant General William H. Simpson's Ninth Army encircled the Ruhr River Valley—Germany's most important manufacturing area and source of nearly 70 percent of its coal—and crushed Field Marshal Walter Model's German Army Group B. Hodges, promoted to four stars (full general), and First Army were scheduled to go the Pacific and lead the invasion of Honshu, but Japan capitulated before that could happen. He died in San Antonio on January 16, 1966.

Joseph Lawton Collins

George Marshall, while commander of the Infantry Training School at Fort Benning from 1927 to 1932 was deft at spotting talent. He would place the name of soldiers who particularly impressed him in an informal black notebook with notations next to their names. One of the names which Marshall would be absolutely right about was Joseph Lawton Collins, who would go on to be one of the most capable corps commanders of the Second World War. He was one of only a small number of commanders who served in both the Pacific and European theaters during the war.

Collins was born in New Orleans, Louisiana, on May 1, 1886. He graduated from West Point in 1917 as a second lieutenant, was assigned to the 22nd Infantry, and was sent to France after World War I. He later taught chemistry at West Point and attended Infantry School and the Field Artillery School.

After Pearl Harbor, Collins, as part of the Sixth Corps staff, was moved to the West Coast and soon was appointed chief of staff of the Hawaiian Department. After promotion to major general in May 1942 he took command of the 25th Infantry Division that relieved the 1st Marine Division on Guadalcanal and remained involved in fighting on the island until the end of all organized Japanese resistance. Collins emerged from the Guadalcanal Campaign with the nickname "Lightning Joe" for the aggressiveness he had shown against the Japanese.

Based on his success in the Pacific, Collins was transferred to Europe and placed in command of VII Corps for the D-Day invasion. He immediately began maneuver and live-fire training focusing on the amphibious assault troops of the 4th Infantry Division. On D-Day VII Corps landed at Utah Beach as part of General Omar Bradley's First Army. The beachhead at Utah would eventually extend seven miles into enemy territory but at the price of 10,000 casualties.

VII Corps seized the port city of Cherbourg June 25. The following month Collins was given tactical command of *Operation Cobra*, a breakout from the Cotentin Peninsula that would be preceded by an attack with heavy bombers over a narrow area. Some of the bombs fell short, inflicting casualties on the waiting infantry (and killing Lieutenant General Leslie McNair, commander of Army Ground Forces); regardless, "Lightning Joe" attacked immediately after the bombardment. No unit reached its objectives, but Collins made the bold decision to commit his armor and mobile troops anyway, which cut through the German resistance and cleared the way for Patton's Third Army to advance. The entire German front collapsed after just six days.

Collins led the VII Corps against Aachen within Germany itself. The fight for the city lasted six weeks and cost the Americans 8,000 casualties. In the end the city would be taken after a vicious fight in which progress sometimes was measured in yards.

Less than two months later the Battle of the Bulge began. British general Sir Bernard Law Montgomery began organizing forces for a counterattack, but troops were needed to hold a portion of the line while he did so. Monty demanded the most aggressive corps commander take that position; he refused to consider anyone but Lightning Joe Collins.

After the Bulge VII Corps went on to seize Cologne and help seal the Ruhr Pocket. On the banks of the Elbe River they met Russian forces advancing from the east. Through it all Collins maintained his reputation as a man who led from the front.

After the war Collins would serve as Chairman of the Joint Chiefs of Staff. He would retire from the army in 1956 and pass away on September 12, 1987, in Washington D.C.

Conclusions

Dwight David Eisenhower could be seen as one of the least likely candidates to lead the D-Day invasion. He had not seen combat in World War I and had served mostly in administrative posts. However, he did possess the qualities needed to organize and carry out this enormous undertaking. President Roosevelt said one reason Eisenhower was chosen was because he was the best politician among those being considered. A good part of the job was political, holding together a coalition of commanders and troops from different nations. In addition, Eisenhower had to deal with men who possessed enormous egos such as Patton and Montgomery. Ike had true compassion for the common soldier, which is best exemplified in the famous photograph of him speaking to members of the 101st Airborne just prior to D-Day.

Sir Bernard Law Montgomery, in command of all ground forces for the D-Day landings and for several months afterwards, could be arrogant and uncooperative at times but was nonetheless an effective commander. He led Allied forces in France during D-Day and for some weeks afterward and led the 21st Army Group across the Rhine River into Germany.

Omar Nelson Bradley became known as the "Soldier's General" for the compassion he showed the common foot soldier. He did not fight in World War I but that did not prevent him from being an excellent commander in the Second World War. After D-Day he was given command of 12th Army Group and would help devise the plan to counter the German offensive at the Battle of the Bulge. After the war he became General of the Army.

Arthur William Tedder, after a successful air campaign in the Mediterranean, became Deputy Supreme Commander directly under Eisenhower. Even though Tedder was British, he pushed Eisenhower to replace Montgomery. Tedder helped conceive the Transportation Plan used for bombing railroad facilities used by the Germans. In 1945 he would sign the surrender document for Eisenhower.

Bertrand Home Ramsay had ensured his legacy well before D-Day for leading the Allied evacuation at Dunkirk in 1940. His background in logistics made him the perfect commander for *Operation Neptune*, the naval component of the D-Day landings, in which he commanded over 3,000 ships.

Trafford Leigh-Mallory was a controversial leader of British air forces during the Battle of Britain. He would go on, despite some opposition, to be appointed air commander under Eisenhower. He was deeply involved in *Operation Cobra*, the Allied breakout from the Normandy Beachhead.

George Smith Patton Jr. was possibly the most colorful and aggressive general in the European Theater. During the war he always seemed to be involved in one controversy or another. In December 1944, he did what some thought impossible—pulled his army out of a winter battle and marched it 100 miles to confront the German forces at the Battle of the Bulge. His army would race across France and into Germany, helping to shorten the war.

Matthew Bunker Ridgway was as "hard as flint and full of intensity," so much so that General Marshall, in effect, told him he should learn to calm down. In a rare move, he would jump with the 82nd Airborne Division over France without having undergone paratroop training. He led the XVIII Airborne Corps in response to the German advance at the Battle of the Bulge.

James Maurice Gavin, in charge of the 82nd Airborne, was the youngest commander of an American division since the Civil War. He made more combat jumps than any other general in history. His personal toughness was not just from Army training but from being raised in a foster home in Pennsylvania coal country.

Joseph Lawton Collins, known as "Lightning Joe," was one of the most capable corps commanders in World War II. He was among the few senior generals who served in both the Pacific and European theaters. General Bradley wrote, "Had we created another ETO (European Theater of Operations) Army, despite his youth and lack of seniority, Collins certainly would have been named the commander."

D-DAY PETS AND MASCOTS

Dennis Edward Flake

OUR PETS, OUR ANIMAL COMPANIONS, PLAY A SIGNIFICANT ROLE IN our lives. They provide companionship and comfort for us during hectic and difficult times. Their antics give us comic relief. They can make our lives less stressful and reduce feelings of loneliness.

What would happen if our lives suddenly became more unpredictable and potentially very dangerous, if we were drafted into the United States military and placed in harm's way in some remote part of the world fighting a tenacious enemy? With our lives turned upside down, wouldn't we want some sense of normality, the kind that an animal can give us?

During World War II pets and mascots were commonplace among the men and women in military service. Following periods of brutal combat or a daring aerial bombardment, just a few minutes a day playing with a dog, cat, monkey, or goat could generate feelings of comfort and a major reduction in mental and physical stress.

Lower Stress, Adopt a Pet

An individual in a war zone might adopt a pet, or an entire unit might adopt a mascot. Initially, the animals were adopted to bring good luck to the unit, but they gave comfort, companionship, humor and friendship, and became a source of unit pride. Often these were animals left homeless by the war.

War correspondents began snapping pictures of soldiers, sailors and others with their animal companions, and these "buddy photographs," as they came to be known, frequently appeared on the pages of magazines or newspapers back home. The photos showed that the animal mascots provided comfort for service members so far from home and made their lives more bearable. The National Archives hosted an exhibit of these endearing images in 1993 entitled "Buddies: Soldiers and Animals in World War II."

Most pets/mascots were dogs and cats, but there were rabbits, goats, donkeys, bears, elephants and many others. In the tropics, exotic mascots like monkeys and birds were common. A Luftwaffe unit in occupied France had a lion cub for its mascot.

The *Saturday Evening Post*, of June 19, 1943, stated that mascots were a symbol of home and that some things were worth the fight. The article said it was common for a mascot to go on aerial bombardments with the air corps, and some died during the missions. Some dog mascots even made parachute jumps with the airborne. A "Naval History blog" declared that dog mascots built morale and were a needed respite from the monotony of sea duty. At least three dogs, Blackout, Pete the Pooch, and Knobby, were on U.S. Coast Guard ships at the Normandy invasion. Some mascots were given military ranks and uniforms.

Women in the service adopted animals just as the men did. When the kitten Glamor Puss, mascot to a WAC unit at Camp Haan, Riverside, California, was "catnapped" a story about it ran in Riverside's *Daily Bulletin* newspaper. A week later the paper reported Glamor Puss had been returned by two GIs who didn't hang around to be identified. (A photograph of the second article appears in *Loyal Forces: The American Animals of World War II*, by Toni M. Kiser and Lindsey F. Barnes; published by Louisiana State Press, 2013. The book also has a photograph of a member of the 502nd Regiment, 101st Airborne, with a very small dog, described as a mascot of the regiment, looking suspiciously at a doggy-size parachute.)

Working for the War Effort

Not all animals were pets or mascots. Some were working animals. Dogs were used as sentries and scouts. Messenger dogs carried communications between units in combat, and medical dogs helped locate wounded soldiers on the battlefield. When Britain's 13th Parachute Battalion was airlifted to France for action behind the lines on D-Day each of the three planes they traveled in had a patrol dog onboard. One of the dogs, Bing, was wounded in action and received a Dickin Medal, awarded to animals for outstanding actions in wartime. Glen, an Alsatian shepherd serving with the 9th Parachute Battalion, 6th Airborne Division, was killed by friendly fire on D-Day, along with his keeper, Private Emile Servais

"Jack" Corteil. The 1st Canadian Parachute Battalion also had an Alsatian shepherd mascot, Johnny Canuck (possibly named for a Canadian comic-book hero introduced in 1941), that jumped with his handler Sergeant Peter Kowalski; Johnny's mission was to sniff out German infiltrators.

Prior to and during the Normandy campaign, American-bred homing pigeons were used to carry messages. The British dropped the birds, wearing specially designed parachutes, from planes over Normandy to be picked up by the French Resistance. The Resistance put messages into a tube on a bird's leg and released it to fly back across the Channel with information on the German forces. In response, the Germans began "pigeon patrols," with men assigned to watch for and try to shoot down the birds. Trained hawks and falcons were also employed to pursue and kill the pigeons. This bird vs. bird war was the basis for the 2005 computer-animated film *Valiant*, with Ewan McGregor as the voice of Valiant the pigeon and Tim Curry voicing the bird of prey Von Talon.

In the real-life Normandy Campaign five pigeons were awarded the Dickin Medal. One of the birds honored, Gustav, delivered the first message from the beaches on June 6. Another, Paddy, flew 230 miles across the Channel in four hours and fifty minutes. Duke of Normandy was the first bird to bring a message from British 21st Army Group on D-Day, a trip that took 26 hours.

Even working animals won the affection of their keepers and their units or shipmates. In extremely dangerous and chaotic conditions, some of the best consolations are animals. It has been said that war hardens the souls of all participants. Maybe having a friendly and loyal animal buddy around softens the rigidity.

Fala, Pat, and Rota the Lion

It can be lonely at the top. Like the men and women who served under them, political and military leaders associated with D-Day found comfort with animal companions.

President Franklin D. Roosevelt had the unconditional love and dedication of his Scottish terrier, Fala, probably the most famous pet in the United States at the time. A gift to the president from one of his cousins in November 1940, the puppy's original name was Big Boy, but FDR changed it to Murray the Outlaw of Falahil, in honor of one of Roosevelt's Scottish ancestors. That was soon shortened to Fala as sort of a nickname.

Fala seemed to have the run of the White House, especially the kitchen. The kitchen staff gave generous portions of table food to the dog until he developed digestive issues. Eventually, only President Roosevelt was permitted to provide table scraps to his dog. He enjoyed showing people Fala's talent for shaking hands and standing on hind legs during the National Anthem.

Fala also met with several important world leaders including Prime Minister Winston Churchill of Great Britain. Fala was named national president of the "Barkers for Britain" program, which raised needed cash for supplies to aid the British people who were under siege by indiscriminate aerial bombing. (The supply program was Bundles for Britain.) Special "Barkers for Britain" dog tags were sold to American dog owners for 50 cents. Fala was given tag number 1.

Fala once joined Roosevelt on a clandestine meeting with Winston Churchill at Newfoundland in Canada. The British prime minister likely enjoyed having the dog there: he was quite an animal lover himself. During his lifetime he owned goldfish, pigs, dogs, cats, black swans, and even a lion named Rota that was given to him to commemorate British victories in North Africa during WWII. After a time, Rota was given to the London zoo. A popular but unproven rumor says Churchill taught his parrot Charlie to cuss Hitler and the Nazis.

Canada's prime minister, William Lyon Mackenzie King, was not a sociable man. When Canada entered the war his primary companion—human or animal—was an Irish terrier he had received as a gift in 1924; it was the first of three Irish terriers he would own, all named Pat. Supposedly the prime minister would observe the first Pat's tail-wagging to help him in policy decision-making, and he once postponed a wartime cabinet meeting to be with his four-footed companion when the aging dog fell ill. When the first Pat died in 1941, King sang "Safe in the Arms of Jesus" to him. Godfrey and Joan Patteson, who had given King the first Pat, also gave him the second shortly after Pat I's death, and Pat II helped him get through the rest of the war years. His diary, published after his own death in 1950, reveals the eccentric prime minister was told during séances that Pat I was with King's deceased family members and was happy. He wrote of his dogs, "We shall all be together in the Beyond. Of that I am perfectly sure."

'You Can't Talk War to a Dog'

General Dwight D. Eisenhower enjoyed the company and unconditional love of a black Scottish terrier from the Duke Street Kennels in London. Initially, the general had the choice of two dogs from the kennel. One was older; the other was only a three-month-old puppy. Ike selected the puppy because he thought it was love at first sight. He said it ran straight towards him and had a tremendous personality.

Eisenhower had asked for a dog for his birthday, saying, "You can't talk war to a dog, and I'd like to have someone or something to talk to, occasionally, that doesn't know the meaning of the word. A dog is my only hope." The pup was officially presented to the general on his October 14, 1942, birthday. He named it Telek after Telegraph House, his rented country hideaway in England, and he was known to feed the friendly dog under the table. Telek enjoyed chasing Ike's golf balls and playing tug of war with an old belt.

There are two very funny anecdotes involving the pup. Ike inadvertently used Telek's name in an official letter between the Supreme Headquarters Allied Expeditionary Forces in London and the War Department in Washington, D.C. Most of the War Department staff were not familiar with Ike's dog and thought Telek was a code name for some unidentified covert operation. Ike said that he had a "chuckle" from the news. The second incident occurred when General George C. Marshall, Chief of Staff of the United States Army, went to North Africa in January 1943 to consult with his subordinate, Eisenhower. Telek got so excited with the Very Important Person's visit that he ran into General Marshall's guest room and wet his bed.

The year after Ike received Telek, his naval attaché and friend, Captain Harry C. Butcher, brought a female Scottish terrier back with him from a trip to Washington, D.C. The female was named Caacie (pronounced *khaki*. Deborah Hopkinson, in *D-Day: The World War II Invasion That Changed History*, said the name was short for "Canine Auxiliary Air Corps). Telek was very happy with this new addition to the family, and they had multiple litters of beautiful black Scotties. Most of the offspring were given to friends and family. At cocktail hour, all the dogs were let into Ike's country cottage to run amuck.

General George Patton, "commander" of the phony First U.S. Army Group that helped deceive the Nazis about D-Day, had a shelter dog that previously was the pet of a Royal Air Force pilot who was killed during an aerial mission. The dog was a Bull terrier—a breed Patton's family had kept over the years—with a yellow spot on its tail.

When Patton adopted the dog, its name was Punch, but Patton, thinking his new dog was fearless like him, renamed him William the Conqueror. Unfortunately, the dog became terrified when he heard loud noises or explosions. The general speculated that Punch had been taken on many precarious bombing missions with his previous owner and did not like the thunderous action. William the Conqueror became Willie. He proved to be an excellent companion and comfort for the general.

Willie had a voracious appetite, snored very loudly, and was very social, especially with women. He never needed a leash but was extremely protective of his master. To add a little humor to the war, Patton presented Willie with a bust of Hitler for a target when he lifted his leg.

During the intense fighting in France after D-Day, General Eisenhower decided to visit Patton, who now commanded the very real Third Army. Eisenhower brought Telek with him. All was going well between Telek and Willie until Telek got too close to General Patton. In a fit of jealousy, Willie let Telek know in no uncertain terms he would not tolerate competition in his home. The dogs were separated and sent to their rooms. Following Patton's death in a vehicle accident in December 1945 Willie lived out his life with the general's widow and died in 1953.

Gen. Dwight D. Eisenhower (left) with his Scottish terrier Telek speaking to Secretary of the Navy Frank Knox in October 1943. *(Image courtesy of the National Archives and Records Administration Collections)*

British general Bernard "Monty" Montgomery had two dogs during World War II. One, a Cocker spaniel, he named Rommel for Erwin Rommel, his opponent in North Africa. The other, a Fox terrier, Montgomery named Hitler. The terrier was born in Normandy and given to the general there by Frank Gillard and other BBC correspondents after Montgomery mentioned to Gillard he missed the animals he'd enjoyed at his other headquarters. (Gillard would retire from the BBC in 1969 with the title of Managing Director Radio.) France has long required all pedigreed dogs born in a certain year be given names that begin with the same letter; in 1944 the letter was "S." Monty's new terrier was originally named Selijc. The story goes that someone said the S must stand for Schicklgruber, which many believed (erroneously) was Hitler's real surname. Thus, with dry British wit, Montgomery renamed Selijc Hitler.

The dogs accompanied Monty throughout the fighting in France, traveling with the caravan that served as his mobile headquarters. He also traveled with two caged canaries. King George VI and Prime Minister Winston Churchill were both photographed petting one of Monty's dogs during a trip to the front in August 1944.

Nazis Needed Animal Friends, Too

Montgomery's old nemesis, German field marshal Erwin Rommel, the man in charge of Normandy's defenses, also had two dogs, acquired in occupied France. Both were Dackels, also called Dachshunds. They were named Monty and Misr. Dackels were originally bred for hunting and were small enough to burrow into holes to flush out foxes and badgers; Rommel's dogs were independent and had the reputation of possessing a stubborn character.

The field marshal had been an early supporter of Hitler but became disillusioned with him, especially on military strategy and decisions, and was implicated in a failed plot to assassinate Germany's leader in July 1944. The government didn't want the embarrassment of publicly executing one of its war heroes, so Rommel was given the choice of execution or suicide. He chose suicide in exchange for guaranteed protection for his family. His son, Manfred, recorded in a post-war memoir that when his father was forced to commit suicide "his little dachshund which he had been given as a puppy a few months before in France, jumped up at him with a whine of joy," and Rommel told his son to shut the dog in the study.

Even Adolf Hitler, for all his cruelty to human beings, loved animals, particularly dogs. In 1941 his deputy Martin Bormann gave him a German shepherd (one in a long line of that breed Hitler had owned), and the Führer named her Blondi. She slept in Hitler's bedroom, had her own caretaker and enjoyed a special diet of lean meat and eggs. She learned a number of tricks, and even during military crises Hitler would take breaks from conferences with his generals to walk her and have her perform her tricks. If she performed well, Hitler was in a good mood and more receptive to his generals' ideas. If not—as one officer said, "I sometimes had the impression that the outcome of the Russian campaign depended more upon Blondi than the German general staff."

Blondi appeared in Nazi propaganda films and on posters, so before committing suicide himself in 1945 Hitler told her caretaker to poison her to keep the Russians from capturing her—and to test the effectiveness of the cyanide he and his mistress planned to take the next day.

MEN AND WOMEN IN UNIFORM

The Germans

Jay Wertz

Like all the other European countries that fought in the First World War, Germany lost many young men in combat who were of the generation born in the years just before the beginning of the 20th century. Many of those who weren't killed outright were physically and mentally scarred by the horrors of trench warfare. Even healthy ex-soldiers remained troubled and confused; they became politically involved in para-military groups that waged street violence in the aftermath of the war's treaties—treaties that also limited the manpower of Germany's armed forces. Hardly a scenario to build a massive fighting force. Yet two decades after the end of World War I, a new generation of males in their late teens and early twenties were poised to take up arms for the Nazi Regime of Germany. On the eve of war in 1939 the size of the German military force was 4.52 million men.

Native-born Germans

The vast majority of these young men had spent their formative years in Germany during the period in which Adolf Hitler was chancellor, beginning in January 1933. Even before the Nazis seized control of the German democracy, the party's programs for youth had been carried out in many areas of the country. The *Deutsches Jungvolk* ("German Young People," for boys 10–14) and Hitler *Jugend* ("Hitler Youth," for boys 14–18) combined physical fitness and Nazi party indoctrination in a club-like atmosphere outside the traditional school system. Some boys also learned the message of the party from teachers and family members.

In Hitler Youth marching and military regimentation as well as activities such as flying, motorcycle riding and sailing—that led to specialized military classification later—were introduced. Before the war officially began, young men 18 and older served for six months in a civilian organization run on military principles, the *Reichsarbeitsdienst* (National Labor Service). They labored in public works projects, building Germany's new infrastructure. As the time for war approached, Germany's military seized control of the *Reichsarbeitsdienst*, and its members were conscripted into the military.

While military service was thus compulsory for young men—except for a percentage exempted for special skills, physical or mental deformities and a variety of other reasons—women were actually excluded from service. Though women made up about one-third of the workforce in 1939, the Nazi ideology was for women to stay at home to bear and raise children. They were given cash subsidies from the party to do so. While many women in Germany worked outside the home during the years of the republic, the number of women in factory jobs began to decline when the war began. Those who did not stay home worked primarily in traditional female careers such as teaching, healthcare and secretarial jobs. The *Jungmädel* (Young Maidens) taught girls 10–14 good health practices and how to be good mothers and wives, as well as indoctrinating them with views of the Nazi Party. The *Bund Deutscher Mädel* (League of German Maidens) for those 14–21 continued to teach how to be good mothers to future Germans.

A select group of young men entered the party security force called the SS (*Schutzstaffel*, "Protective Echelon"), formed in 1923 and rapidly expanded, beginning in 1929, by Hitler confidant Heinrich Himmler. The SS leader grew the security force into a multifaceted organization that had a role in many functions of the party, government and German society. Young men recruited for the SS were screened for racial purity, dedication and physical attributes. Himmler paid particular attention to those whose physicality (blond, blue-eyed, tall and muscular) made them candidates to form the Aryan race Hitler desired to build. Those recruited into the SS were only a minority of Germany's new generation of young males. Most youngsters, even those who were members of the Hitler Youth, completed their formal schooling and entered trade apprenticeships until the Nazi mobilization for war snagged them for military service.

While many of the functions of the SS were internal, charged with intelligence gathering and terror tactics to keep the Nazis in power, the SS also had a military presence in the war. The armed forces branch was called the Waffen-SS (Armed SS). Units of Waffen-SS were formed early in the mobilization for war, and some participated in the invasion of Poland. Though many individuals joined Waffen-SS forces, over time casualties depleted these units. Acceptance standards were lowered to include dedicated men of Germanic heritage but not of German birth and Nazi believers who were of other nationalities. The caliber of equipment and personnel varied among Waffen-SS units; however, the best were formed into 15 panzer and panzergrenadier divisions. In combat, Waffen-SS units were under control of the leaders of the armies to which they were assigned, but in every other aspect they were controlled by the SS headquarters. Several SS panzer divisions were assigned to the Western Front in 1944.

Recruits from Axis Partners and Occupied Countries

Germany also had allies who provided young men for the war effort. Initially these were members of the Axis alliance: Italy, Hungary, Bulgaria and Romania. The Vichy French government that formed in the wake of the conquest of France allied with Germany in some campaigns such as in North Africa. Finland joined Germany for a time during 1941's *Operation Barbarossa* (the invasion of the USSR) to fight the Soviet Union; the small country had fought the Russian giant independently for three months in 1939–40 before being forced to cede more than 10 percent of its territory. By September 1943, Italy capitulated and the majority of Italian men who had survived death, wounding and capture were out of the Axis military service.

Individual recruits and conscripts were drawn from countries Germany occupied before the war, Austria, Lithuania, and Czechoslovakia. Later, countries that were conquered after war began became sources of manpower, primarily the Baltic states of Lithuania, Latvia and Estonia and the Balkan states of Croatia, Serbia and Albania, as well as the western countries of Norway, Denmark and The Netherlands. The SS recruited heavily in these places and also in the Ukraine. Some partisans in the Ukraine and Belorussia fought alongside Hungarians and Romanians during the German retreat. Others were simply taken to serve in the ranks of the SS and Wehrmacht.

By the time 1944 arrived, Germany had been at war for three and a half years and early campaigns, particularly the invasion of the Soviet Union, had depleted the pool of military-age recruits. Conscription age was lowered to 18. Married men were drafted. Some exempt classifications were eliminated. Would the less-than-ideal state of German manpower in the spring of 1944 be advantageous to the Allies?

Preparing to Defend the Western Front

The cross-Channel invasion was not going to arrive in front of a demoralized Wehrmacht as early Allied planners had hoped (*see* Operation Roundup *in Plans for the Invasion*). But the problems facing the German armed forces in France, Belgium and Holland were great and diverse. Despite the German commitment—the appointment of a fighter like Erwin Rommel was designed to bolster morale in this theater—the defense was not solid enough to succeed against an overwhelming Allied force that could land at any of a number of strategic points along the Channel coast.

As early as 1942 Hitler had recognized the danger posed by an Allied invasion along the vulnerable coastline of "Festung Europa" (Fortress Europe) and issued Führer Directive 40, a general plan to defend the coastal areas, particularly those abutting the Western Front. Although the directive placed an emphasis on interservice cooperation in a defense that would use all three branches—land, air and sea—to beat the enemy back before or immediately after landing, the structure of German leadership prevented more than voluntary cooperation among the three. Despite this obvious shortcoming, the directive called for building and manning fortifications, guarding airfields and ports, patrolling undefended areas, maximizing local intelligence and fighting to the last man.

Oberbefehlshaber (Supreme Commander, abbreviated OB) West commander Field Marshal Gerd von Rundstedt was one of the top soldiers in the army and, although not a Nazi, had Hitler's respect. Rundstedt battled with shrinking German resources, mostly in air defense and sea patrols in his command that extended from Norway to the Pyrenees. Yet, his major concern was the quality and quantity of combat troops in the theater and their lack of adequate transportation.

As the war raged on the Eastern Front, the best units in France and elsewhere in the OB West command were constantly being swapped with worn-out units from the East. These Eastern Front veterans were, at best, wounded and war-weary survivors of the brutal struggle against the Red Army. Of lesser quality were new recruits—some previously classified unfit for service, others who had held critical jobs on the home front, and many just very young or old. When these sources began to dry up, the Wehrmacht augmented them with the Ukrainians and Eastern Europeans (*Ost*, or East, battalions) as well as other foreign nationals—many of them prisoners of war—who were drafted into service without the commitment and esprit-de-corps of their German counterparts. They lacked training in the basic fundamentals of combat.

The East-West swap of units and men affected two German military veterans in different ways. Hans Eckhardt, a 17-year old from the Sudetenland, volunteered and received admission into the very competitive Luftwaffe flying personnel program. He was placed on active duty in the fall of 1942.

"We spent a short time in Germany then we were shipped out to France near the west coast for Luftwaffe training regiment. So we did what was called in America boot camp. We were trained with guns, machine guns and mortars and we were also kind of manning the Atlantic defenses. There were three battalions and every third night we were on the alert. We slept in our uniforms, with our boots on, and we practiced that within three minutes we were down out of the barracks and into trucks where we were ready to go to the coast where there were fortifications. This was an early response in preparation for D-Day. It was in late 1942.

"[The Canadian attempt to land at Dieppe] was far away from us, but we heard about it in the newspapers. It was a flop. The Canadians were ill-prepared. One thing that I recall from the reports was the tanks were not prepared for the gravel on the beaches. They got stuck. It was very poor intelligence, they expected sand, but it was gravel."

Before long Eckhardt was reassigned to the Eastern Front and put on a train that took him through Germany and to the Ukraine. Fritz Baresel from Stuttgart volunteered for the army in April 1942 to ensure he was selected for panzer training. His father, a veteran officer, and brother were already in the German armed services. Fritz trained near Stuttgart, had tours of duty in Russia, Hungary and Potsdam, and received the *Panzerkampfabzeichen*, (Tank Battle Badge), the Iron Cross Second Class and the *Verwundeten-Abzeichen* (Wound Badge) for a small wound received in the Ukraine. By April 1944 he was just 20 years old and had already served two years. He was attached to the prestigious Panzer Lehr Division. Like many of those he served with, Baresel had been wounded on the Eastern Front.

"It is a story few will believe. After a tank battle in the Ukraine 1943, we returned to a safe place and stationed the tanks in a circle, cannons facing out. All not on guard duty were allowed to sleep. I crawled under my tank, but the ground was uneven and my legs stuck out. During the night a Russian plane dropped a bomb right in the middle of the assembled tanks and a fragment lodged itself under my left kneecap. As a 20 year old, I was so tired and slept so well that I didn't wake up when the fragment hit me. I saw in the morning a hole in my pants and after investigating, I realized I was wounded. My [envious] crew members drove me to a first aid station, from there [I went] to a hospital in Poland and from there in a long train ride to a hospital in Loerrach at the Swiss border."

His wound eventually gained him a ticket to the Western Front, which nearly all German veterans say was much better than going East.

"We stayed in Hungary 'til April 1944, when we were transported by train to France in preparation of the expected invasion. We camped near Chartres."

Recognizing that sending so many units from the West to the Eastern Front might encourage the Allies to invade France, Hitler issued a second directive for the West. Führer Directive 51 started to improve the situation in 1944; among its provisions was a strict prohibition on raiding units in the West for troops or equipment without the express permission of the Supreme Armed Forces Commander. However, the practice continued.

About the time Führer Directive 51 was issued, Erwin Rommel was setting up his headquarters in a chateau northwest of Paris. His tour of the Atlantic Wall in November 1943 greatly alarmed him about its vulnerable condition. Rommel was now convinced that the coming Allied invasion must be stopped at the beaches. If not, Allied air superiority would pounce on any counterattack and crush it. As the only senior commander in the West to have experienced the overwhelming effects of Allied air superiority (the North Africa campaign) Rommel was being a realist in doubting that a massed armor reserve could succeed in counterattacks against the Allied forces once the beachhead was established. He geared his tactics to defeat the Allied forces on the coast, within 48 hours of landing.

One of the outstanding units that did take position along the Atlantic Wall was posted along part of the Calvados coast in Normandy, where Rommel thought the Allied invasion was likely to occur. The 352nd Infantry Division was a well-trained mobile unit. It its ranks was a young soldier in his first assignment to a combat zone, Karl Wiesmuller. Wiesmuller was born in Bavaria, in a town on the Danube River. His father served in World War I and was a prisoner of the British for three years. Karl had an older brother, born in 1924, who served on the Eastern Front and fought in actions on the Crimean Peninsula. Karl, born in 1926, had finished formal school and was apprenticing as a carpenter when he was drafted.

"I finished my grammar school but I was in my apprenticeship. I started carpentry. I only made about a half a year, then they called me up for *Arbeitsdienst*. We had to play army. Three months. Then I was home, I was only home a couple of weeks. Here was the order—you have to report. Sworn in to the Fatherland (laugh). [Basic training at] . . . in Czech, they say Slaný. [Running] up and down the hills. And then two months later we were in Normandy, in December 1943. I was assigned to Headquarters Company in the 916 Regiment, the light pioneer company."

"We knew [the Allied invasion] was coming, but we didn't know exactly when. Shortly before the invasion, the commander sent a message to the company, 'heavy ship concentration in English ports.' So we knew it was coming soon."

Men and Women in Uniform

British, Commonwealth and Other Allied Forces —America's Indispensable Allies in *Operation Overlord*

Christopher J. Anderson

Shortly after the landing of Allied forces in Normandy in June 1944 Lieutenant General Dwight D. Eisenhower, Supreme Commander Allied Expeditionary Force, wrote a letter to a little boy describing the Supreme Headquarters Allied Expeditionary Force (SHAEF) patch worn by Eisenhower and the other service personnel assigned to SHAEF. The flaming sword, Eisenhower explained, represented the sword of freedom bringing light to a Europe living in darkness, symbolized by the black shield. Over the top of the shield was the rainbow of peace; the colors of the rainbow represented the coalition of Allied powers arrayed against Nazi Germany. Eisenhower was clearly making the point that SHAEF was an allied command, not a solely American one.

Yet, today many books and documentaries, especially in the U.S., often give the impression D-Day was an American operation. In truth, 11 nations besides the United States participated in the landings on June 6, 1944. Collectively they provided more than 5,000 of the 6,000 ships deployed, half the aircraft and more than half of the 156,205 men landed that morning. Allied contingents were also instrumental in the remaining 76 days of the campaign to liberate Normandy. Simply put, without America's partners, the Normandy landings and subsequent liberation of France would not have been possible. Any accurate telling of what Prime Minister Winston Churchill called, "the greatest thing we have ever attempted," therefore, must talk about the men and women of the other Allied contingents on D-Day.

A Multinational Military Force

Four years to the day after HMS *Shikari* took the last boatload of troops away from the beaches of Dunkirk, British servicemen—many of them veterans of that earlier evacuation—and their Allies were in marshalling areas or on troop ships waiting to begin the liberation of Western Europe. It was an incredible feat. The United Kingdom of Great Britain and Northern Ireland, America's closest ally in Europe, was the only country in the coalition of powers arrayed against Adolf Hitler that had fought uninterrupted from the beginning of the war in 1939. This effort had required unprecedented mobilization of Britain's resources both in terms of manpower and materiel. In 1941 Britain converted to a full wartime economy, which meant that until the end of the war more than half of the country's income was dedicated to military expenditure. It also saw manpower mobilization on a vast scale. By the time of the Normandy landings 22% of the available workforce was serving in the armed forces or auxiliary forces, and an additional 33% were involved in military manufacturing.

To make this all possible, Britain was the first nation to order the partial mobilization of women. During the war the number of women present in the workforce increased 42% to more than 7 million; this included a half-million women serving in uniform services, 300,000 in the Civil Service and 200,000 in the Woman's Land Army (women taking the place of male workers in agriculture). Women could be found in nearly every logistics and supporting role prior to the landings as well as manning the anti-aircraft batteries protecting the fleet waiting in England and providing personnel for Allied intelligence gathering efforts, most notably at the Government Code and Cypher School at Bletchley Park where more than 75% of the vital codebreaking workforce was made up of women in uniform. It was through the efforts of these women and their male counterparts that in the lead-up to the invasion Eisenhower had an almost complete picture of German forces in Normandy and, just as important, knew that the enemy had bought the Allied deception effort, *Operation Fortitude*, hook, line and sinker.

The fight had been costly, and by the summer of 1944 Britain was facing manpower shortages that would become more acute as the campaign wore on. It has been argued that the D-Day landings were Britain's last great military effort. "The British Army reached its zenith on D-Day," historian Max Hastings has remarked. "From then on, the British Army was shrinking because it no longer had the men to replace the casualties." While that is so, it would also be correct to say that Britain's last great army was not really British at all, but a multinational force made up of conscripts and volunteers from around the world.

The first great pool of manpower were the forces of empire: countries such as Canada, Australia and New Zealand contributed overwhelming numbers of soldiers, sailors and airmen to the British war effort. They served in national units like Australia's 466 Squadron, which bombed an enemy battery at Maisy that threatened Omaha Beach, or were integrated into formations largely made up of native Britons. Some have suggested that every ship in the Royal Navy (RN), for example, had at least one New Zealander in its crew. More than 15,000 Canadians, all volunteers, would land on Juno Beach.

The second great source of manpower was exiles from occupied countries who refused to submit to Nazi domination. Throughout the early stages of the war, particularly after the fall of Western Europe in 1940, freedom-loving people endured incredible hardships to escape their occupied countries and continue the fight, while others remained behind to resist as best they could.

Czechoslovakian Oto Horovic remembered how he wound up fighting in a British armored unit. "I fled in 1940 because I wanted to fight for our country. I crossed into Hungary, made my way to Yugoslavia and from there on to Italy. I was captured and imprisoned in a concentration camp in Italy for three years, then escaped. I went to Sicily and from there Algeria and finally England. In 1944 I fought in Normandy."

Britain became a haven for governments-in-exile and provided military equipment, training and support to men who, like Horovic, would not submit. They also parachuted badly needed supplies to resistance groups in France. It is estimated that by spring 1944 there were as many as 3,000 active members of resistance organizations in the departments of Calvados, where the landings would take place, and Manche, where the critical port of Cherbourg was located. Prior to the invasion, members of these resistance organizations were crucial in providing intelligence on enemy fortifications and strength. By May 1944 some 3,700 top-secret reports had been smuggled out of occupied France and brought to England. On June 5, resistance fighters were alerted to the impending action and began carrying out "Vert" operations, meant to destroy railroad infrastructure, and "Tortue" operations, meant to attack enemy vehicle convoys. In Calvados resistance groups accounted for eight bridges disabled, more than 100 vehicles destroyed, and several important rail lines cut. All of these efforts paved the way for the landings to begin the next morning.

On D-Day itself, the Norwegian destroyer *Svenner* became the first Allied naval casualty of D-Day when it was sunk by torpedoes; sailors of 24 French ships under Allied command made the agonizing decision of firing on their homeland; and at the very end of the campaign it was soldiers of the 1st Polish Armored Division that blocked the German army's final escape route from Normandy.

An 'India-Rubber' Island

Regardless of where the personnel came from, the contribution of Great Britain to the landings was massive. Even while heavily engaged fighting on other fronts, the British Isles had opened their doors to the millions of men of many nations who would, eventually, invade France. Niall Barr wrote in *Yanks and Limeys: Alliance Warfare in the Second World War*:

> Preparations gathered even greater speed and momentum during the early months of 1944, which saw Britain transformed into a huge storehouse, workshop, arsenal, armed camp and aircraft carrier. Tens of thousands of aircraft and millions of soldiers had flowed into Britain, while thousands of ships of every type and size were anchored in every port and estuary. Rationing, the blackout, the most extensive conscription of men and women of any of the combatant nations, along with wartime shortages, all combined with the massive influx of British, American and many other allied nations' soldiers, sailors and airmen to give the impression that Britain had become an 'India-rubber island' that had been stretched to maximum capacity.

In addition to its logistical support of the buildup, Britain provided much, much more. The initial invasion plan, including the selection of Normandy for the landings, the deployment of airborne forces and the necessity to build temporary harbors was conceived by Lieutenant General Frederick Morgan, a long-serving English officer. A war-weary Britain also provided critical intelligence, most of the naval forces, the bulk of the aircraft, and more than half of the ground forces. In addition, Air Chief Marshal Arthur Tedder, Eisenhower's Deputy Supreme Allied Commander, and the commanders of all air, sea and land forces were British officers.

Royal Air Force

First to be committed were the air forces. It was Royal Air Force (RAF) and U.S. Army Air Forces (USAAF) planes, under the direction of British Air Chief marshal Trafford Leigh-Mallory, which began the bombardment of targets over Normandy in the months prior to the invasion. The role of the air forces was critical to destroying German infrastructure in France as well as in isolating the invasion area from enemy forces on the day of the landings. During these pre-landing missions, the RAF lost 2,000 men and 300 aircraft in just two months. On June 6, the RAF carried out interdiction missions over the landing beaches as well as diversionary raids elsewhere in France. Britain's pilots flew bombing missions and on June 5–6 carried nearly 8,000 British airborne troops to objectives between the Orne and Dives Rivers and flew nearly 6,000 combat sorties (one flight by one plane) in support of landing forces. Allied aerial supremacy gained over the beaches on D-Day continued for the remainder of the campaign. German field marshal Erwin Rommel later remarked, "The enemy have complete control of the air over the battle zone."

On D-Day, Australians, Canadians, New Zealanders, Czechs, Poles, Norwegian and Dutch pilots could be found in the cockpits of RAF planes flying over the invasion beaches. Some of these men flew in British squadrons, others flew in national units. Czechoslovakia supplied pilots and crew for four squadrons. The RAF's 131st Wing, which was made up of Poles in 302, 308 and 317 squadrons, provided aerial support over the beaches. The Royal Australian Air Force (RAAF)'s Lancaster-equipped 463 and 467 squadrons carried out several missions against Pointe du Hoc prior to the U.S. 2nd Ranger Battalion's epic assault. By the end of 1944 one quarter of the RAF was made up of Royal Canadian Air Force personnel (RCAF).

The Naval Armada

With the skies overhead swept free of enemy aircraft and the battlefield isolated, Eisenhower still had to get his invasion force across the Channel and landed securely ashore. This job would fall largely to the Royal Navy—Britain's senior service—and the associated navies operating under British command. In the years leading up to the Normandy invasion, the RN had played a central role in the Battle of the Atlantic, which is rightly seen as one of the most crucial Allied victories of the war. So safe were the sea lanes following that battle that some two million American servicemen had been safely transported from ports in the United States across the Atlantic to Britain by 1944.

On June 6 the Allied naval effort was directed by Admiral Bertram Ramsay, the British admiral who had masterminded the evacuation of troops from Dunkirk in 1941 and later planned the amphibious elements of operations *Torch* (the Anglo-American invasion of North Africa in November 1942) and *Husky* (the invasion of Sicily in July 1943). Following

Husky he began planning for *Operation Neptune*, the landing phase of *Operation Overlord*, as well as the subsequent deployment of two temporary Mulberry harbors.

Like Eisenhower, Ramsay fully appreciated the importance of the Allied landings and also the central role that Allied forces would play on the day. On May 31, 1944, just before the landings were launched, he commented on the pending operation.

"Our task," he wrote, "in conjunction with the Merchant Navies of the United Nations, and supported by the Allied Air Forces, is to carry the Allied Expeditionary Force to the Continent, to establish it there in a secure bridgehead and to build it up and maintain it at a rate which will outmatch that of the enemy. Let no one underestimate the magnitude of this task."

Ramsay's naval force was the largest naval fleet ever assembled up to that point. Canadian Tom Gunning, who served on His Majesty's Canadian Ship *Cape Breton*, struggled to explain what he was part of. "It's impossible to describe the awesome power of it," he later remarked.

To Secure Bridgeheads

Ramsay divided his command into the Eastern Task Force, which would support landings on the two British and one Canadian beaches, and the Western Task Force, which would support the two U.S. landing beaches. Despite the division into British and American zones, the naval effort was overwhelmingly British. Of the 1,212 warships and 4,125 amphibious craft that were part of the invasion fleet 83.5% were manned by British or Canadian crews. British craft could be found supporting landings on all five of the invasion beaches. It was landing craft from the Royal Navy's 551st Assault Flotilla that took Company A, 116th Infantry Regiment, the famous "Bedford Boys," into Omaha Beach and nine Royal Navy Landing Craft Assault (LCA) that took the 2nd Rangers to Pointe du Hoc. The remainder of the fleet was made up of navies-in-exile, including ships of the French, Dutch, Norwegian, Polish, Belgian and Greek navies. In addition to seaborne personnel, the Royal Navy also supplied a number of Royal Marine Commandos to support the landings, particularly around Port-en-Bessin where the British and American sectors met and where *Pluto*, the underwater oil pipeline would be set up.

Ultimately, it was the mission of the air and naval forces to, as Ramsay said, secure a bridgehead for the landing forces—which would be under the overall command of British general Sir Bernard Law Montgomery—on all of the beaches. On the American beaches, Montgomery's subordinate,

Lieutenant General Omar N. Bradley would command the U.S. 1st Army landings on Omaha and Utah. Lieutenant General Miles Dempsey would command British 2nd Army on the easternmost beaches—Sword, Juno and Gold, which stretched 25 miles from Ouistreham to Port-en-Bessin (the latter now shown as Port-en-Bessin-Huppain on maps, following a merger of two towns).

The British Army had come a long way since the earlier disastrous battles of 1940–1941, and the divisions landing at Sword and Juno beach in particular reflected that. The assault divisions on these beaches both had a solid backbone of pre-war regulars and veterans of earlier campaigns in the ranks who brought a great deal of experience to the operation. Many of the men had been fighting since 1940 with little or no respite. Their experience was invaluable, but they could not be faulted for feeling that after four years of fighting maybe they had already done their part. As Lieutenant Geoffrey Picot of the 1st Hampshire Regiment rightly commented at the time, "Many veterans were running out of courage. Most men have a finite amount of this commodity and it can get used up. The Germans had no so such problem. All deserters were shot. Thus, everybody stays in the firing line. The average infantryman has fought in six major attacks without being hit, he knows that he won't last another six . . . Not nice to think that the best that can happen is to be wounded—to get a 'Blighty'" (a wound that will allowed a soldier to be evacuated to England). On the other hand, the airborne troops of the 6th Division jumping from planes or landing in gliders around the Orne River and Caen Canal crossings or the Canadians of the 3rd Division landing on Juno beach were entering combat for the first time—inexperienced but eager.

The Typical British Soldier

Regardless of whether he was a grizzled veteran or an untried rifleman, the typical British soldier would have been in his early 20s—although men from 18 to 50 were eligible for national service—and by this point in the war had most likely been conscripted into the army. After reporting for service, he would have received six weeks of General Military Training (GMT) before being sent to further schooling at a branch school. For most young recruits in 1944, this meant the infantry. After graduation he would have been assigned to a regiment, which was considered his military "family." Typically, the soldier would spend his entire military career in one of the battalions of his regiment.

Originally, soldiers would be assigned to the regiment that recruited in the county where they lived. This, however, began to change as the war went on, and soldiers would be assigned from recruit training to those units most in need of reinforcement. Unlike the United States Army, which assigned three battalions to each of its numbered regiments, the British practice was to have three battalions in a brigade. Each of these battalions could come from a different regiment. This is important to remember when reading accounts of Allied forces in Normandy. Generally, a British brigade was equivalent to a U.S. regiment (i.e., about 3,100 men at full strength). Depending on conditions and losses, a battalion in both armies would consist of between 800 and 1,000 men.

The 'Sharp End'

The infantry divisions were at the "sharp-end" of the landings on the British beaches. By 1944 each British division at full strength was made up of 18,347 men of all ranks; airborne divisions were slightly smaller. Lack of sufficient landing craft and space meant that not all of these men would be landed at once, but in a series of timed waves. The cutting edge of the division, its nine infantry battalions, was supported by artillery and other divisional troops.

On the easternmost end of the 25-mile-long British sector, the 6th Airborne Division, commanded by Major General Richard N. Gale, would secure the high ground between the Orne and Dives Rivers. Doing so would protect the flank of the landings and secure vital river crossings—including the bridge over the Caen Canal at Bénouville that would be forever memorialized as "Pegasus Bridge," after the symbol of the British Airborne taken from Greek mythology, Bellerophon on Pegasus. While many of the men were experienced soldiers, it would be the division's first combat action.

'Ironsides' and 'Fifty Div'

Landing at Ouistreham and advancing inland to relieve 6th Airborne Division was the 3rd Infantry Division. In addition to being made up of regular army battalions, the 3rd was unique in a number of other ways. It is the first, and oldest, permanent division in the British Army. Created by Arthur Wellesley, the Duke of Wellington, in 1809, the 3rd fought at Waterloo and in the Crimean, South African and Boer wars. It earned the nickname "The Iron Division" or "Ironsides" for its performance in World War I. Sent to France at the start of World War II, it was commanded by then–major general Bernard L. Montgomery, who designed its distinctive black-and-red triangle insignia. During the 1940 campaign in France it served with distinction, holding the perimeter at Dunkirk. After escaping from France, it remained in England while other units were sent to North

Africa, Italy and the Far East. It was one of the most highly trained British divisions on June 6 and would have had a number of regular and veteran soldiers in its ranks.

Coming ashore on Gold Beach, the center of all five invasion beaches, was the 50th Northumbrian Division. Their mission was to advance inland from their sector of the beach, which ran for 10 miles from Port-en-Bessin to Arromanches. The division was to seize Bayeux and establish contact with the Canadian 3rd Division to the left and U.S. 1st to the right. "Fifty Div," as it was known in the army, was made up of Territorial Army (TA) battalions that had been recruited from the mining and industrial towns of the Tyne and Tees Rivers, which served as the inspiration for the division's famous double T patch. The TA is equivalent to the U.S. National Guard.

After service in France in 1940, 50th Northumbrian was sent to North Africa. It performed with distinction at the battles of Gazala and El Alamein with the 8th Army. It remained in the Mediterranean and took part in the Sicily operation before being recalled to England in November 1943.

Hobart's Funnies

The final British assault division that should be mentioned had no beach of its own and did not fight together as a unit, but it remains one of the most unusual and important units of D-Day. The 79th Armored Division, commanded by Major General Percy "Hobo" Hobart, was responsible for developing a variety of specialized vehicles used during the landings. The 59-year-old Hobart was one of the pioneers of British armored warfare and the first brigadier in the Royal Armored Corps. Forced into retirement in 1939 because of his revolutionary ideas about armored warfare and the place of the horse on the modern battlefield, Hobart spent time in the Home Guard before being recalled into service. Under Hobart's direction, the officers and men of the 79th developed tanks that could float, clear minefields, crack open concrete positions, deploy bridges and lay roadways. "Hobart's Funnies," as the tanks came to be called, could be found on all five of D-Day's landing beaches, and the crews of these vehicles on the British beaches largely came from the 79th Division.

The All-Volunteer Canadians

Tucked in between Sword and Gold Beaches, Juno was the responsibility of the 3rd Canadian Division, which was entering combat for the very first time. When Canada declared war her entire regular army consisted of only 4,261 men. In just four years, that number grew almost a hundredfold. The 3rd Division was part of that expansion, its men enlisting in militia units from the Maritime provinces and eastern Canada. Many of those in the 3rd Division were in units such as the North Nova Scotia Highlanders and Stormont, Dundas and Glengarry Highlanders, reflecting the large Scottish community in Eastern Canada. There was also one French-speaking unit, Régiment de la Chaudière, which landed in the second wave at Bernières-sur-mer, where they apparently caused great surprise among the local population.

One other unique difference between the Canadians and the other Allies on June 6 was that every Canadian serviceman serving on D-Day had volunteered for overseas service. Early in the war Prime Minister Mackenzie King had introduced conscription, but only for home service in an effort to avoid the discord seen during World War I amongst the French-Canadian population. All soldiers serving overseas had to volunteer to go.

Allied Casualties

As they had shared much of the burden of the landings on June 6, the Allied powers also shared much of the cost. Casualty counts for D-Day are difficult to give with certainty, but work done by Carol Tuckwiller at the U.S. National D-Day Memorial is considered to be the most accurate. Tuckwiller gives total numbers of dead at 2,499 for the U.S. and 1,914 for British and Allied forces. Of the British and Allied casualties, 359 were Canadian, 37 Norwegian, 19 French, 13 Australian, two New Zealanders and one Belgian.

As the Normandy Campaign ground on, more Allied formations joined those already in the field. On July 23, 1944, the headquarters for First Canadian Army became active in France. Besides additional Canadian formations, units from Great Britain, Belgium, Czechoslovakia, The Netherlands and Poland were assigned to this organization.

1st Polish Armored Division

For the men of the 1st Polish Armored Division who joined First Canadian Army, it had been a long trip to the battlefield. Shortly after the Germans invaded Poland from the west in September 1939, Germany's Russian allies invaded from the east. Hopelessly outnumbered, the Poles were quickly crushed, and the victors began carving up the spoils. Unwilling to give up the fight, many soldiers of the Polish army and fliers from the air force escaped. Some 100,000 of these made their way to the Baltic and Balkans and from there to France, where they provided a mountain brigade, three infantry divisions and a cavalry division, as well as pilots for the French air force.

This Polish army-in-exile fought in Norway and then in France following Germany's Spring 1940 invasion. Those who survived the fighting in France and were able to escape to England became the basis of the 1st Polish Armored Division, commanded by Major General Stanislaw Maczek, a veteran Polish armor officer. The division landed in Normandy on August 1st and was assigned to the 1st Canadian Army. It fought with this multinational force through some of the toughest battles of the Normandy Campaign and was the unit that linked up with American and French forces near Chambois when the campaign finally came to a close at the end of August. It was an appropriately multinational end to a campaign that was only made possible through the contributions of all the Allied powers that took part.

'The Blood of Many Nations'

Three hundred and thirty-six days after Eisenhower had written his note to that little boy explaining the SHAEF patch, Ike was sitting in SHAEF headquarters in Reims, France, and he returned to the theme of the Allied coalition. He had just received the unconditional surrender of German forces in Europe. As he had done every day since taking command of SHAEF, Eisenhower sat down to issue his "order of the day."

"After summarizing the Allies' accomplishments and thanking the men and women of his command, Eisenhower continued:

The route you have traveled through hundreds of miles is marked by the graves of former comrades. From them have been exacted the ultimate sacrifice. The blood of many nations—American, British, Canadian, French, Polish and others—has helped gain the victory. Each of the fallen died as a member of a team to which you belong, bound together by a common love of liberty and a refusal to submit to enslavement. No monument of stone, no memorial of whatever magnitude could so well express our respect and veneration for their sacrifice as would the perpetuation of the spirit of comradeship in which they died."

Seventy-five years after the Normandy landings, it is, perhaps, not a bad thing to be reminded of this.

Men & Women in Uniform

The Americans

Lee W. Jones

The Allied assault across the English Channel has been called "the most important day of the twentieth century." While the Allies had achieved air and naval dominance and had constructed a large force of landing craft in a miraculously short time, the battle still had to be won by the Allied infantry, "citizen-soldiers" facing a well-entrenched German opponent. Lieutenant Bert Stiles, co-pilot of a B-17 in the Eighth Air Force, on his way back to England after bombing Normandy on D-Day, wondered how "the poor bastards down on the beach" were doing and realized "We'd be trucking the bombs over (but it was) the boys who take it the slow way (who) had the bright lights on them now." Colonel Charles Cawthon, commander of the 116th Infantry Regiment, recognized this as well, asserting that no matter how excellent the planning or how many supplies were amassed, "the job would come down heaviest upon the infantry."

The 'Mother and Father of all Melting Pots'

By 1944, the year of D-Day, the U.S. Army had become younger and more inclusive (with the notable exception of black soldiers). Half the soldiers sent to Europe that year were teenagers, and historian David Kennedy refers to the Army as "the mother and father of all melting pots," with many divisions mixing together "farm boys and factory hands, old-stock Yankees and new immigrants, rich as well as poor, Protestants, Catholics and Jews." The young servicemen experienced "more social, ethnic, and religious diversity than they had ever encountered or even imagined (*The American People in World War II: Freedom from Fear, Part Two*)."

However, as Colonel Cawthon acknowledged in "Pursuit: Normandy, 1944" (*American Heritage* Vol. 29, Issue 2, February/March 1978), World War II was "essentially white America's war," although in addition to African American troops some 500,000 Latinos, mostly Mexican American, are believed to have served in the military. Most Asian Americans served in the Pacific until the 442nd Regimental Combat Team (which became the most-decorated unit for its size and length of service in U.S. military history) and the 100th Infantry Battalion (incorporated into the 442nd RCT in 1944) were sent to the Mediterranean Theater.

Native Americans provided 44,000 men for the military, a tenth of the tribes' entire population. Women from all of these historically marginalized groups joined women's military auxiliary units like the WACs and WAVES.

Despite government propaganda posters urging "uniting to win," African Americans faced the "extraordinary breadth" of a rigidly enforced Jim Crow military policy that even included the "meticulously enforced" segregation of blood plasma. Blacks were usually kept out of combat and relegated to menial work under white officers. However, due to enormous manpower needs, some 600 black soldiers were placed in a specialized combat role for D-Day—setting up and manning barrage balloons. They were among the first to land on deadly Omaha Beach. All told, 2,000 African Americans arrived early in Normandy, with another 1,400 contributing courageously to the dangerous work of transport, rescuing the wounded and burying the dead.

Also, due to manpower needs the Army became much more tolerant of physical limitations, accepting even the toothless and those who were blind in one eye or deaf in one ear. In a paternalism worthy of the New Deal, the Army made 2.3 million pairs of glasses for the soldiers, extracted 15 million teeth, and supplied 2.5 million sets of dentures.

Cigarettes, Hershey Bars, and Toilet Paper

Indeed, for many the U.S. Army brought an improvement in the standard of living, with decent medical care and a generous diet. In training, the soldiers in the Army consumed 4,300 calories per day and 3.400 in the field, plus a daily ration of 12 cigarettes (for a "satisfying smoke"), a stick of gum ("for thirst and tension"), Hershey bars, and graham crackers at each meal (for "roughage, vitamins and starches"). The invasion army stationed in Britain, where the standard of living had declined 20%, was "the wonder and envy of the British." Kennedy described the British as feeling "lucky to befriend Americans" with their bounty of supplies such as canned meat (Spam), fresh fruit, and 22 sections of toilet paper a day (to only three for the British). In fact, a joke circulated in Britain that only the barrage balloons kept the island from sinking into the ocean under the weight of men, weapons and supplies.

Relations with the British, however, were sometimes strained for various reasons, including jealousy over the Americans' pay, which made them the best-paid military in the world, earning about triple the salary of the British soldiers. As historian Rick Atkinson points out in *The Guns at Last Light,* the contrast to British poverty was quite obvious, with the shortage of soap earning their country the nickname Goatland and a limited supply of glass leading to pub requirements that patrons bring their own beer glasses.

'Oversexed' Americans

Adding further tension to the Allied relationship was the sexual behavior of the Americans. British authorities feared for local girls because the GIs "gave every appearance of being sexually enterprising and hyperactive." British girls were cautioned to "Look before you *jeep* or you'll be *Yanked* into maternity." The U.S. Army's soldier's manual had attempted to control the situation, while acknowledging that sex was "a primary biological urge" and that "those who wear the uniform (have) a special appeal." It admonished "that sexual intercourse without marriage is everywhere condemned as wrong" and that "sexual activity is NOT necessary to maintain good health."

The Army asserted that the soldiers' sexual needs should be "controlled" by outlets like "athletic participation" and "hard physical work," while avoiding things like pin-up girl pictures which, while "fun to have," were also "constant irritants." The guidance failed in its immediate purpose. Atkinson points out that so many British girls were impregnated by GIs that the U.S. government agreed local English courts be given jurisdiction "in bastardy proceedings." (*Postscript: when the Allies advanced into France and took Cherbourg, two bordellos were set up to operate between the hours of 2 p.m. and 9 p.m., for "whites only" and monitored by military police.*)

For the British, the Americans were "overpaid, overfed, oversexed and over here." The Americans countered by labeling the British "underpaid, undersexed, and under Ike." General Eisenhower attributed the boorish behavior of some Americans to "GI hubris," with "Every American soldier coming to Britain . . . almost certain to consider himself a privileged crusader." American "bad behavior" included reckless driving, like racing trucks that flattened hedgerows and sent cyclists and pedestrians leaping into ditches. This prompted some locations to put up road signs cautioning, "To all GIs: please drive carefully, that child may be yours."

Historian Linda Hervieux, author of *Forgotten: The Untold Story of D-Day's Black Heroes, at Home and at War*, describes American drunkenness in public as out of control, and certainly some of it must have contributed to a rash of vandalism that included removing people's gates, eating the royal swans at the king's palace, fishing with grenades and setting fire to haystacks with tracer bullets.

Preparing for Battle

High jinks and sexual escapades aside, the training was intense and focused. For the Airborne, that involved learning "how to kill a man silently by slicing through the jugular and the voice box." They also were forced to crawl through the entrails and blood of hogs as part of getting toughened up. The infantry training avoided such extremes and involved much amphibious landing practice, with the "tempo of (its) preparation . . . constantly stepped up." The tension and anticipation mounted, and as Cawthon described it, "something of a pre–big game atmosphere developed," with the troops feeling like "an enormous first team." He portrayed the general spirit as "light of heart, caught up in the momentum of a mighty effort," but also as a mood of "restrained violence." An American infantryman commented, "All are tense and all are pretending to be casual."

Many soldiers spoke of waiting as the hardest part, and longed for the worst to be over. To ease the tension, the soldiers watched movies (Bob Hope films were favorites of many) and listened to radio music as well as the broadcasts of the Nazi propagandist Axis Sally (American-born Mildred Elizabeth Sisk Gillars), whose reports they didn't take seriously. They read a War Department pamphlet *A Pocket Guide to France*, which informed them that the French are "good talkers and magnificent cooks," and that "Normandy looks rather like Ohio." *Stars and Stripes*, the Army's newspaper, provided more reading material and guidance about the French, telling soldiers not to be surprised "if a Frenchman steps up and kisses you. That doesn't mean he's queer. It means he's French and darn glad to see you." The magazine also attempted to reassure "jumpy soldiers," advising them that "shock kept the wounded from feeling much pain." Other soldiers played cards and, of course, went to pubs.

It was here that the black soldiers relished a newfound equality. Fresh in their minds was the infuriating situation of being barred from public bars and restaurants back home, the very same establishments that would serve some of the 420,000 Nazi POWs held in the U.S. However, all was not perfect in Britain and segregation could be inflicted, as happened when the U.S. military officials interceded to prevent black women in the 6888th Postal Battalion from using a public swimming pool in Birmingham. African Americans were also taken aback by the credulity of some Brits who believed stories that they had tails.

Women in U.S. Military Service

As noted earlier, the U.S. war has been described as a conflict of white America, but that could be amended to "white male America," at least in terms of combat roles. Congress voted in 1942 to allow women to serve in the military through the Women's Army Auxiliary Corps (WAAC). Their status was officially changed on July 1, 1943, to become part of the Army's reserve forces, and the organization was renamed Women's Army Corps (WAC). Every branch of America's military formed similar groups, from the Marine Corps to the Coast Guard.

Stephen Ambrose wrote in *D-Day*, "The contribution of the women of America, whether on the farm or in the factory or in uniform, to D-Day was a *sine qua non* (an essential condition) of the invasion effort."

American women were not able to serve in combat, unlike their Russian "sisters." Forty-nine WACs did arrive in Normandy thirty-eight days after the invasion (female nurses as early as June 10) and performed a variety of roles, such as making maps, analyzing codes, interpreting bombing accuracy, and plotting aircraft missions, (including hitting German V-1 rocket launching sites). The Soviet Union, by comparison, used upwards of 800,000 women in almost every phase of its frontline effort, from nurses to fighter and bomber pilots, tank commanders, and snipers. Rosalind Miles and Robin Cross wrote in *Hell Hath No Fury: True Profiles of Women at War from Antiquity to Iraq*, that in recognition of the vital female role, Russia even created amenities such as 43 "mobile frontline tea shops" that came equipped with hairdressers, cosmetics and extra soap.

Though American women were officially barred from combat roles they did come under fire while serving near the front lines. Nurses were particularly vulnerable to bombing and artillery fire. More than 1,600 nurses were decorated for bravery under fire and meritorious service and 16 were killed in WWII. Women did not receive combat pay or the benefits provided to male soldiers, and they had no protection under international law concerning POWs if captured.

Confidence and Motivation

While the soldiers certainly experienced trepidation prior to the invasion, there was a general feeling of confidence, with one soldier expressing a positive feeling that his group was "as ready as an outfit could be." There was also an upbeat feeling derived from the sense that their naval, air and invasion forces were "overwhelming." The Eighth Air Force had waged a successful five-month battle for air supremacy that made the invasion possible. It cost them 18,400 casualties, however, including 10,000 combat deaths. Thus, according to historian Donald L. Miller, the airmen "deserve an equal place in the national memory" about D-Day (*Masters of the Air: America's Bomber Boys Who Fought the Air War Against Nazi Germany*). Confidence among the invasion forces was further swelled by the misleading report that the German forces were of a relatively old age (average age of some units was 34), which gave hope they would lack a willingness to fight to the death. Intelligence about Omaha Beach, however, had failed to notice that the Nazis had sent the 352nd Infantry Division, primarily comprised of Eastern Front veterans, as reinforcement for this sector.

It is difficult to generalize about the attitude or motivation of the many D-Day troops. However, a common attitude was that of Waverly Woodson, a young black medic who served heroically on Omaha Beach. "For him there was no ambivalence entwined in fighting for his country, even if that country didn't support equality for all its citizens. This was a war he believed in with all his heart . . . to defeat the Nazis and their brutally racist world view," Linda Hervieux wrote in *Forgotten*.

Colonel Cawthon witnessed a similar attitude in another minority soldier, a Native American from the Southwest that he referred to only as "the Chief" in a post-war memoir, *Other Clay: A Remembrance of the World War II Infantry*. Cawthon mused on the mentality of this soldier, whom he describes as "being (in) the first of every attack starting with D-Day," despite it being "essentially white America's war."

In generalizing about the feelings of the GIs of D-Day, historians Rick Atkinson and Stephen Ambrose both emphasize that the young men were amateurs and "citizen-soldiers" whose fighting spirit was "aggressively temporary." While they mostly believed in the cause, "Few voiced enthusiasm for yet another American intervention in northwestern Europe—'that quarrelsome continent,'" Atkinson wrote in *The Guns at Last Light*, adding that a 1944 Army survey among troops in Britain found one-third of those polled had doubts about whether the war was worth fighting, double the number from a similar poll in July 1943. Atkinson argues that the common themes characterizing the views of many GIs were those of "skepticism and irony" about military life. Soldier-writer Irwin Shaw, in *The Young Lions: A Novel*, expresses this ambivalence well: "I expected the Army to be corrupt, inefficient, cruel, wasteful, and it turned out to be all those things, just like all armies, only much less so than I thought before I got into it."

Preparing for the Worst

As the big day approached, there were changes in the grooming of some units. One Navy officer insisted that the crew "shave, shower and wear clean clothes" to lower the risk of germs. Several divisions shaved their heads and many copied the "Mohican fashion" of the paratroopers.

Some soldiers speculated about the outcome. One morbidly wondered how his family would react to his death and felt some comfort that they would receive the military's $10,000 insurance payment as compensation. Another pondered which extreme outcome might ensue, sensing they were "approaching a great abyss—not knowing whether we are sailing into one of the world's greatest military traps or whether (they) have caught the enemy completely off guard." Some wrote final letters to families or loved ones in case of death and taped meaningful photos to the inside of their helmets. Many unwisely had "decadent" last meals, like those in the Navy who were offered "as much steak, chicken, ice cream and candy," as they wanted; others were served large breakfasts of bacon and eggs. This would, unfortunately, produce much vomiting when soldiers got violently seasick on the trip over, causing the men to be quite weak once they got ashore.

Adding to the difficulty of their landing was the excessive weight most soldiers carried. In the desire to be especially prepared, their packs averaged 68 pounds instead of the recommended 43 pounds. Some have asserted that this extra weight bogging down the waterlogged troops may have greatly increased the number of casualties.

As they were about to depart, soldiers heard a variety of speeches, some inspiring and useful, some depressing and questionable. The leader of the 501st Parachute Regiment gave a rousing talk, wielding a commando knife and yelling that he wanted "to stick (the) knife into the heart of the meanest, dirtiest, filthiest Nazi in all Europe." Brigadier General Jim Gavin of the 82nd Airborne said, somewhat ambiguously, that what they were about to go through they wouldn't "want to change for a million dollars, but you won't want to go through it very often again." He finished off his speech by saying, "Remember that you are going in to kill, or you will be killed." A rather depressing talk was the shock tactic of a commander who warned the soldiers of the deadliness awaiting them. He told them to look "to the right . . . and look to the left," and then said "There's only going to be one of you left after the first week in Normandy." A tank commander attempted some humor, telling his men, "The government paid $5 billion for this hour. Get to hell in there and start fighting." General Eisenhower was brief and perhaps most to the point, saying, "The trick is to keep moving . . . The idea, the perfect idea, is to keep moving."

The Big Moment Arrives

Not surprisingly, the reactions to the anticipated combat varied dramatically between the veterans and the novices. The response of the 388th Bomb Group to the invasion announcement was "pandemonium" accompanied by "cheers, whistles and shouts." For the untested infantry, the feeling was not surprisingly one of trepidation, though in looking back, one soldier admitted his worry was "less . . . than in any subsequent one," with "inexperience having much to do with it."

Charles Cawthon felt that a foot soldier's first day in battle "probes new emotional depths," which he feels are "fairly universal." He portrays it as "a conviction that he (the soldier) is "abandoned, alone, and uncared-for in the world." Another "first" emotional extreme was the indelible impression of witnessing a first battle death. He explained that "the image of no one—loved, admired, or disliked—remains more vivid."

The paratroopers were the first to go (some 20,000 flew in over 1,200 planes), and they were quite successful, losing only 21 planes and generally achieving their goal of securing the most vital roads and bridges. After landing they used dime-store clickers to re-establish contact in the dark, though many of them hated the clickers and some preferred the password "Flash," with the counter-response "Thunder." The words were chosen, according to Antony Beevor, because they were thought to be difficult for a German to pronounce convincingly.

The paratroopers' combat was brutal and has been described as the "most vicious of the whole war on the Western Front." The Germans had been told the enemy were criminals released from jail, while the paratroopers had been told not to take prisoners because they would slow them down. With the discovery of several paratroopers whose privates had been cut off and stuck into their mouths, the command was given to "shoot the bastards." One soldier went beyond that order and retaliated with "ear-hunting," sewing a string of dead Germans' ears together. Some shot German prisoners and used their bodies for bayonet practice. This type of fighting exemplified what one soldier described as the "casual and mindless unconcern with which armies . . . wreaked havoc on each other and on all about them." (*Eyewitness to History: World War II*, by Stephen W. Sears)

Carnage on Omaha Beach

At all but one of the five beaches, the troops achieved their initial foothold within hours. On Utah Beach, one of two American landing sites, the boats fortunately debarked in the wrong area, causing them to face fewer obstacles and less fire. On Omaha Beach, however, due to unpredicted circumstances such as ineffective Allied bombardment, rougher seas and a strong German presence, the beach became a chaotic killing zone of exploding horror. One arriving soldier felt "disarmed and naked" facing an enemy much stronger than expected. Some landing craft unloaded too far out, and with numerous men not knowing how to swim and weighted down, there were many drownings. Furthermore, seawater caused malfunction in many radios and guns (despite putting condoms over the muzzles to keep them dry). Soldiers were hit by machine-gun or artillery fire, often as soon as the landing ramps were lowered. One soldier described this phenomenon as men falling "just like corn cobs off of a conveyer belt." The firing was so remarkably intense (Atkinson calls it "demented") one sergeant was moved to make a calculated guess that "at least 20,000 bullets and shells per minute" were being fired. Atkinson notes that soldiers were being hit "by 9.6-gram bullets traveling at 2,000–4,000 feet per second and by shell fragments traveling even faster." On Omaha Beach there would be 4,720 killed, wounded and missing, placing it among the bloodiest single days of the war for Americans.

Sights, smells and sounds on Omaha Beach were horrifying. One shell wiped out a Navy demolition team and tore through the lower body and limbs of one victim, producing a disturbing image described by one sailor as "sticking up in the waterline like a pitiful V for victory." The smell of burning flesh, the sight of dead and dismembered bodies, and soldiers crying out futilely in pain, "I'm hit!" produced immobilized shock and irrationality in some. One captain said of the soldiers he came across, "They were beat up and shocked. Many of them had forgotten that they had firearms to use." Another found many fellow soldiers "out of their heads," crying, moaning and screaming. A soldier from Minnesota recalled that he had "never in his life prayed so much." He did, however, see a different reaction in his 1st Division, with numerous acts of courage: "I've never seen so many brave men who did so much—many would go way back and try to gather in the wounded and themselves got killed." One remarkable hero, Corporal A.E. Jones "went out six times and brought men in" to medical orderlies.

Treating the Wounded

The doctors, medics and nurses worked frenetically under fire to save as many victims as they could. One of those courageous medics was Waverly "Woody" Woodson, from the all-black 320th Barrage Balloon Battalion who, despite being hit twice, saved many wounded. Woodson later said the soldiers "didn't care what color my skin was"; war was the great equalizer. He removed bullets, closed gaping wounds, performed a foot amputation, and resuscitated four drowning men. He then passed out, after having worked 30 hours without rest.

Charles Shay, a Native American medic on Omaha Beach, administered to the wounded and saved numerous soldiers on the verge of drowning. He stated he was so busy he didn't have time to think or concentrate on the possibility of losing his own life. Nurse Muriel Kappler, who worked on Utah Beach, argued similarly that she was so busy she wasn't concerned about morale or fear. Wounded Germans received the "exact same treatment" as Allied troops, a policy that, according to Kappler, was not popular. Medical groups worked frantically because of the number of wounded and because those soldiers suffering from shock were doubly vulnerable to the cold. Those with "combat trauma" were treated with Nembutal to "knock them out."

When possible, wounded were taken to temporary hospital ships before their ultimate return home. Sailors took the dead to the ship refrigerators, and operations were performed in ships' galleys. Battle wounds could be very dramatic and alarming, such as when an injured soldier realized his right leg was missing; he had to be restrained as he yelled, "What am I going to do? My leg? I'm a farmer." Medics at times had to hush sufferers who asked only for a bullet in the brain.

Two remarkable medical stories of reciprocal humanity happened in the midst of this brutal combat. German and American medical officers became POWs and were recruited nonetheless to provide emergency care to the wounded. The German did so "with efficiency" and "assembly-line precision," and the American was "treated . . . as a friend" as he cared for American paratroopers.

Following the 'Wounded Tiger'

Fortunately, by noon things began miraculously to turn around on Omaha Beach, and, as historian Gerhard L. Weinberg puts it, "brave men with strong naval gunfire support" managed to move up and get off the vulnerable beach. Most crucially, the Germans assumed they had won and sent no new forces. Thus, the first day ended with the Allied forces breaking into "Fortress Europe." Rick Atkinson wrote, "Though far from over, the battle was won." The invasion was an event that was, in the view of the Royal Air Force history, "the most momentous . . . in the history of war since Alexander set out from Macedon."

However, the next stage, designed to push the Germans out of Normandy, would be brutal, with Hitler ordering a "fight to the death." Cawthon describes the situation aptly as like "following a wounded tiger into the bush; the tiger turning now and again to slash at his tormentors, each slash drawing blood." Blood was indeed drawn by each side, with German snipers often taking advantage of the hedgerow terrain, motivated by a reward of 100 cigarettes for every 10 kills. Antony Beevor describes this phase of the fight as a "crueler" test with "average losses per division on both sides topping those for Soviet and German divisions during an equivalent period on the Eastern Front."

For the World War II men and women in uniform, combat experiences could be extremely variable, depending on the theater of war, the timing and the strength of the enemy. Cawthon, in his memoirs, seems a kind of warrior-philosopher about the Normandy invasion, thoughtfully capturing the human impact of the experience. He articulates his emotional reaction to the combat and explains his ability to find the strength and fortitude to function effectively day after day. His complex feelings about the war began with a "sorrow . . . characterized by an emotional void" evident when looking back upon friends gone that day. He describes gloom as being a "not unfamiliar emotion" throughout his service, which he characterizes as plagued by "the manic-depressive atmosphere of war."

Yet he was able to stay focused and effective as a combatant because he could overcome the sadness and ever-present fatigue with what he described as "a sense of life forced to a hard bright flame to survive." Overcoming the persistent weariness, sorrow and dread of war produced in him an "exhilaration from the same source at the same moment." It was a kind of excitement that he claimed was naturally accompanied by "dread." When battle approached, he remarkably experienced an "increasing cheerfulness," which he described as a "phenomenon of intensified, illuminated life" in combat.

WHAT HAPPENED ON D-DAY—JUNE 6, 1944

Jay Wertz

June 6, 1944, began with the throaty hum of a thousand C-47 transports carrying the men of two U.S. and one British airborne divisions entering French airspace above the shores of Normandy. It would end 24 hours later with Allied forces rolling over German defenses in some places while clinging to small bits of cliffs or flooded fields in others. Some of the deadliest fighting in France since the end of World War I occurred in the hours between.

The Allied Airborne Operation

The largest airborne operation up to that time, it involved 7,000 Commonwealth and 13,400 American paratroopers in the first wave plus 4,000 follow-up infantry, engineer, medical and Signal Corps paratroopers with heavy equipment. Radar detection of the airborne attack signaled the first warnings of an imminent invasion to German leaders at the northern France headquarters of Army Group B and Fifteenth Army. SS intelligence in Berlin reported the initial intercepts to Admiral Karl Dönitz's Kriegsmarine headquarters, where they were interpreted as an exercise. Due to the lack of solid intelligence data and predictions of continuing bad weather, the news came as a surprise to the German defenders.

Many in the Wehrmacht thought this was just another false alarm of an invasion that had been anticipated for a month. Though Fifteenth Army raised the alert status to the highest level, Seventh Army was less prepared. Field Marshal Erwin Rommel was already in Germany with his wife to celebrate her birthday on the sixth and was also preparing to meet Hitler to lobby for reinforcements for his command. *OB West* (*Oberbefehlshaber* West, Germany's overall command for its armed forces on the Western Front) was still predicting that the invasion would be coming over from Dover, and even when reports came in of parachutists on the ground, they considered this a diversion for the anticipated Pas de Calais–region landing.

The objectives of the American paratroopers were all on the Cotentin Peninsula and aimed at securing exits for the U.S. VII Corps from Utah Beach and slowing any German counterattack there. The drop area for the 101st Airborne Division was planned north of the hub city of Carentan, inland from Utah Beach, and the 82nd Division's drop zones were to the west, straddling the Merderet River near the town of Saint Mère-Église. But some sticks (a stick is one planeload) of the two U.S. airborne divisions ended up as far as 35 miles north or south of their designated drop zones and most of these paratroopers quickly ended up in German hands. Though scattered about, a large group of 101st troopers landed in the vicinity of St. Côme-du-Mont on the southern flank. This was fortuitous because the 101st also was ordered to seize the lock at la Barquette to control the flood plain of the river along with two bridges at le Port. They were also ordered to destroy bridges north of St. Côme-du-Mont to prevent German forces from crossing the Douve River from Carentan.

Using the toy "cricket" clickers they were issued to facilitate making contact with fellow Americans, they searched in the dark for comrades, no matter what their unit. Passwords and the classic baseball challenge questions were also used. Though about 60% of the equipment dropped from the planes was destroyed, the paratroopers had their personal arms. GIs concentrated on finding friends and avoiding the Germans in the early going. The 101st commander, Major General Maxwell D. Taylor, jumped with the first wave and assembled a small group of American paratroopers in the 101st sector. In addition to his aide, a lieutenant, Taylor's group soon included Brigadier General Anthony McAuliffe, a colonel, three lieutenant colonels, three other lieutenants, a few non-commissioned officer (NCO) radiomen and about a dozen privates. Taylor observed, "Never in the annals of warfare have so few been commanded by so many." Taylor then led this unique patrol toward the objective at Pouppeville.

The widely scattered air drops served to confuse Allied intentions in the minds of the Germans. By 4:00 a.m., however, German commanders estimated that the intention was to cut off the Cotentin Peninsula at the narrowest point on its neck. Few German commanders realized that a beach invasion was not far off. The general actions of the German units in the vicinity of the drop areas—the 709th (Static) Infantry Division, 91st

Air Landing Division and the 6th Paratrooper Regiment—were to stay in their prepared defensive positions, making only small local ventures outside them to counterattack. Communication between headquarters units was hampered by telephone lines put out of commission by the French Resistance.

Gradually, larger groups of American jumpers began to form. In the 82nd Airborne Division sector, Lieutenant Colonel Edward C. Krause took the 3rd Battalion of the 505th Regiment to his objective, St.-Mère-Église, and forced the surrender of the German garrison with little effort; the American flag was raised over the first liberated French town. The 507th and the 508th regiments of the 82nd did not have well-placed landing zones in their efforts to straddle the Merderet River and protect the left flank of the invasion. The bridges over the causeways had to be secured intact and this proved to be quite a challenge.

Already the paratroopers were encountering the scourge of mechanized warfare in Normandy—the hedgerows. These were formidable earthen embankments, often topped with trees or bushes, that surrounded Norman fields. Landing a glider within the confines of one of these boxes was difficult at best. To make matters worse, Rommel anticipated glider operations and had installed anti-air-landing obstacles. Nicknamed "Rommel's asparagus," these were stakes topped with mines and connected by barbed wire. Fortunately for the American glider units, most of these obstacles were installed further inland.

Some of the objectives of the two American airborne divisions were secured easily and others would be contested objectives throughout the day. But the paratroopers were astride the main road from Paris to Cherbourg; they were slowly gaining control of the Utah Beach exits and had a foothold along the strategic Douve and Merderet rivers.

An altogether different scenario occurred to the east where the British 6th Airborne Division landed along the Orne River and Caen Canal without initial detection. They came on a direct route south across the Channel to land in the area northeast of the city of Caen. Individual parachutists and Horsa gliders landed on both sides of the Orne and moved to seize or destroy key bridges over the Orne and Dives Rivers.

Six gliders pinpointed their objectives—the bridges over the Dives and Orne Rivers that were to be destroyed. A bridge spanning the Orne River and the lifting bridge at Bénouville over the Orne Canal, vital to hold, were captured in a lightning-strike operation by Major John Howard's D Company of the "Ox and Bucks" Light Infantry. The canal bridge was renamed Pegasus Bridge after the emblem of the 6th Airborne Division.

Another important objective was the battery at Merville that threatened enfilading fire on Sword Beach. The signal went out that the battery was neutralized and naval gunfire, which would have to have been extremely lucky to deal a death blow to the guns casemated in six feet of concrete, could move on to other targets. The British 6th Airborne Division had secured its basic objectives prior to the beach landings and held the flank positions throughout the day. They would be on the leading edge of the first major German counterattack in the afternoon.

Air Operations on D-Day

The Allies put an incredible 10,521 planes in the air on June 6. If D-Day ended in failure, the air forces could not take the blame. How that many planes could be in the air at once without incident is unfathomable, and there indeed were collisions. The 1,200 heavy bombers—B-17s and B-24s of the U.S. Eighth Air Force—had initial targets over the Omaha Beach and Commonwealth beaches. Preceding them, the Royal Air Force (RAF) Halifax and Lancaster heavies worked specific targets, including the Caen railroad station.

But it was the medium bombers of the tactical air commands that had the greatest impact on the beach defenses. The sorties (each sortie is one flight by one aircraft) by the medium bombers of the Ninth Air Force were low-level runs at 500 feet over Utah Beach. These proved to be effective in stunning, and sometimes knocking out, the coastal garrisons there. But flak was heavy and the medium bomber commands sustained some combat losses.

Rounding out the air armada were the fighter squadrons of the Ninth Air Force and the RAF. For these missions, the USAAF used primarily P-47 Thunderbolts and P-38 Lightnings. The P-51 Mustangs were held out of the D-Day flight plans. They were more important to the long-range bombing missions that would soon commence again. The British relied on the venerable Spitfire.

Only a few Allied fighter pilots, those that flew perimeter patrols looking for U-boats or other potential hazards on the flanks of the Channel crossing, saw Luftwaffe planes on D-Day. The cross-Channel convoys were screened by a constant umbrella of fighter squadrons flying 3,000 to 5,000 feet above the water. The P-38s were the only fighters used above the armada because their twin-tails shape could be easily identified by shipboard gunners. Despite this, several P-38s were victims of friendly fire. With only 113 planes lost on June 6 and only one Luftwaffe mission over the landing area—carried out late in the day—the Allies truly commanded the skies on D-Day.

Naval Operations Prior to H-Hour

As impressive as was the showing in the air, the display on the water was truly historic. First in line were the costal minesweepers (YMS) which began working through the wide belt of the main German mine field that extended from the Cotentin Peninsula to the Dover Strait. Five lanes, one for each task force (forces U, O, G, J and S) were opened across the Channel and buoy marked. As the convoy lanes crossed the middle of the Channel and approached the Bay of the Seine, they were split in two: one for fast ships such as destroyers and one for slow vessels such as Landing Craft, Tank (LCTs). The fire support ships arrived at their designated lanes.

As the fire support ships moved into position in the Bay of the Seine and the transports awaited the command "Away all boats!" nowhere was there an indication that the Germans were reacting to the pre-invasion maneuvers. Admiral Theodor Krancke had cancelled water patrols because of weather concerns and his conviction that the conditions were not right for an invasion. Luftwaffe reconnaissance also remained on the ground that night.

A thundering, flame-belching naval bombardment such as the world had never seen was about to add to the misery of the German garrisons occupying the Atlantic Wall. While the pre-invasion bombardment was being carried out by the battleships, cruisers, destroyers and other fire support ships, another critical operation was taking place at sea. Assault units were filling up the Landing Craft, Vehicle, Personnel (LCVPs) and other landing craft bobbing up and down in the water while lashed to transports and the big Landing Ships, Tanks (LSTs). Men climbed down the rope ladders into the landing craft lying well below the main decks of the transports. A few men ended up in the sea and had to be retrieved. Despite the precarious process, none of the landing craft floundered before or during loading.

The Omaha Beach Landing

Omaha Beach was a crescent-shaped beach about 7,000 yards wide. At low tide the beach would run for 300 yards up to a shingle, which was an angled plane of baseball-size rocks where fishing boats beached. By high tide the waves would be lapping this shingle. Beyond that was a four-to-twelve-foot-high seawall on the right and a sand dune line on the left. A beach road, partially paved, that the Germans strung concertina wire across, was behind the wall and sand dune line. Beyond those features the beach extended for an uneven width and contained beach villas inland from the road, many of which had been destroyed as part of the German defensive preparations. A tiny village, Les Moulins, lay on the beach toward the west end where the beach was sandy, but elsewhere marshy pockets punctuated the flat terrain. Behind this sea level area, steep cliffs averaging 100 feet and topping out at 170 feet supported a high ridge that overlooked Omaha Beach. The cliff had folds and scrub vegetation.

The ridge was punctured by five draws (gullies) that supported one paved and three unpaved roads as well as a trail at the east end. These draws were the principal objectives of the first wave. They were also the most heavily defended areas at Omaha Beach. At the top of the ridge three villages were located within a half-mile of the ridgeline—Vierville, St.-Laurent and Colleville, all with the suffix "-sur-Mer" added, meaning "by the sea." To the west of Omaha Beach was Pointe de la Percée and then Pointe du Hoc (Pointe du Hoe) where the Germans had located a major battery of large-caliber, partially casemated guns. East of Omaha Beach the ridge continued in steep cliffs past Port-en-Bessin to the area where the British and Canadian divisions landed on the beach flats. Omaha Beach was the most opportune section between the British beaches and the Cotentin Peninsula to land. Without the landing here, the assault's wings would have been widely separated. The Germans, of course, recognized the value of Omaha Beach and sited guns to cover it from every possible angle with overlapping fields of fire.

Battalions of two infantry regiments, the 16th of the 1st Infantry Division (the Big Red One) and the 116th of the 29th Division, would assault Omaha Beach in companies in the first wave. They were to be preceded by 32 Duplex Drive (DD) tanks (tanks with amphibious capability) of the 741st and 743rd Tank Battalions and covered by the close support fire of tanks and guns firing from LCTs, along with rocket barrages from LCT-Rs.

The beach was divided into eight parts, code named from west to east: Charlie; Dog Green, White, and Red; Easy Green and Red; Fox Green and Red. On the right, the 2nd Ranger Battalion was to land simultaneously and scale the high cliffs of Pointe du Hoc to overwhelm the battery there. What looked neat and logical on paper was about to come apart at H-Hour (the time of day an attack or landing is to begin, in this case 6:30 a.m.), and it would require intelligence, training and improvisation to prevent disaster.

Nearly all the DD tanks were lost in heavy swells immediately after being launched at H-Hour minus 50 minutes. Although the landing was timed between low and high tide to avoid as many of the underwater obstacles as possible and this generally worked out well, the current carried most of the units of the 116th and the 16th too far to the east. Hence, many of the initial assault companies ended up in other beach zones, bunched together.

The air bombardment did nothing to impede the German beach defenses, and the naval barrage did not put the guns facing Omaha Beach out of commission. The German defense system of nests and strong points on the ridge were training their guns on the landing craft coming to shore. Fearing the gunfire, some coxswains (boat drivers) in the first wave stopped their craft far out when they hit sandbars. Those that did come the whole way in were very anxious to drop their loads and take off again.

To Omaha Beach came boatloads of the men in companies A, E, F and G of the 116th, companies A, E, I and L of the 16th, and 96 tanks of the 743rd in LCTs shoved to the beach. They were followed closely by army engineers and naval underwater demolition teams (UDT). To the right, Company C of the 2nd Ranger Battalion landed near the foot of Pointe du Hoc. The German batteries that had opened on American naval vessels at 5:35 now concentrated their fire on the beach invaders, with machine guns and mortars adding to the cacophony of weapons.

Over in the 1st Infantry Division sector, many men of the infantry companies were having the same problems. The machine-gun fire was ricocheting off the metal drop-down ramps of the LCVPs. The men concluded they did not want to be in the front when that ramp dropped down.

The result of the misplaced landings and heavy enemy fire was that only one company, G of the 116th, had any unity, and they were out of position. The others were scattered and intermingled.

Over on Easy Red, only a few units of the initial assault wave landed in the sector, and they recovered reasonably well from the sporadic fire. But all of these men were out of position. Units of the second wave were getting stacked up quickly. The landing craft attempting to make shore, including the larger LCTs and LSTs beginning to make their way in, were hampered by the lack of success on the part of the engineering task force. They milled about in the surf. Men were crowding beach shelters and obstacles in the water. Destroyed radios and lack of communication in general made it extremely difficult for commanders to reorganize units and advance toward the critical beach road and draws. Only one of the six cleared lanes to the beach was marked. The use of amphibious trucks (DUKWs) to ferry in cannons was a complete disaster. Most of these were swamped in the significant swells in the bay that was only briefly and partially becalmed between storms. Tanks were the only firepower ashore for much of D-Day.

The advance up the ridge by Company G, between St.-Laurent and Coleville draws, was paralleled by a Company E advance to their right. Together these independent actions began the movement up the cliffs and inland in the 16th Regiment sector because the draws were still heavily defended. They took the garrison, men from the German 916th Regiment, from the rear and forced them to surrender.

All across the front soldiers, often just groups of beach survivors, banded together to try to get across the beach and up the ridge. Another major development occurred near Les Moulins, where a concerted effort was made to take the Vierville draw. Companies of the 116th Regiment and 5th Ranger Battalion were organized by Brigadier General Norman D. "Dutch" Cota and other senior officers to move on either side of the village and up the ridge. These units struggling to move forward on Omaha Beach were facing the best of the German defenses on the Calvados coast.

Destroyers came in close, to about 200 yards off the beach, to clear out German strong points on the ridge. This was extremely helpful to the soldiers, including Company C of the 2nd Rangers at Pointe du Hoc. They were delayed 40 minutes on the way in, and the work of getting ropes and ladders heading up the cliff face was very slow. Eventually, the Rangers made the crest but the other Ranger companies and part of the 116th Regiment that were to wheel west through Pointe de la Percée were running far behind schedule. The Rangers found the casemate abandoned but then discovered the 155mm guns in a camouflaged position further inland. These were abandoned also. However, the 1st Battalion of the German 914th Regiment counterattacked and pinned down the Company C Rangers who were as yet unreinforced. They would be cut off and alone on the crest of Pointe du Hoc throughout the night.

The American high command was beginning to feel a change in attitude after limited communication in the early morning portrayed disaster. A V Corps staff officer in a DUKW began crisscrossing the beach to give on-the-scene reports. By mid-morning he was able to report that the situation was improving as mixed units got off the beaches, advanced toward the draws and moved up the cliff face to the high ground.

The beach was still laced with artillery and small arms fire, but with the five draws in the process of being secured and the road through the St.-Laurent draw open, beach traffic began flowing in the afternoon as more and more follow-up units came ashore. The toll for taking Omaha Beach was nearly 2,000 American casualties. In order that those who perished would not die in vain, much more progress would have to be made on June 7.

The Landing at Utah Beach

Across the Vire estuary on the Cotentin Peninsula the landing at Utah Beach started out much better for VII Corps than the nightmarish Omaha

Beach experience of V Corps. Logical reasons for this were the more favorable terrain, the more effective beach bombing by the 9th Air Force medium bombers, and the fact that the airborne landings had diverted the attention of the peninsula's German defenders.

All of the units headed to Utah Beach in the first wave were from the 4th Infantry Division, commanded by Major General Raymond O. "Tubby" Barton. The first assault units, as planned, would land on the beach in front of the village of la Grande Dune in a 2,220-yard front. The 8th Infantry Regiment and the 3rd Battalion of the 22nd Infantry Regiment made up this force. Detachments from the 4th and 24th Cavalry Squadrons landed in the St. Marcouf Islands north of Utah Beach, at H minus 2 hours. They found the location heavily mined but abandoned, and the Americans held the islands through the day against German artillery shelling.

The naval gunfire preceding the invasion did not clear out all the enemy strong points, which were well concealed, but the bay was more sheltered off Utah Beach, and the Higgins boats approached without incident. All but four of the 32 DD tanks assigned to the first wave made it in under their own power.

The landing took place 2,000 yards to the south of the planned beach areas, designated "Red" and "Green," and a few minutes late due to a strong, unanticipated current. The assault force escaped the stronger defenses that covered the original landing area. As a result, the Utah Beach landings were accomplished with few U.S. casualties. Engineers and demolition units cleared the beach and landing approaches in one hour. By H plus 3 hours only sporadic gunfire harassed activities on the beach.

Though out of position for their first inland objectives, the light opposition to the landing allowed units to reorganize and move out together. The initiative was taken by assistant division commander Brigadier General Theodore Roosevelt Jr. (son of the 26th president), who personally reconnoitered new routes to the causeways leading over the flooded back beach. For his June 6, 1944, efforts Roosevelt was awarded the Distinguished Service Cross (DSC), later upgraded to the Medal of Honor.

All units were to be on the lookout for their airborne comrades. On Utah Beach the armored units were able to advance inland over the causeways that the paratroopers had secured. The 12th Regiment landed and headed inland. Neither it nor the 22nd Regiment would reach their objectives because once they passed over the secured causeways they were bogged down by natural marshes. The 12th did make contact with the 502nd Parachute Infantry Regiment (PIR) holding the northern flank of the 101st Airborne Division at St. Germain de Varreville.

Except for failing to establish communication with the 82nd and stopping short of their D-Day objectives when the terrain and German defensive maneuvers halted their progress, the 4th Division and attached units had a reasonably successful day. Total casualties for the units landing on Utah were 200, a tenth of those suffered at Omaha Beach.

The Commonwealth Beaches

The success of the operations carried out by the British 6th Airborne Division on the extreme left flank of the invasion area set the tone for how things would go for the landings on Gold, Juno and Sword Beaches and the inland penetration of the British and Canadian forces on June 6. The beaches were separated by the Calvados reefs, which required careful consideration of the tides. The Eastern Naval Task force moved into the area, and the warships pounded the coastal batteries for two full hours. Airplanes had laid down a smoke screen on the eastern flank of the task force because Sword Beach was in range of powerful German guns at Le Havre. Three German torpedo boats did venture out into the eastern part of the bay and launched torpedoes among task force ships. A Norwegian destroyer was sunk in the raid.

The landing troops of the British Second Army were unaffected by this event and loaded into their landing craft to motor over to the beaches, subdivided into sections from west to east as at the American beaches. The Second Army also landed seven commando forces of 500–600 men—British and some French—to fan out quickly and capture key points away from the beaches, such as Port-en-Bessin.

At 7:25 on June 6, as scheduled, one hour later than the American landings because of the tides, the initial assault units of the Second Army made landfall on the three beaches simultaneously. On the right, the British 50th Division came ashore east of Arromanches on Gold Beach. The only ferocious resistance to the Commonwealth landings came at le Hamel on the west edge of Gold Beach, where the German 916th Regiment 1st Battalion defenders fought stubbornly.

To the left of the 50th Division, the Canadian 3rd Division landed on the beach designated as Juno in front of Courseulles. They also had an opportunity for moving lead units off the beach quickly, but beach congestion was a problem at Juno as well. The easternmost beach was Sword, near the mouth of the Orne River. The British 3rd Division landed on Sword in front of Lion-sur-Mer and Ouistreham. Part of this division then turned east to cross the Orne and link with the 6th Airborne.

The lack of serious opposition on the Commonwealth beaches, except on the extreme right where the German 916th soldiers contested the advance throughout the day, allowed the British and Canadian soldiers to move toward the high ground, a ridge called Périers Ridge. It was the next objective for the advance units. The German *Ost* Battalion dissolved, leaving the road to Bayeux undefended. But in the smoke and confusion of the battle the gap was not immediately discovered by British commanders.

The panzer division closest to the Allied beachhead was the 21st. Initially, the 21st was ordered to move to the Orne River to deal with the 6th Airborne paratroopers. However, after the sea invasion commenced they were rerouted to protect Caen. Moving up to the vicinity of Périers Ridge, they launched an attack against British tanks and infantry in the afternoon, but they were unsuccessful. British commanders, however, feeling unsure of their gains, halted short of two important objectives—Bayeux and Caen—on D-Day.

The End of the Day

As darkness crept in on the late spring evening on the Normandy coast, the Allied commanders had to assess how the long and intense planning worked out on D-Day. The most serious problem as the day came to a close was the isolation of the 82nd Airborne Division in pockets along the Merderet River and the high casualties sustained in the division, especially among the glider troops. The paratroopers were in desperate battles around the bridges over the river and with Germans trying to retake St.-Mère-Église.

Elsewhere, the Allied line was stabilizing, although few units had reached the hoped-for D-Day "phase line," the end-of-the-day objectives that ran in a line roughly along the Paris to Cherbourg highway through Caen, Bayeux, Carentan and St.-Mère-Église. The only large counterattack, by the 21st Panzer Division, was contained. But Caen and Bayeux, seemingly there for the taking, remained in German hands.

By the end of D-Day the Germans were digging in, bracing for further Allied advances, with most of their panzer divisions trying to sneak past Allied air cover. One desperate Luftwaffe attempt to bomb Omaha Beach failed miserably as British and American ships used the four enemy Junkers bombers for target practice. Whether or not this June 6 invasion was *the* invasion or another was coming in the Somme River region, the Wehrmacht LXXXIV Corps was going to need some help. The units were coming as fast as conditions on the ground would allow, from all over the OB West command. The invasion had begun; the shores of Normandy were breached, but France was not going to change hands without a great deal more fighting.

MOMENTUM SWINGS

Mark Weisenmiller

TO THE NORTH AND NORTHWEST OF FRANCE THEY CAME DURING THE first week of June of 1944—the Americans, who brought with them everything from battleships to portable ice cream makers; the British, led by peppery General Sir Bernard L. Montgomery, nicknamed "Monty"; and the Canadians, whose 3rd Infantry Division advanced farther inland than any other Allied unit on D-Day.

The Allies' great gamble worked; every beach had been taken by nightfall, but in the coming days and weeks the momentum generated by the largest invasion in history would swing back and forth precariously.

Some of the fiercest fighting on and immediately after D-Day occurred at places that, during peacetime, seem unremarkable—such as the battle for the La Fière Bridge in the Cotentin Peninsula, inland from Utah Beach. The contest for the 500-yard causeway began when a group of paratroopers landed at a farm in La Fière at dawn on D-Day. In the late morning they crossed the arched-span bridge over the Merderet River, which the Germans had flooded, only to be thrown back by a counterattack. Four days of attack, counterattack and maneuver finally ended when the reinforced Americans took control of the bridge on June 9.

At Omaha Beach the Americans had a tough time securing a beachhead, but finally made progress up the draws to the high ground, where they prepared to continue their inland advance the next day. To the east of Omaha, the British and Canadians faced less formidable defenses at Gold, Juno, and Sword beaches and made good progress, but not good enough. Delays allowed the German 21st Panzer Division to reinforce Caen, a port city on the Orne River, and its nearby Carpiquet Airfield, nine miles inland from Sword Beach. That failure would ultimately set the Allied timetable back for weeks; and cost thousands of casualties. The day after D-Day Bayeux—a town known for its many industries and also, dubiously, for being burned in 1105 by England's King Henry I during his invasion of Normandy—became the first city of any size in France to be liberated, when British troops entered uncontested. (The small village of St.-Mère-Église in the Cotentin Peninsula had been liberated by the U.S. 82nd Airborne in the predawn hours of D-Day.)

Progress Measured in Yards

Beyond Omaha and Utah Beaches loomed the bocage country, filled with small fields, most of them about 100 x 100 yards. Separating the fields were hedgerows, banks of earth supporting trees whose roots and limbs had intertwined over centuries, making them impenetrable except where openings existed for passage between fields. German machine guns covered the openings. Vehicles traversing the narrow lanes between hedgerows were easy targets for anti-tank weapons.

"The hedgerows form perfect camouflage in which troops, artillery, and tanks can be hidden," as noted in *D-Day: 24 Hours That Saved The World*. "Each one of these thousands of fields of an acre or less could be defended for days with relative ease; to advance just a single mile, a squad of Allied infantry would have to cross as many as 30 of these 'boxes.'" Progress was measured in yards per day, slowing Allied momentum and allowing the Germans time to reorganize their defensive plans and receive reinforcements.

"Breaking out posed problems," Frank E. Vandiver wrote in his 2002 book *1001 Things Everyone Should Know About World War II*. "In all the meticulous planning the resistance potential of hedgerows had not been cancelled and it definitely helped the Germans."

To break through the hedgerows, "Rhinoceros" tanks were created—a Sherman tank with welded-on prongs made from demolished German beachhead obstacles. (These "hedgecutters" were also attached to some M3 Stuart light tanks and M10 tank destroyers, according to The National Museum of the United States Army). Sergeant Curtis G. Cullin of the 102nd Cavalry Reconnaissance Squadron is usually credited with the innovation. Cullin himself said the idea was originally proposed by "a Tennessee hillbilly named Roberts." Although not a miracle cure-all, the Rhino allowed Allied tanks to break through hedgerows.

On to Caen

In the British-Canadian sector the country was more open, better suited to tank warfare, and here the Allied troops faced German armor more often and in larger numbers. Montgomery believed his forces would capture Caen and the Carpiquet Airfield the day of the invasion. When that did not happen, a two-prong attack to take the objectives was made on June 9 but also failed.

On the western flank of Britain's Second Army, the American First Army's V Corps had pushed more than 12 miles inland from Omaha Beach by June 11 and on the following day forced the remnants of the German 352nd Infantry Division to fall back to St. Lô. This opened a 7.5-mile gap near Caumont on the border between American and British areas of operation. Britain's 7th Armored Division attempted to exploit this gap, outflank the SS Panzer Lehr Division that was determinedly holding the road south from Bayeux, and threaten the German positions east of Caen. On June 13 elements of the 7th Armored entered the small town of Villers-Bocage, in the rear of Panzer Lehr, and approached nearby high ground shown on Allied maps as Point 213. They were attacked by German tanks, including heavy Tigers. The British withdrew after losing almost 60 armored vehicles, including nearly 30 tanks, and close to 220 men; approximately half the losses in vehicles were inflicted within 15 minutes by a single Tiger commanded by *Obersturmführer* (equivalent to a British lieutenant or U.S. first lieutenant) Michael Wittman. The Germans lost six Tigers and two Panzer VI tanks.

Meanwhile, the U.S. forces on the British right also ran into stubborn opposition, a foretaste of what would happen in their efforts to capture the crossroads and rail town of St. Lô. On June 17 Hitler met with his commanders north of Paris and reiterated his orders that their soldiers were not to withdraw an inch but to fight to the last man, although he did agree to a partial fallback south of Cherbourg.

A New Form of Terror

While Britain's 7th Armored Division was being mauled at Villers-Bocage, a new form of terror fell from the sky over London. The first V-1 rocket bomb (*Vergeltungswaffen*, or "vengeance weapon") landed, detonating a 1,870-pound warhead. Soon, up to 100 of these terror weapons a day were striking Britain. More than 6,000 people were killed and 17,000 wounded in an 80-day period. On September 8 an improved rocket, the V-2 strategic guided missile, struck Chiswick, near London; the first of more than 1,000 that would kill more than 2,700 Londoners before war's end. The port city of Antwerp, Holland, also suffered 900 V-2 strikes in the last months of 1944. The rocket bombs didn't alter the course of the war but did cause the Allies to divert resources to knocking out launching and manufacturing sites.

A Port Full of Port

On June 12 the U.S. Army VII Corps, led by Major General Joseph Lawton "Lightning Joe" Collins, captured Carentan in the Cotentin Peninsula, sealing the gap between Utah and Omaha beaches and reducing the chance of a major counterattack. On the morning of June 18 Collins's men reached the peninsula's western coast, cutting off the German troops north of their line.

The Cotentin Peninsula extends into the English Channel. Besides many fishing towns there is the chief port city of Cherbourg, a place few Americans had then heard of. The Allies needed the seaport and naval base as a resupply port, and by the end of the month it was in American hands—but it was a Pyrrhic victory. The Germans had destroyed port facilities and filled the harbor with sunken ships and hundreds of contact mines. By the time it was repaired sufficiently to receive shipments regularly the Allied advance had moved far beyond it. There was consolation for the conquering American soldiers who entered Cherbourg, however.

"Among the troops in Normandy," General Omar Bradley wrote in his 1951 autobiography, *A Soldier's Story*, "Cherbourg's strategic worth was soon overshadowed by the wealth of its booty, and it was there that the term 'liberate' came into popular use in the army." This was another way of saying that certain troops under his command proceeded to steal virtually anything they could touch. "As a result," wrote General Bradley, "we fell heir not only to a transatlantic port but to a massive underground wine cellar."

Charnwood and *Goodwood*

June ended, July began, and the British and Canadian forces still had not advanced far beyond their beachheads. Repeated attempts to outflank Caen's defenders had failed. Now, Montgomery decided it was time to strike head-on and two operations were planned to carry this out. (Because the casualties Britain had suffered between 1940–44 had reduced manpower a head-on assault was always considered a last resort.) The attacks would be preceded by heavy air and naval bombardments.

On July 7 *Operation Charnwood* began with waves of bombers—about half of the Allied bombing forces available at the time—dropping their lethal loads on and around Caen in what is known as "carpet bombing." Guns on warships joined over 650 pieces of artillery in adding to the destruction rained on the German defenders, but most bombs and shells missed their targets, leaving the German positions relatively unaffected while killing nearly 400 civilians. Casualties were heavy as the Anglo-Canadian forces advanced the next day, but they inflicted losses of their own and captured outlying villages. On July 9 the first Allied troops entered Caen, and the Carpiquet Airfield was finally captured. The Germans repositioned south of Caen, near Bourguébus.

Nearly two weeks later a second operation, *Goodwood*, opened on July 18 with 7,700 tons of bombs dropped by more than 2,000 British and American aircraft. While Canadian troops cleaned out the last German resistance in the rubble of Caen, three British armored divisions moved out to break through on the rolling plain southeast of the city in the direction of Falaise. For three hours the tanks advanced rapidly; then they ran into the final defensive line, and the advance ground to a halt. Localized attacks continued until a heavy thunderstorm on July 20 turned the area around Bourguébus into a quagmire. British VIII Corps had captured almost 35 square miles, a monumental leap after the many failures that had preceded *Charnwood* and *Goodwood*, but the corps lost more than 4,000 men and 500 tanks. The Germans, however, had committed their last reserves.

'The Capital of the Ruins'

Below the Cotentin Peninsula, about 20 miles south of Carentan, Germans held on tenaciously to Saint Lô, the capital of the Manche Department. An old Gallo-Roman town, it had been a major fortress in medieval times.

For almost one month, defenders in the hedgerows and marshes around St. Lô thwarted the American First Army the way Caen had thwarted Montgomery's 21st Army. On the night of June 6–7 American bombers pounded the city. (In 1946, former French Resistance member and future novelist and absurdist playwright Samuel Beckett would describe St. Lô as "The Capital of the Ruins.")

Beginning on July 11 the Americans and the Germans, like two heavyweight pugilists standing in the middle of a boxing ring slugging away at each other, fought with attacks and counterattacks, artillery and mortar fire and aerial bombing. By the morning of July 18 all Germans except small pockets of resistance had pulled out of the entire sector. It marked an important swing in momentum in Normandy. Holding St. Lô had allowed the Germans to move troops and materiel effectively. Now its intersecting roads would help the Americans to finally break out of the bocage.

Operation Cobra

Momentum was clearly on the Allies' side. The situation was right for the Americans to make their long-delayed breakout from the constricting hedgerow country. *Goodwood* had focused enemy attention on the eastern edge of the Allied line; now the American First Army would strike the opposite end, breaking out of the Cotentin Peninsula by driving west into Brittany, then making a wide southeastwardly swing. Developed by Major General Omar Bradley, the plan was code named *Operation Cobra*. Tactical command was given to Major General Joseph Lawton Collins. (*See the Allied Generals section.*)

On July 25 some 4,400 tons of ordnance was dropped in carpet-bombing fashion by Eighth Air Force bombers. Colored smoke, to indicate the demarcation between friend and foe, blew back across American lines, causing bombs to explode on American units killing, among others, Lieutenant General Leslie J. McNair, commander of U.S. Army ground forces. Regardless, Collins pressed on immediately. After failing to obtain his first day's objectives, he committed his armor and mechanized units to disrupt German command and communications. Newly arrived lieutenant general George S. Patton Jr., placed in command of VIII Corps while waiting for his Third Army to be activated, drove his men hard and seized Avranches nearly 40 miles south of St. Lô on July 31. Capturing this city, which ended the *Cobra* operation, positioned the Americans to turn the flank of the German Seventh Army. In just six days the entire German front had collapsed.

July melted into August, and on the latter's first day Patton's Third Army began operations as part of Bradley's 12th Army Group. The quiet, studious Bradley and the rambunctious Patton were a glittering example of opposites who work well together; they had each other's respect. (*See Allied Generals section.*)

Rommel Wounded, Hitler Attacked

One of the worst setbacks for the Germans came on July 17 when British Spitfire fighters strafed an enemy command car carrying Field Marshal Erwin Rommel. He suffered serious head injuries in the resulting crash and was sent to convalesce; Field Marshal Günther von Kluge, who had replaced Gerd von Rundstedt as commander in chief in the West on July 3, took over Rommel's duties as commander of Army Group B as well.

On July 20 evidence the war's momentum had swung to the Allies exploded in Hitler's Wolf's Lair headquarters in East Prussia. A group of army officers, convinced the war was lost, attempted to kill the Führer with a bomb planted during a staff meeting. The wounded Hitler had the Gestapo round up anyone suspected of being part of the plot. Rommel's name kept coming up, and on October 14 he was given the choice of a public trial or, in exchange for protection for his family, quietly committing suicide with poison. He chose the latter. Von Kluge had preceded him in death two months earlier, committing suicide on August 18, the day after he was sacked by Hitler, who suspected him of complicity in the assassination plot and of contacting the Allies to negotiate a surrender. German command structure in the west was breaking down.

The Germans Strike Back

Hitler saw the *Cobra* breakout as an opportunity for a counterattack that would slice the rather thin connection between the U.S. First and Third armies. *Operation Lüttich* called for Seventh Army and Fifth Panzer Army to break out to the west and seize Avranches, although the divisions that would carry out the operation were understrength as a result of losses during the previous two months.

On the foggy morning of August 7 the Germans began their attack; it caught the Americans to their front by surprise. (The Allies had received warning through ULTRA intercepts, but the information didn't reach the front before the assault was launched.) In the first hours of *Operation Lüttich*, the Germans advanced seven miles and came within 13 miles of Avranches but ran into stiff resistance, particularly from the 30th Infantry Division around Mortain. Once the fog lifted around noon, American and RAF fighter-bombers attacked the advancing columns. In the following three days more than 100 German tanks were demolished. On the night of August 11–12, the Germans evacuated Mortain and their panzer divisions retreated eastward.

It had quickly become apparent to Bradley that First Army could contain *Lüttich*, and elements of the Third Army that were already fighting around Rennes and Le Mans were not recalled to help in the defense. Instead, they drove eastward to capitalize on a chance to join with Montgomery's army group near Falaise and encircle the German forces.

The Falaise Gap

The day after the Germans launched *Lüttich* to push westward, British, Canadian and Polish forces of Montgomery's command began an offensive to capture high ground north of Falaise. Von Kluge quickly realized his entire force could be encircled and wanted to withdraw. Hitler, however, mistakenly believed the German attack to take control of Avranches would succeed. "To him the equation was still valid that a metre of Norman soil was of more importance than 10 kilometers of ground in any other part of France," James Lucas and James Barker wrote in their 1978 book, *The Battle of Normandy: The Falaise Gap*.

Von Kluge was able to convince the Führer of the need for a short withdrawal to condense his lines; then, on August 16, Hitler gave permission for a two-stage withdrawal. On August 17 German forces began moving toward the 15-mile-wide Falaise Gap, their only hope for escape.

Allied aircraft bombed and strafed them mercilessly as they withdrew, inflicting large numbers of casualties. But logistic problems, disagreement and confusion among Allied commanders slowed the advance on the ground. The gap wasn't closed until August 21, by which time a great many Germans had escaped, leaving their heavy equipment behind.

The 1994 Facts on File reference book *D-Day Atlas: The Definitive Account of the Allied Invasion of Normandy* states, "the Germans put up an astonishing performance, proving masters of the improvised battle group, the hard-fought engagement, and the quick withdrawal. For two days, 500 troops with 15 tanks and a dozen 88s held their ground on the last rise before Falaise."

Decades later, historians still are not certain about casualties in the Falaise Pocket. The Germans lost no more than 10,000 killed, with 50,000 more captured, but 115,000 escaped. Their losses in equipment included 200 tanks, 5,000 other vehicles, 300 heavy guns and 700 artillery pieces. The Allied victory wasn't a complete one, but Hitler's insistence on holding every meter of ground cost his army dearly.

The Allied "race across France" could now begin. Patton's fighting force advanced at such a rapid pace he had to rely on a Michelin road map to constantly update the movement of his troops. There were localized German counterattacks and defensive stands, but the greatest factor in the race to the Rhine was the Allies outrunning their supply lines. To resolve the problem the Americans instituted the Red Ball Express, supply truck convoys that operated 20 out of every 24 hours. (The British equivalent was the Red Lion Express.) The trucks were driven almost exclusively by African American soldiers who, in the segregated army, were more likely to be assigned to supply companies than frontline outfits.

The Southern Invasion

On August 15, another Allied invasion force came ashore in southern France. Originally named *Operation Anvil*, then renamed *Dragoon* after Allies feared the code name had been compromised, it had been planned to coincide with the Normandy invasion but had to be postponed due to an insufficient number of landing craft. The defenses here were not as strong, casualties were much smaller, and inland penetration was faster.

Paris is Free!

Eisenhower planned to bypass Paris, isolating German troops in the French capital, but competing groups of French Resistance Fighters began an uprising in the city on August 19. Twelve days earlier General Dietrich von Choltitz had taken command of German forces in the Paris area, with orders from Hitler to defend the city or destroy it. When promised reinforcements were diverted elsewhere, von Choltitz could read the writing on the wall, and it said the Allies were going to win this war. Unwilling to be known as the man who destroyed the magnificent city—or to be hanged as a war criminal for doing so—he chose to risk ignoring Hitler's demands. Assisted by the Swedish general counsel Raoul Nordling, he worked out a truce with the French resisters but fighting continued. Meanwhile, Brigadier General Charles de Gaulle, leader of the Free French forces among the Allied armies, had changed Eisenhower's mind about bypassing the city. On August 26 de Gaulle led the Free French 2nd Armored Division into Paris, which had been liberated the day before.

Setbacks and SNAFUs

"The main battle for France is over," correspondent Harry Boyle wrote in an Associated Press story of August 24. The next challenge was getting into Germany itself.

On September 17, British, Polish and U.S. paratroopers dropped out of the sky near Nijmegen and Arnhem, the Netherlands, to seize a network of bridges and canals; a British armored force that was moving overland would then use the bridges to cross the Rhine into Germany. *Operation Market Garden* was planned by Montgomery, who had been promoted to the rank of field marshal. It was a spectacular failure that resulted in more than 10,000 Allied casualties and overshadowed Allied successes in September 1944 (the British liberated Brussels, Belgium; the U.S. First Army took control of Luxembourg; and Soviet fighting forces invaded Axis-aligned Romania and were advancing toward Yugoslavia).

The first German city to come under Allied attack was Aachen, which for centuries had been the coronation site for Holy Roman emperors and German kings. Fighting for the city began in earnest on October 13; by the time the city was surrendered on October 21, American casualties topped 3,700; four of every five houses had been damaged or destroyed.

From Aachen, Lieutenant General Courtney H. Hodges, commanding American First Army, intended to sweep into Germany's Rhine plain toward Cologne (Köln). First, he decided, he had to secure his right flank by taking the Hürtgen Forest. Thus began what historian Rick Atkinson, in a November 30, 2018, speech at the National WWII Museum in New Orleans, described as "one of the most ill-conceived, badly led, and pointless American operations in any [World War II] theater."

Smaller than the city of Washington, D.C., the forested area with its narrow, twisting trails presented little opportunity for a significant German counterattack, but it was a defender's dream. The thick forest negated three of the Allies' greatest assets: aircraft, artillery and armor. Beneath the trees, landmines were nearly as common as mushrooms and mutually supporting bunkers made the Hürtgen as dangerous as the slopes above Omaha Beach. Between September 12 and December 16, some 33,000 Americans would become casualties.

A Leader Lost

Despite the setbacks and lengthening casualty lists, President Franklin Roosevelt was so confident of victory that on November 18 he told Prime Minister Churchill that, as Commander in Chief of American forces, he would call for their withdraw from Europe immediately after the defeat of Nazi Germany. Historians know he wanted to be in San Francisco on April 20, 1945, for the first formal session of the United Nations, but what most people do not know is that immediately afterwards he wanted his wife Eleanor "to accompany him to London, Holland, and the (war) front," as noted by Doris Kearns Goodwin wrote in *No Ordinary Time: Franklin and Eleanor Roosevelt: The Home Front in World War II*. It was not to be; FDR would die from a cerebral hemorrhage on April 12, 1945.

Crisis in the Ardennes

The only thing that halted the bloodletting in the Hürtgen Forest—temporarily—was the German offensive that began December 16 south of it. It would become known as the Battle of the Bulge, and for a time it gave the appearance of swinging the momentum back in favor of the Germans, especially after the costly and sometimes unproductive Allied failures of autumn.

The German counterattack came through the Ardennes Forest and caught the Allies by surprise. Spearheaded by some of the most experienced troops in Hitler's armies, equipped with the heaviest German tanks, the attack quickly drove a bulge 50 miles wide and 70 deep into the Allied lines. Bad weather grounded the airpower that had played such a key role in the Normandy Campaign and breakout. Heroic stands by American forces, often in ad hoc groups, slowed the Nazi advance. Montgomery, acting on his own initiative, redeemed some of his reputation by moving his XXX Corps into blocking positions.

The Ardennes Offensive ended officially exactly one month after it began. It cost the Allies—mostly Americans—90,000 men, 300 tanks and 300 aircraft, and set Eisenhower's timetable back by five weeks. The cost to the attackers—100,000 men, 700 tanks, and 1,600 aircraft—was far worse because, unlike the United States, Germany could not replace such losses. There should have been no remaining doubt about which side would win in Europe, but Hitler still had a sucker punch left.

Alsace Offensive

South of the Battle of the Bulge, another German offensive, code named *Nordwind* (*North Wind*) surprised American and French forces in the Alsace-Lorraine region on New Year's Eve and forced them to fall back. Particularly heavy fighting raged for two weeks around the villages of Rittershoffen and Hatten. The offensive was halted January 25. American and French combined casualties may have topped 16,000, but the Germans lost another 23,000 irreplaceable men.

It was their last offensive in the West. The Western Allies still had months of hard fighting ahead of them in Germany and Austria, but on April 25, 1945, American soldiers met up with Soviet Army troops along the Elbe River. That same day, the Soviets completed their encirclement of the German capital, which was surrendered on May 2, two days after Adolf Hitler committed suicide.

Conclusions

At times the Western Allies' campaigns in the late spring and early summer of 1944 seemed to teeter on the brink of failure—the confusion and fierce fighting on Omaha Beach, the slugfest in the bocage, the difficulties in capturing Caen—and their missteps then and after the breakout raised doubts about some commanders' ability to lead. But once Caen fell and *Operation Cobra* got Americans out of the hedgerows, momentum clearly swung to the Allied side. German attempts to regain it—*Operation Lüttich*, the Ardennes Offensive, *Nordwind*—enjoyed only brief success. To Allied planners and people on the Home Front, the battle lines on maps showed clearly the Nazis were losing ground. But to the individual rifleman, shivering in his foxhole or facing another day of close-quarters fighting in some city he'd never heard of before the war, victory must have seemed at times a long way off.

Weary Infantrymen of the First U.S. Army rest in Bastogne, Belgium after the German Battle of the Bulge offensive overran their 110th Infantry Regiment battalion on December 23, 1944. *(Image courtesy of the National Archives and Records Administration)*

A portion of the Omaha Beach Invasion Tableau at the National D-Day Memorial. Bedford, VA *(image courtesy of the Library of Congress)*

The Present

FINDING YOUR D-DAY HERITAGE

Dennis Edward Flake

MOST PEOPLE REACH A POINT IN THEIR LIVES WHEN THEY BEGIN TO ask, "Who am I? What is the meaning of life? Who came before me and how does my life compare to theirs?" Answering the first two questions can be very difficult and challenging, but it is easier to discover the lives of our ancestors and determine what meaning those lives may hold for us today. A good understanding of our ancestor's struggles and failures, their successes and pleasures can provide a direction for our lives in the early twenty-first century.

The generation that participated in D-Day—whether that participation was involvement in combat areas or the Home Front—has been dubbed the "Greatest Generation" by some historians, a term popularized by the 1998 publication of Tom Brokaw's book "The Greatest Generation."

Tragically, most of this generation has passed away. The youngest are in their early nineties. Of the 16 million Americans who served in the military during WWII, only 558,000 were left as of 2017, with 362 passing away each day, taking their oral histories with them and creating an urgency to collect this valuable information and stories. But even if your family includes WWII veterans (or civilians of that period) who have already passed, there are still numerous methods to research, examine, and find your World War II heritage. But before we jump to that, let's take a quick overview of what factors formed the Greatest Generation. More in-depth information can be found in earlier chapters of this book.

Most of this generation was born in the 1910s and early 1920s. They saw in their own hometowns, perhaps in their own families, maimed veterans of "The War to End Wars." The economic boom of the 1920s promised them a golden future before tossing them into the turmoil and hardships of the worldwide Great Depression of the 1930s. In Europe and Asia the rise of militaristic nations during the depression threatened to bring about a new world war—a threat that became reality for America when the Japanese attacked Pearl Harbor on December 7, 1941.

By the time of the Pearl Harbor attack, a peacetime draft had already increased the United States armed forces to 2.2 million, up from only 334,473 just two years earlier. By the end of the war, 16 million American men and women had served in uniform. Additionally, 3.5 million Britons, 1.1 million Canadians, and people from virtually every European nation, Australia, New Zealand, and many countries of Africa and Asia, were in the military on one side or the other, so there is a good chance one or more members of your family or extended family saw military service. Millions of civilians worked in defense industries (a situation that opened factory employment to women and minorities, often for the first time) and government agencies, collected scrap metal, planted Victory Gardens, rolled bandages, sewed socks for soldiers, or otherwise took an active Home Front role. Any member of your family who was old enough to remember living through the World War II years is a source of information about your heritage.

Americans in the assault wave were in the 1st and 29th divisions. These and other Allied commands produced unit histories, held reunions and started commemorative organizations, good sources for research. *(Image courtesy of the National Archives and Records Administration Collections)*

How to Explore Your Heritage

If you are lucky enough to have a family member from the World War II generation still alive, you should start recording their oral history immediately. Apart from their own experiences they can tell you about a husband, brother, sister, aunt, uncle, or other family members. Ask them for any letters, diaries, journals, or any military or government documents. See if there are any old uniforms or souvenirs in a closet or in the attic. The uniforms could contain unit patches that may help in your search. For example, a bright red 1 on the left upper sleeve means that uniform was worn by someone in the 1st Infantry Division, aka the Big Red One. Tell them that the items are not only important for family history but also for American history and should be preserved for future generations. If possible when recording the oral history, try to obtain full names, service numbers, branch of service, and dates of enlistment and discharge.

If there are no longer any members of the World War II Generation left in your family, begin by asking the oldest members of your family about oral history or any documents, uniforms, or souvenirs they are aware of.

World War II veterans, like veterans of other wars, often did not share their wartime experiences with their children. Most of the vets had large families to raise and bills to pay and did not want to talk about painful and traumatic war experiences; however, many became more open about those experiences as the years went by. Hopefully, the veteran in your family opened up to his children at some point in his life and detailed his experiences. The oral history may not be complete or might be somewhat inaccurate (memories fade and get mixed with other memories), but it can be very helpful when researching military and government documents. Once again, when recording the oral history, attempt to obtain full names, service numbers, branch of service, and dates of enlistment and discharge. You'll need that information when you take the next step—approaching government archives.

Government and Public Resources

By far, the best repository for military and government records in the United States is the National Archives, headquartered in Washington, D.C., and in College Park, Maryland. The vast majority of the military and civilian Federal government employee records from World War II, however, are located in the National Archives site in Saint Louis, Missouri.

When you access the agency's website at www.archives.gov there is a tab entitled "Veterans' Service Records" that states, "Request military records and learn about other services for yourself or a family member." When you click on the tab, you will receive a link to request service records online, by mail, or by fax. The great majority of historical military personnel records and medical records exist only on paper and are not available online. Official military personnel files from 1956 or older—the ones that cover World War II veterans—can be requested by anyone. For records created after 1956, the request must be initiated by the veteran or next-of-kin.

Within the Military Records link, there is a section entitled "Online Veterans and Military Documents." Scroll down to "World War II Era." There are online casualty, prisoner of war, enlistment and draft records, as well as photos from World War II. This online section could be very helpful to you if you discover during the oral history that your family member was wounded or killed in action or was captured as a prisoner of war.

After reviewing the main National Archives website, you will mostly likely find it easier to proceed directly to the National Archives website in St. Louis at www.archives.gov/st-louis. All of the personnel records at St. Louis are open to the public because they precede 1956. Another benefit of this website is that it provides information on not only military service but also civilian Federal government employment during World War II. Your ancestor may have worked in Draft Registration, the FBI, or other government agency.

When researching personnel records at St. Louis, be aware a fire in 1973 destroyed or damaged over 16 million records from the years 1912 to 1964. Fortunately, most of the data is still available and the National Archives has been able to reconstruct information from alternative record sources.

There are four links on the left side of the St. Louis website that will assist you in your research for military service. First, there is the Official Military Personnel Files (OMPFs). The link details the branch of services and the dates of service. Some OMPFs have both personnel and active duty health records. The medical records could hold induction and separation physicals and any treatment while in uniform. Second, there is the Selective Service Records. These records will determine if your family member was 1A, available for military service, or deferred from the draft due to an important civilian occupation, a medical issue or other reasons. Third, there are the Deceased Veteran's Claim Files, which could show a relative received compensation from the Veterans Administration due to a wartime wound or injury. And finally, there are the Individual Deceased Personnel Files. These records are similar to the previous files, but the records also show Veterans Administration compensation to the widow or heir of the veteran.

The link for the civilian federal government employment records is also on the left side of the St. Louis website. It is labeled Official Personnel Folders (OPFs). These civilian employee archives date from 1850 to 1951. The personnel data is available from many government departments and agencies, ranging from the Department of Agriculture to the Weather Bureau. Many of these departments and agencies greatly contributed to the war effort.

Remember that these personnel records in St. Louis are only available in paper and not online. There are several ways to access and copy the paper records. Whether you are researching military or civilian Federal employee records, the procedures are basically the same.

You can go in person to visit the Archival Research Room in St. Louis. This way can be challenging and time consuming but very rewarding when you discover your relatives' records. There is no researching fee for this service, but you need to schedule an appointment at 314-801-0850. Once you have located the records, a staff member can make copies for you at 80 cents each, or you can make your own copies for 25 cents each.

If you can't travel to St. Louis personally, your next option is to mail or fax a request letter or the Standard Form (SF) 180, which can be downloaded from the website, to National Personnel Records Center, 1 Archives Drive, St. Louis, MO, 63138. The fax number is 314-801-9195. The request letter or the SF 180 should contain complete name, service number, branch and dates of service, date of birth, place of discharge, last unit of assignment, and place of entry into service. This is why you need to collect as much information as possible beforehand about the family member you are researching.

There is an online record request option, but it is confusing at this time for World War II files. It is called eVetRecs, and it appears to be geared to military service records after 1956. It requires the signature of the veteran or the next of kin. Remember that military records from 1956 or before, which are 62 years after discharge, are open to the public.

The National Archives does not guarantee a specific timeframe for the research, but the website states you can track the status of your order by ten work days. There is a copy fee for the mailed, faxed, or online requests. The amount is a $25 flat fee for five copied pages or less and a $75 flat fee for six copies or more.

If you have a busy schedule, or you find the National Archives records request methods too cumbersome or confusing, there are independent researchers for hire. There are multiple researchers with a specialty in World War II listed on the website. You will have to negotiate a fee for their investigation and for any copies of the documents. Some of the researchers are graduate students in the St. Louis area who are very familiar with the search processes, and they could be worth the cost.

There is very little difference in requesting the Official Personnel Folders (OPFs) for civilian Federal employees compared to the military records. The copy fees are the same, and you also have the option to visit in person the Archival Research Room in St. Louis. For the civilians, there is not a specific request form like the SF 180. A written request including full name, date of birth, name and location of employing Federal agency, beginning and ending dates of service, and Social Security number if applicable, can be emailed to stl.archives@nara.gov or mailed to NARA, Attn: Archival Programs, P.O. Box 38757, St. Louis, MO, 63138. You could also hire an independent researcher who specializes in Federal government employment during World War II.

An alternative to the National Archives is the National WWII Museum in New Orleans, Louisiana. The museum is independent and non-profit, and it has a stellar reputation for interpreting World War II history and its meaning on the United States today. The website is www.nationalww2museum.org. Most of the documents that the museum utilizes to research the military service of a World War II veteran are gathered from the National Archives, the Library of Congress, and from its own extensive collection. The museum's researching fees are higher than dealing directly with the National Archives, but its services may be well worth it.

After you bring up the museum's website, there is a link listed as "The War." When you click on the link, many interesting World War II articles will appear. Return to "The War" link and click the down arrow. An option entitled "Research A Veteran" will appear. Click this option and you have the opportunity to request a free guide. You will need to populate the information in the online request form. You also have the option to sign up for emails from the museum.

To use the museum's paid inquiry services, return to the "The War" and "Research A Veterans" tabs. Click the down arrow and "WWII Research Services Discover Your Veteran's Story" will appear. Following three background paragraphs, the process for beginning the museum's research services are explained in detail. There is also a comprehensive "Frequently Asked Questions" (FAQ) section.

The museum's search services are under its Institute for the Study of War and Democracy. The institute attempts to customize your family member's documents such as rank, training, battles, medals, and citation, and then integrate the materials with what is known about your relative's unit including reports, rosters, maps, and photos.

The first step is to contact a historian at the institute and receive an explanation on the different levels of services. The telephone number is 504-528-1944, x286. To begin the search, you must pay $75 plus taxes, which is an "Initial Research Fee." This amount is nonrefundable and will pay for the institute's search of its own archives, the National Archives records at College Park and St. Louis, and an array of other World War II databases. There is a Veteran Information form that requires name, date of birth, place of birth, service number, branch of service, unit/ship, and rank. This search process normally takes two weeks. Once the historian discovers how much material is available on your family member, he will contact you with the results. Then you can decide if you want additional services.

There are two levels of enhanced services. The "PLUS" package costs $299 plus taxes. The initial $75 fee is applied to this price. The institute will use the newly located documents to compile and detail a one- to two-page summary of your relative's military service. The documents and summary will be sent to you in a museum folder and envelope. The other package is the "Premier." It costs $1,995 plus taxes; you get credit for the initial $75 fee. You will receive the same service as "Plus" and in addition will obtain a detailed military biography of your family member with maps, pictures, and charts in a professionally cloth-bound book. You can order additional copies for other members of your family. You can also choose a leather-bound copy for an extra charge.

Besides the National Archives and the National WWII Museum, there are a few other World War II search sites. You can check your state libraries and county historical societies. Some have extensive records of service members from their states and counties. Normally, it should be more convenient to visit these sites in person and only pay for copies. Paid genealogy websites like Myheritage.com and Ancestry.com can be helpful, but the sites are typically not comprehensive and often incomplete regarding World War II materials. FamilySearch.org, the online service of the huge and storied Los Angeles Mormon Temple genealogy library is another source; its information is general rather than military.

Sharing Your Heritage

Once you have completed an oral history and have located significant documents on your family member, it is imperative to preserve the data. A professionally designed folder or book from the National WWII Museum is nice to have on a coffee table. You might consider creating a website or blog on the wartime service of your ancestor. These online sources will permit other members of your family to examine and to contribute to what you have uncovered. With these online formats, you might discover a distant relative who is also interested in exploring and sharing on the topic.

You might also create a YouTube video on your World War II findings. A video can be an innovative way to reach and emotionally touch certain members of your family who would be less likely to read the information on a website or blog, but it would be difficult to include additional findings and documents. Remember to back up all your World War II files by methods like Google Drive, iCloud, and USB devices.

After gathering your data, you may well find World War II still has an impact on your life today. Do you live in California because your great-grandfather, a United States Navy World War II veteran of the fighting in the Pacific, chose to remain in San Diego or Long Beach instead of returning to the family farm in Illinois? Do you live in the Washington, D.C. area because your great-grandmother chose to continue in Federal government employment after the war instead of returning to her native North Carolina?

One of the biggest social and cultural programs in American history was the post-war GI Bill. The program provided educational and home ownership benefits to thousands of returning veterans. These programs greatly underwrote the enormous post-war economic boom and the remarkable growth of the middle class. Are you the third or fourth generation in your family to attend college? Maybe the first member of your family to go to college was your great-grandfather, who served in the United States Army in France during D-Day and took advantage of the GI Bill. Perhaps you live on Long Island, NY, today because your great-grandfather used his GI Bill housing benefit to leave Brooklyn and to buy his first home in Nassau County.

Learning your World War II and D-Day heritage can be a very rewarding experience. It has been seventy-four years since the end of the war and seventy-five years since D-Day. While this may seem like ancient history, its impact today on our country and the world—and on you—is still profound.

D-DAY IN POPULAR CULTURE

D-Day Books

Gerald D. Swick

NOT SURPRISINGLY, D-DAY IS AN "EVERGREEN" SUBJECT IN BOOK publishing. The sheer scope of the planning and execution of the operation; its high-risk, high-stakes nature; the elaborate deception campaign to misdirect the Germans; the personalities involved; and of course, the stories of valor and sacrifice have been related and analyzed in hundreds of books.

The titles listed here should not be considered a "best-of" list, but an overview of some of the best and most popular books on various aspects of the incredible human drama that played out on the blood-soaked beaches of Normandy on June 6, 1944, and later became weeks of claustrophobic close-quarters action among the hedgerow-lined roads of Normandy's bocage country.

Overviews

Perhaps the most accessible introduction for readers who know little about D-Day and the subsequent campaign in France is Wayne Vansant's *Normandy: A Graphic History of D-Day, the Allied Invasion of Hitler's Fortress Europe*. Vansant's book, published in 2012, consists of only 104 highly illustrated pages but manages to cover the period from the Normandy invasion to the liberation of Paris nearly three months later, Vansant blends "big-picture" information with stories of individual soldiers. The book uses graphic-novel format but is a well-researched and comprehensive overview.

Cornelius Ryan's *The Longest Day* has captivated readers since it was first published in 1959 with its narrative style that reads more like a novel than nonfiction. It is known to contain some inaccuracies but is surprisingly comprehensive for a book of under 300 pages.

Max Hastings's 1984 *Overlord: D-Day and the Battle for Normandy* offers excellent comparisons of weapons and tactics, and his ability to present complex information in layman's terms have kept this book on the D-Day must-read list for over thirty years. *D-Day: June 6, 1944: The Climactic Battle of World War II*, by Stephen E. Ambrose (1994), is the most comprehensive of this historian's three books on D-Day and is noted for his insightful analysis. An illustrated edition was published in 2014.

More recent books have the advantage of mining new information that has come to light or is taken from previously underutilized research sources. *D-Day: The Battle for Normandy*, by Anthony Beevor (2009), drew material from over 30 archives in several countries, much of it previously overlooked, to give greater coverage of the Canadian, French, German and Polish experiences during the campaign than many other books have. Rick Atkinson explores the Normandy invasion as part of the larger war in *The Guns at Last Light: The War in Western Europe, 1944–1945* (2014), the final book in his World War II trilogy that began with the Pulitzer Prize–winning *An Army at Dawn*. Atkinson is skilled at relating details in a manner that not only tells a story but packs an emotional punch.

The subtitle of 2009's *The D-Day Companion: Leading historians explore history's greatest amphibious assault* says it all: thirteen American and British historians examine various aspects of the invasion. Edited by Oxford history graduate Jane Penrose, it features a foreword by Major Richard "Dick" Winters, the real-life leader of Easy Company, 506th Regiment, 101st Airborne, who was depicted in Stephen E. Ambrose's *Band of Brothers*, on which the 2001 HBO miniseries was based.

The D-Day Experience From the Invasion to the Liberation of Paris (2004) sets itself apart with 30 facsimiles of memorabilia such as diaries, sketches and secret memos, color maps, and a 72-minute audio CD of veterans' interviews. Written by British historian Richard Holmes, the memorabilia it depicts was drawn from London's Imperial War Museum and North American archives.

With one or more of these overviews under your belt, you may want to move on to books that examine various aspects of D-Day in more detail. There is no lack of options, regardless of your specific interests.

Planning to Invade Fortress Europa

Beyond overviews, numerous books examine specific aspects of

Overlord and the Normandy Campaign. The earliest work on the planning for D-Day, published January 1, 1945, is *We Planned The Second Front. The Inside History of How the Second Front Was Planned*, by Major John Dalgleish of the Royal Army Service Corps. More recent additions include 2014's *Destination D-Day. Preparations for the Invasion of North-West Europe 1944*, by David Rogers, which includes such information as planning an underwater pipeline to get fuel to the beachhead; creating the Mulberry floating harbors; and strategies for supporting the French Resistance.

The Deception

The Allies used deception and misdirection campaigns to convince the Reich's military planners—particularly Hitler—the invasion would come somewhere other than the Cherbourg-Le Havre area and that any Normandy landing would only be a feint. The overall campaign was code-named Bodyguard.

Roger Hesketh wrote *Fortitude; The D-Day Deception Campaign* at the end of the war but held off on publication until 2002. It is a slog rather than a page-turner but contains a tremendous amount of information. *Double Cross: The True Story of the D-Day Spies*, by Ben Macintyre (2012), tells how British intelligence penetrated and used the German spy network in Britain to feed misinformation to German intelligence.

Air Operations

Ken Delve's 2004 book, *D-Day: The Air Battle*, covers planning, training and other preparations, as well as the events of June 1944. *Air War Normandy*, by Richard Townshend Bickers (2015), focuses on the British air effort. The stories of three American and five British aircrews are incorporated into Stephen Darlow's *D-Day Bombers: The Veteran's Story* (2004), re-released in 2010 as *D-Day Bombers: The Stories of Allied Heavy Bombers During the Invasion of Normandy*.

Naval Operations

Getting 160,000 men and their equipment across the English Channel was critical but usually doesn't get the attention the land war does. Code-named Operation Neptune, it involved nearly 7,000 craft, from landing boats to minesweepers to battleships. Some destroyers closed to within 1,000 yards of shore to provide direct fire support for the men on the beach.

Operation Neptune: The Normandy Landings 1944, by Kenneth Edwards, a senior British naval officer, first saw print in 1946, was reprinted in 2013, and an illustrated edition appeared in 2016. It covers the conception, planning and execution of the largest amphibious operation in history. *Operation Neptune 1944: D-Day's Seaborne Armada*, written by Ken Ford and illustrated by Howard Gerrard (2014), provides a very concise 96-page account.

Also in 2014, Oxford University Press published Craig L. Symonds's *Operation Neptune: The D-Day Landings and the Allied Invasion of Europe.* Symonds, professor emeritus of history at the U.S. Naval Academy, employs decades of research to take the story from the first stages of planning through all the naval operations of the D-Day landings. Also available in audio book.

Airborne Operations

Those who have already read Stephen Ambrose's *Band of Brothers: E Company, 506th Regiment, 101st Airborne from Normandy to Hitler's Eagle's Nest* (2001) or watched the HBO miniseries based on it will want to check out *A Company of Heroes: Personal Memories about the Real Band of Brothers and the Legacy They Left Us* (2010). Marcus Brotherton uses interviews with surviving members of Easy Company or with family of those who had already passed to tell the personal stories of the members of that now-famous company of the 101st Airborne.

The 82nd Airborne's story is highlighted in *Down to Earth: The 507th Parachute Infantry Regiment in Normandy*, by Martin K.A. Morgan (2004), which covers the 507th's thirty-five days of combat. British Airborne troops get their due in *Pegasus Bridge and Merville Battery: British 6th Airborne Division Landings in Normandy D-Day 6th June 1944*, by Carl Shilleto (1999), which tells how the men of the 6th Airborne blocked German reinforcements and silenced a major battery; it also serves as a battlefield guide for visiting the area.

D-Day: The Allied Nations

Most books about D-Day, especially those published in the United States, focus heavily on the American experience. To learn more about the other Allied forces of the invasion you might start with *Six Armies in Normandy: From D-Day to the Liberation of Paris; June 6–Aug. 5, 1944*, by John Keegan. First published in 1982 and revised in 1994, it covers American, Canadian, English, French, German and Polish armies, presenting each in its own section rather than following a chronological timeline. *A short story of 21 Army Group: the British and Canadian Armies in the campaigns in North-West Europe, 1944–1945*, by Hugh Darby and Marcus Cunliffe (1949), concisely covers the activities of the battle group that included British, Canadian, and Polish soldiers. *The Resistance: The French Fight Against the Nazis, by Matthew Cobb* (2013), uses hundreds of eyewitness accounts and recently released archival materials to detail the activities of the French Resistance under German occupation.

D-Day: The German Viewpoint

D-Day Through German Eyes – The Hidden Story of June 6th, 1944, by Holger Eckhertz, captures "the longest day" as experienced by German soldiers who manned the Normandy defenses. This was originally two volumes but was combined into a single paperback in 2016. *The Germans in Normandy*, by Richard Hargreaves (2006), examines D-Day and the Normandy Campaign from the perspective of German commanders as well as common soldiers.

First-Hand Accounts

Omaha Beach: D-Day, June 6, 1944, by Joseph Balkoski (2004), has been called the literary accompaniment to the opening scenes of Stephen Spielberg's movie ***Saving Private Ryan***, providing a minute-by-minute account with personal stories interwoven into the narrative. *D-Day: The Campaign Across France*, by Jay Wertz, intersperses interviews and other first-person sources from veterans of both sides with a comprehensive account of the spring and summer of 1944. Published in 2012 as part of the *War Stories: World War II Firsthand*™ series, it includes original 3D maps and other images.

The Silent Day: A Landmark Oral History Of D-Day On The Home Front, by Max Arthur and others (2015), takes an unusual approach in that it uses first-hand accounts to relate the 24 hours in Britain after the invasion forces set sail and the two years that led up to it. Another unusual account is *My Longest Night: A Twelve-Year-Old French Girl's Memories of D-Day*, by Genevieve Duboscq, in which she recalls the night of June 5–6 when Allied paratroopers arrived out of the darkness at her home. Published in France in 1978, it was translated into English in 1981.

Miscellany

The D-Day Atlas: Anatomy of the Normandy Campaign, by Charles Messenger (2014), utilizes 71 computer-enhanced maps to show the planning and execution of D-Day and the Normandy Campaign. *The Normandy Battlefields: D-Day and the Bridgehead*, by Leo Marriott and Simon Forty (2014), uses mixed media to depict the Normandy battlefields today with then-and-now photos and computer artwork. *D-Day Landing Beaches: The Guide*, by Georges Bernage (2009), is intended for those planning a visit to Normandy, but with over 200 photographs, charts and maps, it is also useful for armchair travelers.

Top: A North American P-51 Mustang in flight. The sleek plane was effective in accompanying bombers to targets in Germany and also in dogfights with the Luftwaffe's best fighters. *(Image courtesy of the National Archives and Records Administration Collections)*

Right: General Dwight David Eisenhower at the time of the D-Day invasion. *(Image courtesy of the National Archives and Records Administration Collections)*

Above: British sailors and American GIs train prior to D-Day in LCA landing craft, which had no drop-down ramps. Soldiers had to go over the sides to disembark. *(Image courtesy of the National Archives and Records Administration Collections)*

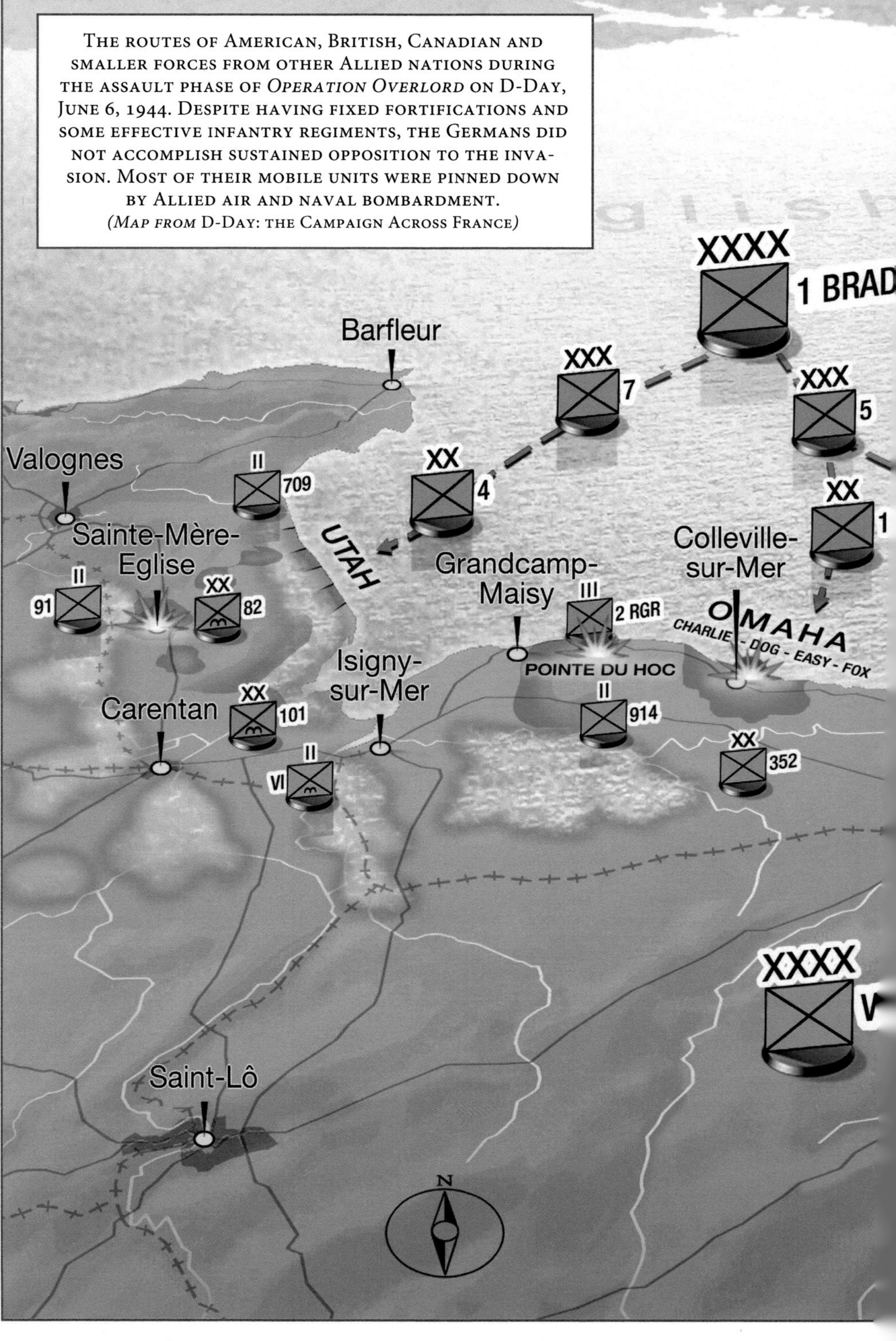

The routes of American, British, Canadian and smaller forces from other Allied nations during the assault phase of *Operation Overlord* on D-Day, June 6, 1944. Despite having fixed fortifications and some effective infantry regiments, the Germans did not accomplish sustained opposition to the invasion. Most of their mobile units were pinned down by Allied air and naval bombardment.
(Map from D-Day: the Campaign Across France*)*

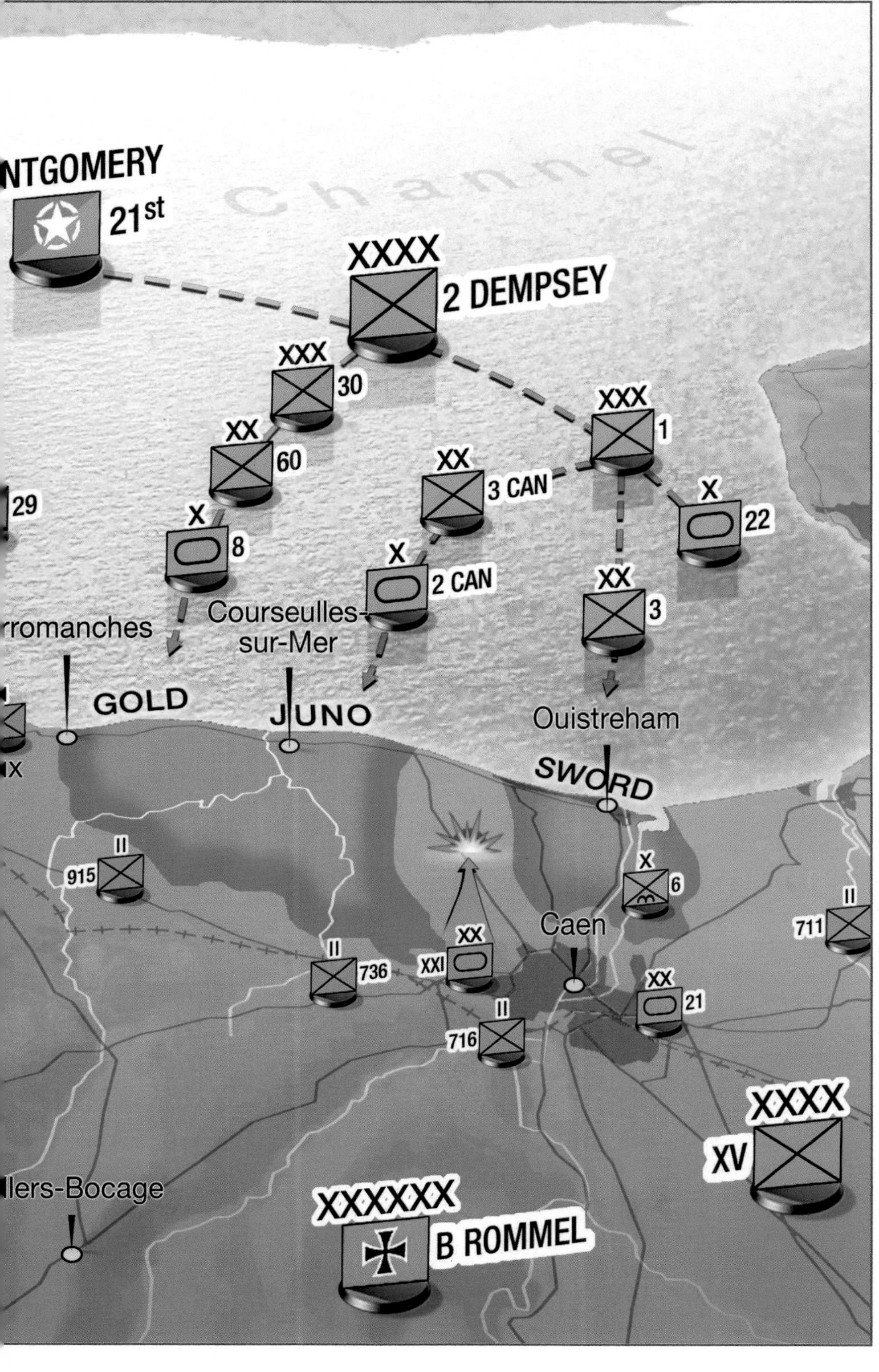

Channel
NTGOMERY
21st
XXXX
2 DEMPSEY
XXX
30
XX
60
X
8
29
XX
3 CAN
XXX
1
X
22
X
2 CAN
XX
3
rromanches
Courseulles-
sur-Mer
GOLD
JUNO
Ouistreham
SWORD
II
915
X
6
II
711
Caen
XX
XXI
II
736
II
716
XX
21
XXXX
XV
llers-Bocage
XXXXXX
B ROMMEL

Left: There are dozens of World War II military vehicles and replicas in private collections in Europe. Owners take to the road for events such as the D-Day 70th Anniversary Commemoration. Here two Allied utility vehicles are parked near the Falaise battlefield. *(Photo by Jay Wertz*

Right: 506th Parachute Infantry Regiment "Easy Company" veteran Earl "One Lung" McClung and Stephen Ambrose Historical Tours guide and historian Chris Anderson at a battlefield site in Europe. *(Photo courtesy of Christopher J. Anderson)*

Above: Historian and WWII veteran Ed Bearss holds a folded American flag during a guided tour of the Normandy American Cemetery. The cemetery was the location of the opening and closing scenes of *Saving Private Ryan*. *(Photo by Robert Desourdis)*

Above: The town church of St.-Mère-Église. The white parachute material on the steeple symbolizes where the 82nd Airborne's Pvt. John M. Steele was trapped by a tangled chute. He was quickly rescued.

Left: The beautiful nave of the church where regular services are still conducted. *(Photos by Jay Wertz)*

Above: Cast members of *Saving Private Ryan.* Front row from left to right: Barry Pepper (Pvt. Jackson), Tom Hanks (Capt. Miller), Tom Sizemore (Sgt. Horvath), Edward Burns (Pvt. Reiben), Dale Dye (War Dept. Col. and Senior Military Advisor), Vin Diesel (Pvt. Caparzo), Adam Goldberg (Pvt. Mellish), Giovanni Ribisi (T-4 Medic Wade) and Jeremy Davies (Cpl. Upham). Back row: John Barnett and Laird Macintosh, soldiers on the beach and assistant military advisors. *(Image courtesy of Dreamworks LLC/Paramount Pictures)*

Left: Historian Ed Bearss inspects the famous World War II German fortified artillery piece at Longues-sur-Mer. The battery was a key part of the German Atlantic Wall defenses overlooking the Normandy beaches. *(Photo by Robert Desourdis)*

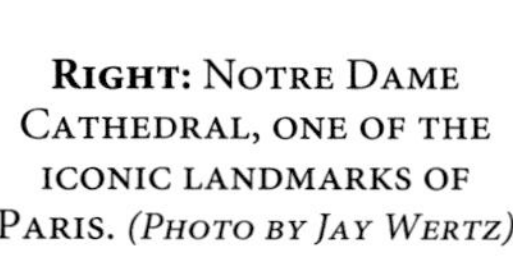

Right: Notre Dame Cathedral, one of the iconic landmarks of Paris. *(Photo by Jay Wertz)*

Above: Aisne-Marne American Cemetery, Belleau, France. This cemetery contains the graves of 2,289 war dead of the American Expeditionary Forces, most of whom fought in the vicinity and in the Marne valley in the spring and summer of 1918. *(Image courtesy of The American Battle Monuments Commission)*

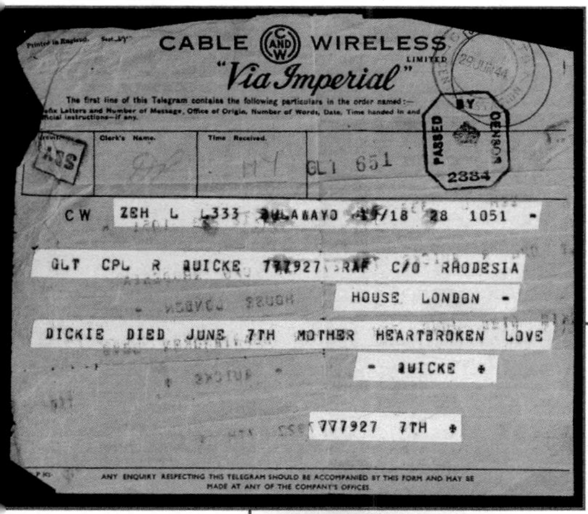

CABLE AND WIRELESS LIMITED

"Via Imperial"

The first line of this Telegram contains the following particulars in the order named:— Prefix Letters and Number of Message, Office of Origin, Number of Words, Date, Time handed in and Official instructions—if any.

Clerk's Name. Time Received.

GLT 651

PASSED BY CENSOR 2334

CW ZEH L L333 BULAWAYO 17/18 28 1051 -

GLT CPL R QUICKE 777927 RAF C/O RHODESIA

HOUSE LONDON -

DICKIE DIED JUNE 7TH MOTHER HEARTBROKEN LOVE

- QUICKE +

777927 7TH +

ANY ENQUIRY RESPECTING THIS TELEGRAM SHOULD BE ACCOMPANIED BY THIS FORM AND MAY BE MADE AT ANY OF THE COMPANY'S OFFICES.

Left: Telegram sent to Cpl. Rolly Quicke informing him of the death of his school friend Andrew 'Dickie' Dickinson, a Lieutenant in the 2nd Battalion, East Yorkshire Regiment. Dickinson was wounded on Sword Beach on D-Day and killed the next day when the ship returning him to the UK was bombed. *(Artifact courtesy of The D-Day Story museum, Portsmouth, UK)*

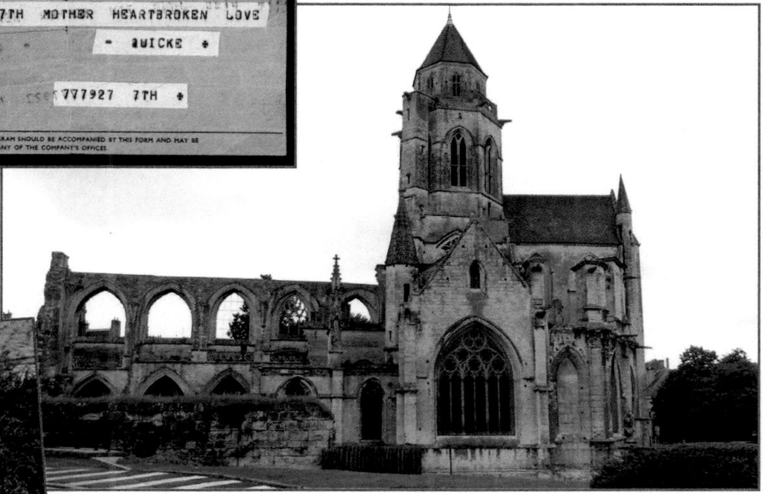

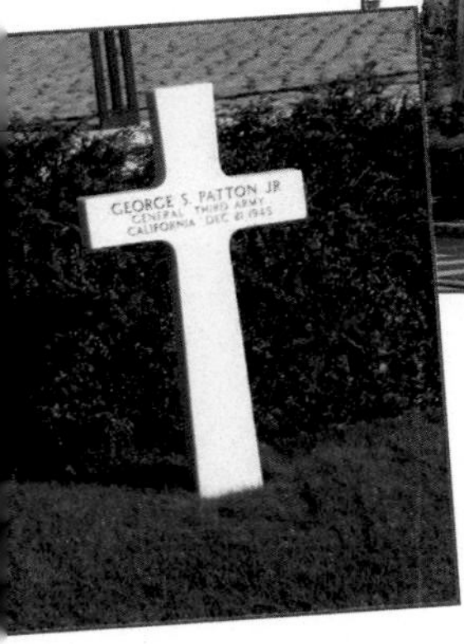

Above: This church in the Norman city of Caen survived intense Allied bombing and fighting between British and German forces, June-July, 1944.
(Photo by Jay Wertz)

Left: The grave marker for General George S. Patton at Luxembourg American Cemetery and Memorial.
(Photo by Robert Desourdis)

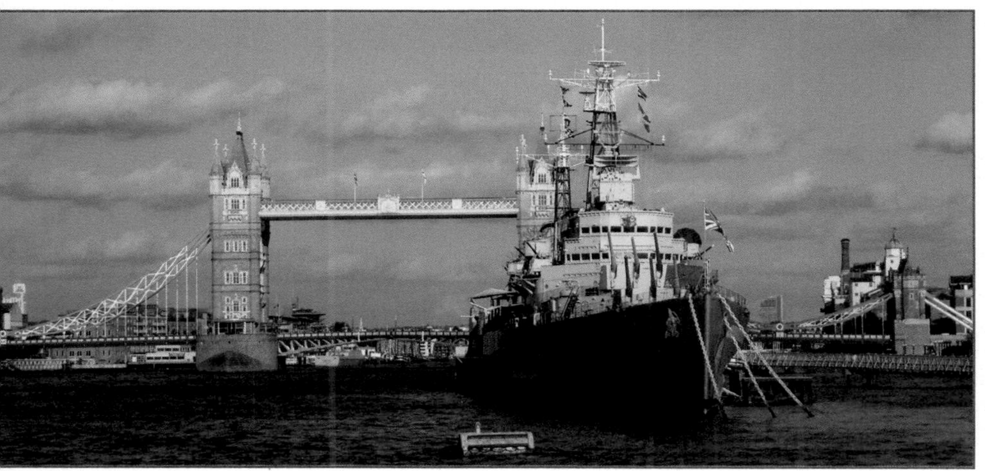

Above: A modern navy warship is pictured here docked near London's Famous Tower Bridge in 2014. *(Photo by Jay Wertz)*

Right: A World War II battle in miniature being fought as a table-top game at the Historicon miniatures gaming convention. *(Photo by Gerald Swick)*

Top left: President Barack Obama addresses World War II veterans, spectators and a worldwide TV audience from the semicircular colonnade at the Normandy American Cemetery during the 2014 D-Day 70th Anniversary Commemoration.
(From a digital recording of the event by Jay Wertz)

Right: The bronze statue, *The Spirit of American Youth Rising from the Waves* at Normandy American Cemetery
(Photo by Robert Desourdis)

Above: Normandy American Cemetery, Colleville-sur-Mer, France. This cemetery contains the graves of 9,386 American war dead, most of whom lost their lives in the D-Day landings and subsequent hedgerow fighting. *(Image courtesy of The American Battle Monuments Commission)*

D-Day Films & Television

Jay Wertz

From the moment the first shots were fired in World War II, cameras were there to record the action. They produced moving pictures with sound—an upgrade over the silent motion picture shots documenting World War I. And only a short time later scriptwriters began working on screenplays to tell the stories of the greatest period of violence the world has ever known. World War II has been the most popular subject for dramatic interpretation of war ever since. The cross-Channel invasion, *Operation Overlord*—most popularly known as D-Day—and the campaign across France that it began have been among the most popular subjects for World War II cinema.

There is nothing in the cinema quite like the action, desperation, pathos and raw human emotion exhibited in war movies. Those qualities are all in evidence in this selected list of scripted cinematic and television interpretations of D-Day. There are, of course, many documentaries of the invasion and the campaign. Most documentary collections of World War II—from the 1950s classic ***Victory at Sea*** and the BBC's ***The World at War***, to the much more recent ***Patton 360*** and ***World War II in Colour*** series—have segments on the campaign. There are also many individual documentaries about D-Day. A listing of documentaries is available on the *D-Day 75th Anniversary—A Millennials Guide* **Readers Only** website. See the back of the book for access.

The Classics

The Longest Day (1962) – In an effort to compete with television, the 1950s and early 1960s were the era of the epic picture in Hollywood. These were big spectacles, often based on historic subjects, using new wide screen camera technology, huge star-studded casts, hundreds of extras and flashy pyrotechnics. None was bigger than ***The Longest Day***, based on the historic novel by Cornelius Ryan, who also wrote the screenplay. The story tells all the key events leading up to the execution of *Operation Overlord* as well as all the action of June 6, 1944. It is filmmaking on a grand scale, commensurate with the story being told.

The principal cast and crew of the Darryl F. Zanuck production are too numerous to mention here (there were five directors) but among the stars in the film were John Wayne, Henry Fonda, Robert Mitchum, Richard

Burton and Sean Connery. Some of the actors who appeared in the film, including Eddie Albert, Henry Fonda and Richard Burton, were World War II combat veterans themselves. Oscars were handed out for Best Cinematography and Special Effects. Among the many movie extras (now called movie atmosphere) charging ashore in the spectacular master shots of the beaches were U. S. Marines. More on the use of Marines in the making of the film follows this sub-chapter. Most of the film was shot on locations in Europe, including Pointe du Hoc on the Normandy coast, where during the war U.S. Army Rangers scaled the cliffs to capture a German artillery battery. ***The Longest Day*** is one of the best war films of any era.

Saving Private Ryan (1998) – The magnificent Steven Spielberg film starring Tom Hanks was famously snubbed at the 1999 Oscars ceremony in the Best Picture category, losing to the romantic comedy-drama ***Shakespeare in Love***. Still the multi-award winning film took home Oscars for Best Director, Cinematography, Film Editing, Sound and Sound Design/ Effects Editing. With its clever fact-based storyline, brutal action scenes, compelling cast and powerful message, is a favorite of a broad spectrum of movie audiences. Stories from the making of the film and an interview with the principal military advisor, Captain Dale Dye, appear later in this part.

Other Theatrical Movies

Overlord (1975) – This British film was shot in black & white, allowing for the integration of World War II combat and archival footage throughout the movie. The director spent three years at London's Imperial War Museum, which assisted in the production, looking through World War II clips to make selections for the movie. Cinematographer John Alcott, a favorite of director Stanley Kubrick, manipulated film stock and processing to achieve a seamless match to the wartime footage. The dramatic use of sound enhances the impact. Laid on this big canvas is a very personal story.

Brian Stirnir plays Tom, a young recruit called up as an infantryman before D-Day. He is not a remarkable character, but an average English boy who goes through the challenges of training, writes to his parents, worries about his dog back home, meets a girl on leave and prepares to die in D-Day's assault wave. Only first names or descriptions of characters are given, making it a universal tale of so many who fought and often died on the beaches of France. A recent 35mm restoration of ***Overlord*** has appeared on the festival circuit, giving viewers an option beyond digital access.

The Big Red One (1980) – Samuel Fuller, a former journalist and pulp novel writer, enlisted in the US Army in World War II and landed at

Omaha Beach as a member of the 16th Regiment, 1st Infantry Division. In the 40s and 50s he wrote and directed a number of movies in Hollywood, mostly military dramas and low budget films on controversial subjects. But over the years he became disillusioned with the studios. He wrote and directed only a handful of projects, mostly TV, in the 60s and 70s. In 1980 he resurrected a film that had been shelved for two decades at Warner Brothers, the landmark, semi-autobiographical ***The Big Red One***. The motion picture was financed by major independent Lorimar, which had a distribution deal with Warners.

The title comes from the insignia for the army's 1st Infantry Division, a red Arabic "1" on a brown field which appears on uniforms and equipment. ***The Big Red One*** follows Sergeant Possum (Lee Marvin), Griff (Mark Hamill—Luke Skywalker of ***Star Wars***), Zab, the character based on Fuller (Robert Carradine), and two others in his squad who survive from the division's first actions in North Africa, through the Sicily Campaign, the D-Day invasion, across France and Germany, and end the war by liberating a concentration camp in the former Czechoslovakia.

Little is revealed about Possum, an army lifer played with appropriate toughness and common sense by Marvin, a World War II Marine. There is some reference to an incident during World War I in which Possum as a private had a life-altering experience, but mostly his character is played out in one curious or violent event after another. This was Fuller's attitude toward war—that it is a series of unconnected events where survival is paramount. Hence, the film plays out in episodes, rather than a building to one big climax. Even the Omaha Beach landing scene lacks a grand scope because Fuller insisted the feelings of those soldiers were that they were landing by themselves, not in the company of 10,000 others. The soldier, the squad, the survival. That was Fuller's focus.

At $4 million, it was a low-budget film for the time but every penny went on the screen. Though Fuller was disheartened the four-and-a-half-hour film he made was cut to 113 minutes for the premiere, he always planned to release a longer version. He didn't live to see that happen but film critic Richard Schickel oversaw a reconstruction of the movie to 158 minutes. That version is available today.

Eye of the Needle (1981) – Ken Follett's novel of suspense and forbidden romance set in the British Isles of 1944 is brought to the screen on the strength of its principal characters, Faber (the "Needle"), played by Donald Sutherland and Lucy, played by Kate Nelligan. Faber is a bitter and ruthless German spy, deeply embedded in wartime England, who has uncovered the ruse of the phony cross-Channel invasion plans to make the Germans think the Allies would land at Pas de Calais. He must get the message of the true invasion destination of Normandy personally to Hitler, but on his way to rendezvous with the submarine that is to take him to Germany a storm off the Scottish Coast shipwrecks him, leaving him stranded on desolate Storm Island. Among the island's four inhabitants are an embittered former RAF trainee who lost the use of his legs in a car crash and his alluring wife, Lucy. Once the film settles into the bleak confines of Storm Island it takes on an aura of sexual tension and dark, foreboding suspense reminiscent of some Alfred Hitchcock films.

The War I Knew (2014) – This direct-to-consumer UK film depicts the experience of a British paratrooper, Private Johnny Barrows (played by Paul Harrison), who is the sole survivor of a D-Day Airborne squad accidentally dropped behind enemy lines. Alone and scared, he manages to avoid German capture as he crosses the French countryside, looking for a way back to friendly forces. He eventually meets with a trio of other misplaced Allied soldiers whose personalities and recent experiences make them an unreliable team. On the way to find their own lines, they capture a German SS officer, interact with French civilians and fight their way out of an ambush. Known in the UK as ***D-Day Survivor***, below average production values and a predictable storyline make this at best a character study of the pressures of war and combat.

Overlord (2018) – J. J. Abrams is a Millennial producer/director who uses tons of computer generated imagery (CGI) to make action, science fiction and fantasy movies. *Overlord* starts off with a compelling and realistic sequence of the jump of paratroopers of the 101st Airborne on the eve of D-Day (realistic except for the African-American paratrooper who plays one of the lead characters—American military units were segregated until the Korean War—and the majority of the CGI scenes involving the transport planes). After that, the storyline and action sequences quickly turn into pure fantasy. A four-man squad stumbles upon a church turned into a zombie-Nazi mill producing superhuman soldiers. Taking on French civilians as allies, the "Screaming Eagles" must fight their way out of the village infested with these undead Nazi brutes. Watch the beginning and then remain only if you are into those kinds of well-worn zombie antics.

Television

Combat! (series: 1962–67) – This gritty, black-and-white, ABC series starring Vic Morrow and Rick Jason helped interest many "baby boomer" kids, myself included, in World War II. ***Combat!*** introduced Sergeant Saunders (Morrow), Lieutenant Hanley (Jason) and their infantry squad to all kinds of characters, friend and foe, as they fought their way across France from Normandy to the eastern border. It was a magnet for established and up-and-coming acting talent. Many in Hollywood, from experienced performers James Coburn and Mickey Rooney to newcomers Tom Skerritt, Ted Knight and Robert Duvall, sought guest appearances on the show. There was always tension—danger literally appearing around the street corners in French villages—as well as plenty of military and human problems for Saunders and his squad to face in the field. It's a well-crafted series – each commercial TV hour-long episode has plenty of drama and action. On Episode 11 of Season 1 Saunders relives his D-Day landing experience in a flashback story told to his squad. ***Combat!*** is available in DVD sets.

War and Remembrance (miniseries: 1988–89) – ***War and Remembrance*** is the second miniseries based on and named for two World War II novels by Herman Wouk. The first was ***The Winds of War*** (1983). Both of these big budget "made for TV novels" were produced by Dan Curtis Productions and aired on ABC at a time when the three major television networks saw motion pictures as their chief competition, rather than the emerging cable networks. Wouk has misgivings about committing his two lengthy and detailed works to the television format but Curtis and studio executives convinced him to do so and he agreed, with certain stipulations and a hand in the writing of the teleplays. The saga follows the extended family of U.S. naval attaché Captain Victor "Pug" Henry (Robert Mitchum), who as a friend and confidant of President Franklin Roosevelt comes into contact with the leaders of the explosive situation of the late 1930s. At the same time Henry's younger son meets a Jewish girl in Rome and brings her extended and persecuted family into the story.

The Winds of War ends with the Japanese attack on Pearl Harbor. ***War and Remembrance***, with a much larger budget and more episodes, follows the story until the end of the war. Episode IX covers the period from May 16 to June 10, 1944 and therefore covers the D-Day landing. While "Pug" appears in the episode, as do Natalie Jastrow Henry (Jane Seymour) and other principal characters, the part of the episode devoted to the invasion and pre-invasion period features characters secondary to the principal storyline, but primary to the history of the invasion. These include General Eisenhower (E. G. Marshall) and other leaders at Southwick House and Eisenhower later visiting the 101st Airborne Division assembly field; Field Marshall Erwin Rommel (Hardy Krüger) at his French headquarters and home; and President Franklin D. Roosevelt (Ralph Bellamy) in the White House. The D-Day invasion is shown as a mix of newsreel film and staged shots filmed in black & white as FDR reads his national address on D-Day in voice-over.

Even without following the storyline of the principal characters and viewing all 19 episodes of the two-parter, Episode IX gives a fine dramatic view of the history taking place beyond the beaches of Normandy.

Band of Brothers

(HBO limited series: 2001)

With the completion of ***Saving Private Ryan***, Steven Spielberg and Tom Hanks were not finished teaming up on World War II projects. In fact, they were just beginning. The historical period and people involved were drawing them into telling those compelling stories. Several years after ***Saving Private Ryan*** had a very successful run in the theaters, they took a screen adaptation of Stephen E. Ambrose's *Band of Brothers* nonfiction account of the 101st Airborne's Easy Company, 506th Parachute Infantry Regiment, to HBO. The premium cable channel was then developing dramatic series that would extend over multiple episodes. ***Band of Brothers*** was a project too good to pass up.

While the storylines focus on lieutenants Richard D. Winters (Damien Lewis), Donald G. Malarky (Scott Grimes) and their platoons, there are many scenes and sequences involving the company as a whole, as well as the major action scenes, like the transports flying to Normandy, that encompass the entire division. Once on the ground in the Cotentin Peninsula the paratroopers lose unit identity. It is the job of Winters and other officers on the ground to gather the scattered airborne troops together to seek out their objectives.

The first three episodes of the series involve *Operation Overlord*. In Episode 1, "Currahee," Winters and Malarky reminisce about their training in Georgia and England in a flashback while awaiting the big D-Day jump. Episode 2, "Day of Days," covers the last few days before D-Day, the flight of the company and other paratroopers to France in C-47 transports and the initial hours on the ground. It features Major Richard D. Winters on camera. Episode 3, "Carentan" chronicles the first big mission – taking the key objective city of Carentan to open the beach exits for the landing forces. The other seven episodes in the series take the unit through the other missions they are assigned to, *Operation Market Garden* and at Bastogne during the Battle of the Bulge, as well as the rest of their experiences in Europe, through the German surrender and the unknowns of their expected re-assignment to the invasion of Japan.

Watch or re-watch Episodes 2 and 3, then read the chapter "In the Footsteps of Heroes: Touring Dick Winters's Day of Days" in *D-Day 75th Anniversary—A Millennials Guide*. If you are in France for the D-Day ceremonies or at any other time, take the tour of historic Normandy from the perspective of Easy Company paratroopers that author Chris Anderson describes in the chapter.

Ike: Countdown to D-Day (2004) – Veteran television and occasional movie actor Tom Selleck takes on the role of General Dwight D. Eisenhower in the dramatic biography made by A&E Television Networks. The story focuses on the preparations for D-Day, the planning and organizational skills exhibited by Ike as he works with his staff and mostly, his tactful handling of the high-ranking Allied officers and political leaders he has to interface with. Selleck's performance has received excellent reviews. The entire production was filmed in New Zealand but with a lack of combat action and sweeping panorama shots, it works.

Into the Storm (2009) – HBO Films in conjunction with the BBC produced a two-part biography of Winston Churchill. ***The Gathering Storm*** (2002) starred Albert Finney and covered the period of the 1930s during Churchill's rise as a chief critic of Adolf Hitler. ***Into the Storm*** stars Brendan Gleeson, who first gained international attention as William Wallace's (Mel Gibson) chief lieutenant, Hamish, in ***Braveheart***. ***Into the Storm*** picks up Churchill's story during his critical years at prime minister of Great Britain and his postwar political and personal life once the sheen of being Britain's savior began to wear thin. Included are scenes showing Churchill's lively discussions with the leaders of *Operation Overlord*. Gleeson is among the best who have portrayed the legendary British politician and statesman; his performance won a Primetime Emmy for Outstanding Lead Actor in a Miniseries or a Movie.

Storming Juno (2010) – Despite having a strong documentary tradition, the Canadian film industry has always operated in the shadow of Hollywood. In 2010 by combining those documentary techniques with American style storytelling, a Canadian company produced ***Storming Juno***, starring Benjamin Muir. It is the under-told story of the Canadian assault of June 6, 1944 on Juno Beach. The action and short character vignettes in the scripted portion of this TV film are quite well done. These are combined with archival footage and interviews with surviving veterans of the landing to make an interesting docu-drama. Every Allied force on D-Day had its objectives and made its sacrifices. It is important that the story of each and everyone be remembered and told.

Rommel (2012) – This German TV production was picked up for US distribution in 2017 by Samuel Goldwyn Films. It focuses primarily on the period of time after the Fürher promoted Erwin Rommel to the rank of field marshal and assigned him to the task of making the Atlantic Wall a strong defense against an Allied invasion of Western Europe. It takes the story through the accusations of complicity with the July 1944 assassination attempt of Hitler and the resulting demise of Rommel's career and life. Though the program is subtitled in English, it's easy to see the strength of the characterization of Rommel by German actor Ulrich Tukur and the overall strengths of the production. Rommel has remained the most popular subject for biopics of all Hitler's lieutenants.

SEND IN THE MARINES!

No American Marines stormed ashore on D-Day, but they did in the movie ***The Longest Day***. After World War II U.S. Marines continued to specialize in preparing for amphibious landings while the Army increasingly focused its assault tactics on the use of planes and helicopters. In March 1943 Army Ground Forces had been relieved of all responsibility for Army amphibious training, under an agreement with the Navy.

In the late spring and early summer of 1961 the 3/6 BLT—Battalion Landing Team of the 3rd Battalion, 6th Marine Regiment—and the U. S. Navy's 6th Fleet were on training exercises in the Mediterranean when the producers of ***The Longest Day*** were to film the beach landing scenes. It provided a rare opportunity to combine Navy and Marine Corps training exercises with filming a Hollywood movie.

From June 21 to June 30, 1961, Marines were involved in the film's rehearsals, as well as staging beach obstacles and scenery. The invasion scenes were filmed near Saint Florent on the north coast of Corsica, an island off southern France. To represent the D-Day armada the 6th Fleet was filmed performing its maneuvers, but this presented a problem: the fleet's aircraft carrier had to be kept out of any shots because no carriers were present at D-Day.

In addition to the nameless "soldiers" debarking from landing craft to hit the beach (one of whom, Howard Swick, was the oldest brother of this book's executive editor, Gerald Swick), some Marines were used in additional scenes as extras. One of them, Staff Sergeant Kenneth H. Long, played an Army major. For more than 50 years he kept the insignia he wore for the part until donating the items to the National Museum of the Marine Corps in Triangle, Virginia.

The Longest Day Marines were part of 23,000 American, British and French troops used in the filming.

D-Day Games

Gerald D. Swick

Reading books or watching documentaries and movies about historical battles often lead to an interest in games on the subject, in which players can try out their own "what-if" strategies. The question wargamers hear most often is, "Do you have to do the same thing that was done historically?"

Absolutely not! The games simulate a historical situation in which players are free to try a variety of strategies and tactics.

There is no lack of options for gaming D-Day, from traditional board-and-cardboard-counters wargames to electronic games ranging from "you are the overall commander" to "you-are-there" first- or third-person shooters.

Each game type has its own advantages and disadvantages. Tabletop games—board games and historical miniatures—require more time to set up and play, and gamers have to keep track of the rules themselves. But these games often provide a better understanding of the historical situation, there's no glitchy AI, and games don't become unplayable because of advances in tech operating systems; the game you enjoy at 15 is still just as playable when you're 50.

Electronic versions require no setup, the software keeps track of the rules, and gameplay generally goes faster. First- or third-person shooters provide an immersive, real-time, sensory involvement, and you can go online for a multiplayer experience. Shooters tend to reward reaction time over real-world tactics, however, and a favorite game may be left behind as operating systems stop supporting older technology.

Tabletop D-Day Games—Board Games

If you've never played board wargames but would like to try some you might consider **Axis & Allies D-Day** from Avalon Hill (part of the Hasbro family of game companies). A variant of the best-selling **Axis & Allies** game that covers all of World War II, **A&A D-Day** is shorter and simpler because of its limited scope and use of cards. Three-dimensional, plastic playing pieces make it a better visual and tactile experience than traditional cardboard-counter wargames.

D-Day (3rd Edition), also from Avalon Hill, offers simple rules, and it is easy to play solitaire if you don't have an opponent to play the game with. Despite its title, *D-Day* actually covers WWII in France from the D-Day invasion to crossing the Rhine. Now out of print, used copies are easy to find. Search online for "used wargames."

Dog Sector from White Dog Games challenges the player to clear obstacles and capture German positions on a generic section of Omaha Beach. (The beach was divided into 10 alphabetically named sub-sectors, from "Charlie" to "Fox Red." The game's title is a reference to the Dog Green, Dog White, and Dog Red sub-sectors. Dog Green is the area depicted in the opening scenes of *Saving Private Ryan.*) It is designed to be played solitaire and is what is known in the hobby as a "beer-and-pretzels" game: not very complex, requiring only a short time to play (about 90 minutes in this case), but still tactically satisfying.

D-Day at Omaha Beach (Decision Games) is another solitaire game although two players can split the American forces between them. More complex than **Dog Sector**, it effectively reflects the confusion on all of Omaha Beach. Card draws generate random events such as which beach sector gets hit by German artillery this turn or a hero emerging to aid American forces.

Frontline D-Day (Dan Verssen Games) puts you in command of a U.S., UK or German squad. Instead of using a mapboard, players lay out cards depicting terrain, not unlike the tile system in the popular *Settlers of Catan* game. Other cards represent individual soldiers or vehicles, each with its own statistics for firepower, morale, etc. You activate soldiers/vehicles by playing Action Cards from your hand. The more terrain you control, the more Action Cards you get. Playable by up to four people, the game comes with a solitaire deck with scripted actions for the opposing side.

Gaming D-Day with Historical Miniatures

Historical miniatures wargames—from which the *Dungeons & Dragons* game was born—use hand-painted figures (affectionately known as "toy soljers") and simulated terrain (think of model railroad layouts) to create an experience similar to Games Workshop's *Warhammer* or *Warhammer 40,000* fantasy and science fiction miniatures games. Several companies have published books filled with D-Day scenarios for miniatures, including Flames of War, Bolt Action, and Iron Fist Publishing.

You don't need to own figures or terrain to try these games; newcomers are welcome to drop in during game days at local stores or at conventions. Type "historical miniatures game clubs" and your location into a search engine or create an account at the Historical Miniatures Gaming Society website and use their database to find groups and conventions around the world.

Electronic D-Day Games

World War II games were once a staple of electronic wargaming, but their popularity faded in the twenty-first century's second decade. In 2018, however, two new console games set in the European Theater were released, possibly signaling renewed interest in gaming WWII.

D-Day Games for Console Gaming

The initial scenario of **Call of Duty: WWII** (2018, Sledgehammer Games) sees Private "Red" Daniels leading his squad ashore to capture fortifications on D-Day before moving on to battle their way across Europe. You also get to take on the identity of soldiers other than Daniels to drive a tank or fly a plane.

Battlefield 5 (2018, DICE) lets you create and customize your company of soldiers, weapons and vehicles. The initial release did not include any D-Day scenarios because Battlefront plans to release WWII campaigns in historic chronology, and when *D-Day, 75th Anniversary: A Millennials Guide* was being written it was not yet 1944 in DICEland.

Computer D-Day Games

In **Panzer Battles Normandy** from John Tiller Software (which has developed numerous simulations for the U.S. military) selecting a stack of board game–like counters brings up a sidebar with the names of the units in that stack, how many men each unit has left and their level of morale and fatigue.

Two computer game companies that merged to form the Slitherine Group in 2010—Slitherine Ltd. in the UK and Matrix Games in the U.S.—continue to "dance with the one what brung them," specializing in award-winning, old-school, top-down-view wargames that emphasize tactical planning over the run-and-gun approach of many console games. Accordingly, game graphics look more like board games than the you-are-there views of first- or third-person shooters. Some are available for iOS and/or for console gaming with multiplayer capability. A few of their options for D-Day games include:

Heroes of Normandie. Play small squads in one of three armies or the French Resistance in a fast-paced game that mixes good tactical decision-making with the feel of a Hollywood B-movie. Graphics are deliberately cartoonish in keeping with the game's attitude.

Battle Academy. Military historian and wargamer Professor John Buckley was involved in creating a realistic AI for this series. You can be part of the British, Canadian, Polish or U.S. forces in the original game or explore the German options with the expansion **Rommel in Normandy**.

The **Close Combat** system has two separate games for PC, **The Longest Day** (originally **Invasion Normandy**) and **Gateway to Caen**. In this platoon/company game your troops may disobey orders if you push them too far or too fast.

iOS D-Day Games

Frontline Commando: D-Day (Glu Games, Inc.) is a third-person shooter with multiplayer capability that comes with 145 single-player missions using movie-style graphics, set on all the D-Day beaches. World War II trivia factoids appear between mission-loading screens.

Tank Battle: Normandy (HexWar Games Ltd.) is a tactical game that allows you to control U.S., UK or German troops, depending on which of its 23 missions is being played. Units and the 3D terrain are viewed from above, reminiscent of board games. Not as visually appealing as FPS or TPS games, **TB Normandy** is an inexpensive ($1.99 at this writing) but engaging intro to D-Day gaming.

The titles listed here represent some of the best entry-level games on D-Day for players with little or no experience in the hobby of wargaming. There are dozens of other games that explore more complex aspects such as supply levels, individual leaders' abilities, and so on. Your local game store can help you find whatever depth of simulation you desire.

D-Day Memorabilia

Gerald D. Swick

Anyone who has seen *Antique Roadshow* on television knows a lot of people like to collect stuff. Some think they can "cash in" on some unusual item from the past, but most people do it for their own enjoyment. World War II items are among the most popular and accessible memorabilia, giving collectors the ability to touch the history; to perhaps hold in their hands an artifact that witnessed the events of D-Day. And while collecting artifacts of history is an enjoyable and educational hobby, traversing the memorabilia marketplace of estate sales, auctions, pawn shops and the internet can be an economic minefield, especially for those just starting to build a collection.

First, a clarification: *memorabilia* is any object of historical interest, especially items associated with a historic figure or event. It can include period clothing, military medals, letters between a soldier and his wife, photographs, cartoons, posters, old newspapers and magazines—basically, anything that is representative of a historic person, event or era. *Militaria* is a subgroup of memorabilia specifically related to the military: uniforms, medals, weapons, vehicles, etc. If you are starting a collection, decide what most excites you and focus on that, be it military weapons or women's hats.

It is not unusual for someone to start buying "old stuff" as an investment, expecting to sell it for a nice profit someday. The reality is that age alone doesn't make something valuable. You can buy coins from Ancient Rome for under ten bucks.

Generally, value is determined by scarcity or by close association to a well-known person or event. In 2016 a U.S. flag that flew on the stern of a boat that carried troops to Utah Beach sold for $125,000. A button from the uniform of one of the men it carried, however, might bring only a couple of dollars on eBay, because millions of uniforms were issued.

In an interview quoted in "10 Most Worthless Pieces of Military Memorabilia," Kenneth W. Rendell, founder and director of the International Museum of World War II in Natick, Massachusetts, said, "anything connected to the Rangers, the Airborne or the Marines" commands a higher price than a standard military uniform because "There's a romance associated with these elite forces that makes their uniforms and equipment particularly desirable to collectors." (Written by Jason Notte, the article appeared in *The Street*, September 11, 2017, and was updated November 12 of the same year.)

Rendell also observed, "American soldiers saved so much of their gear that most U.S. uniform items, helmets and the like are not especially rare and sell for $125 or less." On the other hand, "A standard German army helmet could bring $500 to $1,000. A German *SS* helmet might sell for $4,000 to $7,000."

For years many militaria dealers kept values secret, hoping to pick up items from veterans and their families for far less than the items were worth to collectors, wrote long-time collector John Adams-Graf. In his book *Warman's World War II Collectible Identification and Price Guide* (Krause Publications, 3rd edition, 2014), Adams-Graf suggested that practice tainted militaria collecting's image. Now, he says, sellers and buyers can view online auctions and get an idea of what price specific items fetch—but a little information can be dangerous. Apart from scarcity and historical connection, differences in manufacturing, materials used, special markings, and other variables affect an item's value. Learning the nuances of your favored niche among memorabilia will require a great deal of time and research. Flipping through a price guide won't do it.

Remember that minefield mentioned in the first paragraph? It is loaded not only with variables in value but with fakers and fakes. In any city in Vietnam you can buy "authentic" American dogtags supposedly found in the countryside. In fact, you can even buy superstar Elvis Presley's "found" dogtag—but Presley never served in Vietnam. (Elvis's Army service was in Germany 1958–1960.) Treating newly manufactured items with acid to give them an aged appearance is only one of the tricks employed by professional hucksters.

A private seller may truly believe he or she is selling the genuine article, but it is actually a reproduction. Many people with dollar signs dancing in their eyes have been disappointed to learn that the July 2/4, 1863, edition of the Vicksburg, Mississippi, *Citizen* newspaper printed on wallpaper that they found among grandma's things isn't a valuable artifact. In almost all cases, it is a reproduction printed for Grand Army of the Republic reunions in the 1870s, or more likely one that was sold as a souvenir in 20th century Vicksburg. Sometimes, though, actual artifacts can lay undetected among a family's keepsakes. An authentic and quite valuable 184-year-old copy of the Declaration of Independence was purchased for $2.48 after it was donated to a Nashville thrift store in 2007.

So how do you navigate the minefield? Carefully. Very carefully. Look for organizations dedicated to the type of memorabilia you wish to collect and join them to glean advice from more experienced collectors—and to spend time with people who share your particular passion.

An *Elite Militaria* blog, December 2, 2012, (elitemilitaria.com/blog/) titled "Detecting Fake and Reproduction Militaria" offers some excellent advice for protecting yourself, such as checking out a seller's trading history, length of time the seller has been selling online, and feedback from previous buyers. Only buy from a seller who will give a full refund if you are dissatisfied after receiving the article.

So what are some D-Day artifacts other than uniforms and equipment or letters and diaries? A "Rupert," one of the dummies airdropped to confuse the Germans, sold for nearly $4,000 in 2002, but that was less than half of what was bid for an Omaha Beach medical officer's ensemble in 2013. Also in 2013 a "Holy Grail" of D-Day, a set of the complete plans for *Operation Overlord*, once owned by an assistant to U.S. lieutenant general Omar Bradley, sold at auction for $62,500.

The chances of stumbling across such desirable items are slim, but memorabilia collecting shouldn't be just about money. A renowned collector, Hayes Otoupalik, in an interview by Mike Eppinger for *Military Trader* magazine, published online December 11, 2017, (militarytrader.com/military-trader/10-questions-hayes-otoupalik) perhaps said it best:

"In the end, none of us will take a penny off this planet earth . . . It is all about finding the materiel good homes with museums and collectors who will appreciate its history. That is what is important."

D-Day Annual Events

Gerald D. Swick

"Big number" anniversaries get attention. Events large and small in Europe and North America will mark D-Day's 75th anniversary, as they did in 1994 on the 50th, 2004 on the 60th and 2014 on the 70th (all of which were attended by U.S. presidents and other world leaders in office at the time). See D-Day Calendar of Events later in this section for a list of events for the 75th anniversary.

But what D-Day meant to the world isn't just important every 75 or 50 or even every five years. It was a critical moment in world history, and annual observances take place in remembrance. Any year you want to commemorate the sacrifices and success of D-Day, while taking part in fun and educational activities, you can find plenty of offerings. Here are a few of the annual events you might consider. Not all are held around June 6; check websites for the current year's scheduled dates.

D-Day Festival Normandy takes place near the area of the landings. Since its beginning in 2007 the festivities and observances have grown to over 100 events during the festival, including parachute demonstrations, fireworks, giant picnics, military vehicle parades, book fairs, and dances. For current information, go to bayeux-bessin-tourisme.com/en/event/d-day-festival-normandy.

Across the Channel, the English village of Southwick and Southwick Park partner to take visitors back to 1944 during **Southwick D-Day Revival**. The town's thatched-roof, half-timbered cottages still look much as they did when General Dwight D. Eisenhower made his famous, "Ok—let's go!" decision in a Georgian mansion there known as Southwick House. The Golden Lion public house and adjoining Brewhouse still stand, holding within their walls memories of when the pub was unofficial officers mess for Eisenhower, Field Marshal Bernard Montgomery and other famous leaders along with their staffs.

Southwick's event features a Battle of Britain memorial fly-past, 1940s school lessons in the Old Schoolhouse, swing dance lessons, 1940s dinner dance, and talks by renowned historians. A special treat for history buffs is the large wall map on which staffers plotted the progress of *Overlord*. Southwick is just north of Portsmouth, home to the D-Day Story Museum. Visit southwickrevival.co.uk.

In North America, **The National WWII Museum** in New Orleans commemorates D-Day and the museum's own birthday on June 6 each year. It opened on that day in 2000 as The National D-Day Museum, located in the city where the Higgins boat was created. Following a 2005 act of Congress, the D-Day Museum officially took on its present name on June 2, 2006. Past D-Day commemoration activities include the Victory Belles performing popular songs of the 1940s; special displays of artifacts from both sides of the conflict; a chance for visitors to try on reproduction uniforms, helmets and other personal equipment, and a rare opportunity to go onboard the museum's Higgins boat and interact with reenactors. See nationalww2museum.org.

The **National D-Day Memorial** in Bedford, Virginia, offers many activities leading up to June 6 and on that day. Events in previous years have included a 5K run, concerts, film conference, speakers, recognition of WWII veterans, and the ongoing Lunchbox Lectures series. For additional information go to www.dday.org.

The annual **WWII Heritage Days** at Atlanta Regional Airport-Falcon Field in Peachtree City, Georgia, features historic aircraft and vehicles, demonstrations by reenactors, educational displays and activities, and a 1940s dance. A highlight is "Keep 'Em Flying," a chance to ride in one of the World War II aircraft of the Commemorative Air Force (CAF) Dixie Wing while contributing to their preservation. WWII Heritage Days, which began as a one-day affair in 2003, takes place over two days in April. See wwiidays.org.

The largest annual D-Day reenactment in the United States takes place on the shores of Lake Erie at Conneaut, Ohio. First held in 1999, **D-Day Conneaut** now attracts over a thousand reenactors from the U.S. and Canada to depict American, British, Canadian, French, German and Polish troops. Other living history participants portray civilians.

Mock battles take place along a 250-yard beach adjacent to sloping terrain in Conneaut Township Park that closely resembles the Omaha

Beach area. Reenactments of inland battles like the fight for Foucarville and attacks by French Resistance fighters are held elsewhere in the park. Additionally, there are tank and large-caliber artillery firings, encampments, Higgins boat rides, re-creations of USO performances, and a host of other activities. The website is ddayohio.us.

Another of the Great Lakes is also home to an annual commemoration, known as **D-Day Plus** however-many-years-since-1944, e.g., D-Day Plus 74 for 2018, D-Day Plus 75 for 2019, etc. The centerpiece is *LST 393*, a Landing Ship, Tank, that participated in D-Day. It is one of only two LSTs in the U.S. that remain as originally built. It serves as a museum at The Mart Dock on the downtown waterfront of Muskegon, Michigan (open May–September). Behind a glass display is the actual flag flown by *LST 393* on D-Day. Sailor Paul Grambsch took down the flag, put it in his seabag with a note dated June 6, 1944, and there it remained, unknown to his family, until his death.

During D-Day Plus, a mock air attack staged with vintage aircraft flown by the Hooligan Flight Team is driven off by reenactors firing replica rifles and machine guns. Other popular aspects of the event are Pin-ups for Patriots, a family-friendly 1940s fashion show, a swing dance and beer judging contest, and displays of uniforms, weapons and vehicles. Visit lst393.org.

Paintball enthusiasts have a special event of their own: **Oklahoma D-Day**, a week-long observance generally held the second week of June each year at the D-Day Adventure Park near Wyandotte. Up to 4,000 players maneuver on a 600-acre field that includes mock cities and destroyed tanks and planes. Replica tanks, aircraft, bazookas and heavy weapons are part of the arsenal, and visitors can ride on actual tanks and a helicopter. Check ddaypark.com.

These are a few of the most popular places you can visit for D-Day remembrances. The **D-Day Center** webpage is updated annually with a comprehensive list of the year's events. Go to www.dday.center and select Normandy Today in the menu, then choose Anniversary Events from the submenu.

SAVING PRIVATE RYAN —AN ANNIVERSARY LOOK BACK

The Making of *Saving Private Ryan*

Sandro Monetti

SAVING PRIVATE RYAN IS THE ULTIMATE D-DAY MOVIE AND, MORE than 20 years after its release, remains the most authentic cinematic depiction of the Second World War in Hollywood history. Veterans, historians and critics reserve special praise for its intensely realistic opening sequence, a 24-minute dramatization of the U.S. landing on Omaha Beach. By putting his cameras right there in the surf as the men came ashore and keeping them close to the carnage as German firepower rained down on the landing forces, director Steven Spielberg delivered the kind of gory detail like nothing seen before in a major war movie.

That visceral sequence was part of his plan to help moviegoers understand and feel what a bloodbath Omaha was. In the early morning hours of June 6, 1944, American, British and Canadian troops began storming the Normandy coast. The Americans were at Omaha and Utah beaches, the British at Gold and Sword beaches and the Canadians landed at Juno. By the end of the day, there were 4,900 Allies dead, wounded or missing and 2,000 of those casualties were on Omaha.

Saving Private Ryan, released in 1998, tells of a D-Day squadron that storms Omaha Beach and then must risk life and limb again by marching into occupied France to rescue a lowly paratrooper who has been granted special status by the government as the last surviving son in a family decimated by the conflict.

Spielberg was inspired to make the film as a tribute to his dad, Arnold Spielberg, a World War II veteran who manned a radio in B-25 bombers in India and Burma fighting against the Japanese, and who would later regale young Steven with war stories. Spielberg grew up frightened by his father's realistic accounts of combat and much preferred the fantasy of John Wayne war films than the reality of the stories his father told him. Pretty-looking explosions and neat, heroic deaths were easier to relate to than the grim reality where a man's torso is blown off while next to him his colleague loses an arm. His father's old war buddies used to laugh at the way war was portrayed in Hollywood movies, saying that wasn't the way things really were.

Showing his fascination with the conflict, many of Spielberg's films take place in the WWII era including his very first, an 8mm short film he made when he was 13 called ***Escape to Nowhere*** in which he used firecrackers for bullets. He has called World War II the most significant event of the last 100 years and set out, with ***Saving Private Ryan***, to make a movie reflecting that.

That was also the mission of Don Granger, an executive vice president of production at Paramount, who was looking to add an epic war film to his studio's slate when he got a call from up-and-coming producer Mark Gordon who wanted to come in with screenwriter Robert Rodat to pitch him a war story.

Rodat, who had studied both history and film in college, walked into Granger's office on June 14, 1995, and captured his attention by telling him that every day he passed a war memorial near his home in New Hampshire, that stated one family had lost eight sons in the Civil War. That had inspired an idea: what if the War Department had decreed that an entire family could not simply be wiped out and what would be the implications if several men were sent to save one lone survivor?

Research had revealed that something similar had happened in real life and that came to inspire the story. All five Sullivan brothers perished at sea on the same ship in 1942. Then, in 1944 two brothers from the Niland family of Tonawanda, New York, were killed within 24 hours of each other during the D-Day operation; another brother was (erroneously) believed to have been killed fighting the Japanese the previous month, so a chaplain was sent out to find the fourth brother and bring him home. The Niland brothers story inspired Rodat's tale, "Saving Private Ryan."

Paramount bought the rights to the film, and the search began to attach top talent to the project. Tom Hanks, now a top star thanks to Oscar-winners ***Philadelphia*** and ***Forrest Gump***, was first choice for the squadron commander, Captain Miller, and although he'd long said he had no interest in playing a character who carried a gun, this was clearly something different, dramatic and important. Plus, it played into his love of WWII history. As a teenager in Oakland his favorite viewing was the documentary series ***The World at War*** and he had devoured books on WWII ever since.

Hanks was fascinated by the idea of a captain who had survived the devastation of D-Day but now had to put his life on the line again for one man. The actor brought up the idea of Steven Spielberg directing.

Unbeknown to him, Spielberg was already reading the script—suddenly this project was the hottest property in Tinseltown. Spielberg wanted some tweaks to Rodat's screenplay and hired more established writers Frank Darabont and Scott Frank to polish the material before Rodat, who eventually wrote 11 drafts of the story, was brought back for some final changes.

Spielberg had explored World War II in his previous films, ***1941***, ***Empire of the Sun*** and, most memorably with ***Schindler's List***, as well as in the Indiana Jones movies. But he knew that if ***Saving Private Ryan*** was done right, it could be the war movie to end all war movies.

When preparing the film Spielberg met with D-Day veterans who urged him not to change the reality of the horrors they saw and experienced, as so many moviemakers had done in the past. Among them were veterans who had actually been on Omaha and Utah beaches, and their descriptions of the sights and sounds of combat proved invaluable. So too did his consultation meetings with author Stephen E. Ambrose, who has written definitive books about World War II that provided the core of the film's historical detail.

Part of Spielberg's plan for authenticity at all times was to make sure that the cast, instead of acting like soldiers, could actually *be* soldiers—so he sent them off to a special boot camp. As the trainer who would show them the ropes, he enlisted retired U.S. Marine Corps captain Dale Dye, who had earned three Purple Hearts during his tours of duty in Vietnam. Dye had been so incensed by Hollywood's inaccurate portrayal of military combat in Vietnam that he started his own company, Warriors Inc., to help moviemakers get it right and had already consulted on close to 40 war films, including ***Platoon***.

Dye's boot camp, based at an old British Aerospace facility in Hatfield, England, was a long way from the typical Hollywood star life of red carpets and limousines. After he'd finished with the actors, they would never again complain about minor inconveniences like the water in their trailers not being perfect room temperature.

During the toughest week of their lives, the actors, who had to call each other by their character names at all times during boot camp, learned weapons drills, military lingo, hand signals, close combat, did endless pushups and tackled obstacle courses and the artillery range. That was the easy part.

The troops were wakened after only three or four hours of sleep a night, made to run for six miles and hike for another 12 miles through miserable rainy weather, wearing woolen uniforms and carrying 40-pound rucksacks on their backs before being made to sleep outdoors in their wet clothes.

Amid all this, everyone recalls Tom Hanks calmly standing over a fire with his wet socks on the end of a stick waving smoke from his eyes as the rest of the group sat around aching and complaining. Hanks had been through a Dye boot camp before as preparation for ***Forrest Gump***, so he knew what discomfort to expect.

Nobody enjoyed the army rations they had to eat. Actor Giovanni Ribisi called it "cat food." Co-star Ed Burns lost nine pounds in that single week. But there was no opportunity to call their agents and get a car to drive them to London for a four-course, five-star meal.

Through it all Dye was shouting at them things like "This isn't a high school play!" and referring to his charges as "turds." He ran the place with an iron fist. If anyone called their weapon a "gun" they were down doing 25 push-ups as punishment. If an actor didn't refer to someone else by that person's character name Dye was in his face yelling.

Everyone was exhausted, miserable, tired, achy and wanted to go home. Four days into boot camp the group was considering taking a vote on whether to quit. It was Tom Hanks who talked them out of it.

Addressing his fellow actors, he told them, "Throw down one finger if you want to leave, two if you want to stay." They all threw down one, but then Tom Hanks threw down two and told them, "You guys represent all the guys who died for this country and the guys that died on the beach that day. And I'm not going to let you disgrace their honor."

Hearing about the near mutiny, Dye also addressed them as a group making a similar sentiment, if in less pretty language than that used by Hanks. By the end of that day, no one was left in any doubt what was required from them, as Dye explains in the next chapter of this book. But the tough experiences bonded the actors as a group and made them ready for the two-and-a-half-month shoot in England and Ireland that was to follow.

The only main actor not sent to the boot camp was Matt Damon. That had been a deliberate choice by authenticity-seeking Spielberg so that the other actors might feel a resentment towards him similar to what their characters feel towards his character for having to risk their lives to save his.

Those joining Hanks at the boot camp were Vin Diesel (Pvt. Caparzo), Edward Burns (Pvt. Reiben), Barry Pepper (Pvt. Jackson), Adam Goldberg (Pvt. Mellish), Tom Sizemore (Sgt. Horvath), Jeremy Davies (Cpl. Upham) and Giovanni Ribisi (Medic Wade).

Vin Diesel was not the big name back then he has since become thanks to the ***Fast and the Furious*** films. At the time he was cast in ***Saving Private Ryan***, he was working as a telemarketer and had made only two little-seen films, a short called "Multi-Facial" and a feature called ***Strays***. Luckily for him, film buff Spielberg had seen both of them. The director invited him to the set of ***Amistad***, which he was shooting before ***Saving Private Ryan***, to meet him.

Also invited to the ***Amistad*** set was Barry Pepper, then the San Fernando Valley roommate of another starry-eyed young actor, Ryan Reynolds. The call from Spielberg was a dream come true and one Pepper compared to being invited behind the curtain in the land of Oz.

The script of ***Ryan*** was still going through rewrites, so Diesel, Pepper and the others auditioning for parts were asked to read lines from a World War II movie from a few years earlier, ***A Midnight Clear***.

When he eventually landed the role, Pepper wept. It meant a lot to him as he'd had three relatives who served in World War II—only one of whom came home—and he wanted to honor them.

The movie introduced a whole bunch of talented new actors, but by the time it came out the one playing the title character would be a household name: Matt Damon had won an Oscar months earlier for co-writing ***Good Will Hunting***.

The presence of Tom Sizemore in the final film was not guaranteed for a long time. A recovering drug user, he was required by Spielberg to take drug tests every day during filming with the understanding he would be fired and replaced if he failed just one of them. Sizemore managed to pass all of his tests.

The D-Day landing sequences were filmed first with the scenes shot at Ballinesker Beach in County Wexford, south of Dublin, which would double as Omaha Beach. The scenes involved 1,500 extras, many of whom were members of the Irish Reserve Defence Forces. Members of local war reenactment groups were cast as German soldiers. To portray American soldiers maimed during the landing more than 20 amputees were hired.

Although he had used storyboards on his previous movies for action scenes, Spielberg dispensed with those here so he could get spontaneous reactions to the mayhem. He used lots of hand-held cameras in the middle of the action, placing them mostly at ground level, and also used underwater cameras to better depict soldiers hit by bullets in the water. Forty barrels of fake blood were used to simulate the blood in the sea.

Among the many veterans of D-Day who would later praise Spielberg for showing events as they really unfolded was James Doohan, famous for playing Scotty in ***Star Trek***. He had participated in the invasion of Normandy, landing at Juno Beach with the Canadian infantry.

The gory details which shocked audiences sparked painful memories for many who were actually there on D-Day—so much so that America's Department of Veterans Affairs set up a special 800 phone number to help the hundreds of former soldiers who were traumatized after seeing the film.

From the beach scenes, filming moved to Hatfield, England, where a war-torn French village was built from scratch at the same facility where the boot camp had been held. A total of 500 cast and crew worked on the film, which was run, appropriately, like a military operation. An efficient one, too.

The crew included costume designer Joanna Johnston, who felt more like a quartermaster. She'd hand out uniforms to everyone playing troops with words like, "You look like a 44, take this one." Then there was Simon Atherton, the production's armorer, who brought in 500 pieces of weaponry from small pistols to heavy machine guns and bazooka rocket launchers.

As captain of it all, Steven Spielberg appeared calm and in control of everything. He was editing the film while shooting it so he would know he was getting what he wanted. On the last day of filming, Tom Hanks pulled out a bottle of Jack Daniels and a collection of shot glasses, poured each of his co-stars a drink and said, "Guys, I want to make a little toast about how great an experience it's been working with all of you. I've been to the editing room, I've seen what Steven has cut so far, and I have some good news and bad news.

"The good news is that we are making a pretty incredible film and if the movie turns out like I think it's going to turn out, we're all going to be part of film history. This is a movie that will live on long after we're all gone. Generations will watch this movie after you've all passed. That's the good news. The bad news is that it's all downhill from here."

But the good news continued when ***Saving Private Ryan*** was released in summer 1998 to rave reviews and great box office. The film took $100 million in its first 17 days on release in America and went on to earn $216.8 million domestically, making it the highest grossing film of the year in the United States. But audience enthusiasm was global. The film's worldwide box office total was $481.8 million.

At the 71st Academy Awards, ***Saving Private Ryan*** was nominated for 11 Oscars including Best Picture, Best Original Screenplay and Best Actor for Tom Hanks. It won five; Best Director for Steven Spielberg, as well as the other four mentioned previously in "D-Day Films & Television." In one of the biggest controversies in Oscar history, the film lost Best Picture to ***Shakespeare in Love***, whose producer Harvey Weinstein repeatedly attacked ***Saving Private Ryan*** for supposed historical inaccuracies while lobbying hard for his film.

But history judged ***Saving Private Ryan*** to be not just one of the greatest war films ever made but one of the greatest films ever made. In 2014 it was selected for preservation in the National Film Registry by the Library of Congress being deemed "culturally, historically or aesthetically significant."

Spielberg and Hanks would team up again to co-produce two more highly acclaimed World War II projects, the television drama series ***Band of Brothers*** and ***The Pacific***. But ***Saving Private Ryan*** remains their greatest epic. It's an unflinching account of bravery and grit and remains a powerful and poignant tribute to those involved in D-Day. Members of the Greatest Generation have a great film paying tribute to them.

DIRECTOR STEVEN SPIELBERG AND SENIOR MILITARY ADVISOR DALE DYE ON THE SET OF *SAVING PRIVATE RYAN* WHILE DYE IS IN UNIFORM FOR HIS OTHER POSITION PLAYING AN ARMY OFFICER IN THE FILM.
(IMAGE COURTESY OF DREAMWORKS LLC/PARAMOUNT PICTURES)

An Interview with Dale Dye

Senior Military Advisor on *Saving Private Ryan*

Lowell Dean Gytri

For more than three decades Dale Dye has been among the top technical advisors in Hollywood. He has been the point person on all the major film productions involving war and conflict in recent memory. His screen credits include ***Platoon*** (1986), ***Born on the Fourth of July*** (1989), ***The Last of the Mohicans*** (1992), ***Forrest Gump*** (1994) and ***Saving Private Ryan*** (1998). He has also been senior military advisor on HBO's two pivotal World War II TV series, ***Band of Brothers*** (2001) and ***The Pacific*** (2010). He was born in Cape Girardeau, Missouri, on October 8, 1944, as World War II was entering its final year. He graduated from Missouri Military Academy as an officer cadet but was unable to immediately enter college for financial reasons.

Dye then enlisted in the United States Marine Corps in January 1964. During his 13 years of service he rose from private to master sergeant; served two tours of duty in Vietnam totaling more than four years; and earned numerous decorations including a Bronze Star for bravery and three Purple Heart medals for combat wounds. He entered officer candidate school and received a commission as a warrant officer, quickly rising to the rank of captain. In 1982–83 he served in Beirut, Lebanon, as a member of the multi-national peacekeeping force as that city was torn by racial and religious strife.

Dye retired from the Marine Corps in 1984 and, having earned a BA in English from the University of Maryland, he joined the staff of *Soldier of Fortune* magazine, covering the civil wars in Nicaragua and El Salvador. A year later Hollywood called.

Through his firm Warriors, Inc. Dye has conducted actor training "boot camps" and advised on a wide variety of military authenticity issues on war films of many different time periods. But not all of Dye's work involves military matters. He has been a technical advisor on such diverse films as ***JFK*** (1991), ***Natural Born Killers*** (1994) and ***Starship Troopers*** (1997). He has also been an advisor on video game production. In short, Dye has had just about every job one can do behind a Hollywood camera and, by the way, he has also appeared in 85 films and TV episodes, often playing a gruff, spit-and-polish military leader.

Some twenty years after beginning his work on ***Saving Private Ryan***, Dale Dye is still intensely involved in making movies. He will soon add "director" to his incredible list of credits as he begins a project he has been deeply involved with for several years. Actor and Monroe Publications correspondent Lowell Gytri sat down with Dale Dye at his Los Angeles area home.

LG - ***It's Tuesday, December 11 and I'm with Captain Dale Dye at his command post in North Hills, California. Thank you for giving this time, Captain Dye.***

Most welcomed, Lowell.

LG - ***Your thoughts on your being the senior military advisor for Saving Private Ryan?***

Well, ***Ryan*** is a project that is very close to my heart. It was interesting, Steven Spielberg called me one day, himself, on my cell phone, and said, "Listen, what are you doing?" I think I was shopping for a suitcase or something down on Ventura Boulevard. He said, "Well, you need to come see me, we've got this project." I said, "Sure." So we had a meeting with him, Tom Hanks, and the writer, and they kind of filled me in what the story was. I said, "You know, guys, this reminds me of some stories I've heard." The writer said, "Well, yeah, it's because it's based on a real thing." Steven jumped in and said, "But we're not going to do that specific story, which is the story of three brothers, the Niland brothers, two of whom were in the Army infantry, one of whom was an air crewman in the South Pacific."

The upshot of the Niland story was one of the brothers was killed in action in the ETO [European Theater of Operations] right around D-Day, and it was thought that the other brother, who was in the South Pacific, had gone down, was missing in action. This caused a little bit of a burble at the War Department at that point because they thought, "Oh, my God, we're going to wipe out a family here." There was precedent for that because of the Sullivans who had been sunk aboard the [U.S. Navy cruiser] *Juneau*, all five brothers.

LG - ***And the Bixby family back in the Civil War.***

That's right. And so there was precedent. The chairman of the Joint Chiefs and the Secretary of the Army and everybody else got in the mix and said, "Look, we don't want this to happen, so find the surviving Niland brother and get him home." And that was kind of the genesis of the story from Robert Rodat, who was the writer that I keep speaking about. Bob Rodat's a brilliant writer. So he adapted that story and decided that a small unit of Rangers at this point, the 5th Rangers, would be policed up and sent off to find the surviving private. Not Niland this time, but Ryan. And that was the genesis of the story. Spielberg said, "Okay now, you're going to have to train the actors." He named the actors that we were going to be involved with. "And you're going to have to organize this whole D-Day Omaha Beach thing."

LG - ***You're a Marine. There weren't any Marines at D-Day. Was that considered when you were in the planning stage here?***

Well, two things. First of all, there were Marines at D-Day, but they were on ships' detachments. [Second] I have kind of prided myself on being a military historian. Through a 20-some year career, I've worked with all of the services, and I know their methods. I certainly know the World War II methodology. So the fact that I was a Marine really didn't enter into it until we got into the amphibious stuff for the landing. Of course, my experience with LCIs and Higgins boats and that sort of thing—and I have a lot of that experience—paid off because we had to train the folks to get on and off the landing craft. So it didn't really enter into it as to choosing who would be the senior military advisor. I've always been Spielberg's guy, and thank God for that. He knew what I was up to, and he trusted me to have all the insights that I did.

LG - ***You worked with Oliver Stone, Michael Mann—a number of legendary directors. Was there anything that struck you most about Spielberg's vision and style?***

Well, Spielberg is truly a visionary moviemaker. As you say, I've worked with a bunch of them and top-notch guys. But Spielberg knows the human emotion, he knows where your buttons are, if you're in the audience for one of his films, and he will mash that button. He knows exactly where he's going with these things. And like a lot of creative people, sometimes he doesn't communicate that real well. It's in his mind, it's behind his eyeballs. The key to working with him is to get behind his eyeballs, to understand what he's trying to do.

Usually when you're on a huge project like ***Saving Private Ryan***—and almost all of Spielberg's projects are huge these days—you vie for time with him personally so that you can be sure that he gets what he's after, so you can deliver. You don't want to screw up with a guy like Spielberg. If you look at that picture there, it's Spielberg and I sitting on the beach, and he says, "I never thought I wanted to go to war, and then I met you," or words to that effect. And that's really what it was about. I mean, Spielberg knows when he's got an expert and he defers. You can't ask for anything better than that. His ego is such that he knows what he doesn't know, and he's willing to listen to the people that do know. He's got to trust you and he's got to believe that you are a kindred storyteller. He doesn't have much time for guys who are strictly technicians who say, "Well, it has to be this way." You have to understand that you're telling a story here, and if you've got that plus some technical expertise, then you're Spielberg's guy. Fortunately, I fell into that category.

LG - ***How long was your pre-production? How long was the planning stage before you were actually rolling cameras?***

The planning stage was huge, especially logistics, because we were going to shoot in the UK, and we were going to shoot in Ireland. My particular part of it, he gave me, I think, four weeks, and during that time I had to get over to the UK and arrange with the department heads to be their consultant. The uniform people, the wardrobe people, the armory people, the armored vehicle people and so on. I was always their touchstone. They would ask me, "How about this? How about that?"

LG - ***How did you feel your cooperation with all those departments was? Did you have it for the most part?***

I did, and that's because of Spielberg. Spielberg put the word out that Dale's my guy and you all listen to him. That was classic, you can't ask for a better situation than that. So I had to establish those liaisons, I had to prepare to receive the primary actors and to take them into the woods at Hatfield to train them. And then I had to put some of my staff—I was allowed to bring two people, two of my NCOs—and I had to get them forward to Ireland to start raising this 1,000-man unit of the Irish Guarda, which is kind of like the U.S. National Guard, part-time soldiers. I had to get them raised. I had to get the armored vehicles shipped over there, or had to ensure that that was happening. Had to get the ships at sea, all those small boats. So I was down at Portsmouth [England] for a while where they were working on the small boats and getting ready to get them over to Southeast Ireland where we were actually going to shoot. So for about four weeks, I was busy.

LG - ***Considering all the logistics and the number of departments you were organizing, a month doesn't seem like a lot of time.***

No, it isn't. And fortunately, they were working ahead of me. For instance, the guys who had to find existent Higgins boats for that landing sequence on Omaha Beach, those are like hens' teeth; those are hard to find. And when we did find a few of them, they had to be repaired, the engines had to be juiced up so that we could actually use them in the landing. We had to move a huge bunch of wardrobe, World War II uniforms, over to Southeast Ireland to get people actually wearing these things.

LG - ***So not only were you working with the principals, you're working with a thousand Irish background players?***

Yeah, we had a thing we called the Sausage Factory. We'd put them in at one end as part-time soldiers and they'd go through wardrobe and they'd go through indoctrination briefings and they'd go through weapons workings. And these kids, they'd seen an FN rifle, they'd seen an M16 but they'd never seen an M1 or a Thompson submachine gun or a Browning Automatic Rifle. We had to take them down and run them through this course of fire. One of the interesting things was—and I mentioned this to Spielberg and the armorers—I said, "Look, once this thing rolls it's going to be hell to stop it." So what we need to do is make sure everybody's got enough ammo and knows how to reload that weapon, so that they're doing it on camera. [So] we don't have anybody stopping out there saying, "Hey, my gun doesn't work." Everybody understood that. So when I sent my NCOs forward, it was with an emphasis on teaching them to wear the gear. I mean, those leggings that they wore during World War II, it's very easy to get those on backwards and trip yourself up. We had to check all of that, get all of that rolling.

So I sent my guys over there to get that started, knowing that I would arrive a week later and help pick up the slack. Then I took the principal actors, along with two more of my NCOs, to the field, to Hatfield in England, to get them ready and to prep them. And of course, the weather in England at that point was absolutely miserable. It was raining and muddy out where we were and all I had was old shelter huts to get under. It was cold, and then it was hot, then cold, then it was wet, and it was miserable. And I loved that, because that's exactly what training to fight in World War II was like. The kids didn't necessarily like it very much but they quickly figured out that this is valuable to them in terms of...

LG - (Interrupts) ***So when you say "kids," you're talking about your actors?***

Yeah, I'm talking about Tom Hanks, I'm talking about Tom Sizemore, Jeremy Davies, Vin Diesel and a great Canadian actor, the sniper kid [Barry Pepper]. We trained them . . . and it was a miserable experience for five long days out in the British countryside. Every evening I had what's called a stand-down, which is their time to ask me questions because there's no time for that during the day. And to delve into the mindset of what it was like to be a young drafted soldier or enlisted soldier in the 1940s facing World War II.

We not only trained their body, but we got into their mind and into their heart and into their guts. Young guys like Barry Pepper, they don't talk the way people talked in those days, so you had to get them out of using street conversation. And we were able to do that. There was this business of getting them mentally and psychologically into the period, and that was a task. It always is, because some of the things that people did and thought and said in those days don't make sense to young men today. In that particular instance it was a matter of not only talking about the big picture, which was D-Day and the Rangers' part in it, as much as it was Here's how people thought in those days, here's what they faced in World War II, the Axis powers, and here was the assault on Fortress Europa which took place in 1944, which was four years after the war had started. So there was a lot of that sort of thing we needed to teach them, we needed to get instilled in them. We were able to do that.

And then we moved them. There was a private aircraft and we put everybody aboard, we put all their gear aboard and flew directly to Shannon in Ireland and then went onto the beach. I kind of left them alone to deal with Spielberg. He did some table reads and some rehearsals. I went down in the Sausage Factory and helped my guys get these 1,000 young Irish Guarda kids through their training.

And then we were as ready as we could ever be to go. The tough part was, it was rough out on the Irish Sea at that point, so we were spending a lot of time bobbing around in landing craft out there. All the guys were getting seasick. It was some misery. We had to teach them the way to assault out of the landing craft, not to come straight ahead into the fire, but to go to either side into what are called the "murder holes" which are on either side of the ramp. That was something that I knew from my own research. So once we had all of that done, we were kind of on that cusp, on that brink, and Spielberg said, "Well, okay, I guess we're going to do this." I said, "Well, I guess we are, boss."

We had a final inspection. We looked at everybody's gear, we issued all of the necessary ammunition, and they were loaded down with that ammo because I didn't want anybody running out down there. We had to go over the logistics of the beach, which was a beach called Curracloe near Wexford in Southeast Ireland. We had to go over the logistics of the beach where the German obstacles had been in place, where the explosions were. We couldn't leave any marks. Normally on a set, you'll put a little red flag or a little marker of some kind. In these big shots, Spielberg's got about five cameras running.

LG - ***Did you hear from anybody, "I can't hit any marks while I'm acting?"***

No, I didn't hear any of that, but there was a danger there and Spielberg had talked for a long time about how [he] wanted to shoot this thing. We were dealing with Janusz Kaminski, who was the director of photography. Spielberg asked me one time, "Look, what do you see in combat? What's your perspective?" I said, "Frankly, it's low . . . and it's what I call assholes and elbows." That's what you see, the guys right in front of you, maybe get a look around this way, a look around that way. And he thought about that. I knew I had planted a seed there, but I didn't know what he was going to do. What he decided to do was to send into the chaos, once the drill began, he decided to send cameramen with hand-held cameras, right into it. And I saw some of the most extraordinary camera work. I saw a camera operator, with a camera on his shoulder, run into the chaos. He ran right through one of these detonations that went off. I said, "Oh, my God, we've lost that guy!" When all of the smoke cleared and the debris fell he was still going.

Some of the greatest shots—other than the master which is the big, wide, overall look at Curracloe Beach filling in for Omaha, with all the people and landing craft and armored vehicles and so on coming ashore—some of the greatest stuff was gotten by these individual camera operators who were just charging right into the chaos. There were pieces that Spielberg really wanted. He knew a lot of it was going to be by-guess-and-by-God once the whistle blew. Everything was just going to be wild. But there were certain pieces he wanted. For instance, we had heard a story from a surviving veteran of the 16th Infantry who said that he saw a guy actually walking through the chaos, back toward the surf line, carrying his arm, which had been blown off. Spielberg absolutely wanted that in the film. I've seen a lot of weird things happen to wounded guys in combat, but that one I said, "Damn, are you sure?" And he said, "Yeah, yeah, it's perfect—wonderful!" And he knew the emotional button there. And so we had to labor to get that, because it was amidst the chaos that he actually got that.

LG - (Interrupts) ***So you didn't have a lot of "cut" and "action?"***

No, there was none.

LG - ***Once you set it off, you were going?***

Yes. I said, "Steven, once we roll this puppy, I don't know if we can stop it." He was smart though; he put thousand-foot (film) magazines on his cameras so there was no way we were ever going to run out. And when we went, we went. It was one of the most—I got my Eisenhower fix that day. I was standing up there with a bunch of radios, and I was trying to control all of this chaos and watching the first A.D. [assistant director] and watching Spielberg and watching the guys who were going to do the tiling, and the visual effects guys and so on. I finally realized—I said, "Look, we just have to say 'go' and everybody had better do their job because we can't do this again. It's just going to be what it is." Fortunately, the good Lord shined upon us that day and everything went like it was supposed to be.

LG - ***When you say you got your Eisenhower fix, what was [that]?***

I was watching D-Day, essentially.

LG - ***How long, from when you said "go" till . . .?***

It had to be five minutes until we had literally run out of that master shot. It was now time to get inside it, and find Tom and find Sizemore and find Barry Pepper. I remember I was running—I was up on the cliffs above the German positions—and I had radios in my hand and I was talking to this guy, and talking to this (other) guy. I only had two of my NCOs, who were down on the beach, in uniform, carrying a weapon, with an ear bud, and they could hear me. So if I could see anything dying or anything wrong, I could get them in there real quick and fix it. Nothing really happened, and they say to this day their biggest job was making sure nobody got run over by the tanks. The drivers couldn't see.

LG – ***So you spot something down there. Were you able to key in and give specific instructions to individual camera operators?***

I couldn't talk to the camera operators, but I could talk to my guys who were down in there. I'd see something dying in Sector Two or somebody doing something stupid in Sector Three, and I could rush them over there. I could see them go running toward that, and pick a guy up and throw him forward or something like that. I wasn't able to talk to camera operators and neither was anybody else, I don't think. Back where the master shots were, where the wide shots were, Spielberg could talk to the camera operators and Janusz Kaminski could talk to the operators. But when we launched those guys out there with a camera on their shoulder, they were out of contact.

LG - ***So that sequence ended up being what, about 18 to 20 minutes, something like that?***

The whole sequence until they get off the beach, I think, was 22 minutes. And it was some of the most extraordinary action ever put on film. I didn't know about this at the time, but Steven and Janusz Kaminski had decided that they were going to color-time the film and bleach it so that it moved toward the Ektachrome part of the spectrum as opposed to the Kodachrome part of the spectrum, [where] you get those warm yellows and reds. Ektachrome is faded greens and blues. So they were going to do it that way, and I think that really added something to it. It made it look as miserable out there as it was.

LG - ***Doesn't it also lend itself to all the old newsreels that were black and white at the time? You kind of got that subconscious connection.***

Certainly [for] people who knew the history of World War II and studied what film there is and that sort of thing.

LG - ***Was there anything with Saving Private Ryan with your principal actors, notable incidents?***

Well, I guess the notable incident that you're probably fishing for is what has become an apocryphal story now, that there was a mutiny, and that they decided that they were just way too miserable and needed to get out of this. There's a grain of truth to that, but it is not at all what has been reported to be. One of the actors, who has remained unnamed and will remain unnamed in this interview, decided that he just had enough. He said, "I'm going home. This is ridiculous. I'm cold, I'm miserable, I'm an actor." He clearly had not adopted the mindset that I needed him to adopt. And rather than go to me, because he knew that would be useless, he went to Tom Hanks. And Tom did what I think was one of the most honorable and brave things I've ever seen a guy do in a situation like this. It's one of the things that cemented my longtime friendship with him. He made a speech—I wasn't there, this was reported to me second-hand— and said, "Look, we're actors and we can quit any time we want to. But this is our opportunity to really, really understand what we're doing. Rather than saying lines and hitting marks, we get a chance here to really understand, from an emotional standpoint, the misery that those guys experienced in World War II." He said, "I don't want to pass that up. As an actor I don't want to pass that up. I want that, I need that."

Almost everyone agreed with him. But it was brought to me, when I was finally back in the CP [command post], that this had happened. My First Sergeant came to me and said, "Skipper, look, here's what's happened." He didn't know how they were all going to react to what Tom had to say. I said, "All right, let me talk to them." I gathered them all together and I put them under the one shelter that we had. It was just pissing rain, miserable, cold, rain. I put them under that shelter, and then I stood out in the rain and in the mud to talk to them. It was a bit of psychodrama, I grant you. I spoke to them, and I simply sort of reiterated what I had been told that Tom said. I said, "Look, you have a rare and unique opportunity to represent, in a media that will reach millions of people, the men who fought and died to give us what we have, to give us the opportunity to make all the money that you're going to make and garner all the fame and attention . . . they paid for that with their lives. They paid for that with their blood, sweat and tears. You now have an opportunity to represent them and I, by God, want you to represent them properly. I want you to *understand* what those guys went through because that's important. And it's important to tell this story.'

I may or may not have been eloquent but I certainly was impassioned, and they were paying attention. Once I said that, I said, "Now, this is your decision," and walked away. There was some conversation that went on. I don't know what was said. But I do know that Tom Hanks came to me and he said, "Skipper, never mind about all of that. We're going to go through with this. We're going to make this happen." I said thank you, and I patted him on the shoulder and said, "I'm proud of you. It's important." And he said, "Yes, sir, I understand it's important."

And so we continued. That happened the day prior to the last day, so they didn't have much more to go through. I was very proud of them. I had a troublemaker in there, the guy who will remain unnamed, and I knew what the trouble was, which wasn't the misery of his environment. We got through it, I think, in an excellent fashion.

While we were shooting at Hatfield in England—long after their training, while we were shooting during principal photography—we would have a press day and the reporters would come aboard. And they would talk to Tom and they would talk to Barry Pepper and they would talk to Vin Diesel, and [the reporters] would say, "We understand you had a miserable time in training and everything." The interesting thing is what they had to say. They said, "We simply couldn't have done this without what Captain Dye put us through." And that, of course, was my Academy Award right there. They got it.

LG - ***It certainly shows in the movie.***

I think so.

LG - ***A lot of World War II equipment is in Western Europe and a lot of it is in the hands of private collectors—the equipment that you found, was it serviceable? Did you have to do a lot of modifications?***

When it comes to uniforms and webbing equipment, a lot of that we had to manufacture, but we did it absolutely to specification. We found the actual lasts [patterns] for the old GI boots, and we had the boots made to that specification. We were very careful with the stuff. We didn't want any cheap knockoffs that are made in Pakistan or China or that sort of thing. So we had this gear made really well. The problem was weapons. We needed a pot-full of weapons. We had a terrific armorer who traveled a lot of places, South Korea and places that used old World War II weapons, and we bought a bunch of it. We then had to modify all of those weapons, blank-adapt them. Thompsons, Browning Automatic Rifles, M1 carbines, hundreds of M1 rifles, 30-caliber machine guns—and then manufacture the ammunition for them. Then the Germans: We needed Schmeisser MP-38-40s, we needed MG-42s, MP-34s, a pot-full of Kar98K rifles. So all of that had to be collected and that took quite a while. A man by the name of Simon Atherton, who is probably the top armorer in Europe, got all of that together in the numbers that we needed. And then we had to test fire it all and make sure we had the ammunition for it. It was monstrous, the amount of ammunition.

LG - ***Who gets the contract for that much ammunition? Where did you acquire that?***

Simon had a number of manufacturers that were producing it. Where Simon got it all, I'm not sure, but I know he had major contracts out and we were getting shipments of ammunition in daily (laughs). Especially during the Omaha Beach sequences we really needed a bunch of ammo, and so he had it stockpiled.

LG - ***I've used firearms on sets a lot of times, just never paid any attention to where the ammunition came from.***

There are people, especially in Eastern Europe, that manufacture that stuff by the truckload. And it's specifically blank ammunition. You can get it in various loads, quarter-load, half-load. We insisted that we used only full-load blanks. The problem is, when you blank-adapt a weapon, you're defeating the original engineering. And so you're asking for stoppages and malfunctions. What we found is if we use full-loads it makes the weapon function much more reliably because of the gas produced in gas-operated weapons, and recoil-operated weapons, because the impulse is stronger.

I might say a word about the tanks. We wanted authentic German armor for the village sequence, when the Germans attack. It was tough. We wanted only the most looming and visually deadly German armor that we could find. We found a few small things, we found a German halftrack, we found the Kettenkrad little [halftrack] motorcycle. But the tanks, the main battle tanks, were a problem. We had a guy by the name of Steve Lamensby and I—I've studied tanks for a long time, and worked with them a lot. We sort of got into what we were going to do about this, because we wanted to make Tigers, Mark VIs. We kept looking at what was available, what we could find. There's only one running Tiger, I think, in all of Western Europe at this point, and they were not going to let us have anything to do with it because we were going to blow it up, and shoot at it, and so on.

We were able to find two running Soviet T55s and then we came up with a way that we thought we could change the profile and make it much more angular than a 55 is, especially on the turret, increase the length of the weapon and put the muzzle brake on it so it would look like a Tiger. That was a major drill. We were literally bolting big metal elements onto the hull of the [tanks]. We really did well with it, I think. The only thing that we screwed up, and I heard about it from armor enthusiasts once the film came out, is we didn't get the inner lead road wheels. We tried to make inner lead road wheels on the T55, but they kept falling off. It was just a visual [cosmetic addition], it wasn't functional. The tank would hit something and the road wheels would pop off. We gave up on that. I think they looked great, but it was a big job just getting those tanks ready to go.

There is a scene in ***Ryan*** where they come across a glider wreck, of a Waco glider CG4, and we actually had to call in some old guys from the English countryside who had built gliders during the war. They were [building] Horsas, but they knew about the Waco and they had worked on it. We got these old guys in and had them build us one, and then we wrecked it. There was a lot of that stuff that went on, and that to me was fun. I mean, here we were making Tiger tanks out of Soviet T55s. Here we were recreating a CG4A Waco glider. When you're willing to spend the money and the time to get those kind of things right and to manufacture those, that's [me like] a kid in a candy shop. I loved that stuff, I was down there welding and doing anything I could to help. So, I'm very proud of those things. We really did it well, I think.

LG - ***I think, as far as the end result of the movie, unless you're a real expert or a real aficionado of a specific area of expertise, it looked great, it worked.***

Just one last thing. The Germans. I have always felt that one of the big problems with war movies is that we don't spend any time with the bad guys, the enemy, and they end up looking like cartoon characters who were just there to be shot and disappear. And I always thought that was a mistake, because the jeopardy has got to be real. If they're clowns, there's no jeopardy. If they're tough guys and good combat men, then the jeopardy is jacked up. So when we were doing ***Ryan***, I spent quite a bit of time, especially one of my sergeants who is a German specialist, I had him really work on it. We didn't want them to be clean, pristine, parade ground jack-booted Germans. We wanted them to look like us. We wanted them to look bedraggled and worn by combat. So we spent a lot of time with that, and I'm proud of that. I think the Germans look great there. And we carried that on into ***Band of Brothers***.

LG - ***I think a lot of Hollywood is cliché. Whatever the perceived perception of the enemy is, that's what is.***

I get it. But you know, we found that the Germans had certain ways that they would wear their equipment. They had a tendency to stick grenades, potato-masher grenades, in the tops of their boots and all kinds of things like that. They carried a bread bag and they put the bread bag strap around their helmet so they could stick stuff in there. We found these little touches and we said, "We've got to get these in there." Of course, when we did that, Spielberg loved it. He said, "Oh, these guys look great."

LG - ***What about billeting for cast and crew?***

We were spread all over the little towns of Blackwater and Curracloe. The cast were in the only available four-star hotel. That was in Wexford where the glass factory is. The rest of us were kind of scattered all over. Myself and my crew, my NCO who is the German specialist—a kid by the name of Laird Macintosh who has now gone on to become a successful actor in his own right—Laird and I and John Barnett, who is my First Sergeant, were billeted in an old Scottish castle. It was in Blackwater, which is right adjacent to Curracloe Beach. Little, small town, it's called a two-pub town. It's tiny, and the centerpiece was this castle. A Scottish couple owned it. It was suits of armor standing the in passageways and big broad, sweeping stairways. We loved it. The only problem was, you had to race to see who was going to be the first guy in the shower after work, because it had a limited hot water supply (laughs). I usually got the ice-water shower.

LG - ***Was the company, as far as the business end of it, received well by the people that you contracted and lived with?***

We were kind of a special case. They knew that we had military advisors who were a big deal [and] are a big part of the effort. So we got kind of special treatment. You do a film like ***Saving Private Ryan*** and then you follow with ***Band of Brothers*** and so on.

LG - ***In a geographic area like that, there just had to be an absolute ton of money left behind, a ton of money spent.***

Oh, absolutely. The economy of Blackwater and Wexford, to this day they're still talking about it. It was a unique opportunity. They were just so grateful because in County Wexford in Southeast Ireland, the whole economy is based on the Wexford Crystal glass plant, and there's not much else. Some fishing, and that's it. When we came to town, the place just lit up.

They were just so glad to see us, and would do anything for you. I had a great-aunt, she's dead now, that lived in Cork, which is just to the west of that. I'm from Irish ancestry. And so I got to go see my great-aunt Kate while I was there. It was a huge deal. The whole neighborhood turned out to see Aunt Kate—and she was 80-something at that point—everybody turned out to see Great-Aunt Kate's American nephew who became this guy in Hollywood.

LG - ***Is there still of sense of, as far as reception of Americans over there in that part of the country, that we're the good guys?***

I think so, yeah, especially in Southern Ireland. Everybody, it seems, has some Irish ancestor somewhere in their history, and the Irish people are very aware of that. They know that a generation of Irish kids left during the potato famine and the uprising, came to America. We have a huge Irish heritage in America, and they're appreciative of that, they know that. They'll always pay attention to your name and see if they can and find it on a clan list somewhere.

What I remember, after we finished the Omaha Beach sequence, we had this party for all of the thousand people, and they could bring their families and everything else. We put up huge tents adjacent to Curracloe Beach. We catered it, brought food and things like that in. I had to go around to every tent and meet all of the guys who had been on the beach, and shake hands with them. And the problem was, all of them brought their family version of potcheen, which was Irish moonshine. I don't remember how long that party lasted or what went on, because you have to taste everybody's potcheen. You could tell that they were just so glad.

Nobody had seen any of the dailies or anything else, except for Spielberg and Janusz Kaminski. I hadn't seen a thing. I felt like, if we got this on film, we've got it, we're in good shape. Nobody had seen it, and it just didn't seem to make any difference. Those people were so glad to be a part of that.

LG - ***We talked about your raising your army of background players from the Irish community. Stunt people [also] acting as soldiers, I would imagine?***

The stunt coordinator brought a pretty good bunch. I think it was about 12 that he had on hand regularly. They did the body burns and getting blown in the air and that sort of thing. But we tried to minimize that. Steven Spielberg isn't that big on stunts. I've always told him, and I tell most of the directors that I work with, that one of the pathetic things about death is that it happens in such a mundane fashion. I mean, a guy's walking down the street and he gets hit, and he's dead before he hits the ground. It's just like if you had a puppet and you cut the strings, he just collapses.

There's no doing the funky chicken and calling for mama, it just doesn't happen. And I think Spielberg liked that. He said, "Yeah, that's the way it should be. It should seem casual, because that makes it effective." To me that was Spielberg understanding the emotional buttons, and he certainly pushed them in that regard. So, in terms of stunts, we did a few, especially when we hit the big German bunker, and there were some guys that fell out of it [holding their] firearms. We did a few of those, but stunts were not a big deal, we didn't do that many of them.

LG - ***Did you have any kind of language issues with the people you were working with?***

Thank God, no. If you hear a real serious Irish brogue, sometimes you have to listen closely to pick it out, but we caught up with it very quickly and they caught up with our American English very quickly.

LG - ***Visual effects in the film, used sparingly, were effective and sophisticated for 20 years ago. Most of the special effects and stunts in Saving Private Ryan were done on the set. Better that way or the modern, heavier reliance on CGI [computer generated imagery]?***

I understand the need for computer-generated imagery and in fact I'm going to use it pretty extensively on a new film I'm preparing. But I think, and Spielberg believes, that in a story like ***Saving Private Ryan*** where you're using a historical incident or event as a basis for your storytelling, they should minimize that sort of thing, unless there's no other way to reach the spectacle bar. We didn't do a lot of that. I remember, in practical terms, we wanted to see bullets hitting the water as people waded ashore at Omaha. The natural instinct of a modern filmmaker would be, "Well, we'll just put that in in post, we'll get the bullets zinging through the water." Not Steven. We went to Hatfield, and dug a trench and filled it with clear water, lined it with Visqueen (polyethylene plastic sheeting) so it wouldn't get muddy, and walked these stunt guys in. We fired pellets down through the water and the camera was under water, so we could see those rounds coming through. That's an example of doing it practical rather than immediately falling back on CGI. That said, we did what is called tiling, or replication, on the beach sequence. We had a thousand men, but we needed more than that. We needed it to be deeper than it was going to be. So at some point after the mass chaos was over, we actually moved people down the beach deeper and then shot it again. But that was after we had gotten the master. That was to fill in and make the beach look deeper. We could have computer-generated that; we could have just recreated people down there, but we didn't want to do that. So we actually took the guys we had and moved them down.

LG - ***So, when we see the landing craft out in the water, those are actual landing craft?***

Those are actual Higgins. We had five of them, three of which were semi-reliable and the other ones didn't float a lot (laughs). The reliable ones would motor toward the beach. The others, maybe they'd motor, maybe they wouldn't. It kind of depended.

LG - ***You are a prolific character actor, including playing a U.S. Army officer in Saving Private Ryan. What do you prefer, acting or being a military advisor?***

It's hard to say. I get to play [experiment] a lot more when I'm an advisor. I get to do things like going down and helping to build a tank. I'm that sort of mechanical, hands-on guy. I get to play a lot with weapons—make them, fix them and make them happen. That appeals to me hugely. On the other hand, I am an actor and I'm a storyteller and I like the idea of helping to tell the story in a credible fashion in front of the camera. So what I've done throughout the years is, I've tried to double-dip. I've tried to mix-and-match. So where I'm the military advisor, I will very often find a role I want and tie that into the deal.

LG - ***What is your pitch if you're going to do that?***

Usually they come to me and say, "We want you to be this military advisor. Tell us how much you're going to need, tell us what you want, and tell us what we ought to pay attention to." Nowadays, they come to me rather than me going to them. There's been so much publicity, they know the Captain Dye method and they don't argue with it.

I'll shoot a target of opportunity. I'll find out where we are in the situation, and I'll get next to the director rather than talk to producers or casting directors—*the* director. And I'll say, "Listen, you know, the role of Colonel 'Umpyfratz?' I could eat that alive. You'd be hiring a guy who not only is an actor, but who's been the colonel, or been a version of that colonel." That usually works. The reason is because it's rarely a leading role. It's some kind of supporting role, and they're very happy.

LG - ***Your role in Saving Private Ryan—you brought in an entirely different perspective to the planning of the mission . . .***

And that's the military perspective—hard-headed, practical military perspective. Sometimes there's so much [military] jargon that has to be spit out, that actors who have never spoken that language can't get their head around it. They put the wrong em*pha*sis on the wrong *syllable*. I know exactly how to say that. All I've got to do is repeat that line real quick and they say, "Oh yeah, I believe him, he knows what he's talking about." Sometimes I'm hired just for my voice, which has kind of a drill instructor growl, and they want to hear that. That is what they think most people sound like in the military.

LG - ***You must have consulted a number of D-Day veterans in your planning stage?***

Yeah, absolutely. For ***Ryan***, I talked to several people who had landed on Omaha, who were specifically in the 1st Infantry Division, 16th Infantry (Regiment). I found a bunch of the guys who were in Regimental Combat Team 16. They were aging survivors at that point. I talked to them specifically about how they moved up the beach. We talked about the use of Bangalore torpedoes. I found two of these guys here in California; one was in Tulare and one was south of here, Newport Beach. Old gents. I found them through the 1st Infantry Division Association, and I called them. All you've got to do is drop the Spielberg name on them, and these guys will say, "Sure, I'll talk to you." And then I'd go see them. And I talked to a guy in Texas who had been a glider pilot.

LG - ***Did you have any cooperation from Germans?***

One of my NCOs might have. Laird Macintosh might have talked to some, but I don't think so. I think he would have told me if he did.

LG - ***Did you consult during editorial?***

Yeah, especially on sound and that sort of thing. In fact, one of the things you might be interested in, Steven wanted—he's a big sound guy—and he wanted some post work done so he called me and I arranged to go onto a police range where I could use live ammunition, here in L.A. I bought a side of beef, hung it, and then we mic'd the beef so that I could fire 9mm subsonic (bullets) into the carcass. It would hit bone and crack; it would hit meat and thud. It's a very distinct sound. And then I went up to Northern California to another range with a friend of mine who had some machine guns. We put five microphones at various distances down-range, and I locked off the machine gun so that it would fire within three inches of the mics. We fired the rounds down there, and what you got was the Doppler effect of a close round. When a round is very close to your ear it'll snap, it'll pop, and it's breaking the sound barrier next to your ear.

LG - ***What was your impression of the completed motion picture the first time you saw it?***

Well, I hate to use a cliché, but it was mind-blowing. Steven invited me down to see it at a theater on the Universal lot. It was being shown to some studio executives. I think Tom Hanks was there. We took a look at this thing and I was kind of shocked into silence, I didn't know what to think. I said, "My God, that's powerful. That's *huge*." I'd *never* seen anything like it. Frankly, it was a little humbling to know that I had something to do with making that first 22 minutes happen.

LG - ***Tell us a little bit about your new movie, your directorial debut, No Better Place to Die.***

No Better Place to Die is going to be one of the more eye-popping stories to come out of the World War II genre. If you think of ***Saving Private Ryan***, this is a prequel. This is what happened when the airborne assault went in, prior to the beach landings. It's the story of scattered paratroopers all over the Cotentin Peninsula who managed to cobble themselves together [into small combat units] and take and hold vital bridge crossings. One particular is the bridge at La Fière.

I borrowed the title of [Robert M. Murphy's book]. It's the story of how the Able Company of the 505th Parachute Infantry Regiment was able to take the bridge at La Fière and hold it against German tank counter-assaults. Had they not held that [bridge], the Germans would have blown right across, down onto the beach and thrown D-Day into the sea. So it's not hyperbole to say that fights like the bridge at La Fière saved D-Day. I'm surprised that nobody ever told that story on film so I wrote a script. Whereas ***Saving Private Ryan***, for that opening sequence, was Omaha Beach, mine is going to be in the air with people jumping out of airplanes. Gliders and everything else. So you'll see gliders crash and wreck for the first time.

LG - ***Didn't they [the Germans] raise posts, tree trunks, stuff like that?***

Yeah, "Rommel's asparagus" (they called it), to stop glider landings. You're going to see all of that.

LG - ***To me that's got to be insane, to be in an aircraft without power, and try to land.***

And jumping out, with all the anti-aircraft coming up and the formations breaking up and the paratroopers being just dumped out willy-nilly. S.L.A. Marshall, the military historian, has called the fight at La Fière the bloodiest small unit engagement of the war. So I want to do that story. And we're very lucky: Tom Hanks is the executive producer.

LG - ***Will Tom be in the movie?***

Tom's going to do a cameo for me. He plays the CO [commanding officer] of a troop carrier wing. We're building a supporting cast and major actors. One of the interesting elements of it is that I have made a commitment to use as many genuine veterans, young men from Afghanistan and Iraq and so on, as many as I can find that have the capability. I'm going to use them in front of the camera and behind the camera. All these guys and gals who write me letters and say, "How do I get into show biz?" Well, here's your shot.

LG - ***What's your timeline on that?***

It looks like June next year, which would make it a summer 2020 release.

La Fière Bridge and the Merderet River, near St-Mère-Église, the area central to the story of *No Better Place to Die*. *(Image courtesy of the National Archives and Records Administration Collections)*

THE D-DAY 75TH ANNIVERSARY COMMEMORATION

How to Get Around Normandy for the D-Day 75th Anniversary Events

Especially for those who have never been there

Martin Robert Galle

I have been to many ceremonies in and around Normandy for many years and there are some tips and tricks that should help you. As June 6th is on a Thursday, all events will take place Thursday until the following Sunday.

NORMANDY IN GENERAL

Weather: In June it can change from bright sunshine to pouring rain, back to sunshine and rain again often on one day, so be prepared. It is the coast, so winds bring in all kinds of fast changing weather. Mornings might be chilly, burning sun around noon and cold again in the evening. You will also experience daylight from about 4 am to 1130 pm, so there is really time to see a lot.

People: The people in Normandy are very friendly and know how important this event is to Americans and other visitors to the region. Please do not run across farmers' fields to see a bunker or to take a short cut. They have growing crops out there from which they live. In the cities people are in more of a hurry so may be less courteous; this does not just happen in the French countryside.

Food: Typical French cuisine. During this time of the year (and especially during this event) there will be a wait at most restaurants. A speciality of the region is seafood platters. Different from the USA, the seafood is often served cold with an assortment of dips, so ask the waiter if the seafood is served hot or chilled. Roadside trailers that offer BBQs and pizzas are under government control and offer a good snack alternative.

Local Drinks: Cider farms where you can buy locally produced cider and Calvados—which is made by distilling cider twice, thereby increasing the alcoholic content—can be found all along the coastal roads.

Prices of alcohol are quite high at restaurants and hotels. Shop at the local supermarkets which usually have a good stock of beer and wine.

Toilets: It is important for Americans travelling to France to note that many of the old bistros only have one for all! In France the traditional 'seat' has always been gender neutral.

Driving and Gas Stations: Get your gas when the tank is half empty. There are some areas in northern part of Normandy where gas stations are far apart.

Police / Gendarmerie: In France you find different types of police - the local police and the Gendarmerie nationale. The Gendarmes are usually nice but, as they are part of the military, they will not tolerate any taunting or unlawful behavior.

Hospitals: Are all free in France if you have an emergency. In Normandy they quite often have someone who speaks English but don't rely on that at night. I have spent many nights with clients at hospitals where not a single English-speaking person was around.

If you have any kind of ongoing health problems, make sure to take a letter of your medical status and medications with you in French. This is also important if you need any medication at a pharmacy.

Souvenirs: There will be many military sales stands and flea markets around the D-Day event. Please check with your airline, customs office or, for American travellers, the TSA website to learn what you can take home in your suitcase.

BEFORE JUNE 6TH

Many reenactors and owners of WWII vehicles will start arriving the weekend before and you will be able to see quite a few shows, parachute jumps, camps and so on before the 6th. (See "Calendar of Events" following)

During these days you will encounter lots of traffic and police securing the events.

So, drive carefully and stay away from alcohol when driving. If you have travelled in Normandy during other times of the year keep in mind that some town centers like Bayeux, St.-Mère-Église and Carentan might be blocked off from vehicle traffic and parking is sometimes way out of town. You'll find helpful information at the tourist offices.

! JUNE 6TH 2019!

The 75th anniversary will most likely be the last event with living veterans, so there is a huge interest in the event from all around the world.

If you haven't booked a room by early 2019, it will be very difficult to get any kind of accommodation in the areas of Caen, Bayeaux, St-Lô, Carentan and Cherbourg. This includes camping spaces and legal spaces for motor homes and travel trailers. You should reserve a rental car, which is best done in Paris, well in advance. Joining a tour group specifically designed for the D-Day ceremonies may be the best way to attend the event.

Even if you have a car or tour going to the beaches on June 6th, consider this day to be a nightmare of congestion. All major roads along the beaches are either blocked for VIPs or overcrowded by tourists.

There will be almost no parking space available around the ceremonies along the beaches. If you don't have a special pass ("Laisse Passer" in French) you will not be able to get near to the beaches or cemeteries except by event buses.

Police barricades and detours are not taken down until very late in the day on the 6th so it may take a while to get to your hotel or planned nighttime activities.

AFTER JUNE 6TH

After the ceremonial events of the 6th are over, heavy traffic will continue on Friday, Saturday and Sunday as more tourists come to the area. Delays will occur not just on the A13 interstate from Paris but also on the N13 national highway. The narrow coastal roads will be cramped with vehicles of all sizes and vintage. You will be sharing the narrow streets and roads with jeeps, halftracks, WWII motorcycles and many busses. In the areas of historic sites. including Omaha-Beach, Utah Beach, Carentan, Grandcamp-Maisy, Pointe-du-Hoc, Longues Gun Battery, Arromanches, Gold, Juno and Sword Beaches, Ouistreham and Pegasus Bridge, traffic will be very slow. In the small seaside villages, parking will be very limited.

So, take your time and shop at the local supermarkets. Many of the restaurants and snack bars will be filled with tourists. I always make sure to have at least two six packs of water and soda in the car plus some cookies. Most bakeries in France make "sandwiches." It is usually a French baguette with everything on it you desire. If the weather is good, shop at the supermarket or bakery and have a picnic on the beach or in a public park. This is tasty, fun and you don't have to rely on restaurants, cafes and snack bars.

Other than the D-Day ceremonies, the major event you may want to go to is the big parachute event at St-Mère-Église **on June 9th.**

HERE IS THE PROGRAM:

From 10 am to noon around the church square: exhibition of military vehicles (7 tanks, 20 vehicles)

From 11 am: Great military and historic parachute drops at Sainte-Mère-Église and La Fière. These are historic parachute jumps of men in original uniforms using military parachutes - American, German and British paratroopers (more than 1,000 military paratroopers and 30 aircraft)

From 6 pm: A great parade of military vehicles for the returning troops; at least 20 WWII veterans are expected to be in attendance

From 11:30 pm: Fireworks

Thousands of people will be attending. If you are not at Sainte-Mère-Église before 9:00 am there will be almost no place to park near the town. The approach from all other sides will also be full of vehicles. On the 70th anniversary, I was late getting to this event and spent three hours on little dirt roads trying to get even near St. Mère-Église. Make sure to have a very good breakfast before you go. Plan to have enough water, soda and snacks for a minimum of five hours. The BBQ and beer stands will be overcrowded. For this event bring a backpack, good hiking shoes, and an umbrella, which will be useful whether there is rain or bright sunshine.

For more information:

https://www.airborne-museum.org/en/program-of-the-75th-anniversary-of-the-d-day-landings-in-sainte-mere-Église

CELEBRATION EVENTS CALENDAR

For the 75th Anniversary of D-Day

Edited by Sharon Gytri

THIS CALENDAR IS ORGANIZED BY COUNTRIES WHERE EVENTS ARE being held. Keep in mind that the official events for June 6 at the American Cemetery are only available to dignitaries, WWII veterans and their families and need to be arranged ahead of time. However, there are many ceremonies available in nearby towns in Normandy.

It's best to reserve places as soon as possible since Normandy will be extremely crowded at this time. This calendar was created months before dates of events, so there may be changes and additional events not listed. Where prices are given in Euros, visitors from outside Europe should check the current exchange rate.

Here is a list of the most complete event websites to check if there is no website address at the end of an event entry:

D-Day Center: http://www.dday-anniversary.com/
D-Day Overlord: https://www.dday-overlord.com/en/normandy/commemorations/2019/agenda
Normandy Tourism: http://en.normandie-tourisme.fr/calendar-of-events-120-2.html/

IN FRANCE

ONGOING EVENTS:

Gold Beach Guided tours for 75th on Gold Beach area Port-en-Bessin. Ticketing & start at Tourist Office. March 6- October 6: (except June 6 & 7) Mondays – Fridays.

Occupation, Liberation and Oil Port: 10:30 am–1:30 pm.
Info: 02 31 21 92 33.

Bayeux, the Miracle! From the Occupation to Général de Gaulle's Speech: 1½ hrs.
Departure (**10:30 am & 2:00 pm**)
Info: 02 31 51 28 28.

Arromanches: Occupation, Liberation and Artificial Port:
Duration 1½ hrs. (11 am / 2 pm / 4 pm).
Info: 02 31 22 36 45.

Longues-sur-Mer: German battery of Longues-sur-Mer:
Duration 1 hr. English language: **10:15 am / 3:40 am.**
Info: 02 31 21 46 87
http://en.normandie-tourisme.fr/calendar-of-events/june-603-2.html/.

"In Their Footsteps" Exhibit at Juno Beach Centre, Voie des Français Libres, BP 104.
14470 Courseulles-sur-Mer, France.
April -November: Numerous displays related to Canadians' D-Day experience including the film *They Walk With You.* A large volume of visitors is expected in the museum from June 2 to 9, 2019. Reserve at mailto:aresa@junobeach.org. Closed June 5 and 6.
https://www.junobeach.org/.

Saturday June 1st

Guided Historic Hike – Footsteps of 101st Airborne Paratroopers at Hiesville.
Guided historical hike (5.5 mi /9 km) in the footsteps of the paratroopers of the 101st Airborne in June 1944 (3:00). Follow signs in the village. Limited places.
Price: 2 €/person, under 10 free.
Mandatory registration at the Tourist Office: +33 (0)2 33 21 00 33 or ot.sme@ccbdc.fr.

Harley Davidson Run at Sainte-Mère-Église. Run and display of more than 60 military Harley Davidson motorcycles from the 1940s. **9:30 am;** planned return by 5 pm.
Info: 02 33 21 00 3.

Sunday June 2nd

Harley Davidson Run at Sainte-Mère-Église.
Run and display of more than 60 military Harley Davidson motorcycles from the 1940s.

9:30 am; planned return by 5 pm. Info: 02 33 21 00 3.

World War II Foundation International Film Festival Red Carpet Event at the Utah Beach Museum. With actors from the *Band of Brothers* television miniseries, D-Day and other World War II veterans. Special guests also attending. Ticketed event. Includes access to museum, food, drink, music, autographs and photos with actors and veterans.
7:00 pm–11:00 pm €75 per person. www.wwiifoundation.org/events/film/.
Pay online in advance.

Monday June 3rd

***Band of Brothers* Autographing** at Utah Beach Museum.
11:00 am: *Band of Brothers* actors signing autographs. €20 per person. Does not include admission to the museum. www.wwiifoundation.org/events/film/.
Pay online in advance.

***Band of Brothers* Film**
at Utah Beach Museum
Special screening of a short film chronicling several ***Band of Brothers*** actors returning 18 years later to where they did their "boot camp" or training for the series. (*For information on this boot camp, see Secrets of Production in the* Saving Private Ryan 20th Anniversary *section of this book.*) The 30-minute film, shot in England, was produced and introduced by Rick Warden, who played Lt. Harry Welsh. It will be followed by a panel discussion with the actors from ***Band of Brothers*** at Utah Beach Museum. The topic is "Behind the Scenes of Episodes 2 & 3" of the series, "Day of Days" and "Carentan."
6:00 pm–8:00 pm €20 per person. www.wwiifoundation.org/events/film/
Pay online in advance.

Ceremony for Peace at Carentan-les-Marais (Manche).
6:00 pm: Location to be specified.

Tuesday June 4th

Ceremony at USAAF Monument at Picauville (Manche). **10:00 am.** Info: +33 (0)2 33 41 00 18.

Military Welcome Dinner at Carentan-les-Marais or Sainte-Mère-Église (Manche).
6:00 pm: Welcome of military personnel and families for dinner. To participate: +33 (0)2 33 42 74 00.

Film at D-Day Experience Museum, Saint-Côme-du-Mont (Manche).
8:00 pm: First public release of the movie *The Girl Who Wore Freedom*, depicting the lifelong ties between the people of German-occupied

Normandy and the soldiers who liberated them.

VIP Dinner with *Band of Brothers* Actors at Carentan (Manche).
8:00 pm: Pont D'ouve restaurant in Carentan. Space is limited. www.wwiifoundation.org/events/film/. Pay online in advance.

Wednesday June 5th

Daks Over Normandy Parachute Jump at Caen Carpiquet Airport. All of the Douglas DC-3/C-47 Dakota aircraft (Daks) participating in the event will fly in formation across the English Channel to drop a large group of paratroopers into an original 1944 drop zone in Normandy. https://www.daksovernormandy.com/ & https://rcptusa.org/news/6301737.

Exhibition of Historic Military Vehicles at Sainte-Mère-Église.
10:00 am: Exhibition of historic military vehicles.
Info: 02 33 21 00 33.

507th (U.S.) Parachute Infantry Regiment Ceremony at Amfreville (Manche) – Rue du Moulin
11:15 am.
Info: +33 (0) 2 33 41 00 18.

Carentan Liberation Conference at Carentan-les-Marais (Manche). Schedule to be confirmed: Carentan Theater, rue de la Halle. Info: +33 (0)2 33 42 74 00.
11:30 am: Men in WWII uniform parachuting near the Purple Heart Lane (RN 13, north of the city) from C-47 aircraft. Subject to favorable weather conditions.
4:30 pm: Ceremony at Carré de Choux, in the presence of American veterans (Saint-Côme-du-Mont road).
5:30 pm: Ceremony at the Signal Monument (facing the town hall, Boulevard de Verdun).
6:00 pm: Military parade to the port.
9:30 pm: Concert by actor Nick Aaron, who played Robert E. "Popeye" Wynn in *Band of Brothers*, at the port of Plaisance.
11:30 pm: Fireworks at the harbor.

Band of Brothers Concert at Carentan, Manche.
8:00 pm: Free Concert in Carentan Square (in front of Salle du Théâtre) featuring actors from *Band of Brothers*, who will bring their own incredible musical talent to the stage. www.wwiifoundation.org/events/film/
Reserve place on website.

Concert Evening at Foucarville (Manche).
9:00 pm: "Foucarville Bunker" with the West Celtic Pipe and Drum Band.

Historical Parachute Jump at Sainte-Mère-Église.
10:45 pm -11:15 pm: Pathfinders

(paratroopers in charge of marking and securing jumps areas in the early hours of D-Day) demonstration at La Fière, with commentary. Info. 02 33 21 00 33.

Thursday June 6th

Official American D-Day Ceremony at Normandy American Cemetery. Details of event will be finalized closer to the event. If you're interested in learning more, email dday75@abmc.gov. If you are a family member of an individual who is buried or memorialized in Normandy American Cemetery or will be traveling with a World War II veteran, please include that information in your email. American Battle Monuments Commission https://www.abmc.gov/news-events/news/75th-anniversary-d-day-normandy-american-cemetery/.

Official Canadian D-Day Ceremony–Juno Beach Centre, Voie des Français Libres, BP 104 14470 Courseulles-sur-Mer, France. You must pre-register to attend the 75th Anniversary of D-Day at the Juno Beach Centre. Please contact Veterans Affairs Canada, vac.normandy2019-normandie2019.acc@canada.ca. https://www.junobeach.org https://www.abmc.gov/news-events/news/.

TRIBUTES TO THE ALLIES ON LANDING BEACHES

Held at the exact time of the D-Day landings on the five landing beaches. Participate in one of the gatherings with a simple flower in memory of fallen Allied soldiers. Organization: Association D-Day Overlord.

6:31 am: Utah Beach (on the beach, near the Utah Beach Museum, behind the Higgins landing craft).

6:35 am: Omaha Beach (beach of Saint-Laurent-sur-Mer, near the monument "Les Braves").

7:20 am: Sword Beach (Colleville-Montgomery Beach, facing "Place du Débarquement" and Bill Millin Mon.

7:25 am: Gold Beach (16-30 Boulevard de la Plage, 14114 Ver-sur-Mer, near the beach rescue station).

7:25 am: Juno Beach (Bernières-sur-Mer beach, in front of the House of Canadians, 32-34 Promenade des Français).
Association D-Day Overlord.
https://www.dday-overlord.com/

Arromanches D-Day Celebration at Arromanches
6:00 am -10:30 am: Exhibition of 250 historic vehicles on Arromanches beach.
5:00 pm–6:00 pm: Parade of historic vehicles, with commentary.
9:00 pm -12:00 am: Live show of the biggest '40s standards with 17 musicians and 3 singers on stage. Fireworks at the end of the show. Info. 02 31 22 34 31

Canadian D-Day Celebration at Bernières-sur-Mer (Calvados).
8:00 am: Commemorative ceremony at the Maison des Canadiens, 32 Promenade des Français.
9:30 am: Ceremony at the monument of 288, route de Bény.
11:30 am: Ceremony at the Canadian Monument, rue Queen's Own Rifles of Canada.
9:00 pm: Commemorative ceremony at the Maison des Canadiens, 32 Promenade des Français.

Run to Pegasus. At Ouistreham, Calvados.
8:30 am: Runners come together at the port and depart on the towpath towards Pegasus Bridge. To commemorate the 75th Anniversary of D-Day and to honor the men who spearheaded the invasion, this highly successful event was first staged in 2009. On 4th June 2019, a group of 186 sponsored runners will set off from the site of Tarrant Rushton Airfield in Dorset and make their way into the New Forest and down to Portsmouth, covering 62 miles in under 24 hours. The ferry arrives in Normandy at 6:45 am on Thursday 6th June, around the same time that men began to land on the beaches, 75 years earlier. After a brief and well-earned rest at the ferry port, the group will then gather to complete the journey to the legendary Pegasus Bridge.
2:00 am: Once assembled at the Landing Zone in Périers-en-Auge Calvados, the group will be transported to the River Dives where a commemorative plaque will be unveiled at the spot where the men of 22 Platoon, on no4 Glider, landed, having been towed off course.
2:30 pm: "22 Platoon" will lead the group on a march back to Pegasus Bridge.
5:00 pm: In Ranville, Calvados, the arrival of "22 Platoon" group from Périers-en-Auge, will complete the 10 mile route they had to take on D-Day to rendezvous with their comrades. This will take the total distance covered to 75 miles for the 75th Anniversary of D-Day.
https://www.veteranscharity.org.uk/rtop/.

In the Footsteps of 47 Royal Marine Commando at Asnelles to Port-en-Bessin.

8:45 am: Following the movement of the D-Day landing of 47 Royal Marine Commando on Gold Beach, near Asnelles, and 20km march behind enemy lines with the objective of liberating Port-en-Bessin. Start from Asnelles, main car park by the bunker. Arrival in Port-en-Bessin.

Tribute to Airborne Troops at Leadership monument at Sainte-Marie-du-Mont (Manche), 913 Provincial Road ("route départementale") to Utah Beach.
Commemorative ceremony at the Major Dick Richard Winters Monument. Time to be confirmed.
Association D-Day Overlord.
https://www.dday-overlord.com/.

Utah Beach Ceremony at Utah Beach–Sainte-Marie-du-Mont (Manche).
10:00 am.

Celebration of D-Day at Sainte-Mère-Église (Manche).
10:00 am–12 pm: Exhibition of historic military vehicles.
2:00 pm: Reenactment of the embarkation of paratroopers in period dress at church square.
2:00 pm: Paratroopers demonstration about June 1944 boarding with comments at church square
4:00 pm: Ceremony at the Stele of Alexandre Renaud, former mayor of Sainte-Mère-Église.
4:30 pm: Mass in the church.
5:30 pm: Ceremony at the monument of AVA, place of June 6th.
8:30 pm: Concert for peace at church square.
2:00 pm: Paratroopers demonstration about June 1944 boarding with comments at church square.
Info: 02 33 21 00 33.

Band of Brothers Actors Autographing at Saint-Côme-du-Mont, Manche.
8:00 pm: Signing session at the D-Day Experience (Dead Man's Corner Museum). €20 per person. Does not include admission to the museum. www.wwiifoundation.org/events/film/.
Pay online in advance.

French Play at Carentan-les-Marais (Manche)–Théâtre de Carentan–Rue de la Halle.
9:00 pm: French play "*Les Voilà!*" written to commemorate the anniversary of the Normandy landings. Free.

Friday June 7th

Round Canopy Parachute Team at Ranville, Calvados.
Time TBA: Mass parachute drop by over British Drop Zone "K." Aircraft will return to Cherbourg Maupertus Airport following the drop. https://rcptusa.org/news/6301737.

D-Day Landings Ceremony at Sainte-Mère-Église (Manche).
9:00 am: Ceremony at the stele of the 3 temporary cemeteries. Info: 02 33 41 31 18.
9:30 am: Mass of the Memory in the church Notre-Dame-de-l'Assomption.
10:45 am: Ceremony at Signal Monument, 6th of June place.
11:35 am: Wreath-laying at milestone 0 in tribute to the civilian victims, facing the town hall at No. 6, rue du Cap-de-Laine.
11:45 am: Wreath-laying at the stele of Generals Gavin and Ridgway.
7:00 pm: "Banquet of Liberty," Friendly meal with the military of several nationalities. By reservation at the Tourist Office at Sainte Mère Église: +33 (0)2 33 21 00 33 or ot.sme@ccbdc.fr. Prices: Adults: 36 € – Children (7–12 years; free for children under 7 years old): 15 €. (payment before April 15th mandatory, check payable to AVA, limited places).
9:00 pm: *La Jazz en vadrouille* concert, Place du 6 Juin, then *Ladies for Liberty*.

D-Day Landings Ceremony at Carentan-les-Marais (Manche).
10:00 am: Ceremony in the presence of American paratroopers of the 101st Airborne Division, Republic Square.
11:30 am: Departure of the Carentan Liberty March. Information: carentanliberty-march@outlook.com.
Schedule to be specified: Ceremony at the Cole Monument, inauguration of the Purple Heart Lane (RN 13, north of Carentan) in the presence of troops of the 101st (US) Airborne Division.

***Band of Brothers* Actors Autographing** at Catz (Manche).
11:00 am–1:00 pm: Actors' signing session at the Normandy Victory Museum in Carentan. €20 per person. Does not include admission to the museum. www.wwiifoundation.org/events/film/.

D-Day Landings Ceremony at Chef-du-Pont (Manche).
12:00 pm: Country meal near the Rex Combs Square.
2:00 pm: Ceremony at the Rex Combs Square.

D-Day Landings Celebration at Arromanches.
2:00 pm to 11:00 pm: Commemorative overflight of 75 WWII PIPER L4 planes. Squadron flight of 3–6 planes for 1 hour.
The songs of Glenn Miller and Andrews Sisters will take you back to the days of the famous Boogie-woogie. Sing and dance all day long. Info: 02 31 22 34.

Liberation of Port-en-Bessin Ceremony at Port-en-Bessin.
3:00 pm–6:00 pm: Parade of

historic vehicles with reenactors wearing period outfits.
7:00 pm: Concert by Royal Marines orchestra. Info: 02 31 21 92 3.

D-Day Landings Ceremony at Beuzeville-au-Plain (Manche).
5:00 pm: Ceremony at the stele, Place Bienaimé Agnès.

D-Day Landings Ceremony at Picauville (Manche).
6:30 pm: Ceremony at 90th ID monument, followed by a meal on registration. Info: +33 (0)2 33 41 00 18.

WWII International Film Festival at Carentan (Manche).
8:00 pm: Award-winning films from the World War II International Film Festival will be shown at Salle du Théâtre in Carentan square. Awards presented by *Band of Brothers* actors. Free event. Reserve at www.wwiifoundation.org/events/film/.

Saturday June 8th

D-Day Landings Celebration at Sainte-Mère-Église (Manche)
9:00 am to 8:00 pm: D-Day Memorial Parade organized by Historic Programs, with 3,000 musicians from 15 US states.
9:00 pm: Musical entertainment with the group Les Refrains d'entour.
10:45 pm: Rehearsal demonstrations on the camp Géronimo (3 km from Sainte-Mère-Église, towards Picauville). Use of anti-aircraft searchlights.

Celebration Day at Tilly-sur-Seulles.
1:30 pm: Festival Hall, "Participation of the Native Americans in WWII": An official Comanche delegation will introduce this culture, the role of the Comanche Nation, and above all the Code Talkers.
1:30 pm: Stadium "Panoramic view over the Battlefield." A hot air balloon will provide a view over battlefield.
8:30 pm: Stadium. Brass Band concert playing 1940s music with the participation of traditional Comanches dancers and singers. Outdoor event followed by a firework and open-air dance. Info: 06 07 59 46 02/. association@tilly1944.com.

Commemorative Ceremony at Angoville (Manche).
10:00 am.

D-Day Landings Celebration at Ecausseville (Manche)–Dirigible hangar, La Lande.
10:00 am: Inauguration of the monument in memory of American soldiers and civilians of Ecausseville. This event will be followed by a reception.
3:30 pm: Parachuting close to the hangar of reenactors. Parachute

jump around the shed by men in period uniforms like those worn during the night of June 5th to 6th. Subject to favorable weather conditions.
Info: +33 (0)2 33 08 56 02.

D-Day Celebration at Ranville British War Cemetery (Calvados) 1 County St. Louis de Rohan Chabot, 14860.
Time TBA**:** Ceremony in honor of the Commonwealth soldiers who fell during the Battle of Normandy, with participation of the members of the Poppies of the Commonwealth war graves sponsorship program. Organization: Association D-Day Overlord. https://www.dday-overlord.com/.

Liberation's Parade at Bretteville-l'Orgueilleuse, Rue de Caen. 3:00 pm: In an old-style main street, come to see the liberation as if you were there. A walking parade with civilians and soldiers dressed in 1940s outfits preceded by a Scottish pipe band composed of 30 musicians will be followed by more than 150 civilian and military WWII vehicles and other surprises. Drink and souvenirs on site.
Info: 07 77 31 86 20 /. upthejohns@gmail.com.

Historical Hike at Amfreville (Manche).
4:30 pm: Guided historical hike of 5 mi/8 km. Comments on the battles of the 82nd (US) Airborne Division. Meet at the parking lot of the communal hall. Reenactors allowed without a real or dummy weapon. Limited places. Price: 2 €/pers. (under 10 free). Mandatory registration at the Tourist Office. +33 (0)2 33 21 00 33 or ot.sme@ccbdc.fr.

D-Day Landings Celebration at Carentan-les-Marais (Manche).
4:30 pm: Parade with the arrival of the exodus on the place of the Republic followed by the arrival of Carentan Liberty March. In the presence of 101st Airborne soldiers and American veterans.
8:30 pm: Liberation ball, rue de la Halle. Entry: 10 €. On-site catering. Organization: Carentan Liberty Group.

Great Aerial Meeting at Arromanches. Reenactor paratroopers dropping in the evening.
Info: 02 31 22 34 31.

Join up the Johns! Liberty Ball at Bretteville-l'Orgueilleuse.
7:00 pm: Fourth edition of the Liberation Ball organized by Up the Johns! Association, in a warm and redesigned atmosphere. Celebrating the liberation of the village with 1940s classic songs played by the band Dancing Day. Food and drink on site. Info: 07 77 31 86 20 / upthejohns@gmail.com.

Sunday June 9th

Celebration at Ste-Mère-Église–le Bourg la Fière (2mi/3km de Ste-Mère-Église direction Picauville).
10:00 am–12:00 pm: Exhibition of historic military vehicles.
2:00 pm to 3:00 pm: 1940s–1950s talent show.
3:15 pm to 5:45 pm: Musical performances.
6:00 pm: Parade of historic military vehicles in the streets.
8:45 pm to 10:00 pm: Musical performance with The Four Nation Country Blues Orchestra.
10:15 pm to 11:30 pm: Mimile and the Ramulots.
11:30 pm: Fireworks.
Info: 02 33 41 31 18.

Ceremony Honoring 101st Airborne Division at Brévands (Manche).
11:00 am: Ceremony honoring American paratroopers. Information: filthy.13@hotmail.fr.

Liberation Parade at Bayeux, Rue Principale.
11:00 am: Parade of British historic vehicles and pipe bands in the main street of the first liberated town of continental France.
Info: 02 31 51 28 28 / info@bayeux-tourism.com.

Ceremony Honoring Fights of Maisy Battery at Grandcamp-maisy (Calvados) – Maisy Battery.
11:00 am: Led by the 5th (US) Ranger Battalion, organized by the Maisy Battery Museum. Participation of the D-Day Overlord Association. https://www.dday-overlord.com/.

Reenactor Parachutists at La Fière (Manche).
11:00 am: In WW2 outfits with the participation of Liberty Jump and the Round Canopy Parachuting Team. Subject to favorable weather conditions.
1:00 pm: Parachute jumps with 1,000 paratroopers and 30 aircraft from several nations. Subject to favorable weather.
3:00 pm: Ceremony at the Iron Mike Monument.

Celebration of Liberation at Sainte-Mère-Église–**la Fière** (2mi/3km de Ste-Mère-Église in direction of Picauville).
11:00 am: Historical parachute jump with men in WWII uniforms.
1:00 pm: Great military parachute jump with paratroopers from different nations (subject to weather conditions).
11:00 am–2:00 pm: German Choir "Voix de la Paix partagée". Musical animations with "52è Rue."

Footsteps of XXXth British Corps around the Battle Museum and Tilly Fairground.
1:00 pm: Reenactors for British

liberators presenting WWII equipment and 200 British vehicles. Info: 06 07 59 46 02 /. association@tilly1944.com. info@bayeux-tourism.com.

Peace Ball at Ecausseville (Manche)–La Lande.
8:30 pm: At the dirigible hangar.
Info: +33 (0)2 33 08 56 02.

Monday, June 10th

Saint-Hilaire-Petitville (Manche)
10:00 am: Inauguration of the Fresco for Liberty at rue d'Isigny.
11:00 am: Ceremony at the Tucker Monument.

Celebration at Sainte-Mère-**Église** (Manche).
11:00 am: Meeting of May, Escher and Steele families
11:30 am: Musical entertainment with the Harmonie de l'Etoile Sottevastaise.
12:00 pm: Normandy Day Picnic.
12:30 pm–6:00 pm: Musical entertainment with Howlin' Fox and other shows. American equestrian performance on the equestrian ground next to the American military camp, near the market hall. Free. Info: 02 33 41 31 18.

Prison Ceremony at Foucarville (Manche).
3:00 pm: Ceremony at the former German prison camp.

Liberation Ceremony at Carentan-les-Marais (Manche).
Details TBA: Ceremony commemorating the liberation of the city. https://www.dday-overlord.com/.

IN UNITED STATES

"The Final Salute," the 75th Anniversary of D-Day at National D-Day Memorial Bedford, Virginia.
Wednesday, June 5th: Dedication of the U.S. Naval Academy Plaque.
Thursday, June 6th: Aerial Tribute to the Veterans of WWII–**10 am.** "The Final Salute" Commemorative Observance–**11:00 am.** Roll Call–Approximately **12:30 pm.** (The annual gathering around the "Homage" sculpture will take place immediately following the roll call.)
Friday, June 7th: Regular admission and tours of the Memorial & Outdoor Concert and Canteen. Time TBA.
https://www.virginiawwiandwwii.org/.

For additional listings of events in the U.S. see the D-Day Annual Events section of this book.

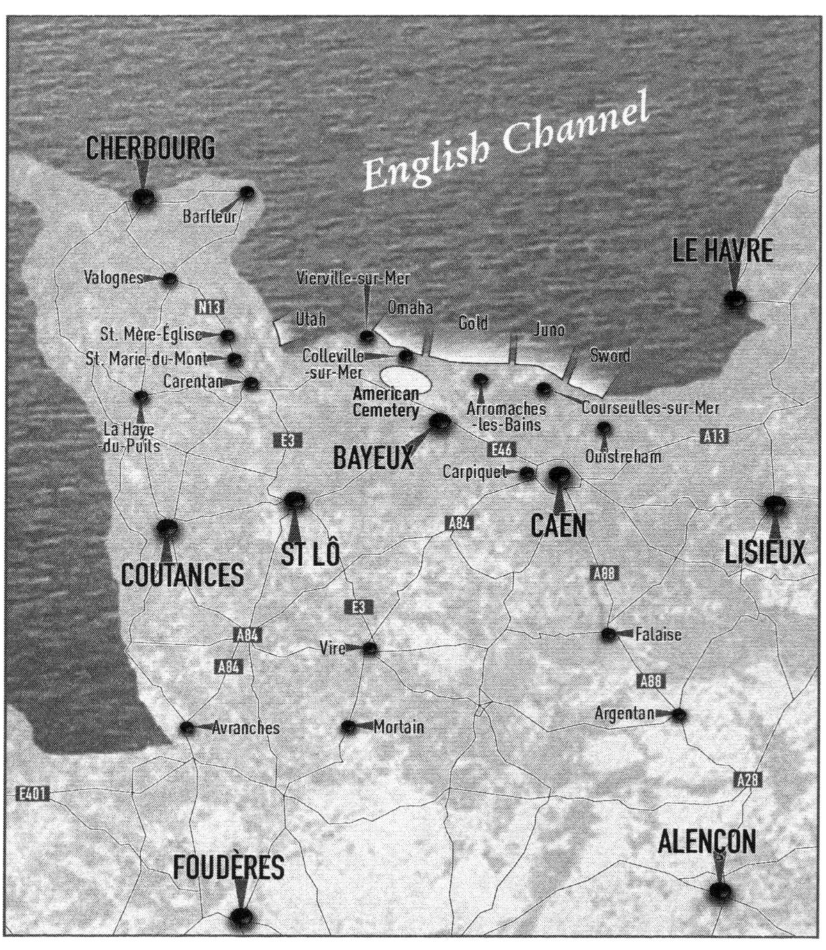

This map shows the location of major points of interest in World War II Normandy. For more information, consult the *D-Day 75th Anniversary—A Millennials Guide* **READERS ONLY** online website.

IN GREAT BRITAIN

Run to Pegasus at Tarrant Rushton Airfield in Dorset. **Tuesday, June 4–Wednesday, June 5.**
8:30 am: To commemorate the 75th Anniversary of D-Day and to honor the men who spearheaded the invasion, the Run to Pegasus, which was first staged in 2009, is being repeated. On June 4 a group of 186 sponsored runners will set off from the site of and make their way into the New Forest and down to Portsmouth, covering 62 miles in under 24 hours. Leaving Tarrant Rushton in the evening, the group will follow a 62-mile route overnight, to Portsmouth. After arriving at the ferry port, the group will sail at 10:00 pm on Wednesday, June 5 to Normandy. www.veteranscharity.org.uk/rtop.

Daks over Normandy at Duxford Airfield, UK.
June 4 & 5: The June 4th jump will be a mass practice jump in the United Kingdom. On that day C-47s participating in the event will fly in formation across the English Channel to drop a large group of paratroopers into an original 1944 drop zone in Normandy. https://www.daksovernormandy.com.

D-Day 75th Land Run at Walton-on-Thames, Surrey–the Xcel Leisure Centre. **June 6–8 at 9:30** am daily. D-Day runs are 6-hour timed events where participants choose from 5km to ultra-marathon. Participants can complete as many or as few laps as they like of a 3.28 mi/5.3km out and back course along the beautiful River Thames. Runners of all abilities welcomed. Anyone who completes even one lap will get a medal. Places limited. £37.95 (Affiliated) or £39.95 (Unaffiliated). https://www.phoenixrunning.co.uk/events/d-day-75th-land-run.

Normandy 75 – Global War Studies at Portsmouth, Hampshire. **July 22–July 25.**
This International Conference will bring together scholars, students, and the public from a variety of disciplines. Second World War historians will discuss the wide-ranging, international implications of the campaign. Registration will continue to July 5 via the online store. http://www2.port.ac.uk/portsmouth-business-school/conferences-and-business-events/normandy-75/.

Southwick D-Day 75 Revival at Southwick Hampshire on 8th–9th June.
Historic days at the nerve-center of Operation Overlord. Also see D-Day Annual Events section of this book.
www.southwickrevival.co.uk

VALOGNES
BARFLEUR
NO SIGNAL!
ROAMING NOT AVAILABLE.
A LOUR FOR RENT
USA
OH SNAP!
CHILL, DUDES. I GOT US COVERED!

JUST FOR FUN

D-DAY LANDING QUIZ

Sharon Gytri and Jay Wertz

Are you a scholar of WWII? Check out your knowledge on this quiz of the Normandy D-Day Landings. See how you do at the end. Good luck!

1. **The Allied landing forces mainly consisted of which soldiers?**
   a. Canadians, British and Americans
   b. Polish, French and Italians
   c. Belgians, Dutch and Russians
   d. All of the above

2. **The Allies tricked the Germans in which way?**
   a. They transmitted fake broadcasts between England and the French city of Dover conveying to the Germans that Calais would be the place of the Allied attack.
   b. They projected dummy paratroopers from lasers at fake invasion sites.
   c. They used "phantom" armies with fake tanks and planes near places the Germans expected attacks.
   d. The British sent in the famous spy Mati Hari to distract Hitler.

3. **Which film is about the Normandy D-Day Landings?**
   a. "The Longest Day"
   b. "The English Patient"
   c. "A Bridge Too Far"
   d. "The Hateful Eight"

4. **Why was the invasion postponed by one day when the planned invasion was for June 5, 1944?**
   a. The Allies knew that German Field Marshall Rommel's wife was having a birthday party June 6th and so they knew that Rommel would be absent from France.
   b. British meteorologists convinced General Eisenhower of probable stormy weather.
   c. An Irish psychic predicted that June 5th would be a risky day to attack the Germans.
   d. American astronomers predicted a lunar eclipse making visibility poor for paratroopers.

5. **What does the "D" stand for in D-Day?**
   a. "Done" since the Normandy D-Day Landings ended the war.
   b. "Doom" standing for doomsday for the Germans.
   c. "Day" the military term D stands for Day.
   d. "Da" the Welsh word for done.

6. **What was the name of the cliffs that the Rangers scaled on D-Day that aided the Allied Forces landing on Omaha Beach?**
   a. White Cliffs of Dover
   b. Orly Cliffs
   c. Point du Hoc Cliffs
   d. Mesa Verde Cliffs

7. **What was so significant about the D-Day Landings?**
   a. It was the largest seaborne invasion in history.
   b. Hitler watched the D-Day Landings from Point du Hoc Cliffs.
   c. It began the liberation of German occupied France.
   d. Both a & c.

8. **The two beaches that Americans landed on D Day were?**
   a. Silver and Utah
   b. Sword and Nevada
   c. Omaha and Utah
   d. Malibu and Waikiki

9. **Which D-Day Landings beach had the highest number of casualties?**
   a. Silver Beach
   b. Omaha Beach

c. Nevada Beach
d. Sword Beach

10. Who was not a commander/leader at the D-Day Landings?
a. Dwight D. Eisenhower
b. Gerd von Rundstedt
c. Bertram Ramsey
d. Ronald Reagan

11. How long was the planning phase for D-Day?
a. Two weeks
b. Two months
c. Two years
d. Immediately after Germany invaded France

12. What music did the Allies use to lure Germans in Normandy to surrender by creating an atmosphere of nostalgia? (Suggested by Mark Weisenmiller)
a. Louis Armstrong blues
b. Johann Strauss waltzes
c. "De Valkieries" by Richard Wagner
d. "Yankee Doodle Dandy" by George M. Cohan

13. What happened at the end of the day on D-Day?
a. The Germans drove the Allies forces back to their boats.
b. The Allies moved off the beaches and established positions inland.
c. The invading soldiers spent a cold, dreary night on the beaches.
d. After many were killed, the survivors were withdrawn to England.

Answers to D-Day Landing Quiz:

1. A	**2.** C	**3.** A	**4.** B	**5.** C
6. C	**7.** D	**8.** C	**9.** B	**10.** D
11. C	**12.** B	**13.** B		

9 or 10 correct—You are definitely a brilliant scholar of WWII or perhaps just smart and caring enough to really pay attention to the stories of a father, grandpa or relative who fought bravely in WWII. Then you probably had the intellectual curiosity to learn more of the facts about the history of the D-Day Landings. You are a person deserving of admiration.

8-6 correct—Um, were you a middle child or just an excellent guesser? At any rate, you are concerned about the World around you and how past history can influence the events of today. Kudos to you.

5-0 correct—You were the like cool, popular kid in high school. Were you a cheerleader or a football hero? Maybe you were voted the biggest flirt or the class clown. People loved to talk to you in school since you were a wonderful conversationalist. However, you probably have matured more now to know learning about important events in history can be interesting too. After all, you're reading this guide!

OVERLORD CROSSWORD PUZZLE

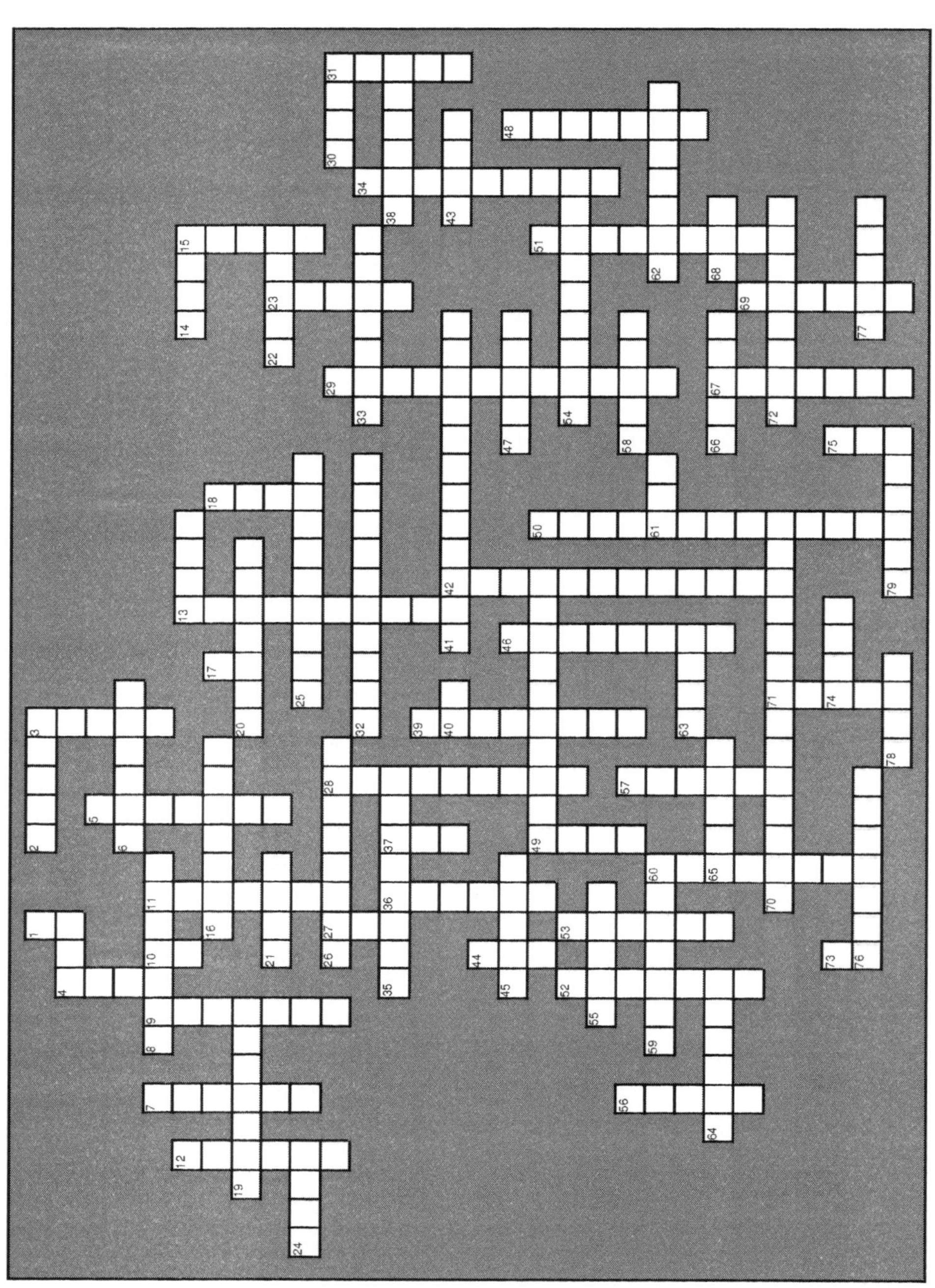

ACROSS

2 German pistol manufacturer
4 Ship with bow doors (abbr.)
6 French Underground organization
8 Queen Elizabeth II's husband
13 D-Day objective for British
14 British slang for a glass of beer
16 Virginia home town of famous American unit
19 Mythological name given to bridge
20 American gum maker
21 D-Day beach exit/sketch
22 Wife of Supreme Commander
24 Code name for beach on Cotentin Peninsula
25 Largest American bomber in D-Day campaign
26 International symbol of medical forces
30 Higgins boat (abbr.)
32 American novelist and war correspondent
33 U. S. president – D-Day 50th anniversary
35 Handheld American machine gun
38 Commander of 101st Airborne Division
40 American ally (abbr.)
41 German beach obstacles used at Normandy
43 WWII hospital diagnostic tool
45 There's no looking over the white cliffs of ______
47 Star of Saving Private Ryan
49 English port city
54 Military vehicle with tires and treads
55 City in central France
58 First Aid giver
59 U. S. Army special forces unit at D-Day
61 Compass direction, Normandy from England (abbr.)
62 ________ PIGEON
63 Pork shoulder and ham
64 Famous American tank commander
65 ID system using radio waves (abbr.)
66 Japanese-American generation fought in WWII
68 Code name for beach group on Omaha's east side
70 Allied truck route across France
72 Key river taken by 82nd Airborne troops
74 American made glider
76 Fast American pursuit plane
77 Important French river objective after D-Day
78 Month of D-Day landing
79 Riviera invasion site/film festival resort

DOWN

1 U. S. Navy patrol boat (abbr.)
3 Slang for American wartime female factory worker
4 First name of Nazi documentary director
5 BARRAGE ______
7 The "D" in FDR
9 Chocolate bar maker
10 U.S.state of Higgins boat shipyard (abbr.)
11 British Isles country neutral in WWII
12 Some non-German D-Day defenders
13 American D-Day military cemetery (short form)
15 Nickname of heavy German tank
17 Slang for American serviceman (abbr.)
18 Code for beach where Canadian 3rd Division landed
23 Nickname of D-Day ground forces commander
27 European Theater of Operations (abbr.)
28 German U-Boat base (abbr.)
29 Location of practice landing disaster
31 French capital
34 American actor/U. S. Navy lieutenant commander
36 Band leader killed in Europe
37 Not present on Normandy morning of 6-6-44
39 High speed train under English Channel
42 Nickname of USA Seventh Corps commander
44 Popular GI mascot
46 Slang for German V-1 rocket
48 American paratrooper's communication device
49 Rockwell magazine (partial)
50 Author of famous D-Day novel
51 American handheld torpedo
52 Street name of British PM residence
53 Clergyman/American self-propelled gun
56 American air force in WWII (abbr.)
57 U. S. Navy battleship off Omaha Beach
60 Field officer's main man
67 Popular American tank
69 One of two German-held British islands on French coast
71 First name of German field marshal
73 Time of day for D-Day landing (abbr.)
75 International distress signal (abbr.)

Answers to Overlord Crossword Puzzle on page 221

```
C X Y G E N U J S C R E N Z S O R N T V O A B T N S J
S O B N C M T L K L A R R O N R I A S S R N L M I J Y
S F R M C I M S N I T I D U E W E H D E O B A R J J B
O D H N O O D T A N S A J R R G C G L A A P A L G O D
R L A T E B L E H T O Z E E E E I L N R R P B G E I L
C N L N E L Z L M O R A R N Z G I P R A L U G E R D M
D U F E A R I Z E N U N E C I M I A R Y R G P V C L G
E S T T G M E U U V E T L I N E G T Q E N R M N Q P Q
R R R N N Q R D S B I S O O S E S X Y I I D N Q R N B
P E A O A Y Z E R R N L S U B O S K N A B R I A F M P
J D C M T K E O H E Y P L A R D R W S D T X R P X J K
E B K Z S Y T S A S M A L E O S O E D R A W H A N B Q
O A T M U E D C E O N L N V N D R Y Y V P I T M C H J
J L S T M U T A H P O S E T A G N A I G L E B P T D Z
G L Y D E R J T D O J R Q Y E P W Q Y L L L T U T V G
N E T K N K S E N N A C R A N G B D I I L N O M A P S
I X R D U A C Y Y T N K N D N V N P B A M M F A A S U
N P Y O R B S I E V T T T I W A G E G D S N E V A D A
T R E P L O K N R L W J M N L Z R M B T H E R S H E Y
H E S D D A F Y O C G M P E I A L T R P E G A S U S Q
G S R T B M G D N T E I R A T P Z O T A Y L O R Q B L
I S E T Y P B N E H P I R O T V P M A Q U I S Q T L Y
L D J M A M I E A B T A R W C T N I S E I Y A R N X D
L E K R D P Y G D B Y W L D B A O Y T B W R D M D J V
J W N V R R G M V Q L Q M S N K W N K G Q M B L R L J
R D K I T X Z T D Z M L T J D J M T W X D D P R G T N
```

WORD SEARCH

AM
BANGALORE
BARRAGE BALLOON
BEDFORD
BELGIAN GATES
BUZZ BOMB
CAEN
CANNES
CARRIER PIGEON
CLINTON
COLLEVILLE
CORNELIUS RYAN
CRICKET
CZECHS
DELANO
DOG
DOVER
DOWNING
DRAW
ERWIN
ESE
ETO
EUROSTAR
FAIRBANKS
FOX
GI
HALFTRACK
HANKS
HEMMINGWAY
HERSHEY
IRELAND
JERSEY
JUNE
JUNO
LA
LCVP
LENI
LIBERATOR
LIGHTNING JOE
LST
LUGER
MAMIE
MAQUIS
MEDIC
MERDERET
MILLER
MONTE
MUSTANG
NEVADA
NISEI
PARIS
PATTON
PEGASUS
PHILLIP
PINT
PORTSMOUTH
POST
PT
RADAR
RANGERS
RED BALL EXPRESS
RED CROSS
ROSIE
SEINE
SERGEANT
SHERMAN
SLAPTON SANDS
SPAM
STNAZAIRE
SUN
TAYLOR
THOMPSON
TIGER
TOURS
UK
USAAF
UTAH
WACO
WRIGLEY
X-RAY

Answers to Word Search on page 221

MILLENNIAL SUDOKU

				1	8	2	6	
6	9				3		7	
			6	7			1	
	7			2	6			
9	6		7	4				
	3		8			7	5	
7				3		4		
	4					3		
3							2	

Answers to Millennial Sudoku

4	5	7	9	1	8	2	6	3
6	9	1	2	5	3	8	7	4
8	2	3	6	7	4	5	1	9
1	7	5	3	2	6	9	4	8
9	6	8	7	4	5	1	3	2
2	3	4	8	9	1	7	5	6
7	8	6	5	3	2	4	9	1
5	4	2	1	6	9	3	8	7
3	1	9	4	8	7	6	2	5

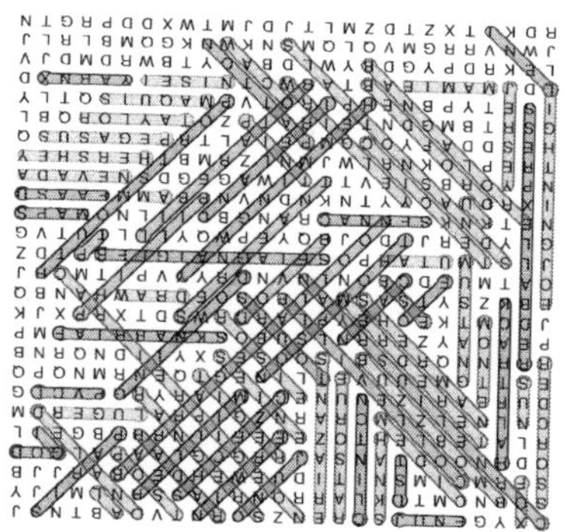

Answers to Word Search

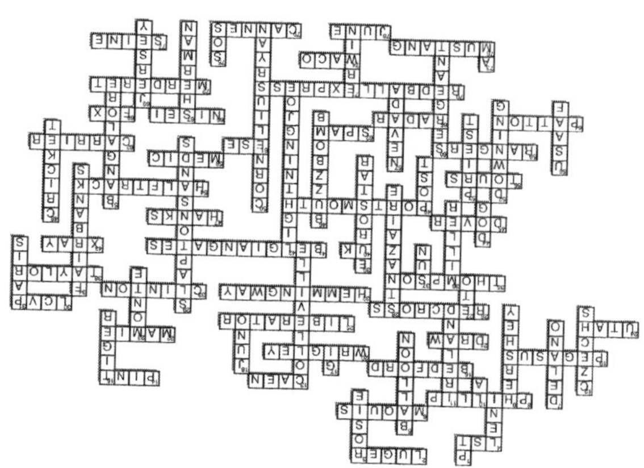

Answers to Overlord Crossword Puzzle

MAN, AMERICAN FLYBOYS IN THOSE COOL LEATHER JACKETS! THEY MUSTA CHARMED THE LOCAL LASSES BIG TIME!
York

ALLIED FLYERS EPIC PUB CRAWL

A Pub Crawl Down Memory Lane

Sandro Monetti

Many of the East of England pubs where American airmen drank when stationed there during WWII are still standing today. Most of them look largely unchanged from the years when GIs played darts and dominoes in them, downed pints and charmed the local girls.

A pub crawl around these Suffolk hostelries is like a step back in time, as several are full of wartime memorabilia in honor of the U.S. pilots who fought the air war in Europe's deadly skies before, during and after D-Day.

That bucolic county was home to more American airfields than anywhere else in Britain. For a brief time these sprawling bases transformed the landscape of the farmland area known as East Anglia.

Memories of the airmen and ground crews of the United States Army Air Force live on in the region today at places like the Airmen's Bar in Lavenham's Swan Hotel. The signatures of dozens of American fliers appear on a wall there, several of them members of the 487th Bombardment Group, which flew 185 missions from Lavenham Airfield (operational from March 1944 to August 1945) in B-24 and B-17 bombers. Among their missions was bombing airfields in northern France in preparation for D-Day.

In their free time the Americans would walk from their Nissen huts on the base across several fields to the pub, leaving their muddy flying boots at the door to collect when they left.

Talking of leaving things behind, The Swan Inn in the village of Lawshall has coins nailed to its timber beams that were hammered in by servicemen to reclaim on their return. The large number of unclaimed coins there remain as a permanent reminder to honor those from the village and much further afield who lost their lives in war.

The Swan Inn is everyone's idea of a typical English country pub. Around since the 18th century, it's a thatched-roof, timber-framed paradise in a picture-postcard-perfect sleepy village. Recently lovingly restored, it retains the period features that made it such a picturesque home away from home for the American servicemen.

Another beautiful Suffolk village is Horringer, where you can find one more long-standing pub, The Beehive, which used to be swarming with servicemen. It had the same owners from the start of World War I right through to the late 1980s and still retains the same welcoming family atmosphere now. Time has moved on, of course, but this corner of the world in Suffolk has changed very little from how things were in 1944.

Meanwhile, little has changed in 500 years at timeless pub The Weeping Willow at Barrow with its beautiful flower beds and secluded corners creating a relaxed ambience that must have seemed to the servicemen a world away from war and its terrors.

Sometimes beautiful things come out of horror-filled times like wars, and such is the case with the Appleby Rose Garden in Abbey Gardens. The picturesque spot in Bury St Edmunds is a quiet place for reflection and houses a number of memorials to war veterans. Visitors there can sit on a bench made from the wing of an actual American Flying Fortress bomber. The rose garden is named after American John Appleby, who served with the 487th Bomb Group in Lavenham, and was funded by the royalties from *Suffolk Summer*, a book he wrote about being stationed there in WWII.

Airmen like him were admired and idolized by the locals. The kids wanted to be them and the women, well, wanted them. These exotic creatures brought with them Coca-Cola, peanut butter, chewing gun, jitterbug dancing, good manners and great looks. With all those handsome, suntanned men in the countryside it must have seemed like Suffolk had been invaded by Hollywood movie stars.

Speaking of film stars, Clark Gable served in the USAAF and came to Polebrook, Northhamtonshire, to shoot film for ***Combat America***, a propaganda-recruitment film about air gunners. Officially, he went on five combat missions as a gunner, but flew on many more to capture 50,000 feet of film. The head of the Luftwaffe, Hermann Göring, reportedly offered a sizable reward to any pilot who shot down the "King of Hollywood," but the reward was never claimed.

The Americans would have such a positive impact on the local communities in East Anglia and elsewhere that their arrival was known as "the friendly invasion." Some of the locals became more than just friends, of course. Among them was Suffolk's May Rose Lockwood, a member of the Women's Land Army, who met and fell for Robert Kirschner when he was stationed in her region with the 56th Fighter Group. They were married in Coddenham, Suffolk, in 1943 and moved to Syracuse, New York, after the war where they lived happily ever after, enjoying 51 years of marriage.

But in wartime there are sometimes conflicts even when you are on the same side, and not all the men of Suffolk shared the same enthusiasm for their American cousins. Some simmering resentment overheated during a notorious February 1945 bar brawl at the White Horse Tavern in Sudbury.

Three Brits, or "Limeys" as the Americans called them, were in there loudly singing the praises of their services commander, "Monty" (Field Marshall Sir Bernard Law Montgomery) who had taken the credit for defeating the Germans in the Battle of the Bulge, a German offensive on the Western Front, December 1944–January 1945.

That caused no end of ill-feeling with the U.S. Armed Forces as so many Americans had given their lives in that battle—the 19,276 American fatalities making it one of the most lethal campaigns in their country's history.

In the pub, a heated discussion between Brits and Americans about the battle swiftly turned into a shouting match and then plenty of pushing and shoving until the punches started flying. Tables were overturned and bottles smashed as a full-on brawl broke out. Military police eventually arrived at The White Horse to sort out the mess, take the worst offenders away and try to cool the situation, which was seeing just about everyone letting off steam in a full-on melee. (For more information on the tensions between Americans and British in England, see the "Men and Women in Uniform – Americans" chapter of this book.)

Perhaps some of the frustration felt by the Americans that dark and cold December night was fueled by their difficult living conditions at the air bases. Their Nissen huts were heated only by a tiny stove, the washrooms were unheated and the latrines were primitive to say the least. But the conditions and the weather were the least of their worries. The specter of death loomed large.

Many colleagues had been lost in action, and most days the airmen practiced the skills of close formation flying, gunnery, navigation and bombing, knowing their lives were likely to depend on such training.

It's hard to imagine what it must have been like for these young men to find themselves half a world away from home, facing death or glory on a daily basis.

Yet an escape from the tensions and fears came with trips to the local public houses where two cultures came together over a few pints and the hostelries provided a welcome break from hostilities.

In 1944, in the lead-up to D-Day, half a million members of the USAAF were based in Britain, on 200 airfields. Each base would house around 2,500 to 3,000 servicemen. That was much more than the population of the villages surrounding each base.

Suffolk villages with names like Holton, Bungay and Parham had experienced very little in the way of global, or even national, impact up to that point, but they were to play a significant part in World War II, housing thousands of servicemen and their aircraft who helped turned the course of the war. B-17 Flying Fortress and B-24 Liberator bombers along with fighters like P-38 Lightnings, P-47 Thunderbolts and P-51 Mustangs routinely broke the silence over the peaceful Suffolk countryside.

The job of the members of the USAAF was to man and maintain aircraft that would attack German targets, and the locals were overjoyed to see them and live under the American air armada's protection.

But flying in England was a big challenge to master for the U.S. pilots, who were used to the massive airfields of Texas, California and Arizona, where there was much clearer visibility. In East Anglia clouds were often below 1,000 feet and visibility less than five miles.

The Suffolk airfields were frequently described as "the size of a dime" and not all of those who lost their lives in the skies did so while attacking the Germans; training accidents and crashes in Anglian fields were all too common.

The mission of the Allies was to crush the German war machine, and the strategy used to achieve it in the air was a round-the-clock bombing campaign. The Royal Air Force would bomb by night and the USAAF by day. Just as the RAF were returning to their bases west of Suffolk after a night of bombing, the Americans would take off, form into large formations and head east towards their targets. Those lucky enough to make it back to England would repeat the procedure over and over again.

Fond memories of those heroic fliers are preserved by volunteers who manage websites, museums, memorials and more all with the aim of

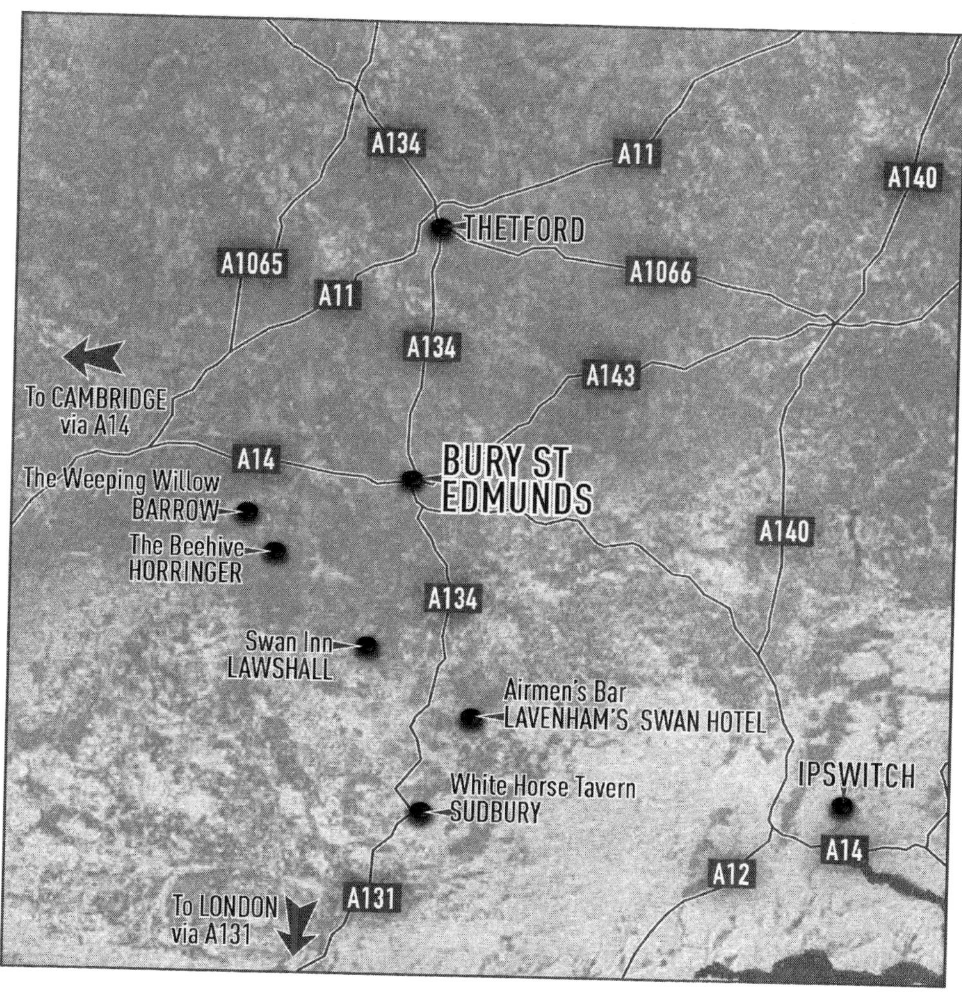

Engaging in a "pub crawl" to follow the route of East Anglia drinking establishments is easy using major routes or rural roads. Most U.S. bomber units in 1943-45 were stationed at bases on the right side of this map. If driving the route, remember to use caution, especially if you are not used to driving on the left side of the road; please respect local laws and do not drive while intoxicated.

informing current and future generations about the magnificent men in their flying machines.

One memory that should never fade is the contribution such heroes made to D-Day, when air power was a key part of *Operation Overlord*'s success. Without support from the skies, the Normandy invasion would have been impossible.

The Allied air campaign for the invasion of Europe began with an attempt to wipe out as much of the Luftwaffe as possible. It worked. Months of warfare in the air inflicted heavy losses on the German forces and in May 1944 alone 25 percent of Germany's fighter pilot force was killed. By the time of the June 6 invasion, the Luftwaffe was unable to muster much of a defense at the battlefront.

During the D-Day invasion itself, 171 squadrons of American and British fighters flew air support for invading forces, protecting ships and striking at inland targets. The invasion swept in like a sudden storm, and Allied air power was deadly and decisive.

Waves of casualties from D-Day were treated at the biggest U.S. Air Force hospital in Western Europe, the 65th General Hospital at the village of Botesdale, Suffolk. All that remains of the since-demolished hospital today is a small plaque on a brick wall half a mile outside the village.

As we reach the 75th anniversary of D Day, the plaques, the wreaths, the memorials and the history books that accompany the occasion all serve to remind us of the sacrifice and splendor of the brave souls who fought in that never-to-be-forgotten moment of history.

Following VE Day in 1945, the USAAF departed England as quickly as they arrived and the airfields were deserted, many later demolished. But in the pubs and in the minds and hearts of the locals, those American airmen will never be forgotten. So as you sit enjoying a last pint in the King's Arms or tossing darts at the Cock Horse Inn before heading back home, try to imagine the scene in those surroundings some 75 years ago. Back then the Yanks were not only a mission to defeat Hitler but also to absorb themselves in as much local flavor, including barley and hops, as possible.

IN THE FOOTSTEPS OF HEROES

Touring Dick Winters's 'Day of Days'

Christopher J. Anderson

Since their first run up Mount Currahee in the summer of 1942, the men of the 506th Parachute Infantry Regiment (PIR) had been preparing for this moment. At approximately 1:15 a.m. in the flak-filled skies over France, 6,600 young paratroopers of the 101st Airborne Division began leaping from 490 C-47s and descending on enemy-held positions in Normandy. They were the vanguard of the long-anticipated invasion of France. If they failed in their mission of clearing the four causeways that ran over the flooded fields behind Utah Beach, the landings could not succeed. And if the landings on D-Day's western-most beaches were unsuccessful, the fate of the invasion itself was in doubt.

As readers of Stephen E. Ambrose's *Band of Brothers* and viewers of Stephen Spielberg and Tom Hanks's HBO mini-series of the same name know, the story of what Easy Company and the rest of the 101st Airborne Division accomplished on D-Day is one of the most compelling of World War II. Even today, 75 years after what Major Richard Winters remembered as his "Day of Days," many of the places talked about so dramatically in the book and shown in the series remain as they were on the morning of June 6, waiting for *Band of Brothers* fans to visit and explore. Armed with some imagination, good maps, car, a suitable pair of walking shoes and the directions and accounts provided in this chapter, you too will be able to walk in the footsteps of heroes and see for yourself where the history depicted so graphically in the HBO miniseries actually happened. You will follow Major Winters from his eventful landing outside the village of Ste. Mère Église to his incredible assault on a German gun battery at Brecourt Manor; arguably one of the most crucial actions of D-Day. As Major Winters remarked to this writer on more than one occasion, "*You can't possibly understand how things happened on D-Day unless you go there, study the terrain and walk the same ground as me and my men.*"

Your first stop should be in the village of Ste. Mere Église, as it was for so many of the men of the 101st and 82nd Airborne Divisions. Best remembered as the place where the 82nd Airborne's John Steele found himself caught on the church steeple while the battle raged below, the village is also where several Easy Company men landed early on the morning of June 6. Begin at the world-renowned Airborne Museum just off the main square, which will give you a good general overview of the entirety of the U.S. Airborne operations on D-Day. After exploring the museum, cross the square and stand facing the entrance to the church. Look up. If you had been standing here just after 1:15 the morning of June 6, 1944, you would have seen the C-47s of the 439th Troop Carrier Group passing overhead roughly from your left to your right. The aircraft were heading toward Drop Zone C, about four miles away. Unfortunately, due to a series of circumstances that are still debated to this day, the formation of C-47s had broken apart and soon paratroopers of the 101st Airborne were being dropped all over the peninsula—some as far away as Cherbourg.

Return to your car. If you parked in the lot across from the museum, drive into town until you reach Voie de la Liberte and turn right in the direction of Cherbourg. At your first intersection turn left onto the Rue De Verdun. Drive a very short distance, pass under the overpass for the N13 and stop your car at the intersection. On the morning of the invasion one of the 20mm anti-aircraft guns that wreaked such havoc on planes carrying the 506th was located here. Nearby was an MG42 machine gun that then-lieutenant Richard Winters remembered firing on him as he descended.

"*Jesus Christ, there's the green light!*" Winters later wrote in his diary, *We're down to 150 miles per hour and still eight minutes out. OK—let's go, Bill Lee, God damn—there goes my knee pack, and every bit of my equipment. "Watch it boy, watch it! Jesus Christ, they're trying to pick me up with that machine gun." Slip, slip, try to keep close to that leg pack. There—it landed beside that hedge. There's a road, trees—I hope I don't hit them. Thump—well, that wasn't too bad. Now to get out of this chute.*

Burton Christenson, who jumped immediately behind Winters, later remembered just how lucky the lieutenant had been.

As Winters left the plane a heavy burst of 20mm hit the tail. I thought for certain he had gone right into it. I was out the door behind him in another second. The 20mm anti-aircraft gun shut down for a moment. With so much action and confusion going on, I don't think I did anything I had been trained to do, but suddenly I got a tremendous shock when my parachute opened . . . A C-47 off to my right, its left engine on fire, seemed to be disintegrating.

Winters landed on the edge of an orchard that was located behind the farm building on your right as you pass under the overpass, and not in the woods as shown in the series. He could hear machine-gun fire coming from the town and could see the church steeple silhouetted by a fire near the square. Although he did not yet know where he was, he knew immediately that he had been dropped in the wrong place. Drop Zone C, where he was supposed to land, was located just outside of Ste. Marie du Mont, which was unique in having the only church in the area with an onion-shaped dome. The church steeple he could see had the typical square Norman tower.

Not wanting to get trapped in the town and anxious to get on with his mission, which was to secure the town of Ste. Marie du Mont and Causeway Numbers 1 and 2 leading off of Utah Beach, Winters prepared to move. Shortly after setting out he was joined by another mis-dropped paratrooper. As they emerged onto the Voie de la Liberte across from the Hotel de Ville, which you can see to your right, they encountered Carwood Lipton. After landing behind the Hotel de Ville, Lipton had stumbled across a road sign marked Ste. Mère Église, so he was able to tell Winters where they were. After consulting a map, the three men headed northeast in the direction of Ste. Marie du Mont.

It is now time for you to leave Ste. Mère Église. Before leaving, purchase any supplies you may need for the remainder of the day. Also, you are encouraged to go to one of the souvenir shops around the square and buy a copy of the *IGN Series Blue Map 1311OT Valognes Utah Beach*, which covers the area of airborne operations on June 6 in some detail.

Drive out of town on the D-17 in the direction of Beuzeville-au-Plain. Upon entering the village, just past the church you will see a gravel parking lot with a monument. Stop here. The marker is a memorial to the crew and passengers of Stick 66, which was the group of men in the C-47 carrying Easy Company's new commanding officer First Lieutenant Thomas Meehan and the company's headquarters section. ("Stick" refers to a group of parachutists who jump or are scheduled to jump from the same exit door onto the same drop zone.) Originally from Baker Company, Meehan was promoted to Easy Company command after the relief of Captain Herbert Sobel. The plane, piloted by Lieutenant Harold Cappelluto, was most likely hit by anti-aircraft fire from guns located near Ste. Mère Église.

Lieutenant Frank De Felitta, who was flying directly behind Cappelluto's plane, remembered what he saw:

As we flew over Normandy Harold's plane got hit several times. I could see flak shrapnel going right through his plane. After maintaining its course and speed for a while, the plane left formation and slowly initiated a right turn. I followed with my eyes and noticed its landing lights coming on. I thought it was going to be all right. Then, suddenly, it came crashing down a hedgerow and instantly exploded.

The fire from the explosion was so intense that the plane burned for three days. Forrest Guth remembered that as he made his way toward Ste. Marie du Mont in search of the rest of Easy Company he passed the still-burning wreck of the plane. He took a quick picture but said he could not get too close to inspect the wreckage as the heat was too intense. Many other members of Easy Company tell a similar story of passing Meehan's burning plane but being unable to stop. Meehan's death meant that command of the company would fall upon Winters later that morning.

Just to the right of the monument is a dirt road bordered by tall hedgerows. Walk down the road a short distance and you will get a feel for what the terrain was like in June 1944. Cappelluto's plane crashed in the field to your left. Return the way you came. When you get to the edge of Beuzeville, make a left onto Rue Saint Thomas (D115). Stay on this until you reach the intersection with the D67 and then stop.

Winters' "command" now consisted of approximately a dozen men; most of whom, including Winters, had lost their weapons and equipment on the jump. Soon after moving out of town, they ran into a larger group of men commanded by Lieutenant Colonel Robert G. Cole from 3rd Battalion, 502nd Parachute Infantry Regiment. Cole, who would later receive the Medal of Honor for his actions outside Carentan and be killed in action in September 1944, told Winters to just join the rear of his column. *"The rest of the night,"* Winters remembered, *"was spent walking down the road while the senior officers tried to find a way to the objective."* As the group continued on, other Americans from the 502nd and 506th joined it.

You are now at the dogleg intersection that was the location of the ambush that you see in the miniseries. Having heard the approaching German wagons, Cole decided to spread his men across this intersection so they could shoot as the wagons became separated traversing the turns. As soon as the first two wagons had reached where you now stand, the GIs opened fire, cutting down the horses and men around the first two wagons while two other wagons were able to gallop away. Easy Company was not directly involved in the firefight and Winters did not yell at Bill Guarnere to cease fire. As Winters explained, "*We were at the rear of the column and did not have weapons. I don't know how we would have been able to shoot at anything. We were there, but it was Cole's men who destroyed those wagons.*" Continue on the D115.

Not long after ambushing the German column, Cole broke up his group. The 506th men, which included Winters's party, headed toward their objectives near Ste. Marie du Mont while Cole and the men from the 502nd set out to secure Causeways 3 and 4. Alone again, Winters was able to find an American rifle under the seat of an abandoned German wagon. "*Finally armed,*" Winters remembered, "*I was happy once again.*" About 6:00 a.m. Winters ran into Captain Jerre Gross of Company D and his party of approximately 40 men. Together the two groups moved toward Ste. Marie du Mont.

Continue on the D115 until you come to another T-junction. Turn right; this is the D14. It was most likely in the area of this intersection that Winters ran into Gross. To your left, approximately two miles away, is Utah Beach. On D-Day morning, Winters and his group walked up this road until they came to the small settlement of Le Grand-Chemin. By the time they arrived at approximately 7:00, the landings had already begun and the company was nowhere near completing its mission—it was not even much of a company. Its company commander and headquarters platoon were all dead and, of the 139 men who jumped that morning, as the day began Easy Company consisted of two officers (Winters and Lynn "Buck" Compton), nine riflemen, two light machine guns, one bazooka with no ammunition and a 60mm mortar with no baseplate.

As Winters's men rested, they could hear fire coming from the direction of the beach but, perhaps more alarmingly, they could also hear gunfire coming from behind the village. Winters, who knew where he was, remembered that he was surprised to hear German guns firing nearby. There was not supposed to be a German battery anywhere near Le Grand-Chemin.

Amazingly, given all of the intelligence gathered by the Allies prior to the invasion, the German battery dug in at nearby Brecourt Manor had escaped detection and now, as the landings began, this battery of 105mm guns was firing directly down Causeway Number 2 which, due to confusion within the landing forces, was precisely where the bulk of the 4th Infantry Division was coming ashore.

Winters remembered that, after only about 10 minutes, "*Lieutenant George Lavenson came down the line and said, 'Winters, they want you and your company up front.'*" When Winters arrived he was greeted by a cluster of 2nd Battalion officers. Winters wrote, "*Captain Clarence Hester turns to me and says, 'There's fire along that hedgerow there (pointing behind the last farmhouse in the village). Take care of it.' That was it.*"

Things now began to happen quickly. Winters ordered Compton to get the men ready. While they did, he went behind the farmhouse on the opposite side of the street and moved along a hedgerow running perpendicular to the road until it intersected with a second hedgerow. From there he looked across the corner of an open field to another hedgerow where he could see a gun firing over Le Grand-Chemin in the direction of the beach. To his left he could hear three other guns firing. He knew a battery that size would have at least 40 men to work the guns. He also knew that it was likely there would be infantry to help defend the battery, so he estimated he would be facing anywhere from 40 to 60 men. Undaunted by the odds, Winters quickly formulated a plan of attack and returned to Le Grand-Chemin. It was now about 8:30.

Continue out of the village until you come to your first intersection. Turn right and immediately stop. You will see a monument with a tablet that explains the action at Brecourt Manor. The three guns that Winters could hear firing were located behind the trees on the opposite side of the field in front of you. The gun Winters saw during his reconnaissance was behind a hedge on the right that ran perpendicular to this one.

Winters split his party into two assault teams, each supported by a .30-caliber machine gun. The first machine-gun team consisted of Cleveland Petty and Joe Liebgott, in support of Lieutenant Buck Compton and Sergeants Bill Guarnere and Donald Malarky. The second team was made up of Winters, Corporal Joe Toye and Private Gerald Lorraine supported by John Plesha and Walter Hendrix. To provide additional covering fire, Compton sent Carwood Lipton and Mike Ranney out along a hedge to the flank of the position.

Winters hoped that by making the best use of fire-and-movement tactics he could get into the enemy position with his assaulting parties relatively intact. This would allow him to attack the first gun while also providing some cover to knock out each of the other guns in turn. As Winters once remarked, "*The easiest way to take an enemy trench-line or fortified position was not by frontal assault but to get into it and roll it up from the inside.*"

On Winters's signal, the support teams opened fire and Compton's party rushed the trench to the left of the first gun position. Just on their heels Winters's group charged toward the first gun position to the right of Compton's party. It only took seconds from the start of the attack until the first gun was taken. During the assault on the first gun Robert "Popeye" Wynn was wounded, but Winters was now in the enemy position.

Three of the Germans tried to make their way to safety on the other side of the field. It was a foolish decision. Winters quickly dispatched one of the Germans. Unlike what is shown in the series, Lorraine, who was armed with a Thompson submachine gun, was able to hit the second German. It was Guarnere, also armed with a Thompson, who missed his target. Seeing this, Winters finished off the third German with a shot in the back.

Winters then directed fire from the first position onto the second gun while he readied a second assault party. Relying on what he called his "sixth sense," Winters waited until he felt that the enemy fire had slackened slightly before rushing the second gun under a hail of grenades and small-arms fire. With the second gun eliminated, Winters paused and sent a runner back to Le Grand-Chemin to request additional ammunition and reinforcements. A half-hour later two men, one of whom was John D. Halls, a mortarman from 2nd Battalion Headquarters, arrived from Le Grand-Chemin with badly needed ammunition.

In the Sainte Marie du Mont town square, 101st Airborne Division, 506th PIR, Easy Company paratroopers (front L to R) Forrest Guth, Frank Mellet, David Morris, Daniel West, Floyd Talbert, and C.T. Smith pose with soldiers from the U.S. Army's 4th Infantry Division on June 7, 1944.
(U.S. Army photo by Walter Gordon)

Repeating the procedure that had worked on the second gun, Winters waited until he could sense the fire had slackened before launching his assault party in an attack on the third gun. Leading the assault this time was Private Halls (misidentified as Hall in both the book and the series). While the gun and six prisoners were quickly taken in the assault, Halls was killed during the attack.

As Winters was trying to consolidate the position just taken, he spotted Captain Clarence Hester, who brought him three blocks of TNT and an incendiary grenade. These were used to disable the three guns that had been taken. Hester told Winters that Captain Ronald Speirs from D Company would be up shortly with five men to attack the fourth gun. While he waited, Winters examined the positions he had already taken. At the second gun position he found a map with the location of all the German battery positions behind Utah Beach. He passed that and his prisoners along as the reinforcements came up. Speirs rushed the final gun and eliminated it, but Private John "Rusty" Houck was killed in the attack and Private Leonard Hicks was wounded. Mission accomplished, Winters evacuated his men from the position.

At a cost of four dead and six wounded, a badly outnumbered force of American paratroopers engaged in their first major combat action and killed 15 Germans, captured 12 others and eliminated a German battery that was threatening the landings at Utah Beach. It was an impressive accomplishment. As Carwood Lipton later remembered:

Here (at Brecourt) the training paid off. We fought as a team without standout stars. We were like a machine. We didn't have anyone who leaped up and charged a machine gun. We knocked it out or made it withdraw by maneuver and teamwork or mortar fire. We were smart; there weren't many flashy heroics. We had learned that heroics was the way to get killed without getting the job done and getting the job done was more important.

Back at Le Grand-Chemin, Winters came across lieutenants Harry Welsh and Warren Roush, who had reached the village with about 30 men. He divided this force into two assault platoons and waited for tanks coming up from the beach. During this interlude Winters had his first shot of Calvados, the powerful Norman cider, "*I was thirsty as hell and I needed a lift.*" Around 12:30 Nixon arrived with four Sherman tanks. Winters mounted the lead tank and directed the armor against remaining German targets around the manor while Welsh and Roush's men secured the position. By early afternoon Brecourt had been secured and Easy company could move into Ste. Marie du Mont.

After taking in all of the information at the monument, head down the small road leading to the manor. Drive slowly and you will soon pass the field on your right where the guns were located and on the left the manor house where the de Vallavielle family lived alongside the German gunners during the occupation. While this is a public road, the manor is a working farm and private property. Please respect the family and do not leave your car to walk around the field or enter the manor. At the end of the road turn left in the direction of Ste. Marie du Mont. Upon entering the village park in front of the Hotel de Ville.

Sainte Marie du Mont was in the heart of the 101st Airborne's area of operations. It sits on a ridge that dominates Causeways 1 and 2 leading off of Omaha Beach and, with the distinctive dome of its church, drew mis-dropped paratroopers to it like a magnet. By the time Easy Company arrived on the afternoon of June 6, the village had been secured, but a good deal of fighting had gone on earlier that morning. Visitors are encouraged to follow the historical markers around the town that describe the fight in the town itself. After you do, stop in front of the monument with the WWI soldier on top.

During occupation, the Germans made the locals take the French soldier down but allowed the pedestal to remain. It was in front of this memorial that soldiers from the 101st and 4th Divisions mingled and had their pictures taken, including the famous picture taken with Guth's camera on June 7 that appears on the cover of the *Band of Brothers* book. In the front row of the picture, from the left, are Private Guth, Private Francis J. Mellet, Private David E. Morris, Private First Class Daniel B. West, Sergeant Floyd M. Talbert and Private First Class Campbell Smith. The men in the back row are unknown.

After taking a moment to snap a picture of your own, take the road to the left of the monument out of town. This is the Rue du Joly (D70). Take your first left onto the Route du Limarais (D329E1) in the direction of Culoville (shown on modern maps as Caloville). After approximately two and a half kilometers you will come to a large farm house on your left. Stop the car. This is the farm of Culoville where 506th Regimental commander Colonel Robert Sink set up his headquarters on the afternoon of D-Day and where Winters brought Easy Company at the end of the day.

Winters placed his men on the perimeter around the farm to protect the headquarters and after a short patrol returned to the farm. He walked a short way down the road opposite the entrance to the farm and prepared for sleep. Before he dozed off, Winters later remembered:

I got down on my knees and thanked God for helping me to live through this day and to ask His help on D+1. I would live this war only one day at a time and I promised myself that if I survived, I would find a small farm somewhere in the Pennsylvania countryside and spend the remainder of my life in quiet and peace.

You have completed your tour of Easy's D-Day battles. However, if time permits, you are encouraged to drive a short distance to Utah Beach to see the museum and the site of the historic landings of 75 years ago. If you choose to do this, return to your car and continue on the road until you enter the village of Vierville, which was the 506th's objective for D+1. When the road ends, turn left onto the Rue de la Galie (D913). You are now on what, on June 6, 1944, was Causeway Number 2, the causeway that led off the main landing site at Utah Beach. Stay on this road for a little over five miles (8.5km)—passing through St. Marie du Mont along the way—until you reach Utah Beach and the Utah Beach Landing Museum, which is full of wonderful exhibits that explain the airborne battles and landings in this area.

Easy Company had jumped into Normandy on June 6 with 139 men. When they were finally relieved from combat 23 days later there were 74 men present. Of the Easy Company men killed in Normandy, most were returned to the States after the war. The families of five of the men chose to leave their loved ones' remains in Normandy. They are buried in the American Battle Monuments Cemetery at Colleville-sur-Mer.

Cemetery	Name	Plot	Row	Grave
	Robert Bloser	H	21	23

Robert Bloser was born May 30, 1922, in Harrisburg, Pennsylvania. He was a member of 1st Platoon. He was killed when he left cover to go to a wounded American paratrooper who was screaming for help.

	Everett J. Gray	F	24	42

Best friend of William Dukeman, who would be killed in Holland in October 1944, He was from Colorado but enlisted with Dukeman in California. Killed near Angoville au Plain. He had one year left of high school when he enlisted.

	Terrence C. Harris	B	22	16

Born 1920. Rose to the rank of staff sergeant before he was busted for his part in the NCO mutiny that led to Captain Herbert Sobel's relief from command of Easy Company. He was transferred to A Company. He volunteered for Pathfinder training and was killed by a sniper.

Joseph M. Jordan	D	24	37

Born July 25, 1922, Muncie, Indiana. Killed while trying to help another soldier who was wounded.

Benjamin J. Stoney	H	10	39

Benjamin Joseph Arthur Stoney, a Maidu Indian, was born in Yankee Hill, Butte County, California, on October 10, 1921. He was killed during the attack on Vierville. David K. Webster memorialized Stoney. "*Stoney was our only casualty in Vierville. Stoney, the quiet, stocky Indian from S-2. But every village had a Stoney, or two Stoneys, or many more, because that is how wars are finally fought and won—not by rich factories and the coddled Air Force, but by the infantry, who take the ground and kill the enemy, and the infantry is Stoneys.*"

Two other graves of interest in Colleville are John D. Halls, who was killed at Brecourt Manor and Lt. Harold Cappuletto, who was the pilot of Stick 66, the plane carrying Lt. Thomas Meehan and the Easy Company Headquarters Section.

John D. Halls	C	10	32

Born March 24, 1922, in Mancos, Colorado. Part of service company (not Able company as in series). Most likely a Mormon, given large Mormon community in that part of Colorado.

Harold A. Capelluto	A	9	19

Born 1918 in New York. Prior to America's entry into World War II Capelluto had volunteered for, and served with, the Royal Canadian Air Force. He transferred to the U.S. Army Air Forces in World War II.

BEYOND D-DAY TRAVEL

Hot Tips for England, France, Belgium and the Netherlands

Miki Garcia

WOULD YOU LIKE TO MAKE THE MOST OF TRAVEL OPPORTUNITIES after visiting D-Day events and war memorials in Normandy? Here are some ideas to help you plan a long weekend in England, France, Belgium and the Netherlands—countries deeply affected by the war.

There is no doubt that the top reason to visit Europe is history. From Neolithic sites and fairy-tale castles to the wisdom of Descartes and Spinoza, Europe is filled with iconic landmarks and sophisticated cultures. You can feel the history just by walking down the streets. Each building and narrow alleyway has been a witness to the fascinating past.

Living in a cultural epicenter of the world, local people appreciate the finer things in life. Europe is home to some of the most spectacular museums. You can indulge your taste buds in authentic regional restaurants and enjoy high-end luxury or vintage/antique shopping.

You can travel by car, train or plane within the four countries, but the Eurostar is quite handy. It is the high-speed train that runs from London to Amsterdam via the northern provinces of France and Belgium. Trains run two times a day (three times beginning June 2019) from London's St Pancras to Amsterdam Central, taking 3 hours and 41 minutes.

For information on obtaining Eurostar tickets and other detailed travel information, go to the *D-Day 75th Anniversary—A Millennials Guide* Readers Only website. Access to the web and mobile information is in the back of this book.

England: Whether you are travelling alone, or with your friends and family, England offers something for everyone. From popular places to off the beaten path, there are simply too many things to do and see in England, so you will be spoiled for choice. It has lots of castles, historical sites, world-class museums, restaurants, gardens, hills and lakes, not to mention tons of entertainment options such as music festivals and plays. Don't forget to visit an old pub; more than a place to drink and eat, it is the heart of the community. Every pub has its own charm, traditions and fascinating stories.

London: Ever since the Romans built a settlement called Londinium, the capital of England has been a magnet for newcomers. To this day, London attracts people from all walks of life. Particularly, if you are a researcher or writer, London is one of the best places in the world to conduct research, as there are plenty of world-class libraries and archives. Fun-loving, exuberant, quirky, multicultural London won't bore you. The 18th-century writer and compiler of *Dictionary of the English Language* Samuel Johnson was so right when he quipped, "When you are tired of London, you are tired of life."

Tower of London: Officially called Her Majesty's Royal Palace and Fortress of the Tower of London, it is actually a castle of 20-odd towers, equipped with a secure fortress, royal palace, and infamous prison, where two kings and three queens met their death and countless people were imprisoned. To understand its gruesome history and the Tower, a guided tour with one of the Yeoman Warders, or Beefeaters, is a must.

Imperial War Museum: Founded in 1917, the museum was intended to record the civil and military war effort of Britain and its Empire during World War One. The museum has a research center if you wish to conduct some research. Its collections include archives of personal and official documents, photographs and oral recordings.

British Museum: It is arguably the most visited attraction in London. The country's largest and one of the oldest museums in the world has a substantial collection of artifacts at Egyptian, Etruscan, Greek, Roman, European and Middle Eastern galleries. If you try to see everything properly, it will probably take more than a day.

Victoria and Albert Museum: Named after Queen Victoria and her husband and consort Prince Albert, it was opened in 1852. The museum has the world's largest collection of decorative arts and design from Middle Eastern rugs and Western furniture to fashion and Asian paintings.

National Gallery: Conveniently located by Trafalgar Square where the 170-foot (52 meter)-high Nelson's Column stands, the gallery has some 2,300 European paintings on display, such as works by Leonardo da Vinci, Michelangelo, Van Gogh and Renoir.

St Paul's Cathedral: Designed by the renowned architect Sir Christopher Wren, this Anglican cathedral was built between 1675 and 1710 after the Great Fire of London. Its world-famous dome is one of the most recognizable features of the English capital's skyline. A plethora of historical services have been held here, such as the funerals of Admiral Nelson, the Duke of Wellington, Sir Winston Churchill, and Baroness Margaret Thatcher, as well as the jubilee celebrations for Queen Victoria and the wedding of Prince Charles and Lady Diana.

Westminster Abbey: British monarchs have been crowned here since 1066. Its architectural styles are considered as the finest example of Early English Gothic (1190–1300).

Houses of Parliament: Officially called the Palace of Westminster, it is the meeting place of the House of Commons and the House of Lords, the two houses of the Parliament of the country.

Theatres: London is home to world-famous theatres. If you are into plays and musicals, you might want to visit the West End. Even if you can't make it to the show, just chill around and admire the atmosphere after dark. There are lots of theatres including National Theatre, Royal Court Theatre, Old Vic, Young Vic, and Donmar Warehouse, among others. Across the river, on the south bank of the River Thames, there is the Shakespeare's Globe Theatre. This place was designed to resemble the 1599 original as much as possible. It has the arena open to the skies.

Tate Britain: Tate Britain features traditional British art from the 1500s to present, such as works from Blake, Hogarth, Gainsborough, Whistler and Turner. This is one of the largest museums in England.

Royal Air Force Museum London: This museum is located on the former Hendon Aerodrome, which was a crucial center for aviation throughout

WW1 and WW2. There are a lot of things you can experience hands-on, such as trying on an RAF uniform and learning how to fly a Gnat subsonic fighter in a simulator. There is also Royal Air Force Museum Cosford in Shropshire.

Buckingham Palace: It was built in 1703 for the Duke of Buckingham. Queen Elizabeth II divides her time between here, Windsor and Balmoral in Scotland. She is here when the yellow, red and blue standard is flying.

River Cruising: About 2,000 years ago, the Romans established a settlement along the River Thames. The area was initially developed as a Roman port, and the river has played a major role in the development of many towns. There are actually quite a few companies that offer various cruising tours including hop-on hop-off cruises, circular loop tours, lunch and dinner cruises. You can have a birthday party on the ship as well.

Windsor: Windsor Castle

It takes about one hour by train, bus or car from the city center of London to reach Windsor Castle, located in the west of London, not very far from Heathrow Airport. The distance between Heathrow and Windsor is about 7 miles (11km). It is relatively straightforward to get there from the airport as there are regular bus services from Heathrow. This is one of the Queen's main residences. When she is at home, the Royal Standard is flying from the Round Tower. It is the oldest and largest inhabited castle in the world.

Stratford-upon-Avon: Shakespeare's Birthplace

This was the hometown of William Shakespeare, one of the most popular poets and playwrights in the world. He was born in Stratford in 1564 and died here in 1616. You can see all of the original five Shakespeare houses here: his birthplace, a restored 16th century house; Anne Hathaway's Cottage (family home of Shakespeare's wife); Mary Arden's House (childhood home of Shakespeare's mother); Hall's Croft (home of the husband of Shakespeare's daughter Susanna); and Nash's House and New Place (Shakespeare's family home from 1597 to 1616). There is the Shakespeare Centre Library, which holds collections covering all aspects of his life.

Salisbury: Stonehenge

Britain's most iconic monolithic stones were built by ancient Britons in several phases between 3000 BC and 1600 BC. It is the world's most iconic stone monolith and one of its oldest. Some sections date back to 4500 BC.

Bath: Roman Baths

Bath is such a charming city. The Georgian architecture of grand townhouses, crescents and Palladian mansions is simply breath-taking. But the most popular attraction here is the Roman Baths. Bath is where the Romans built bathhouses above the city's three natural hot springs 2,000 years ago. This health resort became the place to visit by high society and is one of the best-preserved ancient Roman spas in the world.

France: Ancient castles and churches are scattered across the country. Because the French enjoy and appreciate the old things and traditions, France—also called the Hexagon by the French people for its roughly six-sided shape—still functions in an old-fashioned way in so many respects. Life may not be super convenient, but you will definitely capture *joie de vivre*—the joy of being alive.

Paris: No one can resist the delightful French capital. Chic, gorgeous and absolutely romantic, the City of Light is simply irresistible. From first-class cuisine and fashion to the Parisian way of life, the world's trendsetter has so much to offer.

Eiffel Tower: The most recognizable symbol of Paris is the Eiffel Tower. It was constructed by Gustave Eiffel as a temporary exhibit for the 1889 World Fair (Exposition Universelle). Nicknamed *la Dame de Fer* (the Iron Lady), it receives about seven million people a year, making it the most visited monument in the world.

Triumphal Arch: The Triumphal Arch of the Star (*Arc de Triomphe de l'Étoile*) is the monument to Napoleon's 1805 victory at Austerlitz. One of the most iconic monuments in Paris is located at the western end of the Champs-Élysées, and the best way to reach it is to walk up that grand boulevard. This iconic main thoroughfare of Paris is where Jean Seberg walked up and down calling out "New York Herald Tribune, New York Herald Tribune," in Jean-Luc Godard's new wave film ***Breathless*** (***À Bout de Souffle***).

The Louvre Museum: The Musée du Louvre is the largest art museum in the world. It displays 35,000 works of art from Mesopotamian, Egyptian and Greek antiquities to masterpieces by great artists such as da Vinci,

Michelangelo and Rembrandt. The iconic Da Vinci's *La Joconde,* or *Mona Lisa,* painting is on display here.

Orsay Museum: Musée d'Orsay was the former Gare d'Orsay railway station. The architecture of the building is absolutely impressive. It is the home of France's national collection from the Impressionist, Post-Impressionist and Art Nouveau movements.

The Paris Catacombs (Les Catacombes de Paris): Created in 1810, the catacombs are ossuaries that hold over six million people. The underground cemetery is actually quite deep: you will have to go down 130 steps. The walking route is about 1.25 miles (2 km).

Notre Dame Cathedral: Cathédrale Notre Dame de Paris is a masterpiece of French Gothic architecture that can accommodate more than 6,000 worshippers. You can climb to the top and the bell tower. The medieval cathedral is located on the charming Île de la Cité.

La Conciergerie: Directly across the street from Notre Dame, le Conciergie is a 14th century royal palace that became a prison a century later. Here you can get the real story of the bloody time of the late 1700s when France struggled to obtain its democratic identity. Displays detail the dark days of the French Revolution, when the condemned spent their last days here waiting to be executed on the guillotine. Marie Antoinette was imprisoned here. A short time later revolutionary leader Robespierre, who condemned Marie Antoinette to death, awaited his own appointment with the guillotine.

Les Invalides: Hôtel national des Invalides was built in the 1670s by Louis XIV to house 4,000 invalides (disabled war veterans). On July 14, 1789, a mob broke into the building and seized 32,000 rifles and then headed to the prison at Bastille. This was the start of the French Revolution. Les Invalides is a complex of buildings containing museums and monuments. Be sure to visit the Musée de l'Armée with its incredible collection of military miniatures and other exhibits. Among the most visited attractions are the tombs of some of France's war heroes, Napoleon in particular.

Place de la Bastille: The symbol of the French Revolution is the Bastille. The largest prison in Paris was stormed on the first day of the French Revolution in 1789. Though the prison building is gone, the square has great meaning for Parisians. Participants gather here to stage political and human rights demonstrations, and to begin or end street marches.

Shakespeare and Company: This is a bookshop that sells second-hand and new English-language books. The original shop was the meeting point for Hemingway's "Lost Generation."

Sacré Coeur: Paris has many churches and cathedrals that are landmarks for the ages. This beautiful church sits atop Montemartre, one of the highest points in Paris and a very romantic spot with its cafes and street artists.

Cimetière du Père Lachaise: It is the largest cemetery in Paris, which opened in 1804. It houses 70,000 tombs. Some of the most visited are American rocker Jim Morrison from The Doors (Division 6) and Irish writer Oscar Wilde (Division 89).

La Rive Gauche: The "Left Bank" of the Seine River (the south bank) is the heart of Paris's coffeehouse culture. It is also known as the Latin Quarter. Many small cafes, restaurants and bars sprang up in the neighborhood of the Sorbonne, the largest university in Paris, as students and intellectuals met to discuss studies, world affairs and life over a pastry, a cup of espresso or *le petit dejeuner*, a French breakfast of bread, meats, cheeses and, of course, coffee.

Panthéon: The building in the Latin Quarter was originally a church and it is now a mausoleum. Since 1791, it has been the resting place of such great thinkers such as Voltaire, Rousseau, Braille and Hugo.

Les Deux Magots: Known as the rendezvous of the literary and intellectual élite, it is arguably the most famous cafe in Paris. Located in St-Germain des Prés, this was a place where Simone de Beauvoir, Jean-Paul Sartre, Albert Camus, Pablo Picasso and Ernest Hemingway used to hang out.

The Statue of Liberty: In 1886 France gave the U.S. the Statue of Liberty. In 1889 a smaller replica was given to Paris to commemorate the centennial of the French Revolution. It is located on the southern end of Île aux Cygnes, a tiny artificial island on the River Seine in the 15th arrondissement.

River Cruises: Bateaux Mouches are open excursion boats that carry passengers along the scenic Seine River. The 9 mile (15 km) journey through the heart of Paris will take you past such icons as the Orsay Museum,

Louvre, Notre Dame Cathedral, and 37 bridges. You can also have lunch and dinner, which includes a three-course meal on the boat.

Versailles: Palace of Versailles

Initially built as a hunting lodge for Louis XIV, his successors expanded it with extravagant architecture and turned it into a monumental chateau in the mid-17th century. It was the seat for the royal court from 1682 until 1789, when revolutionaries massacred the palace guard and dragged Louis XVI and Marie Antoinette back to Paris to be guillotined. The Palace of Versailles is located 17 miles (28 km) southwest of Paris. The Palace is listed as a World Heritage Site. Besides the magnificent palace and grounds, you can visit the Hall of Mirrors here and see the table on which the Treaty of Versailles, between the First World War's Western Allies and Germany, was signed.

Carnac: Alignements de Carnac

The Neolithic stones stretch for miles across the Breton countryside. The largest megalithic complex of its kind in the world was erected between 5000 BC and 2000 BC, during the time when the tribes lived in large houses made of wood and clay.

Normandy: Mont St-Michel

The Abbaye du Mont St-Michel is located on an island opposite the coastal town of Pontorson, connected to the mainland by a narrow causeway. The Abbey Church (Église Abbatiale) incorporates elements of both Norman and Gothic architecture. At low tide, it is surrounded by bare sand for miles around, while at high tide the bay causeway and nearby car parks can be submerged. Make sure to get the tide table (the *horaire des marées*) at the tourist office. When the tide is out, you can walk all the way around Mont St-Michel.

Belgium: This petite, bilingual country is simultaneously cosmopolitan and provincial. You can see some of Europe's finest art and architecture. And most importantly, Belgium offers great beers and scrumptious waffles. After dark, head for a restaurant for mussels and chips *(moules-frites)*, and try some of the boutique-brewed Belgian beers. Don't forget to buy some delicious chocolate for friends and family back home.

Antwerp: Belgium's second city Antwerp (Antwerpen in Dutch and Anvers in French) was one of northern Europe's foremost cities in the 17th century. Historically, its port played a major role in the development of the Low Countries (Belgium, Luxembourg and the Netherlands). Located 55 miles (88 km) inland, it has easy connections to road and rail. The port is still used as a major seaport in the region. Currently, it is home to the largest integrated oil and chemical cluster in Europe, and many other items come through, namely rough diamonds.

Rubenshuis: It was home to Peter Paul Rubens, the most influential artist of Flemish Baroque tradition. The 17th-century studio of Rubens was restored and houses 10 of the painter's canvases. One of the most visited attractions of the country.

Diamond Quarter: Antwerp is known for its diamonds; 80% of all the world's uncut diamonds are traded here. At the Diamond Museum, you can see live gem-polishing demonstrations. If you cannot afford one of the gems, enjoy window shopping.

Bruges: Definitely one of the most picturesque and romantic cities in Europe, the pint-sized medieval city (Brugge in Dutch) has cobblestone lanes, canals, and is simply delightful.

Belfort: UNESCO-listed 14th century Belfort (belfry) is a bell tower, the most recognizable icon of the city. It has a magnificent view from the top.

Groeningemuseum: The gallery offers Flemish Primitive and Renaissance works including Jan Van Eyck's 1436 masterpiece, *Madonna with Canon Van der Paele.*

Brouwerij De Halve Maan: Founded in 1856, this is the last family *brouwerij* (brewhouse) in Bruges. If you want to experience some local beers, it is worth a visit.

Brussels: The capital of Belgium is now also the capital of the European Union. Brussels has a number of examples of Gothic and Renaissance architectural styles. As with the rest of Belgium, waffle restaurants and beer houses are in abundance.

Galeries Royales St-Hubert: Saint Hubert Royal Galleries is like a modern shopping mall—only it was started in 1847. The gallery-like structure of three connected wings boasts neo-Renaissance architecture and loads of shopping possibilities.

Royal District: The center of Brussels culture and government is the Royal District. The Royal Palace of Brussels and the Belgian Parliament are here. So are the Royal Library of Belgium, the Royal Museums of Fine Arts of Belgium and the Museum of Cinema as well as the unusual and fascinating—at least for musicians—Musical Instrument Museum.

The Netherlands: Almost a third of the country is situated below sea level. Water is everywhere in Holland. Canals run like veins. You can see it from the sky when you fly into Amsterdam's Schiphol airport. Dutch people have been living with water for centuries, and it has an extensive influence on their lives. Join a canal cruise tour, hire a boat, or rent a bicycle to visit places where you can enjoy picturesque canals, sleep in a houseboat, and drink coffee in a canal-side cafe. It is a great way to explore Dutch culture and society.

Amsterdam: Amsterdam is often called a city of contrasts—a mixture of a magnificent array of 17th century architecture and a modern urban setting. For a relatively small country, it produced a considerable number of painters during the Dutch Golden Age. There are currently more than 400 museums in the Netherlands. If you want to visit more than three museums, buy a Museumkaart (museum card). Amsterdam's famous Museumplein (museum square) in the Museumkwartier (museum quarter) is the area where some of the popular museums are located.

Rijksmuseum: This is the Dutch equivalent of the Louvre. One of the main attractions is the building itself. It has the world's finest collection of paintings from the Golden Age of Dutch art. Rembrandt's masterpiece *Night Watch* (1642), and lots of paintings by Vermeer, van Gogh and Jan Steen are on display.

Van Gogh Museum: As you would expect, this place offers the world's largest Van Gogh collection. You can also see paintings by other artists, such as Gauguin, Toulouse-Lautrec and Monet.

Rembrandt House Museum (Museum het Rembrandthuis): This was Rembrandt van Rijn's original Amsterdam studio, where he worked and lived from 1639 until he went bankrupt in 1656. There are many etchings and sketches. The house is located in the historical Jewish Quarter by the canal.

National Marine Museum (het Scheepvaartmuseum): The first Dutch company to amass a fortune did it through maritime trade—namely, VOC (Vereenigde Oostindische Companie), or the Dutch East India Company, which was originally established in 1602. You can explore 500 years of maritime history in the museum. The historic building was the former arsenal of the Admiralty of Amsterdam ('s Lands Zeemagazijn), which was built in 1656. A VOC ship moored alongside the museum is an exact copy of a ship lost on her maiden voyage in 1749. There is a very stylish library here if you want to read old books or conduct some research.

Royal Palace of Amsterdam: The palace (Koninklijk Paleis van Amsterdam) was built as a city hall during the Golden Age in the 17th century. It is located on the west side of Dam Square, right opposite the war memorial and next to New Church (Nieuwe Kerk, built in the 15th century).

Anne Frank Museum: The most visited site in the Netherlands draws one million visitors annually. This is where world-famous diarist Anne Frank hid with her family for more than two years during the Second World War.

Cafe Karpershoek: This "brown pub" is the oldest bar in Amsterdam. It was opened in 1606 as an inn for the seamen of the Dutch East India Company.

The Hague: Amsterdam may be the capital of the Netherlands, but The Hague, or Den Haag, is the political hub. It is home to the Supreme Court and has been the seat of government since 1588. The Binnenhof houses the States General of the Netherlands, and the Royal family live in the city. If you sit back in a cafe in Het Plein (town square) and watch the world go by, you will probably run into friendly Dutch politicians. If you are into history, it is worth a visit.

Mauritshuis: This compact museum was the old palace. Vermeer's *Girl with a Pearl Earring,* Rembrandt's self-portrait, Dr. Nicolaes Tulp's *The Anatomy Lesson* are all on display. If you visit the Hofvijver (Court Pond), the Prison Gate Museum (Museum de Gevangenpoort) and Prince William V Gallery (Galerij Prins Willem V) are within about a five-minute walk.

Peace Palace : Peace Palace (Vredespaleis) opened in 1913. It is an international law administrative building that houses the International Court of Justice, the Permanent Court of Arbitration, The Hague Academy of International Law and the Peace Palace Library. Opposite the Peace Palace, there is a Resistance and Liberation memorial.

The International Criminal Court: This was built on the site of the Alexander military barracks, where 66 military personnel and 110 cavalry horses were killed during a German bombing attack in World War Two; a plaque commemorates them. You can visit the court and attend public sessions of Court hearings. There is an exhibit, gardens and cafe.

The Atlantikwall Museum Scheveningen: It is a selection of actual German bunkers from World War Two. The museum offers various events and is open every Sunday from March to October. It is run by volunteers, however, so the museum is not open all the time. Check the website before you visit.

THE VILLAGE OF COLLEVILLE IN 1940, ON THE NORMANDY COAST HIGH ABOVE WHAT WOULD LATER BE CALLED OMAHA BEACH.
(IMAGE COURTESY OF MARTIN ROBERT GALLE)

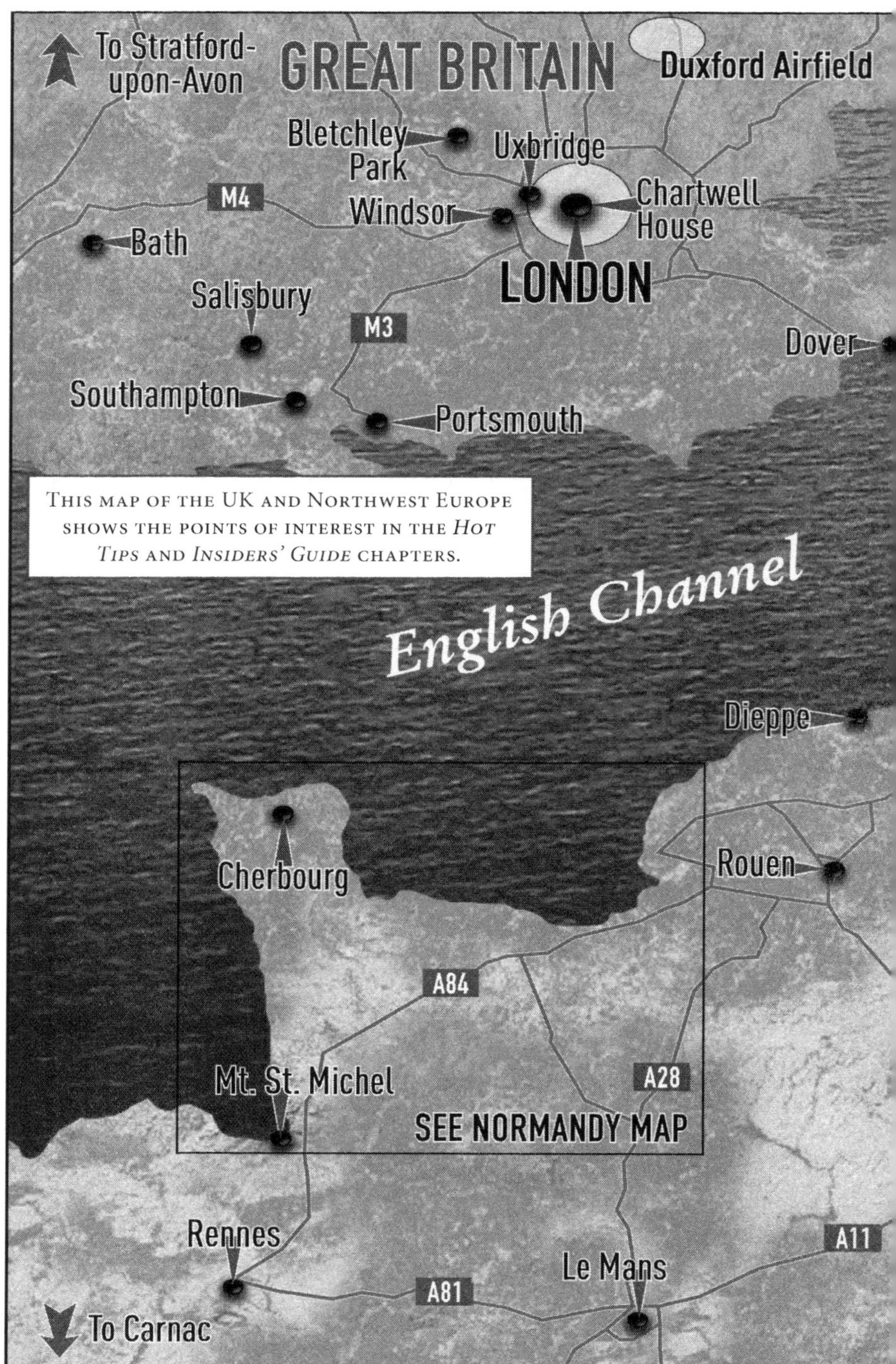

To Stratford-upon-Avon
GREAT BRITAIN
Duxford Airfield
Bletchley Park
Uxbridge
M4
Windsor
Chartwell House
Bath
LONDON
Salisbury
M3
Dover
Southampton
Portsmouth
THIS MAP OF THE UK AND NORTHWEST EUROPE SHOWS THE POINTS OF INTEREST IN THE *HOT TIPS* AND *INSIDERS' GUIDE* CHAPTERS.
English Channel
Dieppe
Cherbourg
Rouen
A84
A28
Mt. St. Michel
SEE NORMANDY MAP
Rennes
A11
Le Mans
A81
To Carnac

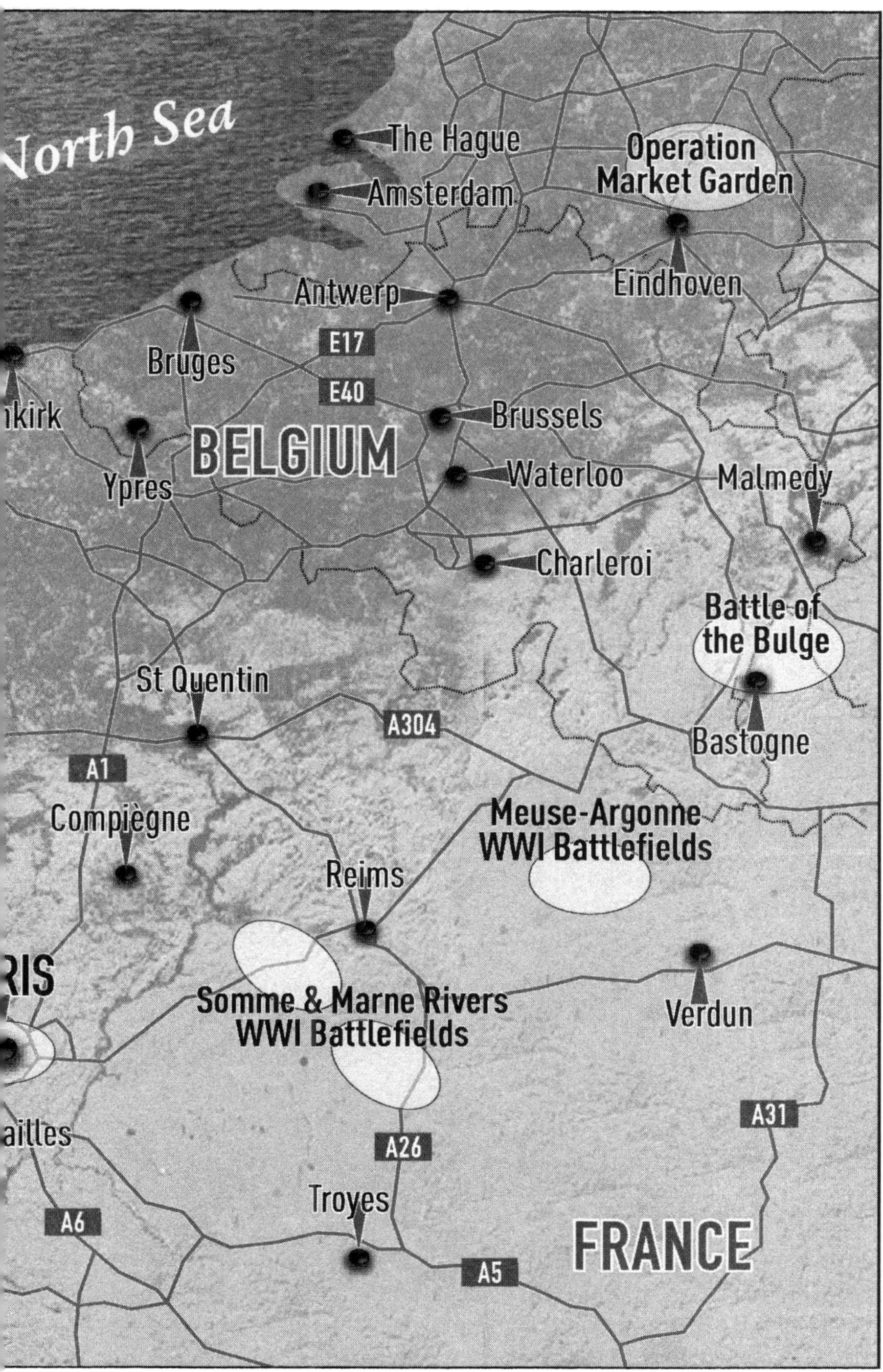
North Sea
The Hague
Amsterdam
Operation
Market Garden
Eindhoven
Antwerp
Bruges
E17
E40
Brussels
BELGIUM
Ypres
Waterloo
Malmedy
Charleroi
Battle of
the Bulge
Bastogne
St Quentin
A304
A1
Compiègne
Meuse-Argonne
WWI Battlefields
Reims
Verdun
Somme & Marne Rivers
WWI Battlefields
A31
A26
Troyes
A6
A5
FRANCE

INSIDERS' GUIDE TO WESTERN EUROPEAN MILITARY SITES

Edwin Cole Bearss
& Robert Irving Desourdis

United Kingdom

The UK offers several historic sites important in the Allies' (United States, Britain, and the Soviet Union) conduct of and final victory in World War II. While visiting these sites, there are many peripheral sites of historical importance that are convenient to visit as well. Here, we focus on World War II and peripheral sites that were visited by the authors.

London

The Imperial War Museum (IWM) London on Lambeth Road is a British museum covering the history of warfare, including major events and exhibits related to the First World War, and it contains several permanent displays from World War II to current conflicts in Iraq and other places. It is one of the best war museums in the world and evolves as new exhibits are built and made available to the public, so there's always something new to see.

The Imperial War Museum also manages several locations offering tours and museum experiences at the heart of Allied success in World War II. The IWM website contains valuable visitor information, maps and ticketing prices for all museum sites. It is among the website listings on

D-Day 75th Anniversary—A Millennials Guide **Readers Only** website. See the back of the book for access.

Churchill War Rooms: In London, the IWM Churchill War Rooms off King Charles Street in London houses three permanent museums including the underground command and control bunker under Westminster.

Cabinet War Rooms: The Cabinet War Rooms show the meeting and map rooms, telephone communications with switchboards, and other areas where the major strategic decisions were made that guided British warfare in World War II. Its underground location was in response to concern over bombing the Germans had done in World War I using zeppelins and large aircraft.

Churchill Museum: The onsite Churchill Museum contains artifacts from the life of Winston Churchill. He served as British prime minister and dynamic leader of Britain during World War II and afterwards. Although a casual visit can be done in 90 minutes, spending time with each exhibit could take half a day.

Undercover: Life in Churchill's Bunker – Integrated with the War Rooms and Churchill Museum, the rooms and corridors that supported life belowground are also on display. Sleeping quarters, kitchen and eating facilities, water and backup power, all needed to support the people who would be belowground for extended periods of time—including Churchill, who might be there for several days during crises.

Royal Air Force (RAF) Bomber Command Memorial: The British bombing campaign against Germany was waged at night because bomber losses were too great in daylight. Since precise targets could not be hit at night, the RAF began wide-area incendiary bombing of German cities. The RAF Bomber Command memorial in London's Green Park commemorates the more than 55,000 British air crewmen who died in World War II, many perishing in a fireball plummeting to earth. The monument depicts a bomber crew and was unveiled by Queen Elizabeth II in 2012.

Outside London

The Battle of Britain Bunker: In September 1940 the German Luftwaffe went beyond just attacking British convoys in the English Channel and began striking at the radar sites (briefly) and the Royal Air Force (RAF) Fighter Command airfields. A Luftwaffe night raid accidentally hit London when jettisoning its bombs, and Britain retaliated with a sequence of night-bombing raids on Berlin. As a result, Hitler focused his Luftwaffe on hitting London and other major English cities, leading to the Battle of Britain air war from July 10 to October 31, 1940. After failing to defeat the RAF, German focus shifted to nighttime bombing raids on London and other British cities from September 7, 1940, to May 11, 1941, a period known as "The Blitz."

The heart of command and control for British fighter defense during the Battle of Britain was the underground bunker near Uxbridge, about 15 miles west of the center of London. This facility was a central command, control and communications center where British radar reports of German aircraft groups assembling over Western France and reports from spotters were received. The staff at Uxbridge used filtered radar data from the fighter command bunker about German aircraft, their numbers, direction and altitude to calculate the target area. They also received status reports of RAF fighter squadrons in 11 Group, such as Biggin Hill (arguably, the most well-known), and determined where 11 Group squadrons should intercept German planes. The site provides a docent to explain the features and functions of all positions in the control room, as well as to relate stories about one of its more famous workers, the actor Rex Harrison. Access from London is by tube (London Underground), then taxi or a one-mile walk.

Duxford Imperial War Museum and Airshows: Regular airshows with a variety of vintage aircraft, vendor stalls and bomber-crew reenactments occur at the Imperial War Museum facility located near Duxford. Scheduled airshows include Hurricanes and Spitfires; Messerschmitt 109s (modified) and many other British, German and American aircraft (a B-17G bomber, PBY Catalina seaplane and others). The schedule of Duxford airshows is available on the previously mentioned IWM website. The airshow provides visitors a sense of the Battle of Britain experience, especially in conjunction with visiting the Uxbridge underground bunker.

Chartwell House: Sir Winston Churchill's country home, Chartwell House, is about 20 miles southeast of London. Maintained by the National Trust, Chartwell House preserves the home, its rooms, decorations, a display cabinet of his uniforms, and the grounds much as they were when Churchill lived there during World War II and through the rest of his life. The grounds and gardens with signed walkways include ponds where unusual black swans are readily seen. The site contains a visitor center, gift shop and restaurant and is accessible from London by train and taxi.

Bletchley Park: An absolutely critical Allied advantage during much of World War II was provided by the successful code-breaking of the German Enigma and Lorenz ciphers by Alan Turing and others at Bletchley Park—a sort of Manhattan Project for breaking German secret codes. The site, about 40 miles northwest of London, contains a museum with artifacts, video, audio and live demonstrations, and a park area largely as it was during its heyday before and during WWII. The intellectual capabilities of the code-breakers at Bletchley saved lives, likely shortened the war, and provided a basis for future automatic data processing (computer) equipment. The Park also includes an independent site called The National Museum of Computing. Turing's contributions to computing were honored with the creation of the A.M. Turing Award, frequently referred to as the "Nobel Prize of Computer Science."

Dover: The city of Dover, about 70 miles southeast of London, is near the closest point between England and Calais in France and is the access point to the Chunnel to Calais under the English Channel. The famous White Cliffs of Dover (white chalk cliffs formed by the natural chalk formation underlying the terrain) can be seen for several miles from anywhere along the waterfront. There are several important World War II sites near the famous Dover Castle, itself a famous tourist attraction.

Dover Museum: The Dover Museum downtown has a large number of artifacts and exhibits from early human history in the area, including one of the oldest boats ever found; it is preserved intact in a climate-controlled room. The museum contains displays from Dover's role in WWI and WWII, including the sacrifice of its citizens in defending the United Kingdom over many years.

Dover Shelling Memorial: Dover, being close to Calais and being an important port, was shelled by the Germans using long-range cannon. The largest of these guns was an improved version of the famous Paris Gun that shelled Paris from 75 miles away in World War I. The memorial is in a small park near the downtown area, close to the water.

Bleriot Memorial: Louis Bleriot piloted the first airplane across the English Channel on July 25,1909, as part of a prize-sponsored challenge, landing near Dover Castle. Today, a stone monument in a secluded area marks his landing spot. His peacetime flight took on a wartime significance some 30 years later, given the Battle of Britain with hundreds of aircraft flying and fighting far above the Channel in World War II.

Dover Castle: Dover Castle has several self-guided and guided tours, including climbing irregular stairways to the parapets for an excellent view of the countryside, the English Channel, and—on a clear day—Calais, France.

Operation Dynamo Bunker—Dunkirk Command Post and Underground Hospital: Between May 26 and June 4, 1940, an ad hoc fleet of Royal Navy vessels and hundreds of civilian boats successfully evacuated over 330,000 soldiers from Dunkirk, France *(Operation Dynamo)*. They were given time to carry out this incredible rescue because Hitler was reluctant to send in his panzer divisions, and the Luftwaffe failed to destroy the soldiers trapped on the beach, as it had promised. The command and control bunker that directed the Dunkirk evacuation is located on the entryway to Dover Castle. The bunker is accessible in periodic group tours that are free once you get tickets at the castle complex entrance. An underground hospital facility conducts group tours starting a few yards from the tunnel entrance.

Dover Command, Control and Communications Building: On the way up the castle access road there is an exit to a walking tour of a command, control and communications building. It has played a role in the defense of the historic Dover Harbor since 1874 and served in several roles through World War II, including a Fire Command Post, Port War Signal Station, Royal Navy shore signaling station, and air-attack early warning station. The site also contains a former artillery battery site and a statue of Admiral Sir Bertram Ramsay, who was Vice Admiral Dover 1939–42 and commander in chief of the D-Day naval operations.

Chain Home—Swingate RDF Site: The British RDF (Radio Direction Finding) sites at the heart of Battle of Britain success, code-named "Chain Home," consisted of metal transmitting towers and all-wooden receiving towers (wood does not reflect radio waves, which would distort RDF accuracy) along the UK coast. Although the receiving towers have been removed, the metal towers are still used for microwave and other signaling systems. The Swingate RDF site transmition towers are visible from the parapets of Dover, and similar towers still exist at other locations in the UK.

Portsmouth: Portsmouth Historic Dockyard served as a major port facility for the vast D-Day armada of ships. Many thousands of soldiers, armored vehicles, transport vehicles, and all forms of supply needed by a ground army set out for Normandy on June 5th. There are paid tours of the harbor as well as excellent museums.

HMS *Victory*: The ship-of-the-line HMS *Victory* was the flagship of Admiral Lord Horatio Nelson when he defeated a French fleet at Trafalgar in 1805 during the Napoleonic Wars. Nelson was mortally wounded by a sniper during the battle, but his victory at Trafalgar ensured Britain's naval supremacy for more than 100 years. The *Victory* is permanently on display in the Portsmouth dock area, and you can access all deck levels and cabins. In an adjacent museum there are also displays and video experiences to bring the Battle of Trafalgar to life.

HMS *Warrior*: HMS *Warrior* is docked in Portsmouth as well, an 1860-vintage ship that was once the pride of Queen Victoria's navy—the largest ship built up to that time and Britain's first iron-hulled, armored warship. You can walk aboard the ship and explore its decks and history.

Supreme Headquarters Allied Expeditionary Force (SHAEF) Headquarters: The Southwick House near Portsmouth was the D-Day Command Post for General Dwight Eisenhower and others as they planned the operation. On display is the original map wall of the southern coast of England and the Normandy coast, showing all units and their movement for June 6, 1944.

The D-Day Story

Portsmouth's latest World War II attraction is The D-Day Story. This museum run by the city has just undergone a full refurbishment and anyone interested in the D-Day landings will want to include it on a visit to the south coast of England—during the 75th anniversary or anytime. The museum tells the story of D-Day through the personal accounts of people who were there. The museum's unique collections range from D-Day landing craft and vehicles to a coat with military badges from several nations sewn onto it; the badges were given to Gosport's five-year-old Betty White (not the venerable actress, who was already making movies and serving in the Women's Voluntary Services in the U.S. at that time) by soldiers on their way to Normandy. Displays are brought to life with stunning audio/visual presentations.

The D-Day story is told in three parts: Preparation; D-Day and the battles of Normandy; and finally "Legacy and the Overlord Embroidery." The Legacy Gallery features the magnificent Overlord Embroidery commissioned to remember those who took part in D-Day and the Battle of Normandy. It is just one of a number of themed displays that immerse the visitor in all aspects of what made *Operation Overlord* a singularly complex and ultimately successful campaign.

The D-Day Story
Clarence Esplanade, Southsea, PO5 3NT
023 9288 2555
www.theddaystory.com
Open daily 10:00 am–5:00 pm
(5:30 pm April–Sept).
Closed Christmas Eve,
Christmas Day & Boxing Day.

Ticket Prices
Adult: £10.00 Senior: £8
Child & Student (aged 5 up to 17): £5
Family ticket (up to 2 adults & up to 3 children): £25
Children under 5: Free
Normandy Veterans: Free

8th Air Force Sites

Strategic Bombing from England: As mentioned in the earlier chapter "Allied Flyers Epic Pub Crawl," about 100 American airfields populated East Anglia in the UK by the end of WWII. These airfields were home bases for the American B-17 and B-24 bombers and the interceptor (fighter) aircraft that protected the bombers from Luftwaffe fighters.

8th Air Force Control Towers: Many of the children in these towns with adjacent airfields got to know the Americans of the U.S. Eighth Air Force. The aircrew and others at these airfields, far from their homes, could—despite their death-defying missions—feel more at home by meeting and greeting these children. In some cases, many decades later these children worked to preserve the control towers as a suitable place to remember the Americans who once flooded the area.

Several American control towers and portions of the aircraft taxiways have been preserved rather than being reclaimed by the farmers whose fields were borrowed to provide bomber bases. Often, these facilities are maintained and include museums with displays from those days when thousands of young American men populated these airfields and, for socialization, the nearby towns. These senior citizens bring back some of their memorable youth by preserving these places. The collections of artifacts, photos and models—and the people themselves—enhance these important American historical sites in England.

France

Normandy

The northern provinces of France and the waters surrounding the region have endured plenty of bloodshed over the centuries, something that increased exponentially here in the high-tech world wars of the 20th century, when new weapons and the scale of the fighting produced millions of casualties. Once you have toured the sites where the events of World War II's D-Day landing took place, travel east to the haunting battlefields of this and earlier wars. Additional sites important to the campaign, such as those at Bayeaux, Caen and Cherbourg, can be found on the **Readers Only** website.

The Allied Invasion of Europe on D-Day, June 6th 1944, would eventually free Western Europe from German control and Nazi terror. It began on the night of June 5–6 with airborne landings and ended with the corridor of death and closing of the Falaise Gap in August, in front of Polish forces who were fighting as part of the Allied troops in Normandy. It is fitting that the Poles would be there to seal the fate of the German 7th Army in this pocket, payback for the unprovoked Nazi invasion of their homeland nearly five years earlier.

Atlantic Wall: Hitler's army had to defend a coastline of more than a thousand miles, from Norway to Southern France, where invasion from England was feasible. He had the Atlantic Wall built, with reinforced concrete bunkers (many still in place) for artillery and machine guns, plus millions of land mines, anti-landing-craft and glider obstacles, and mobile panzer forces held in reserve. There are many vestiges left of this wall today, the guns of which provided indirect artillery fire inland and direct fire on the coastline.

Longue sur Mer Battery: One of the artillery batteries behind the beaches on the coast of Normandy was the Longues Battery. It contains four pillboxes and an observer's bunker facing the ocean. Two of its four large cannons were destroyed, one by a direct hit from an offshore Allied warship bobbing on what was not a "calm" ocean. The ship put a shell through the thin gun shield from several miles away. This location offers a self-guided tour, so you will want to bring a local guide with you.

Azeville Battery: The Azeville artillery battery behind the Normandy beaches is another indirect-fire battery with several gun positions. No guns exist today. There is an underground complex of tunnels linking rooms in several bunkers, an antiaircraft battery mount and other facilities accessible by the public with ticket purchase. This battery is operated by a local enterprise and includes a small museum. Damage caused by a shell hitting one of the pillboxes is apparent in several rooms, where it passed through the walls, bounced off the floor, and went outside without detonating.

Airborne Landings

The paratroopers arrived over Normandy first, around midnight, to capture key positions, such as strategic bridges and crossroads that would control access to the beach areas where infantry and armor would land. The access was necessary both to make sure these points were not destroyed or defended by German soldiers, and to insure they could be used by Allied soldiers coming off the beaches.

Pegasus Bridge: The first military action happened at midnight when British 6th Airborne commandos landed in gliders at the foot of a bridge over the Caen Canal. It was at this action where the first British soldier, Den Brotheridge, and the first German soldier would be killed on D-Day. The original bridge, showing minor battle damage, is on the grounds of an extensive museum including memorials adjacent to the site of the replacement bridge and both a mock-up of the British Horsa glider used and protected remnants from a real Horsa (not one involved at the bridge). There are also stone memorials marking where each glider came to rest.

St. Mère Église: St. Mère Église was a major American 82nd Airborne objective prior to the seaborne landings. The town has the famous church where paratrooper John Steele's parachute got caught (and is depicted on the church steeple). There is a major airborne museum in the town, which includes a C-47 and a Waco glider, American artifacts and several multimedia exhibits with audio provided for rented headset when in close proximity to each display.

Merderet River Bridge: American paratroopers moved south of St. Mère Église to guard a bridge over the Merderet River where they created a defensive roadblock to prevent Germans forces from crossing the bridge and threatening the town. Heroic actions, where a Medal of Honor was earned by Pfc. Charles DeGlopper, prevented French-made German tanks from crossing the river. These are commemorated by several monuments, including a metal table diorama surrounded by a simulated canopy (parachute) showing the bridge and DeGlopper with his bazooka.

Seaborne Landings

American infantry, Army Rangers and the soldiers of several other nationalities debarked from a variety of landing craft onto the beaches of the Calvados coast just after 6:00 a.m. June 6, Paris time. A wide range of resistance was met, resulting in great casualties suffered across these beaches.

Pointe du Hoc: U. S. Army Rangers practiced for months taking the German gun positions above the 100-foot cliffs of Pointe du Hoc between the American beaches codenamed Utah and Omaha. Although suffering over 60% causalities (killed, wounded, and missing), the Rangers captured these positions after scaling the cliffs but found the guns were not there. They had been removed because of the aerial bombing of this obvious target in the weeks before D-Day. The Rangers found the guns further inland and destroyed them while under fire from German soldiers nearby. Today there are pillboxes, including the observation bunker on the point of the cliff's edge, reinforced concrete gun casemates, antiaircraft positions, and many craters, including a few massive ones from the bombing.

Omaha Beach: Omaha (Allied codename for the particular stretch of sand) was the bloodiest beach on D-Day. Included in the dead were 19 of the 35 young men from Bedford, Virginia, who landed near Vierville Draw (a sloping beach access between steep cliffs), which is why there is a monument to them in that small Virginia town. Paraphrasing a veteran who landed on the sector of the beach designated Easy Red, "It wasn't easy, but it was plenty red." General Omar Bradley, who was the ground assault commander, almost pulled the men off the beach, but by the time that move was considered, several penetrations of the German defenses had been made.

Many Americans were mowed down when they left their landing craft because the Allied bombing, naval shellfire, massive rocket launchers, and floating DD (Direct Drive) tanks (most of which sank from rough seas) failed to crater the beach or provide armored direct-fire support to these men. There are monuments at Vierville, as well as German fortifications. Other monuments and fortifications are located at Colleville Draw, at the other end of Omaha Beach, below the major American cemetery and monument to the missing. Many thousands of American dead are buried here, each with a unique and moving story.

Utah Beach: The 4th Division met less resistance coming ashore on the beach codenamed Utah, where there were dunes but no cliffs. The oldest son of the former president Theodore Roosevelt was among the officers who landed here. There are monuments and a nearby museum that includes many displays and artifacts, including a B-26 Marauder bomber, artillery, photographs, and a variety of exhibits.

Juno Beach: Although smaller in total number, casualties among the Canadians who landed at Juno Beach were a higher percentage of the force involved. There are some remaining German bunkers and several monuments to the Canadian forces. The Cross of Lorraine marks where Charles De Gaulle made his long-awaited return to French soil several days after the invasion.

Sword and Gold Beaches: The British beaches code named Sword and Gold are on either side of Juno Beach. Though some resistance was offered from German positions, many of the defenses were hit by the Allied pre-landing bombing and shelling, allowing the British to obtain successful landings on both Sword and Gold with relatively light casualties. They were able to advance rapidly toward Caen, a key objective, but the advance ground to a halt in front of the medieval walled city and layers of German defenses. Sword was famous for the arrival of Lord Lovat and his bagpiper Bill Millin, who walked up and down the beach piping his men ashore. German prisoners taken in the fighting said they had not shot at the piper because he was a "Dummkopf" (foolish person).

In 2016, we met John Jenkins, then 97 years old, in Portsmouth, England. He had come ashore on Gold Beach and told us about his first day in

Normandy. He said his unit thought they'd lost a sergeant, but it turned out the fellow had drunk a whole bottle of Calvados, fell into a slit trench and was "out" for several hours. Sword and Gold beaches contain monuments to the British Army units that landed there.

Caen-Normandie Memorial

The Caen-Normandie Mémorial, located in the city of Caen, is a museum complex with a variety of themed exhibits. A large number of permanent exhibits are dedicated to World War II subjects, including D-Day and the Liberation of Caen. The museum also offers several fascinating satellite exhibits, all with WWII themes and all at locations important to the June 1944 Allied invasion of France and German preparations for it. In 2019 a large amount of rotating exhibit space is dedicated to exhibits on the D-Day theme.

Full visitor information, in English and French versions, including ticket prices, hours of operation and transportation alternatives for planning a visit is available at:

http://www.normandy.memorial-caen.com

Caen-Normandie Mémorial
Esplanade Général Eisenhower
CS 55026 – 14050 Caen cedex 4
+33 (0)2 31 06 06 45

Here are the other exhibit areas that are operated by the Caen-Normandie Mémorial:

Falaise Memorial—Civilians at War: Located in the town of Falaise, where the Falaise Pocket trapped a number of German units at the end of the Normandy phase of the campaign, the exhibit space here is dedicated to the experiences of Norman civilians during the war.

Mémorial des civils dans la guerre
Place Guillaume le Conquérant
14700 Falaise
02 31 06 06 45

Arromanches 360 Circular Cinema displays a 360-degree circular presentation on nine continuous screens. The narrated film features archive footage from around the world. The Arromanches 360 Circular Cinema is built on the remnants of one of two Mulberry artificial harbors sent across the English Channel to handle the massive influx of *Operation Overlord* supplies.

Arromanches 360
Chemin du calvaire
14117 Arromanches-les-Bains
02 31 06 06 45

1944 Radar Museum – Also on historic ground on the coast near Bayeaux is the 1944 Radar Museum, which features bunkers and equipment from a German defense position where radar operators scanned the skies for incoming enemy planes and checked the progress of Luftwaffe interceptors. A unique way to visit the Dover-la-Délivrande radar station is aboard an authentic World War II truck operated by the D-Day Academy.

MUSÉE RADAR 1944
Route de Basly
14440 DOUVRES-LA-DELIVRANDE
Tel. 02 31 06 06 45

D-Day Academy Centralizer
15, route de Bayeux - 14980 Rots - France
Telephone: + 0033663835190
Email: jp.benamou44@gmail.com
Website: www.ddaca.com

St. Lô

American units fought the Germans in St. Lô, after the town had been totally destroyed by Allied bombing. The cemetery, and one mausoleum in particular, was famous as the local (protected) American headquarters. Concrete chips from gunfire are still visible in the cemetery, though much of the rest of the city had to be rebuilt. More than 500 French citizens, some members of the same family, killed in the Allied bombing of the city are buried in the cemetery.

Avranches

General George Patton's men took Avranches, which completed the process of sealing off the Cotentin Peninsula from the Germans. There are plaques on a critical bridge in town and in an area called Place Patton, which memorializes Patton's rapid move to capture the city before moving on.

Mortain

American units captured a strategic hill adjacent to the town of Mortain, which blocked a German counterattack on Avranches. Though taking casualties, the Americans on the hill were able to see down the highways east and called in artillery and fighter-bomber attacks that crushed the German counterattack. The Allies had gained air superiority in the months prior to D-Day, and many German fighters that might have been used for defense in France were now protecting Allied bombing targets in Germany.

Falaise Gap

With Patton's army swinging in an arc east toward Argentan and British, Canadian and Polish forces coming down from the Caen area, the German 7th Army was in a bottle with the open end in the area around Mont-Ormel, a low mountain west of the gap between the towns of Trun and Chambois.

Chambois

Polish and American forces linked up in Chambois at an English-style castle in the middle of town. We drank Polish Vodka at that spot, as they had done, commemorating the closing of what became known as the Falaise Pocket, surrounding the German Seventh Army.

Mont-Ormel

Polish forces, though suffering major losses, were able to eventually stop escaping Germans from the heights of the Mont-Ormel, where there is a major Polish monument (named Montormel) and, below it, a museum.

Along an unmarked road south and east of Mont-Ormel, there is a sunken road at the crossing of the Dives River. It has been the subject of photographs famously showing dead horses, men and shattered equipment, the results of continuous Allied fighter-bomber rocket and bomb attacks. This road and its destruction represented the finality of the Allied Normandy Campaign.

Northeastern France

Compiègne

By the autumn of 1918 in the First World War the pressure of British, French and Americans on the German front line, combined with food riots and Bolshevik-led unrest in Germany and capped off by a gradual dissolution of their chief ally, Austria-Hungary, led Germany's "military masters" to request an armistice through contacts with U.S. President Woodrow Wilson. French General Foch ordered the ceremony to occur in a railroad car pushed onto a siding in Compiègne. Today, the location identifies the site of the railway car, which was destroyed in WWII. An accurate replica sits in an on-site museum. When his armies brought France to capitulation in May 1940, Hitler insisted on using the same railway car to have the French sign their unconditional surrender to Germany. To "rub salt in the wounds of defeat," Hitler sat in the same seat as Foch had used when Germany signed the armistice 22 years earlier.

When touring Versailles, be sure to visit the Hall of Mirrors, pictured here just before the delegates met in 1919 to sign the Treaty of Versailles. *(Image courtesy of the Library of Congress)*

Verdun

Verdun is arguably the penultimate modern killing ground in warfare. It had all the ingredients, including a long military history even before the Germans captured Verdun during the Franco-Prussian War in 1870. Subsequently, there was a national conviction to never let Verdun be captured by the Germans again, so a ring of forts was built around it—despite Napoleon having reportedly stated that whatever side remained within its fortifications was beaten. German commanders therefore believed that if they made an effort to take Verdun, the French would exhaust themselves of men and material to hold on to it, and they were right. Verdun was an epic battleground in both world wars.

As such, when you visit Verdun, you see the shell holes (now covered by grass, trees and other vegetation); walk on the blasted terrain (with the preserved or eroding trenches); view destroyed villages (left as memorials to destruction of civilization); tour the remains of forts (with stalactites and stalagmites forming where water seeps in from above); and walk among the many graves, these symbols of man versus man that contain a sea of human remains. All of these experiences are available at Verdun.

The Citadel

The major ramparts of Verdun, the city itself, contain a vast underground complex of rooms and tunnels called the Citadel, now turned into a Disney-like mobile-cart tour experience. It takes you through preserved or recreated military planning, cooking, cleaning and sleeping facilities. After the mobile cart ride ends you walk to a memorial area and ultimately to a museum/gift shop. Equivalent to a virtual experience, complete with the smell of the underground, it helps you *feel* the environment and receive a small amount of the emotional impact that must have been felt by soldiers living there during WWI.

Douaumont

Defending Verdun from its ramparts proved to be disadvantageous because direct-fire artillery technology allowed the guns to reach the city itself. As a result, forts were built far enough away to avoid direct-fire attack on the city, and with enough steel-reinforced concrete and earth covering them to be protected and be able to strike back. However, long-range, indirect-fire weapons were developed and improved to a point that Verdun, and eventually Paris, could be hit by large-caliber, high-explosive shells from ten or more miles away.

The largest, best-preserved fort northwest of Verdun is Fort Douaumont. Its survival would come down to keeping away soldiers equipped with gas bombs, grenades, dynamite, flamethrowers and other weapons capable of penetrating its apertures. For this reason, machine-gun positions on the reverse slopes of Douaumont in the surrounding dry moat were to stop infantry access to the apertures. It was then necessary to have men in trenches outside the fort to keep enemy infantry from approaching close enough to attack the fort. In the end, it meant men must face men and their infantry weapons to successfully storm shell trenches and take those lines of defense before assaulting the fort itself.

Fleury: Since it was near Fort Douaumont and Verdun, the Germans shelled the village of Fleury. Its inhabitants vacated the town, and it was shelled periodically over many months until it was devastated. At that point, it was not considered worth returning to rebuild—especially considering the amount of unexploded ordnance in the area. The site has small placards that identify the type of business or operation in the center of town that was blasted out of existence and never rebuilt. Now overgrown with trees and weathered over a century, many shell holes have trees growing from them, and some of the roots have pulled up pieces of building foundations.

The Ossuary: It is impossible in WWI and WWII combat, characterized by massive high-explosive indirect shelling, to account for all the dead. A shell making a direct or even a close hit on one or more humans can vaporize them and, as was said about bomb-disposal units in England after the Battle of Britain, "only the birds find you." This is one reason—and there are others, such as a plane crash—that a soldier's name may be placed on the "wall of the missing" at many monuments. There is literarily nothing recognizable left of them.

In between the extremes of complete destruction and having an identifiable body to bury there are a range of cases in which body fragments survive the explosion. Sometimes these explosions cover bodies (such as in a trench) or a body fragment is blown some distance and not found at the time. Animals and decay remove all flesh, and you are left with bones. Sometimes, even today, farmers, hikers, pets and passersby occasionally find these bones. The Ossuary at Verdun has the bones from an estimated 130,000 soldiers (and perhaps others) visible through windows that let people outside the building peer into the remains.

Bayonet Trench: There is a monument to what many believe to be a group of men buried by an explosion—such as mentioned above—that filled in the trench. A number of bayonets were found sticking out of the dirt, and the assumption was made that there were people holding onto their rifles who were buried alive. Many World War I veterans were skeptical, but a memorial site that draws large numbers of visitors was built over the trench of bayonets.

World War I Battlefields in the Area of the Rivers

Beyond Verdun, the greatest number of World War I battles occurred in Northeastern France in a large region traversed by three meandering and roughly parallel rivers, the Meuse, the Marne and the Somme. Trench warfare's stagnation of maneuver made this area a killing ground. Ironically, the speed of the German blitzkrieg in 1940 and the equally rapid eastward movement of the Allied forces in 1944 resulted in little combat in the region of these three rivers during World War II.

The Somme: The Somme River valley was part of the original German 1914 conquests, and they pulled back to here and dug in after the French Army from Paris and the British Expeditionary Force (BEF) forced a retreat from east-northeast of Paris to higher ground. The Germans were able to improve their defenses on the Somme for over a year, particularly on the high ground of Thiepval Ridge, before the war moved to them. Many curtains of barbed wire and trench lines with overlapping fields of machine-gun and artillery fire were in place by 1916.

Thiepval Ridge: Thus, on the first day of the Somme offensive, the British suffered the greatest loss of men in their history, with more than 57,000 killed, wounded and missing—including more than 19,000 killed—in that one day. Many more died over the following months. Visiting Thiepval Ridge in 2018 enabled us to view some German defensive positions as well as the Thiepval memorial to the missing (with more than 72,000 names etched on the walls) above a cemetery of mostly unknowns. Another exhibit shows the Commonwealth daily death toll in WWI. This memorial includes a miniature wrapped corpse placed on the ground with a standard cross "remember" marker for each day in the war. The number of soldiers who died that day is written on the markers. This representation made the casualties from the first day of the First Battle of the Somme—followed by several others at different locations in the region—very apparent.

Belleau Wood: United States Marines have a historical connection to the woods adjacent to the French town of Belleau about 45 miles east-north-east of Paris. German units, bolstered on the Western Front by many divisions freed from the Eastern Front as a result of Russia's Bolshevik Revolution, launched a number of attacks toward Paris during their 1918 Spring Offensive in hopes of ending the war.

The Marines made a major sacrifice in repeatedly striking at Belleau Wood before finally pushing the Germans out. The Aisne-Marne Cemetery, curved around the base of Hill 142 at the foot of Belleau Wood, contains the graves of many of the Marines killed in that fight. The hill and the cemetery are now American land in France commemorating the dead, wounded and missing sons who fought a relentless battle there, often facing German mustard gas, machine-gun fire, artillery barrages, and ultimately close-quarters bayonet and hand-to-hand fighting.

Meuse-Argonne: Once America entered the war the commander of its Expeditionary Force, Major General John J. Pershing, sought to demonstrate what an American army could achieve when fighting in its own sector with its own battle plan, as opposed to acting as part of a French or British Army. Pershing chose an area between the Argonne Forest and the Meuse River, which had been part of the old Verdun battleground. The Germans had had many months to build their defenses, including machine-gun positions with overlapping fire, not only facing the enemy axis of advance but also facing to the rear to cut down an enemy approaching from behind. It was into this cauldron that Americans attacked in September 1918.

Lost Battalion: Major Charles Whittlesey's 1st Battalion of the 308th Regiment of the 77th Division became isolated in a ravine when units believed to be moving forward on its flanks were stopped. Whittlesey's men were surrounded for several days, hit with machine-gun and rifle fire, grenades, mortars and artillery, including friendly fire, in their pocket. Of the 600 men who went in, about 200 were killed, 150 were missing (many captured) and about 200 survived. It became known as the Lost Battalion. There is a marker off the road that includes showing German positions and a marker pointing down to where foxholes and probably shell holes can still be found, though people walking there will gradually cause them to erode away.

Sergeant York: Corporal Alvin Cullum York was awarded America's Congressional Medal of Honor and received awards from a grateful French nation as well, as a result of an action in a ravine near Chatel-Chéhéry. He and a 16-man patrol were detailed to infiltrate behind German machine guns that were holding up the advance of the 2nd Battalion, 328th Infantry on the morning of October 8, 1918. The patrol surprised a group of 90 or so Germans who were eating breakfast. After a short firefight in which six of the patrol were killed and others wounded, York single-handedly dispatched 21 of the enemy. The German officer surrendered his men, and York and the patrol led off prisoners to the American lines. He had captured 132 German soldiers. He was promoted to sergeant.

York's marksmanship was well known. Back in his home village of Pall Mall in the Valley of the Twin Forks, Tennessee, he had learned to shoot using "black powder" weapons at the many turkey shoots that were held there.

For many years, historians wondered where in the Argonne Forest in France the action took place. In the early 2000s, the Nolan Group, using historical records along with modern GIS technologies and an archaeological survey, discovered the actual site in the forest. One of the most important records was from the American Burial Records (Graves Registration Service or GRS), whose department officials buried the six dead where they fell. They were exhumed at the end of the war, and the coordinates of the burials were recorded. Using these records, the Nolan Group was able to locate where those burials took place. A large number of artifacts were recovered, many of them German and American; some of the latter were clearly marked with York's unit, "328 Co. G"—328th Infantry, Company G. The Nolan Group was able to identify some American and German ammunition that could have been from York's weapons and from the German officer who was shooting at York.

The account of how the Nolan group painstakingly pieced together evidence over a number of years is an intriguing detective story. A book has been written by the British military historian and battlefield guide, Michael Kelly, in which all the relevant American official accounts and the German diaries, together with the patrol survivor affidavits, are examined. Nearly 200 color maps and photographs are produced to assist the reader to a better understanding. This book's publishing information is in the bibliography at the back of this guide.

Monuments

Monuments to Allied victories in WWI battles, including cemeteries, are readily found in all areas where men fought and died. There are several massive American monuments to such victories. These monuments represent victory over established German fortifications, all on high ground. Often, this high ground contained hills that had no names and so were identified by the height of the hill above sea level (i.e., Hill 142). This naming practice continued in World War II and later conflicts. All American monuments are managed by the American Battlefield Monuments Commission (ABMC). Access information to ABMC resources are on the **Readers Only** website. These monuments are very well done and cared for and are a natural destination for any American in Europe, as are the American cemeteries. They clearly demonstrate the American commitment and sacrifice to our European allies, then and now.

Château-Thierry Monument: This monument memorializes the American units that fought with the French along the Marne River, notably at Château-Thierry, where America joined the war, preventing the success of the German Spring Offensive. The monument sits near the summit of Hill 204 and overlooks the Marne River and Château-Thierry. It includes a map of the area around the monument and has a vector map giving the direction and distance to various French towns. There is a museum under the monument, which has video presentations and artifact displays. Some of the largest WWI monuments include this one on Hill 204, Montsec and Montfaucon.

Montsec: The Montsec American Monument commemorates the success in attacks on the German St. Mihiel salient. The site is at the summit of Butte Montsec near Thiaucourt, France. The monument includes carved names of the cities and towns liberated by the American First and Second armies from September to November 1918. A large, circular, columned, open-roofed monument, it contains a metallic embossed map of the area oriented geographically in line with the surrounding terrain. On the stone adjacent to the column bases are etched arrows pointing in the direction of French cities and towns involved in the American actions and shown on the relief map. In this way, the monument not only commemorates American military commitment, but also provides an excellent visual geographic understanding of the forward movement of American success in assuring the war would soon come to an end.

Montfaucon: The Montfaucon American Monument, approximately 20 miles from the Verdun battlefields of 1916 and near the village of Montfaucon-en-Argonne, sits atop Montfaucon and commemorates the American Meuse-Argonne Campaign, which lasted from September 26 until the Armistice on November 11, 1918. Remains of a church sit behind the monument, and the ruins of German strongpoints are adjacent to the monument and on the approaches to the site. Over 200 steps bring you to the enclosed top, where doors open to a walled veranda for an excellent view of the region on all four sides. The names of surrounding towns are etched in the top of the veranda walls, which provide an excellent view of the location of trenches from the campaign.

Cemeteries

The ultimate sites to appreciate American and Allied sacrifice in WWI are the cemeteries that contain the remains of thousands of Americans who fought first with the French and then in their own campaign on the Meuse-Argonne region. As you walk along the rows of graves, which are perfectly placed and randomly positioned, (that is, no special placement of officers or politically connected individuals), it is easy to see the cost of freedom.

Walking among the graves and monuments in the peace and quiet, it is easy to imagine those resting there saying to you, "We've all done our best, how about you?" We highlight several American cemeteries here, but there are other American and hundreds of British and French cemeteries to visit throughout northern France and Belgium. For example, the Tyne Cot Commonwealth War Graves Cemetery, the largest WWI British Cemetery, still includes German fortifications whose machine guns may have shot down many who are buried nearby. Note that the cemetery's design, the type of marker stone and its design and engraved content, landscaping around these stones, and vegetation, including trees, are all unique, with explanation about the country of origin of each.

Aisne-Marne: The Aisne Marne American Cemetery contains Americans, many Marines, who fought and died on the adjacent hill containing Belleau Wood. The cemetery arches around part of the hill, forming curved marker lines unusual for an American military cemetery. The cemetery sits at the end of a tree-lined driveway ending in a monument to the missing, whose names are etched on the interior. The cemetery contains over 2,000 names as well as many unknowns, and the names of over 1,000 Americans still missing. Clearly, some of the names of the missing would likely match remains in graves of the unknown, but few have yet been identified using family DNA.

Oise-Aisne: The Oise-Aisne American Cemetery includes American dead from the surrounding geographic area commemorated by the Chateau-Thierry American Monument. It contains graves of notable Americans, including Joyce Kilmer, who wrote the famous poem "Trees." He was shot by a German sniper just several hundred yards from where he rests today. The cemetery contains over 6,000 burials, and the names of over 200 missing appear on the walls of the chapel in the monument at the top of a gradual hill on the other side of the cemetery from the Visitors Center. In all cemeteries, the superintendents eventually learn the moving stories of soldiers buried there, and often greet relatives who come to visit the graves.

Mine Warfare

One of the lesser-known types of WWI warfare was the underground war—digging deep tunnels under enemy positions where large vaults or caverns would be carved out and filled with high explosives. Sometimes this digging was detected from above and counter-tunnels dug to interrupt the enemy's efforts by setting off adjacent mines (called camouflets) to collapse tunnels or by engaging in underground close-quarters combat in the dark. Tens of thousands of pounds of high explosives would be set, and when detonated at the onset of a new offensive, would eliminate imposing and lethal fortifications, eviscerating and maiming many soldiers.

Lochnagar Mine: A major mine was detonated by the British Army in chalky ground near the French town of La Boisselle on the morning of July 1, 1916, the first day of the Somme battle. It formed a crater about 100 feet deep and more than 300 feet wide.

Tanks

Very few WWI tanks are still in existence. The Germans built about a dozen tanks and the Allies more than 4,000. The remains of a British "female" tank (i.e., one equipped only with machine guns), long buried and recently uncovered, are visible in the Cambrai Tank museum adjacent to the Tyne Cot Commonwealth War Graves Cemetery, where several of the tank's crew are buried. In addition to the tank museum, there is a memorial to the first large-scale use of tanks, at the Battle of Cambrai on November 20, 1917. In WWII Cambrai again saw tanks in action as the German 5th Panzer Division bore down on the community in a race with the 7th Panzer Division, under Erwin Rommel, to cut off Allied forces in Belgium in mid-May 1940.

Belgium

Waterloo: Napoleon was a French emperor who dominated the European continent through military victories following his rise in power during and after the 1789 French Revolution. He was known for bringing modern strategic and tactical guidance to warfare. He invented military rations because he knew the army moved "on its stomach," including bottled food boiled to kill germs (a discovery during that time by the scientist Louis Pasteur). He was also famous for implementing legal and administrative systems and building his power through the use of propaganda in the areas he conquered.

Eventually countries, led by Britain and Prussia, formed military coalitions against Napoleon. They captured Paris. Napoleon was deposed and imprisoned but eventually escaped and regained power. In 1815 the last of the allied coalitions met and defeated Napoleon's army at Waterloo, southwest of the Belgian capital of Brussels. The battlefield remains a place to visit, though some of the land has reverted to active farming. Some structures remain from the battle. A high point on which steps have been installed allows visitors to climb to a height where they can gaze over much of the battlefield.

Ypres: World War I was a killing machine in several small areas that are well preserved and memorialized today under national, local or commercial private care. Ypres (pronounced E-pra) is spelled Ieper in Belgium and was pronounced "Wipers" by the British soldiers (Tommies) in the years 1914 to 1918. A major Belgian city within 25 miles of the English Channel, it sits below ridges that were occupied early in the war. That made it an artillery target for years, so the town was devastated, with most buildings turned to rubble. In World War II, Ypres was the site of a high-level meeting of British, French and Belgian military leaders on May 21, 1940, to discuss a breakout from the pocket the Germans were forcing them into, centered on the French port town of Dunkirk.

Ypres has many WWI sights, as well as great restaurants, chocolates, shops, hotels, a cathedral and other attractions. Nearby, the coastal town of Nieuport (now spelled Nieuwpoort) was on the left flank of the Allied defense line in the Dunkirk Pocket and was fiercely defended by a handful of Belgian units at the end of May 1940.

Cloth Hall—Flanders Fields Museum: Since the Middle Ages there has been a large building on the main square in Ypres, called the Cloth Hall because it had once been a place where cloth vendors sold their wares. The building was a target for German artillery from the surrounding ridges and eventually it became a pile of rubble but was later rebuilt. A museum along the city's ramparts (medieval wall) includes a diorama of the city during its WWI destruction—showing it blasted into rubble; dirt and brown dust cover the ruins of all structures. It is an important image to have in mind when you see the city today.

Today, the Cloth Hall houses the Flanders Fields WWI Museum, which has many displays from the Great War; a small amphitheater showing a video of actors portraying soldiers and nurses in uniform speaking from written letters; and a dynamic lighted-relief map of the Ypres area, with accompanying video, to provide a quick understanding of the strategic and tactical plans and actions throughout the war. The rooftop is accessible from inside the museum if you buy the extended ticket. You climb stone spiral stairs to the bell tower, then go up again to an exit on the roof. Plaques with color imagery from the rooftop identify the various buildings visible from that side of the Cloth Hall.

Menin Gate: The Menin Gate is a medieval gate to Ypres along the main thoroughfare into the center of the town. It is used for a major remembrance ceremony for the many thousands of Commonwealth soldiers killed in the Ypres Salient, whose names are carved into the walls. Every night—that is, every night of the year, every year—a large crowd gathers on either side of rope guides, clearing the main roadway for the ceremony. Buglers and a kilted bagpipe player enter one end of the gate and play the "Last Post," beginning at exactly 8:00 p.m. When the music is over, several small groups of people place wreaths in one of the gate's stairways.

Ramparts and Rampart Cemetery: An ancient earthen wall around Ypres is still walkable around much of the eastern side of the city from the Menin Gate. It contains the Ramparts Cemetery (Lille Gate), with 198 graves, which is overseen by the Commonwealth War Graves Commission. You can access the wall at the Menin Gate and walk along a wide trail with the watercourse (a kind of moat) on one side and the city on the other.

Flanders Fields: An American contingent fought near Ypres in support of a British offensive near the end of World War I. Many of the dead from this fight are buried at the Flanders Field American Cemetery and Memorial near Waregem, Belgium. It contains the graves of over 350 American soldiers, and 43 other names are inscribed on the Wall of the Missing inside the chapel. The visitor center has a film with scheduled showings. It tells how the cemetery came to be there and includes stories of local Belgian citizens who have adopted graves. The adopters bring flowers and, if the subject is not an unknown, will write letters attempting to contact relatives of their grave's namesake. All graves have been adopted. It is the only American WWI cemetery and memorial in Belgium.

Pool of Peace: This pool, called the Spanbroekmolen Crater, was created in 1917 by the explosion of 91,000 pounds of ammonal high-explosive under a German position on Messines Ridge that looked out over British positions during the Third Battle of Ypres. In 1929 Lord Wakefield purchased the crater to preserve it as a memorial site. Now, there is a peaceful, water-filled pool there and plaques commemorating the action and the consequences.

Messines and Passchendaele: The high-ground towns of Messines and Passchendaele just to the east of Ypres were controlled by the Germans, so they built up their defenses (trenches and bunkers). The British dug mines to destroy key points along the line. Shelling combined with infantry assaults through often muddy terrain finally took these positions with great human loss. Vestiges of the fighting at both these ridge sites include restored trenches, cemeteries, monuments and displays which recount the grinding battles fought here.

Battle of the Bulge: Adolf Hitler was losing his Third Reich to the Russians in the east and the west was falling to the Allies, who were on the doorstep of Germany. He knew that Antwerp was a major Allied port and thought that taking it would slow supplies to the Western Allies and split their forces. He gathered his armor reserves to make a quick decisive strike—as the Germans had done in WWI and the Wehrmacht had repeated in 1940—through the Ardennes Forest. Into this assumed "quiet" sector the Americans had placed a new, untested division alongside a veteran division that needed an easier assignment to rest after the grueling advance across France. The Germans attacked on December 16, 1944.

Bastogne: Bastogne is a Belgian town with a major crossroads, one of which went in the direction of Antwerp. The 101st Airborne Division was available and trucked into the town to support units retreating from the German attack. They formed a defensive perimeter around the town. Today, there is a Battle of the Bulge museum in Bastogne as well as a major American monument to the fighting in the area.

Foy and the Easy Company Foxholes: To defend Bastogne, units of the 101st Airborne Division, including Easy Company, which was depicted in the ***Band of Brothers*** series, were stationed above the town of Foy in the forest of pines. There is a monument erected by Steven Spielberg on the road approaching the tree line. A sign on one of the trees just off the road states "Easy Company foxholes." A short walk into the trees reveals a number of foxholes, slightly eroded over time and covered with pine needles, indicating where the company dug in.

Malmedy Massacre: Outside the town of Malmedy more than 80 captured American soldiers were machine-gunned in a field by German armored units commanded by Joachim Peiper. SS troops walked among the dead and injured, shooting anyone who made a sound or whose breath was seen in the freezing air. Others were shot down or were machine-gunned when they ran from a building the Germans set fire to. Many Americans "played dead," then got up and ran after some time had passed. Americans troops found the remains of these soldiers when the Germans were pushed back. Eventually those Germans believed to be involved, including Peiper, were tried and convicted. There is a memorial near the massacre site.

The Netherlands

Operation Market Garden

In September of 1944, Field Marshal Montgomery's plan to end the war by Christmas was attempted. Depicted in the movie ***A Bridge Too Far***, American parachutists were to capture several bridges from the Allied jumping-off point along a single road to the city of Arnhem in the Netherlands, which was on the western side of a Rhine River bridge providing a bridgehead into Germany. A mobile British XXX Corps armored force was to move up the road (Highway 69, later called "Hell's Highway") with the protected bridges, get to Arnhem, and cross the Rhine into Germany. British airborne troops were to capture Arnhem and the bridge over the Rhine there. The airborne element was codenamed *Market* and the ground attack by XXX Corps was named *Garden*.

Eindhoven: The 101st Airborne took bridges north of the city, though the Son bridge was destroyed and had to be replaced with a portable, pre-fabricated British Bailey bridge over the Wilhelmina Canal. XXX Corps passed through them and headed north toward Nijmegen.

Nijmegen: The 82nd Airborne landed south of Nijmegen, took two of four bridges assigned to them and fought for days to capture the major bridge over the Waal Canal, critical to operation's success.

Arnhem: British and later Polish forces landed at a distance from their objectives and local SS units not expected in the area eventually killed or captured most of the 8,000 men who landed there. About 2,000 escaped. Plans for *Operation Market Garden* were taken from a dead American officer who brought them with him for the landing, giving the Germans details about the operation. XXX Corps was not able to get to Arnhem in time to save the paratroopers there, in part because of delays taking bridges along the route and defending the captured roadway. The Airborne Museum at Oosterbeek provides a variety of exhibits and artifacts from the British attack on Arnhem.

Pictured here are the delegations of the Union of Soviet Socialist Republics and Cuba during the first session of the United Nations General Assembly, which opened on January 10, 1946 at Central Hall in London. *(Image courtesy of the United Nations Photo Collection)*

The Future

D-DAY ANNIVERSARY TAKEAWAYS

Mark Weisenmiller

IN THE 1920S AND 1930S PARADES AND SPEECHES FREQUENTLY HONORED the generation that had served in the First World War. But the Second World War eclipsed the First in public memory. The baby boomers, born between 1946 and 1964, had millions of World War II veterans living among them (though many veterans would not talk about their experiences until late in their lives). Movies, TV shows, novels and comic books set in WWII were part of baby boomers' pop culture into the mid-1960s. They grew up aware of the history and significance of WWII.

Seventy-five years have passed since that war's D-Day landings and subsequent Normandy Campaign. For the millennial generation the Second World War is as distant and fading as the First World War was to baby boomers. We have focused attention on millennials in this book to help them better understand why this period of history holds meaning for them and to show that lessons gleaned from WWII, particularly from D-Day, are as valuable today as ever, both for society and for the individual.

The chapters in this book about visiting D-Day sites, *The Present*, and learning your family's connections to the Normandy Campaign are designed to help readers find their personal connections to the events of '44. The information on books, movies, games and other areas of popular culture is there to inspire readers to explore D-Day's history and what-ifs for themselves. And, of course, the chapters found in the section titled *The Past* provide historical detail and context for learning about WWII and particularly the campaign in Normandy.

History's DNA

Several chapters in *The Future* show how events of 75–80 years ago continue to influence our world. Just as your DNA was created by genetic traits passed down through generations, so too, the events of history live today in modern conflicts (and sometimes in conflicts avoided); in regional beliefs and ideologies; in the existing boundaries and ethnic makeup of nations; and in scientific and technical research that builds upon previous discoveries. The United Nations, born out of Allied cooperation in WWII, was created to improve international relations and to try to forestall future wars. Economic institutions such as the International Monetary Fund were established to prevent worldwide financial crises like the Great Depression of the 1930s that made countries more vulnerable to demagogues like Hitler. The past is always present, even when we are not aware of it.

Here are a few concepts we, the publishers and authors, hope you will take away from reading *D-Day 75th Anniversary—A Millennials Guide.*

Cooperation and Personal Sacrifice

Personal desires must sometimes be sacrificed for the greater good. Mutual cooperation is more successful than "going it alone."

Military and political leaders who planned and executed D-Day and the Normandy Campaign were strong-willed, sometimes opinionated men whose careers could benefit from personal glory in the war. Yet, time and again, they put aside personal desires for the benefit of the greater cause. They shared information and ideas, worked under the leadership of others even when they felt they should be the leader, and though they often disagreed and quarreled, they never lost sight of their ultimate goal: destruction of the totalitarian government of Nazi Germany that had enslaved most of Europe and threatened the entire world.

Contrast this setting aside of egos and willingness to listen to opposing views with what happened in Germany. Adolf Hitler believed his instincts were invariably correct. Early successes when he overruled the advice of his military advisors strengthened his belief that he knew more than they did. As a result, he failed to heed the advice of men like Erwin Rommel and Gerd von Rundstedt in preparing to repel the coming Allied invasion. He refused to recognize Allied superiority in numbers and equipment. He clung to the belief that what he wanted to happen *would* happen, even when facts clearly showed he was wrong.

The Allies set aside, at least temporarily, their differences, cooperated with each other and won. Hitler insisted he alone was right and lost.

Planning

Plans often fall apart once implemented, but extensive planning increases chances for success and helps prepare for contingencies when things don't go as expected.

Allied planning—the choice of time and location, the types of equipment and size of forces required for victory, the extensive deception campaign to keep the Germans uncertain about Allied intensions, and much more—allowed them to successfully pull off the largest amphibious invasion in history. When things went wrong on the beaches and inland, the extensive planning insured resources were available to overcome unexpected setbacks.

Logistics Matter

When preparing for a major undertaking, don't ignore logistics.

There is a saying: Amateurs study tactics, professionals study logistics. Most of the D-Day planning centered around logistics. The most powerful army in the world isn't much use if it can't get its troops to the battlefield or keep them supplied there. Similarly, individuals, organizations or countries that don't consider the steps and resources needed to succeed at what they hope to accomplish will almost certainly fail.

Communication

Success requires effective communication. Acting on incomplete data can lead to bad decisions.

Communication among the Western Allies wasn't always perfect, but overall they communicated effectively. During D-Day itself, however, communications from the chaotic situation on Omaha Beach to General Omar Bradley aboard the cruiser USS *Augusta* were all but non-existent; what news he was receiving made the landing sound like a disaster. He considered withdrawing the troops and redirecting them to Utah Beach or the British sector—until he received a message around 1:30 p.m. that the men were off the beach and advancing up the slopes. He sent two officers to personally observe and make a report; that report ended any thoughts of calling back the Omaha Beach invasion—but when communications were wanting, Bradley nearly made a bad decision based on inadequate information.

Consider the Germans during the Normandy Campaign. Airborne troopers cut communication lines behind the beaches, and the French Resistance further interrupted German ability to communicate with the front. Allied air power destroyed the German communications net during the subsequent campaign. The inability to get adequate information at crucial times limited German ability to effectively respond to Allied moves.

Effective communication can influence beliefs and behavior. (For example, the disinformation campaign the Allies used to mislead the Germans.) Nations of both sides made effective use of propaganda to demonize and dehumanize their opponents. Propaganda also served to keep up morale and determination among their own people, an example of the latter being a poster with lettering in large black font that demanded, "DELIVER FOR D-DAY!" to encourage thousands of Americans to work harder and faster.

Excluding People Excludes Talent

Never underestimate a group of people just because they are different from your own group.

The Allies mobilized all segments of their society for the war effort, though the United States in particular still clung to negative, stereotypical beliefs about Americans descended from Africans, Hispanics, Asians, Jews, and certain others. Often, these groups were limited in where they could go, what they could do, and how they could serve the war effort. (As two examples of the latter, African Americans were far more likely to be assigned to supply duties than to combat units, and some Jews found themselves barred from participating in service organizations to aid the war effort.) Still, minority groups were not completely excluded from participating in the war, and their contributions added to America's military strength.

Likewise, women were utilized to fill traditionally male jobs that women supposedly were incapable of performing. All Allied nations utilized their women in roles from manufacturing—"Rosie the Riveter" became an American icon during the war and decades later served as a symbol within the women's rights movement—to pilots ferrying planes and training male pilots for combat, to the code breakers of Bletchley Park who played a crucial role in decoding and interpreting Axis messages.

Meanwhile, Nazi Germany relegated most women's role to that of wife and mother, producing and raising a new generations of Aryans for the Fatherland. German women could have taken the place of men in the workforce to free those men for military service, as in the Allied countries. Jews, a potentially large group from which to recruit men to fight the Soviet Union, were not only excluded from the military, they were removed from industry, transportation and other jobs critical to Germany's war effort and sent to die in concentration camps. Hitler had little regard for the field of physics (think "atom bomb") because he believed it was a "Jewish science."

Research, Experiment, Innovate

Science, mathematics and technology can find solutions to monumental problems when adequately funded and encouraged, but be observant—sometimes the search for one thing leads to the discovery of a different innovation.

The demands of the Second World War posed numerous challenges, but researchers and innovators in mathematics, physics, chemistry, biology/medicine and other fields came through. As the Space Race of the 1960s would later reaffirm, when sufficient resources are made available and high goals set, virtually nothing is impossible; some breakthroughs just take longer than others.

The word "science" is a deviation of the Latin word *scientia*, meaning knowledge. Much knowledge was gained and expended in this, the largest war in history. Advances in cryptography, jet propulsion, anti-aircraft weapons, radar and sonar were the result of scientific advances. The list of scientific and technological discoveries and of products that existed in an embryonic state but were improved during the war years is extensive. (Some discoveries such as the microwave oven and the Slinky toy were unexpected byproducts of wartime research.)

In no particular order, here are but a few of the advances made: airplane pressurized cabin; nylon; Teflon (used for gaskets and lining in the atomic bomb); polyester; and synthetic fuels (the Germans accelerated their prewar supply exponentially); the electron microscope; and the kidney dialysis machine. M&M candies were introduced commercially in 1941 but sold exclusively to the military during the war because the hard outer candy shell made it less likely the chocolate would melt.

It could be said a weatherman, not a general, set the final date for D-Day. On June 5, 1944, Scottish meteorologist Group Captain J.M. Stagg told General Dwight Eisenhower there would be "a gleam of hope for you, sir"— there would be a brief clearing the next day in the storms lashing Normandy, and the invasion could proceed. Ike said simply, "OK—let's go," and the window of opportunity proved to be wide enough.

Wars Transform Nations

The uncertainty and upheaval of war generally upset the status quo; no nation that goes to war will remain unchanged. The U.S. and the USSR, both secondary in prominence to Europe's older nations in the 1930s, emerged from WWII as the world's two superpowers while "the old guard" fell from their long-time position as the leaders of the world.

The Second World War devastated many cities of Europe. Bombed-out buildings remained in Britain, France, Germany, and elsewhere for decades after the war ended. Conversely, American cities grew as workers moved into them from small towns and farms to do war work; finding living space for them became a headache in many cities.

World War II also changed the American military. A Joint Chiefs of Staff was formed to have an equivalent of the British model for planning the invasion of Europe and to have the different branches of the U.S. military work together more efficiently. Between 1941 and 1943 the Pentagon was constructed across the Potomac from the nation's capital to house in a single place personnel that were scattered across 17 buildings in the city. Comprised of five concentric pentagonal rings connected by radial corridors spread over more than 6 million gross square feet, it has become the symbol of American military might. In his 1988 book *Washington Goes To War*, journalist David Brinkley related one of the jokes inspired by the unprecedented size and labyrinthian corridors when this building was new. A woman told a Pentagon guard she was in labor and needed help in getting to a maternity hospital. The guard said, "Madam, you should not have come here in that condition." "When I came here," she answered, "I wasn't."

A United Nation is Stronger

When the majority of a nation's population believes the path their leaders have taken is a necessary, even righteous one, the nation is stronger.

Most of the winning countries of WWII had people who resolutely believed in protecting and preserving something (a royal monarchy; civil liberties; freedom for all; preservation of a country's natural and mineral resources; the socialist dream; etc.) and saw the Axis nations as a threat. This unified their people in accepting the sacrifice of lives, both military and civilian, and in enduring rationing and other privations. (Note, though, that by 1944 most American soldiers in Europe were draftees, and war bond sales were declining. Newspapers continued to assail the domestic policies and leadership of politicians of the party the paper did not support.)

The people of the Axis nations, it must be said, also believed their cause to be right (fighting communism, national expansion, taking their "rightful place" among the world's nations). They, too, were willing to sacrifice much for their country's cause. The July 20, 1944, attempt on Hitler's life showed clearly, though, that some among his military officers no longer believed in the Führer. Only after the war did the world learn this was one of many unsuccessful attempts on Hitler's life once his armies stopped winning victories.

Takeaways from D-Day's 75th Anniversary

While we hope readers will come away from this book with a better understanding of D-Day and of WWII in Europe, let us also mention three things worth learning from the 75th anniversary itself.

First, certain historical events must never be forgotten because their impact on human history is so great. If D-Day had not succeeded, more years and more lives would have been required to destroy Nazi Germany; conceivably, Germany might have been allowed to hold onto at least some of its conquered territories in exchange for peace. Even a strongly dedicated nation can become war weary and demand a less-than-desirable negotiated settlement.

Second, current and future generations must understand what great sacrifices have been made in the name of protecting freedom and opposing tyranny, to know what previous generations did to pass on a better world to those yet unborn.

And that brings us to the third takeaway from this anniversary: the need for valor. The Airborne troops climbing into aerial transports and the soldiers descending rope ladders into landing craft in the pre-dawn darkness of June 6, 1944, didn't know if they would still be alive in two hours. But they accepted the challenge that was laid down because they understood the stakes, understood that this invasion was a critical part a cause far more important than the life of any one individual.

If you ever get to visit the Normandy beaches and the cemeteries beyond them, perhaps on a day when sunlight cuts through white cumulus clouds in an azure sky and bounces off white marble headstones, imagine officers and sergeants shouting to their men leaving landing craft to "Get on that beach!" Imagine cries of wounded men, or seeing young men dying noiselessly as they fall into the sand. Imagine the fear men felt as they waded ashore under heavy fire, and ponder for a time how we might find within ourselves the valor they displayed if called upon to do so.

CONFLICTS OF THE LATE 20TH CENTURY

Gerhard L. Weinberg

In response to information about the initiation of developing atomic bombs by Germany, the British and American governments began such projects also while taking some measures to interfere with the German effort. By February 1945 the American project was far enough along for the drafting of an announcement to be released when first one was dropped. The plan was to utilize those available by late 1945 in support of Operation Olympic, the planned invasion of the Japanese home island of Kyushu in November 1945 which President Truman, the successor to the deceased President Franklin D. Roosevelt, authorized in mid-June. American decoded intercepts of Japanese diplomatic exchanges contributed to a new decision. In response to the advice of several Japanese diplomats in Europe, especially Ambassador Sato Naotake in Moscow, that Japan surrender rather than follow the German policy of fighting until the country was occupied, Japan's foreign minister replied that the Japanese governing Council had met and had unanimously decided not to follow this advice. President Truman decided in agreement with several advisors that a maximum of two atomic bombs would be diverted from support of *Operation Olympic* in the hope that the dropping of one and, if necessary, of two would lead to a new meeting of the Council in Tokyo and hopefully a different decision.

The End of World War II

From bombers flying from the earlier conquered island Tinian in the Marianas two atomic bombs were dropped on Japanese cities, the first on Hiroshima and the second on Nagasaki. While the American air commander in the Marianas was ordered under no circumstances to use a third atomic bomb, the governing Council in Tokyo met and split evenly on whether to surrender or not. Emperor Hirohito thereupon ordered that Japan surrender. A coup attempt to keep the war going failed when the man who was to lead it, War Minister Anami Korechika, committed suicide in the dilemma between his belief in continuing the war and his loyalty to the emperor. Thus the road was clear for a surrender ceremony in September 1945 which ended the war that in London and Washington had been expected to last into 1947 or 1948.

There would be more conflicts in the 20th century that will be reviewed briefly, but none covered the globe in death and destruction as the two world wars had. A major contribution to this development was that the Germans and the American people and government had each drawn an important lesson from World War II. The German people saw a major change in war. Their wars against Denmark in 1864, against Austria-Hungary and some other German states in 1866, against France in 1870–71, and against the Allies in 1914–18 had all been fought almost entirely outside Germany. That very obviously changed in World War II when bombing and fighting ravaged the German home country. The Germans learned that if you do not want your house to burn, it is best not to set the world on fire.

The Birth of the Cold War

As the Americans worried about the advances of the Soviet Union, they not only decided on a policy of deterrence but, unlike after 1918, proceeded to implement it for decades by maintaining quite substantial military forces and participating in alliances of which NATO, the North Atlantic Treaty Organization, was the most important. The policy of deterrence so implemented cost a great deal of money and occasionally cost some lives, as when planes crashed during the 1948–49 airlift to supply the Western Sectors of Berlin during a Soviet blockade, but it worked. The leaders of the Soviet Union could quite easily see that the United States was serious in its effort to deter Soviet advances, and although there were some moments of crisis, as over the installation of Soviet missiles in Cuba in 1962, the incentive for restraint was understood. The Cold War, as it was called, lasted from 1946 to 1991; but although the war in Korea in 1950–53 was hot indeed, it remained geographically limited in spite of the intervention of Communist China.

There were essentially local conflicts in the second half of the century. Some were in effect the result of uprisings in European colonies, and some were conflicts between the newly independent former colonies over territory or related subjects. Into the former category belong the Vietnam conflict of 1946–54 (into which the United States became involved 1964–75), the Algerian War in 1954–62, the Mau-Mau uprising in Kenya, and the conflict over the Suez Canal in 1956.

In the latter category were the wars between India and Pakistan in 1947–49, between India and China in 1962, between Iran and Iraq in 1980–88, and within Nigeria over the possible separation of Biafra in 1967–70. Perhaps the Bosnian civil war of 1992–95 and the conflict between some of the local population in East Timor and the government of Indonesia in 1975–2002 can be considered as also belonging in this category.

Middle East Instability

The Jewish inhabitants of the area now often referred to as Palestine had waxed and waned from about 1200 before the Common Era, and had after about 1800 years been joined by immigrating Arabs starting in the Seven Century of the Common Era. Beginning in the late Nineteenth Century, both forms of immigration had increased substantially, the Jewish both because of the persecution of Jews in Europe and the emergence and impact of a Zionist ideology, and the Arab because of the economic development of the area that was a significant facet of the Jewish immigration.

Britain conquered the area from the Ottoman Empire in World War I and secured a "Mandate" of it in the peace treaty. It then divided the mandate into two along the Jordan River and prohibited Jewish immigration into the far larger eastern area first called Transjordan and now known as the Kingdom of Jordan. In the 1930's the British had to cope in what was now the Palestine Mandate with an Arab uprising and both restricted Jewish immigration and fought the uprising. The British considered dividing the mandate into an Arab and a Jewish state, but in anticipation of war with Germany appeased the Arabs by further restricting Jewish immigration so that the troops fighting the uprising could be utilized in the expected war. When that war ended in Allied victory but included the Holocaust already mentioned, the British, who no longer needed the area to protect the northern flank of the Suez Canal to a newly independent India, in 1947 returned control of the mandate to the United Nations Organization (UNO) as successor of the League of Nations. The UNO thereupon in 1948 decided to divide the former mandate into two states and an international portion around the city of Jerusalem.

While the people and government of the Jewish state as defined by the borders set by the UNO regretted some aspects of the division, they accepted the decision and declared their independence. Both the leaders of the Arabic part of the population and the nearby newly independent Arab states rejected the UNO decision and attacked the new state of Israel. In a war in 1948-49 and in several subsequent wars they tried unsuccessfully to destroy the state of Israel. By 1978 Egypt grew tired of the repeated failure of these efforts and made peace with Israel; a procedure followed thereafter for the same reason by the Kingdom of Jordan. The leadership of the Palestinian Arabs continues its rejection of the concept of a separate state into the year 2018 as this account is written, and no effort by the Israeli government or outsiders to settle the conflict has succeeded.

The Twentieth Century would see several additional local conflicts. An attempt by the government of Argentina to seize the Falkland Islands in the South Atlantic in 1982 led to a war with Britain that the latter won. The attempt by Iraq to occupy and annex the state of Kuwait at the western end of the Persian Gulf was thwarted in 1990-91 by the military intervention of the United States. There has also been a pattern of occasional violence in Ireland between the Irish Free State and the Ulster portion of the island that remains a part of the United Kingdom.

For one century, all the foregoing would appear to be more than enough. It must be noted, however, that the Israeli-Palestinian conflict continued thereafter, that other aspects of the Middle East could and did give occasion for more military actions. Furthermore, the originally rather peaceful dissolution of the Soviet Union into a series of separate independent states could and subsequently did provide for the possibility of military attempts by the remaining Russian Federation to reclaim parts or all of one or more of the successor states. If there is any positive side to the high level of conflict in the century it may well be that the creation of nuclear weapons, now held by a considerable number of countries, has provided a truly major incentive for caution in international relations.

THE WORLD SHAPED BY WORLD WAR II

Erin Mahan

[The views expressed in this chapter are those of the author and do not necessarily represent those of the U.S. Department of Defense or the United States Government.]

THE SECOND WORLD WAR WROUGHT UNPRECEDENTED DAMAGE AND hardship to almost every nation. Almost 60 million died, with roughly 10 million of those the victims of ferocious ethnic cleansing not only from the Nazi-initiated Holocaust but also in the Soviet Union, Asia, and elsewhere. Hundreds of thousands more were left displaced and became refugees. Great cities were reduced to rubble. Economic austerity and chaos were left in the wake of the war. The societies of the vanquished powers and to a lesser extent those of the victors were tattered and weary. The world as it had been known before the war was gone.

The Second World War transformed the world for the remainder of the 20th century and even into the 21st century, and the events of that cataclysmic global conflagration shaped the world view of those who came into political power afterward. From Dwight Eisenhower (1953–1961) through George H. W. Bush (1989–1993), the United States elected presidents who came to maturity before WWII and saw active duty during the conflict. The same held true in most other countries. The events of the war forced a fundamental reassessment of how leaders viewed the global order. For Americans, the lessons they learned were many but two stand out: avoid appeasement of dictators and prevent a return to the economic nationalism and autarky (limited national trade) that led to the Great

Depression of the 1930s and that helped give rise to the dictators Adolf Hitler and Benito Mussolini.

The Munich Syndrome

The first lesson learned, that of not appeasing dictators, fueled what is often called the Munich syndrome, which guided U.S. and other Western leaders for the following half century and beyond. The syndrome arose from the belief that French and British appeasement of Hitler at the Munich Conference of 1938, which acquiesced to the Nazi invasion of Czechoslovakia, was misguided because conflict was not averted. Postwar leaders on both sides of the Atlantic evoked the Munich analogy to justify military action and strong-arm tactics throughout the rest of the century.

Presidents Harry Truman and Dwight Eisenhower used the Munich analogy to explain the need to stop communist aggression in the Korean War (1950–53). Presidents John Kennedy and Lyndon Johnson were guided by the Munich syndrome at crucial moments during the Vietnam War in the 1960s. British prime minister Margaret Thatcher evoked Munich over the Falklands War in the early 1980s against Argentina. Most recently, presidents George H.W. Bush and his son George W. Bush used rhetoric of avoiding appeasement to convince the American public that Iraqi dictator Saddam Hussein's takeover of Kuwait in 1991 and then his alleged pursuit of weapons of mass destruction in 2003 could not stand unchallenged.

The entire half century after WWII was regularly marked by military actions pursued under the specter of "another Munich." For better, and often worse as many pundits would argue, policymakers after WWII repeatedly misused this lesson of the Second World War. Too often the Munich analogy used by national leaders on the eve of war proved imprecise, exaggerated, and even gravely misapplied.

The World Economy

The second lesson learned from WWII that had lasting impact on postwar leaders was that only a global economy based on free and open trade could prevent another 1930s-style international economic depression. The Great Depression had started in the United States with the 1929 stock market crash, and affected countries' Worldwide Government Domestic Product (GDP) fell 15%. Unemployment was rampant, international trade plummeted, and prices, revenues, and personal incomes dropped precipitously.

In the last months of WWII, policymakers from almost 45 allied nations came together at Breton Woods, New Hampshire, and forged agreements resulting in the creation of two international institutions—the International Bank for Reconstruction and Development (later renamed the World Bank) and the International Monetary Fund (IMF)—meant to foster long-term international investment and maintain exchange stability. The delegates agreed that the dollar would serve as the global reserve currency. The creation of the General Agreement on Tariffs and Trade (GATT), which provided a framework for reducing trade barriers through periodic bargaining, soon followed. These economic legacies were profound and went a long way towards promoting economic growth, ensuring currency exchange rate stability, and preventing competitive devaluations.

The Marshall Plan

In the aftermath of WWII, however, the recovery of the industrialized nations of the Western world required immediate attention lest those nations plunge further into economic disarray. Army Chief of Staff general George C. Marshall, who is celebrated today as the architect of the plan bearing his name, helped resurrect and save postwar Europe. Between 1948 and 1952, the European Recovery Program—or "Marshall Plan"W-supplied grants and credits totaling more than $13 billion dollars to the nations of Western Europe, including West Germany. The postwar assistance to defeated powers became a hallmark American practice in the conflicts that followed, whether in South Korea or most recently in Iraq—and even to the former Soviet Union when it collapsed in the early 1990s.

Superpowers Emerge

The United States emerged from WWII as a world power. The Soviet Union, though it suffered more in physical and economic losses, rose as the other global superpower. The rivalry between the capitalist United States and the communist Soviet Union, which hid under the veneer of military cooperation during the World War, rapidly came to define the new era. The Marshall Plan foreclosed cooperation between the United States and the Soviet Union, which found the European Economic Recovery program ideologically incompatible with communism.

The struggle for predominance between the two superpowers would affect other nations in all facets. In Europe, the demarcations were drawn along the lines of Eastern and Western occupation forces. In just a few years after the end of WWII, what was called the Iron Curtain fell upon the continent, dividing it between the camps of the two superpowers. Regional defense pacts formed along the two superpower blocs. West European nations became members of the North Atlantic Treaty Organization (NATO) while East European nations joined the Warsaw Pact. That proverbial curtain across Central Europe was given concrete form in Germany when the communists built the Berlin Wall, dividing the city in 1961.

Around the globe other regional defense groupings formed along lines similar to NATO. The Southeast Asia Treaty Organization (SEATO) followed in 1949, and the Rio Treaty, enacted in the same year, involved most Central and South American nations. The Soviet Union did not establish as many formal treaty organizations but certainly kept many nations in its orbit through military alliances and economic assistance. Both superpowers tried to influence other nations through the United Nations, created at the end of WWII. The Allies had committed in 1941 to the broad principles of this new international organization, which was intended to be a forum to resolve postwar political issues. These organizations and alliance structures shaped the global power structure over the next 70 years.

The Cold War

Perhaps the most iconic image drawn from the end of WWII is that of the mushroom cloud ushering in the nuclear age. On August 6, 1945, the United States dropped an atomic bomb on the Japanese city of Hiroshima, reducing it to smoldering rubble. An estimated 100,000 Japanese were killed, and tens of thousands more injured. Three days later the United States dropped a second atomic bomb, on Nagasaki, forcing Japan to surrender and bringing WWII to an end. With this grim forewarning of what the future might hold, the nuclear age began.

America's atomic monopoly was short-lived. The Soviet Union detonated its first atomic bomb in August 1949. The nuclear age that followed WWII was dominated by the adversarial relationship between the United States and the Soviet Union. Divided by deep ideological and geostrategic differences, the two nuclear superpowers began an arms race with each side seeking to exploit and gain supremacy in a quantitative and qualitative buildup of their nuclear forces. At the height of the Cold War, which is considered to have lasted from 1945 to 1990, the combined nuclear arsenals of the former Soviet Union and the United States held over 60,000 warheads. Today the United States possesses upwards of 8,500 nuclear weapons and Russia approximately 11,000.

The 'Nuclear Club' Expands

The great power status conferred by these weapons and the deterrent mystique they offered made other nations seek nuclear arsenals of their own. Soon after WWII, the nuclear "club" expanded as Great Britain developed its first atomic bomb in 1952, France in 1960, China in 1964, India in 1974, Pakistan in 1998, and North Korea in 2006. Although Israel does not acknowledge having nuclear weapons (and the United States also neither confirms nor denies their existence), it is widely believed to have a major nuclear weapons program. Over 20 other nations from South Africa to Brazil to Norway have at one time or another started a nuclear weapons program. Even with the collapse of the Soviet Union and the end of the Cold War in the early 1990s, the nuclear age did not pass.

Biological and Chemical Weapons

While there has been no use of nuclear weapons since August 1945, WWII brought other weapons of mass destruction (WMD), namely chemical and biological weapons (CW and BW), to the fore. The moral repugnance following the indiscriminate use of chemical weapons by German forces against the Allies in WWI perhaps restrained both sides during WWII from using chemical weapons in combat, with the blatant exception of Japanese employment of biological weapons against Chinese soldiers and civilians. The Japanese also conducted vile biological weapons experiments on prisoners of war, and the Nazis killed millions of Jewish and other prisoners in concentration camps with gases suitable for chemical warfare.

The United States was not immune from either stockpiling or using CBW. Napalm, often described as jellied gasoline, is an incendiary gel that congeals to skin until it burns to the bone. Concocted in 1942 in a secret Harvard University laboratory for use during World War II, the U.S. military employed napalm to great effect against Imperial Japan—killing over 87,000 in one bombing of Tokyo alone on the night of March 9–10, 1945. By 1966, when U.S. engagement in Vietnam was at full throttle, the use of napalm had become central to its war effort. About 4,500 tons of napalm was dropped over Indochina monthly. Iraq used sarin gas in its eight-year war with Iran (1980–88), and the Soviet Union may have used CW in Southeast Asia and Afghanistan in the last quarter of the 20th century. Fears of WMD attacks by either nation-states or terrorist groups remain a common feature of today's landscape.

The End of Colonialism

World War II had ushered in an age of totalitarianism and of nationalism accompanied by a decline of colonialism—trends sparked by the First World War but accelerated by the Second. The eclipse of European nations' power during the war essentially destroyed whatever legitimacy their colonial regimes possessed. In the first decades after the war, the sweeping tide of nationalism coupled with the economic exhaustion and war weariness of the colonial powers precluded any successful efforts to reestablish their authority. The major European colonial empires were dismantled between 1945 and the early 1960s. With the exception of India, which was granted independence from Great Britain in 1946 and became an independent nation in 1947, decolonization did not occur without bloodshed. After bitter fighting, the Netherlands, for instance, lost Indonesia in 1948. The French fought unsuccessfully against the communist-led Vietminh in Indochina from 1946 to 1954. And after brutal fighting against Algeria in an eight-year guerrilla war that had atrocities on both sides, France failed to retain its hold on that territory.

The Cold War amplified colonial struggles; what started as wars of nationalism became proxy superpower conflicts. For the United States, Vietnam—a part of the former Indochina—was the most glaring case. The world after WWII gave way to a seemingly endless succession of insurgencies and counterinsurgencies, protracted wars of nationalism, and massacres. It is clear from the U.S. failure in Vietnam and its inability to establish a functioning democratic institution in Iraq that imposed democracy and capitalism did not work for all countries. The Soviet Union and Communist China supported and encouraged colonial revolutions. And within what was then called the Third World a generation of nationalist leaders grew up who were skilled in guerrilla tactics.

Segregation and Integration

The Second World War not only changed the nature of international relations but also set into motion social changes within many nations. In the United States prior to World War II some of the most famous military officers, including General George Marshall, and civilian government officials were outspoken in objecting to the racial integration of the Armed Forces. During World War II, the number of African Americans in the Army increased from 4,435 in 1940 to over 700,000 by September 1945.

Not surprisingly, then, after World War II there were increasing calls for racially integrating the military services, which met with opposition by powerful voices in the military and Congress. After all, President Harry S. Truman's bold decision in 1948 to issue an executive order calling for racial desegregation of the military put the Armed Forces ahead of the American legal system. State laws codifying segregation were still in place in many parts of the country. The president was well aware that although his order would mean that African Americans and whites would train together and share barracks, they would have to return to obeying rules of the segregated South when they left their bases and went into town.

Truman's order directing equal treatment and opportunity for blacks came six years before the Supreme Court's *Brown vs. Board of Education* decision toppled the legal basis for segregation and 16 years before the 1964 Civil Rights Act required the desegregation of public accommodations throughout the Southern states. Racial equality has not been a smooth journey for America. For many decades and arguably today, African Americans have suffered from varying degrees of de facto resistance to racial integration and still struggle for equal opportunities, but WWII was a major catalyst for the Civil Rights Movement.

'The Affluent Society'

Societies changed after the war in numerous other ways. For many countries, especially in the West, the affordability of manufactured goods made what were once luxuries before WWII—refrigerators, television sets, and of course, cars—common to most households.

The continuing communications revolution was another major global change. First came the cheap transistor radio, then satellite television, then mobile telephones, and now smartphones. Few countries, with the possible exception of North Korea and to a much lesser extent China, can impose on their populations the sort of isolation from outside influences as the Soviet Union was able to before WWII. And many key technologies that shape our world today owe their origins and dissemination to WWII. The first programmable computers, which have fueled the communications revolution, were invented by British codebreakers between 1943 and 1945.

Scientific Breakthroughs

Although the British scientist Alexander Fleming accidently discovered the antibiotic penicillin in 1928, he stopped working on it in 1931. It was not until WWII that the first patient was treated successfully with penicillin, in 1942 in the United States. By the end of the war, U.S. companies were making over 650 billion units a month. Penicillin has clearly revolutionized modern medicine.

Then there was German V2 rocket technology, which after the war Americans and Soviets refined to make satellite launches, opening up all sorts of space technologies. Radar was also perfected during the Second World War and is widely used in many industries today. The technology for jet engines came into existence between 1939 and 1945. And WWII witnessed a slew of somewhat more prosaic inventions.

Superglue was invented accidentally by an American chemist who was seeking to manufacture gun sights, and it became a commercial product in 1958. The ballpoint pen, which had been patented just before the outbreak of WWII, came into wide use during the war by the Royal Air Force because its pilots could use them at high altitudes without the leakage common to fountain pens. Even photocopying and freeze-dried coffee came into use during the Second World War.

Out of the rubble of World War II, then, came the seeds for a new world order. In so many ways, the Second World War was a decisive event in the formation of our current world and still casts long shadows over the politics, economies, and societies of many nations. As the decades after the war marched on, the United States moved from reluctant global player to activist internationalist. For the remainder of the century and well into the 21st century, the U.S. was the standard bearer of an interventionist, democracy-promoting, open-trade-oriented international order. The post-1945 world, often called *Pax Americana* (American Peace), remains formed largely in the image of the United States even though now, 75 years after D-Day, there are signs of waning world dominance amid the rise of other great-nation economic and military competitors.

MONUMENTS AND CEMETERIES

Honoring Those Who Sacrificed

Robert J. Dalessandro

THE FILM *SAVING PRIVATE RYAN* BEGINS AND ENDS IN THE NORMANDY American Cemetery near St. Laurent-sur-Mer, France. Most of the 9,386 Americans at rest here lost their lives in the D-Day landings and the subsequent hedgerow fighting. An additional 1,557 names are inscribed on the memorial walls to commemorate those missing in action or lost at sea.

It is a fitting way to bookend a film that focuses on the ultimate selflessness of a group of American soldiers in the opening days of the Normandy Campaign who are assigned a mission to return a soldier home to a family that had already sacrificed too many sons in combat. It was a mission they could not fully comprehend and did not agree with. The film places us with them in a story that communicates service, sacrifice, honor and valor.

That cemetery, along with 30 memorials and 25 other American cemeteries, are scattered across France and in other places around the world where Americans fought and fell. All are administered by the American Battle Monuments Commission, a small agency of the U.S. Federal Government.

The Question

During the commemoration of the 75th anniversary of the June 6 landings, it is appropriate to ask ourselves why it is important to remember those Americans involved in the D-Day cross-Channel assault on Hitler's

Atlantic Wall, including those at rest in Normandy American Cemetery, and to mark these significant historical events in general.

On its face, D-Day's importance seems easy to explain. Arguably, it is the most famous military action in the storied history of the American armed forces, perhaps even eclipsing Yorktown or Gettysburg as a feat of arms. The names associated with D-Day are known throughout the world; Roosevelt, Churchill, Marshall, Eisenhower, Montgomery, and of course, Hitler and Rommel.

It is the classic story of good versus evil, the struggle between democratic peoples and Nazism's tyrannical leaders with the simple aim of restoring peace to the European Continent and, by extension, the world.

So the importance of D-Day—the opening day of the final phase of World War II in Europe, the beginning of the end of German Nazism, the beginning of America's rise to superpower—all seem valid enough reasons to mark this significant moment in time. But I would contend there is much, much more significance, even more consequence to our nation, far beyond the aforementioned.

The Generation That Went Before

In order to understand the true significance of D-Day, we need to look back to the America of the fathers and mothers who begat the "Greatest Generation." They were the generation who fought in World War One to "Make the World Safe for Democracy," who brought America into the modern age—and in doing so, virtually guaranteed that their sons and daughters would return to Europe to fight Germany and its allies again.

As the final observances of the centennial of the First World War fade, we need to understand how that war shaped America and ultimately influenced American actions during the Second World War.

In 1916, the United States was an agrarian, debtor nation, and an inward-looking, minor power on the world stage. It was a much smaller country—less than a third of the present population—and it was more rural; more Americans lived on farms or in the countryside than in cities. More often than not, their homes did not have electricity or running water or an indoor toilet. Their family probably did not own a car; many of them had never seen an automobile, much less an airplane. A great many had never traveled outside the county in which they had been born.

The world regarded America very differently. It was recognized as a potential powerhouse, a land of industry and invention, of enormous farms that produced food to feed its own and plenty for others, but it was provincial and isolated and underpopulated. Americans had the machines, but the United States was not a world power. It was hardly entitled to stand in the room where big decisions were made, much less sit at the table. Americans were not viewed as leaders, let alone world leaders.

Changed by the First World War

The First World War changed all that. Two million Americans went to France as soldiers. Many others went over as nurses, telephone operators, volunteers with the Salvation Army and other support organizations. Two million more were in uniform at home, waiting to be shipped out, when the war ended. Hundreds of thousands of farm boys left for France, where they saw things no other American had ever seen before, things they could not have ever imagined.

When you take two million Americans from their small towns and ship them overseas; when they visit New York City before waving goodbye to Lady Liberty and deploy across the Atlantic, where they pass through England and Paris and then they return, you forever alter the fabric of the society. As a popular song of the period asked, "*How you Gonna Keep 'em Down on the Farm after They've seen Paree*?"

Our beliefs and prejudices about women, race, and citizenship were tested during the war, and all were shaken to the core.

Before the war it was generally believed that women were far too fragile to serve as nurses on the front line. But 11,000 "Yeomanettes" enlisted in the United States Navy; the first time women served in uniform in any branch of the American armed forces. Untold numbers of other women worked for the War Department or in munitions factories or provided humanitarian service abroad, changing their role in our society forever, and shortly after the war earning their right to vote. When General George Marshall decided whether to admit women into the armed forces in World War II, he did not hesitate, because he had seen their service in World War I.

Before the war it was generally held by whites that "the negro" was unfit for combat, too servile from hundreds of years of slavery. But 350,000 African-Americans, most of them residents of Jim Crow communities that prohibited them from voting, shipped out to fight in France; many of them served with distinction.

They also experienced a society that was relatively color-blind, and they returned home expecting Jim Crow to end, because people of color had bled and died for their county. Sadly, that change would not come until well after World War II, but the returning African-American veterans gave new strength to the civil rights movement.

Before the war it was believed that new immigrants to America might not be "trusted" to loyally fight for their adopted county. But more than half a million "hyphenated Americans" shipped off for the continent they had only recently left, and in the process became Americans. (*Italian-American, Polish-American and other groups, including African-American and Mexican-American, were written with a hyphen at that time, giving rise to the term "hyphenated Americans."—Editor*)

The farm boys who crossed the ocean to Europe and back again, the African-Americans and immigrants who served in our armed forces, and the women in the military, in industry, and in humanitarian service abroad, saw their lives changed, which in turn sparked a wildfire of change in American society.

And the world they and we live in was changed forever.

The Past is Present

The fall of the Ottoman Empire, the secret Sykes-Picot Agreement that divided between Britain and France most of the Arab lands of that former empire, and the Balfour Declaration (a 1917 letter by British foreign secretary Arthur James Balfour saying his government favored the establishment of Palestine as a national home for Jewish people) reshaped the Middle East, creating new nations and new hatreds. The conflicts in Syria, Iraq, Israel and the Palestinian State today are direct outgrowths of these agreements.

The fall of Germany and the Austro-Hungarian and Russian empires and the rise of the Soviet Union echo today in the Balkans, Crimea, and Ukraine.

By war's end the United States was a creditor industrial nation and the world's leading economic and military power. Americans now saw themselves as active and influential participants, for the good, in world affairs. President Wilson played a significant role in the peace talks at Versailles and, perhaps, had the Allies paid more heed to the American delegation's advice to soften the harsh terms of the Versailles Treaty there might not have been a second world war.

In April 1917 a small, agrarian nation entered the world stage. Eighteen months later it was an industrial powerhouse and, for better or for worse, was here to stay.

And every decision made during World War II was shaped by the American experience in World War I. On the Home Front, the decision to rely on women as factory workers directly flowed from the contributions of women during the previous war. The armed forces were organized differently, not just organizationally, but demographically. Hundreds of thousands of African-Americans, Hispanics, Asians, and other hyphenated Americans served in the armed forces in a full range of missions, both combat and logistical support. World War I had changed the way we thought about ourselves as a nation.

New Ways to Honor Heroes

And World War I changed the way America remembered her fallen. The World War I generation and their children did not want memorials to great men mounted on great horses. They did not want overly memorialized former battlefields, leaving them cluttered with shrines to states and regiments and great moments in warfare, as at the Gettysburg battlefield.

They wanted memorials that spoke to service and sacrifice, reminders of those who served and those who fell. So when the guns went silent after World War I, America faced the challenge of both memorializing the deeds of the men and women of the American Expeditionary Forces and respectfully laying to rest the 120,000 that had perished.

Almost immediately, Congress recognized the need for federal control over the commemoration of American armed forces overseas. On March 4, 1923, President Warren G. Harding signed legislation that established the American Battle Monuments Commission, designating the new agency responsible for the construction and care of monuments honoring the American Expeditionary Forces.

The American Battle Monuments Commission worked feverously, following the vision of its first chairman, General of the Armies John J. Pershing, to see that "Time will not dim the glory of their deeds." They erected 13 monuments and markers in Europe, commemorating significant campaigns and engagements of World War I.

Final dispositions of the remains of those who died in World War I were carried out under the provisions of newly enacted legislation entitling the next-of-kin to select permanent interment of a family member's remains in an American military cemetery on foreign soil—designed, constructed and maintained specifically to honor in perpetuity the dead of the war. Alternatively, the next-of-kin could have the remains repatriated to the United States for interment in a national or private cemetery; about one-third chose burial in the overseas cemeteries.

Soon after, Congress directed the American Battle Monuments Commission to construct memorial chapels in the eight permanent military cemeteries in Europe, which were at the time maintained by the War Department. In 1934, President Franklin Roosevelt issued an Executive order that shifted the responsibility for the management and maintenance of these hallowed grounds from the War Department to the American Battle Monuments Commission.

At the close of the Second World War, the United States Government followed the successful World War I template, directing the American Battle Monuments Commission to execute a commemorative program consisting of monuments, memorials and markers on foreign soil, along with several memorials in the United States.

Meanwhile, the U.S. Army had established several hundred temporary World War II burial grounds around the world. In 1947, fourteen sites were selected in foreign countries to become permanent American cemeteries for our World War II dead. The chosen locations of these cemeteries corresponded with the course of military operations. They were turned over to the American Battle Monuments Commission after the interments had been completed by the U.S. Army.

In addition to landscaped grave areas and nonsectarian chapels, the World War II cemeteries would ultimately contain memorials, sculptures, battle maps and narratives depicting the course of the war in the region, along with a visitor reception area.

Today, the American Battle Monuments Commission administers, operates and maintains 26 permanent American burial grounds and 27 separate memorials, monuments and markers on foreign soil; it also maintains three memorials in the United States.

There are 124,000 American war dead interred in these cemeteries, of which 30,973 are at rest in World War I commemorative cemeteries, 92,958 in World War II commemorative cemeteries, and 750 fallen from the Mexican-American War of the 1840s. Additionally, more than 15,000 American veterans and others are interred in the Mexico City National Cemetery, Corozal American Cemetery in Panama and Clark Veterans Cemetery in the Philippines. More than 94,000 American servicemen and women who were missing in action, lost, or buried at sea during World War I, World War II, the Korean War, and the Vietnam War are commemorated by name on tablets in American Battle Monuments Commission cemeteries and memorials.

And to this day, the American Battle Monuments Commission stays true to General Pershing's charge, "That time will not dim the glory of their deeds." The United States Government has invested a great deal to honor the memory of service to the Nation by its armed forces.

So now we must return to our pivotal question: Why is it important that we do not forget those men and women and the deeds they accomplished three-quarters of a century ago?

Perhaps it is important for us to make a personal connection to a generation quickly disappearing. Perhaps we should reach out to our grandparents and great-grandparents before it is too late.

Like the parents and grandparents of the World War I generation, the World War II generation—a generation later called "The Builders"—accomplished incredible deeds, both on and off the battlefield. They were a generation who believed anything was in reach through modern science and engineering. World peace and prosperity, elimination of hunger and even opening a path to the stars could be attained. They cultivated a mindset where everything seemed within reach; all the human race had to do was grasp it.

Looking back nearly half a century to May 25, 1961, it seems incredible that a United States president would set a goal of reaching our distant moon within a decade when the American space program was lagging and the challenges to such an endeavor seemed impossible to overcome. Yet, not only did this generation accept that goal, they accomplished it! It was their trademark quality—America could achieve anything!

In one of the closing scenes of *Saving Private Ryan*, we witness a critical interaction between Ryan, who has courageously fought his last combat action before returning home, and his mortally wounded commander, Captain Miller. Miller, in his dying breath, declares that Ryan should "Earn this!" These two words nicely summarize the root answer to my question: Why is it important to remember this quickly disappearing generation?

Archibald MacLeish, poet, playwright, and Librarian of Congress states the importance of remembrance in a far more eloquent way. In his 1941 poem, *The Young Dead Soldiers*, he writes:

> *They say, Our deaths are not ours: they are yours,*
> *they will mean what you make them.*
> *They say, Whether our lives and our deaths were for*
> *peace and a new hope or for nothing we cannot say;*
> *it is you who must say this.*
> *They say, We leave you our deaths; give them their meaning . . .*
> *We were young, they say.*
> *We have died. Remember us.*

MacLeish, who had lost his brother in World War I, understood far better than most. Why must we remember them? Because of their valor; their selfless sacrifice was made for YOU.

Saving Private Ryan closes with a panoramic shot of the Normandy American Cemetery, Latin crosses, row on row, punctuated by Stars of David, fill the screen. Ryan, now an old man, and surrounded by his family, kneels at the grave of Captain Miller and asks himself and his loved ones if he has been a good man and lived an honorable life.

Seventy-five years after D-Day, we should ask ourselves the same question.

PASSING THE HISTORY ON

A Millennial's Perspective

Matthew DeWinde

"I don't see why you can't just teach us history, instead of always harping on about the past." –Glinda, the future Good Witch of *Oz, Wicked*

"Why am I taking this subject? How is this going to help me? How does this relate to my life? Why is history important?"

THESE ARE THE QUESTIONS I AM BOMBARDED WITH BY MY STUDENTS at the very beginning of each new school year. Now, the philosopher George Santayana created a simple answer for us beleaguered social studies teachers to echo: "Those who cannot remember the past are condemned to repeat it." But is that good enough? Is it good enough as an answer to my students' questions about why they are taking my class?

I don't think so.

I was born in 1996, the end-year for the generation known as the millennials, according to the Pew Research Center. I am part of a generation that has been criticized for being "lazy," while also being praised as "creative." I am part of a generation that is focused too much on "Me, Myself and I," while also being considered team-oriented in our approach to learning and carrying out our work. My generation spends too much time on our phones, supposedly too busy tagging and tweeting on social media to look up and see what is around us. So, as a card-carrying member of this generation, why would I think history is so important that I chose a career teaching it?

Birth of a Passion

I grew up in New York before I moved to Kansas to teach history. I fell in love with the subject when I was in fourth grade. For an entire year my class focused on the American Revolution, from the origins of the Thirteen Colonies to the war's virtual conclusion with the Battle of Yorktown.

I enjoyed watching documentaries and reading as a child, and after my fourth-grade experience I wanted to discover all about the past. I found the mid- and late-20th century to be my area of fascination. I wanted to know all about World War II—its causes, its heroes and villains, the technology of the era, and ultimately its conclusion and the birth of the Cold War. I found it all intriguing, and in college I committed a lot of time to my studies involving 20th century world politics and wars and analyzing the cultures of the time.

It seems only fitting that two years after my birth a historian, Peter N. Stearns, published an essay called, "Why Study History?" He starts out by saying that "People live in the present. They plan for and worry about the future." So why, then, do we study history, if history is studying about the past? After all, parents want to have their children become productive members of society (i.e., have a good-paying job) when they are done with the American education system, and history can seem rather counterproductive to that philosophy. Welcome to the STEM generation.

Since the beginning of this millennium, the American education system has rapidly changed. With people trying to predict the future of American society and to meet the needs of its people, many politicians and economists theorized that the fields of gainful employment would be in the Science, Technology, Engineering and Mathematics areas—STEM. The humanities, the "liberal arts" courses designed to provide broad and diverse areas of study, are nowhere to be found in the promotion of the specialized fields within STEM.

But learning history provides skills just as important as those of STEM fields and, in fact, complement them. History is a science unto itself. Those who acquaint themselves with the past have a deeper understanding of present events and are better able to predict future outcomes. They are better equipped to make wise choices in voting and contributing to the society in which we live. They may find inspiration for their own lives in the lives of those who lived before them. And their knowledge of history can open doors to interesting, well-paying jobs in many fields, including those of STEM.

Analytic Skills

In studying history students develop analytical and research skills. They must analyze historical documents including letters, diaries, newspaper reports, speeches, and such things as the Magna Carta, the American Declaration of Independence and the constitution of their nation. They must understand the society in which those documents were written, and they must learn to objectively analyze conflicting information taken from differing perspectives and learn to evaluate the reliability of an information source. In short, they must learn how to conduct research and develop the critical-thinking skills many employers say are essential in the modern workplace.

Many students with a degree in history go on to become attorneys, paralegals, legislative aides, or journalists. The skills listed in the paragraph above are all essential to those careers.

The Facts About Artifacts

In history classes students have the opportunity to look at artifacts and determine how they were used in earlier cultures. By learning the stories of these artifacts they are also learning how the concepts behind those items have been adapted to new uses.

New inventions rarely spring out of nowhere. The creators of new technology and of advanced medical treatments almost always build their ideas upon the work of others. Often, the person or people credited with inventing something revolutionary actually created improved versions of things that already existed or that were based on already known concepts.

Tabitha Babbit, the Shaker woman often credited with inventing the circular saw didn't invent it; by observing the motion of her spinning wheel, she created an improved circular-saw design that made the device more stable and, therefore, more practical. The Wright brothers studied the results and conclusions of other aviation pioneers on their way to creating the first successful powered flight (they did research that was both scientific and historical). Today's smartphones, with their ability to deliver messages by both text and voice are the descendants of the telegraph and the first telephone.

When working in the fields of science, technology, medicine and the like, a good knowledge of history can provide inspiration for something new that might revolutionize society. And, speaking of inspiration, that leads to the next good reason to study history.

Finding Inspiration

Young people, from grade-school students to young adults, are trying to figure out who they are, what their place in the world will be, what ethics they will embrace, what they want to accomplish in their lives. History, perhaps more so than any other area of learning, can lead them to answers, can help them find inspiration through the stories of people who lived before them.

I fell in love with history because I was enchanted by the stories. Unlike fiction, where the characters, settings and plot are imaginative, history offers real people, real places, and actions that had real consequences. As I got older the themes of humanity—truth, justice, honor and duty—resonated and made a far deeper impact on me than any fictional story. In today's world, where film and television comedies and "reality shows" often seem to appeal to the worst in human nature, the most powerful stories from history inspire us to embrace the best human qualities. Nowhere is that more evident than in the story of D-Day and the Normandy Campaign, where thousands risked and sacrificed their lives to break open a pathway for eliminating a cruel, racist, dictatorial regime that was oppressing most of the peoples of Europe.

History and Job Opportunities

So studying history can help us become better people and better citizens, but we still have to earn a living. That brings us back to those "productive members of society" our parents want us to be when we finish our formal education, as stated above. Other than teaching history or writing history textbooks, what can studying history offer us when we are choosing a career?

As already mentioned, the research and critical-thinking skills we develop as we study history have helped many to find careers in law, politics and journalism. As also noted earlier, a knowledge of history can give us a boost in developing new devices, technology and medical care. But here are a few other options for those want to use their love of history to help them find a job they can love as well.

The film and television industries need researchers and advisors to help them tell historical stories in more realistic ways. (*See the interview in this book with Capt. Dale Dye and Alessandro Monetti's piece on the secrets of production in making* Saving Private Ryan.) The video game industry needs the same skills when developing games like *Call of Duty* or *Battlefield* (and even some fantasy and science fiction games with a historical or military basis). Creating massive multiplayer online (MMO) games like *World of Tanks/Planes/Ships* requires someone (or many someones) to do a tremendous amount of historical research into weapon technology. Imagine combining a degree in computing sciences or game creation with a minor in history—you've got a leg up on job-hunting in the game field.

There are even career opportunities for history enthusiasts in international relations, working for the United Nations, the International Monetary Fund, or government.

Apart from these are the more obvious opportunities: librarians, museum directors/curators/archivists, event planners and publicists for historic sites, archeologists and anthropologists, and authors of nonfiction and historical fiction (which can include historical romances and historical detective stories).

No one should be dissuaded from studying history because "it won't help you get a job." The people who figured out how to let us view mummies without removing the mummy's wrapping had to be familiar with more than tech skills. Increasingly, museums must offer visitors something more than an artifact behind glass. The person who can combine a knowledge of history with creative thinking and tech skills will be in demand.

So when asked the question, "Why Study History?" the answer is not just so we do not end up making the same mistakes as in the past. **It is also to allow our children and our society to thrive off the hard work of our predecessors and to provide a future full of opportunities that embrace and expand upon what previous generations have done.**

Production Staff

Bill Breidenstine
Publisher and Marketing

Gerald D. Swick
Executive Editor

Barbara K. Justice
Art Director & Book Designer

Kevin Johnson
Map Designer

Benny Jordan
Illustrator

Zachary Bathon
Photo Editor

Sharon Gytri
Indexing

Ivana Goga
Proofreader

SPECIAL THANKS TO:

Julia Dye, Noemy Wertz, Dony West, Alexandra Giffen, Larry McCallister, Pat Grove, Valerie Smith, Monika Heck; the "teams" at Casemate UK and Casemate US

FURTHER READING & WEBSITE CONTACT:

Learn how to access Bonus Material by visiting
www.ddaymillennialguide.com

BOOKS:

Ambrose, Stephen E., *D-Day June 6, 1944: The Battle for the Normandy Beaches* London: Simon & Schuster, 1994

Balkoski, Joseph, *Omaha Beach: D-Day June 6, 1944* Mechanicsburg, PA: Stackpole Books, 2004

Barr, Niall, *Yanks and Limeys: Alliance Warfare in the Second World War* London: Vintage, 2016

Beevor, Antony, *D-Day: the Battle for Normandy* New York: Viking, 2009

D'Este, Carlo, *Eisenhower: A Soldier's Life* New York: Henry Holt and Company, 2002

Griess, Thomas, E., Editor, *The Second World War: Europe & The Mediterranean* Wayne, NJ: Avery Publishing Group, Inc. 1989

Harrison, Gordon A., *Cross-Channel Attack* Washington, DC: United States Army Center of Military History, 1993

Hart, B.H. Liddell, *The Rommel Papers* New York: Da Capo Press, 1953

Hervieux, Linda, *Forgotten: the Untold Story of D-Day's Black Heroes* New York: HarperCollins, 2015

Hirshson, Stanley P., *General Patton: A Soldier's Life* New York: Harper Collins, 2002

Hull, Isabel V., *Absolute Destruction: Military Culture and the Practice of War in Imperial Germany* Ithaca, NY: Cornell University Press, 2006

Keegan, John, *Six Armies in Normandy* New York: Penguin Books, 1994

Kennett, Lee, *G.I.* New York: Charles Scribner's and Sons, 1987

Miller, Donald L., *Masters of the Air* New York: Simon Schuster, 2007

Miller, Merle, *Ike the Soldier: As They Knew Him* New York: The Putnam Publishing Group, 1987

Murray, Williamson, *Strategy for Defeat: The Luftwaffe 1933-1945* Maxwell Air Force Base, AL: Air University Press, 1983

Overy, Richard, *Why the Allies Won* New York: W.W. Norton, 1995

Sears, Stephen W., *Eyewitness to World War II: Best of American Heritage* Boston: Houghton Mifflin, 1991

Weinberg, Gerhard L., *A World At Arms* New York: Cambridge University Press, 1994

Wertz, Jay, *The World Turns to War* Hummelstown, PA: Monroe Publications, 2017

MORE INFORMATION, INCLUDING REFERENCES USED IN THIS WORK, CAN BE FOUND ONLINE. USE SEARCH SUBJECT ENTRY AT:

http://www.bbc.co.uk
http://www.arlingtoncemetery.net
http://www.pattonthirdarmy.com
https://www.eisenhower.archives.gov
https://shsmo.org/historicmissourians/name/bradley
https://dday.org
https://www.cam.ac.uk
https://armyhistory.org/the-dogs-of-war
http://www.dday-anniversary.com
https://www.southwickrevival.co.uk/
http://www.historyofwar.org
https://www.virginiawwiandwwii.org/
http://www.wwiiwarstories.com
http://www.wwiifoundation.org/events/film/
https://www.dday-overlord.com/en/normandy/commemorations/2019/agenda
http://en.normandie-tourisme.fr/calendar-of-events-120-2.html/
https://www.abmc.gov/news-events/news/75th-anniversary-d-day-normandy-american-cemetery

Index

A

B

C